GW00598419

Elizabeth A. Smith

About Children
and
Children-No-Longer

The New Library of Psychoanalysis is published in association with the Institute of Psycho-Analysis. Its purpose is to facilitate a greater and more widespread appreciation of what psychoanalysis is really about and to provide a forum for increasing mutual understanding between psychoanalysts and those working in other disciplines such as history, linguistics, literature, medicine, philosophy, psychology, and the social sciences. It is intended that the titles selected for publication in the series should deepen and develop psychoanalytic thinking and technique, contribute to psychoanalysis from outside, or contribute to other disciplines from a psychoanalytical perspective.

The Institute, together with the British Psycho-Analytical Society, runs a low-fee psychoanalytic clinic, organizes lectures and scientific events concerned with psychoanalysis, publishes the *International Journal of Psycho-Analysis* and the *International Review of Psycho-Analysis*, and runs the only training course in the UK in psychoanalysis leading to membership of the International Psychoanalytical Association – the body which preserves internationally agreed standards of training, of professional entry, and of professional ethics and practice for psychoanalysis as initiated and developed by Sigmund Freud. Distinguished members of the Institute have included Wilfred Bion, Anna Freud, Ernest Jones, Melanie Klein, John Rickman, and Donald Winnicott.

The series is under the general editorship of David Tuckett; Eglé Laufer and Ronald Britton are associate editors.

IN THE SAME SERIES

1 *Impasse and Interpretation* Herbert Rosenfeld
2 *Psychoanalysis and Discourse* Patrick Mahony
3 *The Suppressed Madness of Sane Men* Marion Milner
4 *The Riddle of Freud* Estelle Roith
5 *Thinking, Feeling, and Being* Ignacio Matte-Blanco
6 *The Theatre of the Dream* Salomon Resnik
7 *Melanie Klein Today: Volume 1, Mainly Theory*
   Edited by Elizabeth Bott Spillius
8 *Melanie Klein Today: Volume 2, Mainly Practice*
   Edited by Elizabeth Bott Spillius
9 *Psychic Equilibrium and Psychic Change:*
   Selected Papers of Betty Joseph
   Edited by Michael Feldman and Elizabeth Bott Spillius

NEW LIBRARY OF PSYCHOANALYSIS
—— 10 ——
General editor: David Tuckett

About Children and Children- No-Longer

COLLECTED PAPERS 1942–80

PAULA HEIMANN

Edited by Margret Tonnesmann

TAVISTOCK/ROUTLEDGE
LONDON AND NEW YORK

First published in 1989 by
Routledge
11 New Fetter Lane, London EC4P 4EE

Simultaneously published in the USA and Canada
by Routledge
a division of Routledge, Chapman and Hall, Inc.
29 West 35th Street, New York, NY 10001

Set by Hope Services (Abingdon) Ltd.
Printed in Great Britain by
Richard Clay Ltd, Bungay, Suffolk

British Library Cataloguing in Publication Data
About children and children-no-longer: Collected Papers 1942–80. Paula Heimann,
(New library of psychoanalysis; 10)
1. Psychoanalysis
I. title II. Tonnesmann, Margret (ed.), 1924–
III. Series
150.19′5

Library of Congress Cataloging in Publication Data
Heimann, Paula.
[Selections. 1989]
About children and children-no-longer: collected papers 1942–80, Paula Heimann
/ edited by Margret Tonnesmann.
p. cm.—(New library of psychoanalysis; 10)
"Complete bibliography of Paula Heimann's publications": p.
Bibliography: p.
Includes index.
1. Psychoanalysis. I. Tonnesmann, Margret, 1924–   . II. Title.
III. Series.
RC509.H452   1989
150. 19′5—dc20   89–10487
ISBN 0–415–04118–X
0–415–04119–8 **Pbk**

Contents

Preface

The collection of papers by Paula Heimann has been arranged in chronological order to allow the reader to trace 'the development of her work-philosophy including changes in her approach to the subject-matter', as she said in a draft introduction when she herself prepared a publication of her papers in 1978. The first date of the papers refers to the presentation of the paper, the second one to its publication. Two papers, chapter 9 and chapter 20, are published here for the first time. Five papers, chapters 8, 14, 15, 18, and 23, appear here for the first time in English. Chapters 21 and 22 were first published in American journals and the original spelling has been maintained in this book.

Not all publications could be included in this book. We were partly guided by Paula Heimann's own selection when she prepared her book in 1978 but we had to eliminate some additional papers. We have, however, compiled a complete bibliography of all her publications as far as they are known to us. As she has published in several languages, we may have missed some of those which have appeared in foreign-language journals unknown to us.

In view of the fact that Paula Heimann prepared her papers for presentation in various countries, it is inevitable that some of the papers show in part a nearly identical repetition of a point she had made before. We have included such papers in this collection when they set these repetitions in a new context affecting their subject-matter.

In the earlier papers quotations and references to Sigmund Freud have been taken from the Collected Papers and other earlier translations. Care has been taken to refer in the Notes to the respective translations from the Standard Edition.

All text in square brackets is editorial comment.

Acknowledgements

I am grateful to Pearl King for her contribution to this book of Paula Heimann's papers. There is no analyst of the British Psycho-Analytical Society better suited to write these memoirs than Pearl King. Her personal knowledge of Paula Heimann's contribution to the life of the Society over many years, of Paula Heimann's accounts of her professional curriculum vitae which she discussed with her in great detail for the Archives of the Society, and also her personal appreciation of Paula Heimann as a colleague and former teacher have augmented a valuable introduction to the reader of Paula Heimann as a person.

I wish to thank David Tuckett, the editor of the New Library of Psychoanalysis, for his help and repeated encouragement with preparing the manuscript.

Ann Hayman, Pearl King, John Padel, and Eric Rayner have given me help and valuable assistance with writing the Editor's Introduction and I wish to thank them for it.

Special thanks are due to my colleague and friend, Faith Miles, who has given me support and a great deal of time-consuming help with editing Paula Heimann's unpublished papers. Her contributions were particularly valuable as she was supervised by her for several years.

My secretary, Yvonne Jackson-Browne, has been willing to type and re-type the manuscript with cheerful patience and she deserves my thanks for it.

The generosity of Paula Heimann's family, executors of her literary estate, has made it possible to include in this collection seven papers which have not been available in the English language before.

I should also like to acknowledge the help of the Board and Finance Committee of the Institute of Psycho-Analysis which made loans available to finance the translations and editorial work.

The editor and publisher would like to thank the following for permission to reproduce copyright material: *The International Journal of Psycho-Analysis* (chapters 1, 4, 5, 6, 7, 11, 12, 13, 16, 17, 19); The Hogarth Press Ltd and The Institute of Psycho-Analysis (chapter 2); *The British Journal of Medical Psychology* (chapters 3, 10); The Institute for Psycho-Analysis, Chicago (chapter 21); *The Journal of the American Psychoanalytic Association* (chapter 22); *Nouvelle Revue de Psychanalyse* (chapter 24). Every effort has been made to obtain permission to reproduce copyright material throughout this book. If any proper acknowledgement has not been made the copyright holder should contact the publisher.

Paula Heimann's quest for her own identity as a psychoanalyst: an introductory memoir

PEARL KING

President of the British Psycho-Analytical Society 1982–4

I welcome the publication of these papers by Paula Heimann which have been put together by Margret Tonnesmann. Her introduction to the papers focuses on Paula Heimann's theoretical and clinical approaches to her work as a psychoanalyst and gives the reader a useful commentary on the development of her many contributions to psychoanalysis.

In this introductory memoir I have been asked to delineate her background and the events that most influenced her writings and her contributions to psychoanalysis. I have drawn not only on my personal knowledge of Paula Heimann as a warm, encouraging, and creative colleague, but also on information which she gave me when I interviewed her in 1974 in the course of my researches into the history of the British Psycho-Analytical Society.

Paula Heimann was born in 1899 in Danzig and died in 1982 in London. Both her parents were Russian and they had four children. The third child, a girl, died, and then came Paula. She always felt she had been conceived as a replacement for this child and that her mother was very depressed when she was born. She felt she had to comfort and look after her mother most of her childhood. Her mother was, however, very appreciative and grateful to her daughter for her support. This family situation is important in the context of her later analytic and extra-analytic experiences.

Paula Heimann did her medical and psychiatric training in a number of German universities, which was the practice in Germany at that time. During her medical training she married her husband, who was a specialist in internal medicine, and in 1925 their only

1

daughter, Mirza, was born. They finally settled in Berlin. There she became interested in treating psychiatric patients, and then a colleague asked her why she did not think of training as a psychoanalyst. She applied to do so in 1928 and she was interviewed and accepted by Max Eitingon, President of the Berlin Society. He sent her to Theodor Reik for analysis, who had recently moved from Vienna. Her teachers included Fenichel, Hanns Sachs, Franz Alexander, Karen Horney, and Rado. She was critical of the approach of some of the analysts in Berlin, as she felt they underemphasized the role of aggression and the importance of the death instinct. In 1932 she qualified as an Associate Member of the Berlin Psycho-Analytical Society. When Hitler came to power in Germany in 1933, Ernest Jones wrote to Eitingon in Berlin to offer to help any of the Jewish psychoanalysts who felt threatened, and invited them to come to London. Paula was warmly recommended by Eitingon, who had a soft spot for her as they both came from a Russian family background. About this time, Paula's husband got a job in Switzerland and he left quickly, as his left-wing interests had put him in especial danger from the Nazis. While Paula was considering whether or not to come to London (the Swiss Government would not give her and her daughter, Mirza, a visa to join her husband), the Reichstag fire took place, and someone tried to implicate her, on the grounds that a party she gave in their flat was a celebration of the success of that fire. The police arrived and arrested her while she was seeing a patient and took her off for questioning. They removed many of her books, but eventually the charges were withdrawn. It was enough to make her see that her life was in danger in Berlin. She left for London as soon as she could obtain a visa, with another psychoanalyst, Kate Friedlander, and her daughter was looked after by a Roman Catholic family until she could find somewhere to be with her in London. It was obvious that she could not return to Germany to fetch her, so an Aryan friend collected Mirza and brought her to London. Paula and her colleague were given visas to practise psychoanalysis in the East End, at that time a very poor district. So they booked into a guest-house and started their search for a consulting room in that area, for visas were only given to refugees to work in areas where they would not endanger the jobs of other residents in Britain; hence the designation 'East End' on their visas. Eventually they found somewhere to start work, but their patients kept complaining about being watched. At first they thought they had several paranoid patients, but when they compared notes with each other, it became obvious that their consulting rooms were part of a brothel and that the 'madam' who ran the place checked up on their patients as they came and went. They were then able to move into the West Central area of London, which proved more appropriate.

Paula had arrived in London in July 1933 and as it was a holiday period it was some time before she met any analysts. Jones gave her a list of those on whom she should pay courtesy calls and this included Melanie Klein. In November 1933 she was elected an Associate Member of the British Society. She found the Scientific Meetings much more stiff and formal than those she had attended in Berlin. She described to me how Melanie Klein, Joan Riviere, and Susan Isaacs used to sit in the front row, and it was obvious that Melanie Klein was at that time very highly regarded by most people in the British Society. She said that there were two couples who were good to her when she arrived: Melitta and Walter Schmideberg, Melanie Klein's daughter and son-in-law, who were both psychoanalysts whom she had known in the Berlin Society; and Helen and William Gillespie, whom she met for the first time when she came to London.

In April 1934 Jones announced that Melanie Klein's elder son had been killed in a climbing accident. Paula wrote a note of condolence to her, and received, through Walter Schmideberg, Melanie Klein's son-in-law, a message that she would like Paula to visit her. Paula had seen Melanie Klein at the Wiesbaden Congress in 1932 and was in sympathy with the emphasis that Melanie Klein placed on the role of aggression and the death instinct. Paula told me, 'Of course I did visit her, and she was distraught, naturally.' Melanie Klein told her many things about herself, not connected with her bereavement. Paula had asked her why she had turned to her, Paula – a stranger – and not to one of her English friends, like Joan Riviere. The English were too alien, and anyhow they could not speak German, Melanie Klein had replied. Paula Heimann said she had responded to her need, and at her wish she visited her regularly. When Melanie Klein decided one morning to make use of some of her experiences of dealing with her mourning for her son's death, and to write a paper, Paula offered to act as her secretary. As time went on Melanie Klein recovered from her bereavement. She must also have become aware of Paula's need for help, for at this time her marriage had broken down, she lived in emotional isolation with no close friends, and was very insecure economically, as well as having to cope with being a refugee and being cut off from her former friends and relationships in Germany. One day Melanie Klein interpreted to Paula that she thought she wished to have analysis with her, but Paula said she couldn't possibly pay for it. Melanie replied that she would reduce her fees. She went on to say that she would not have a vacancy, anyhow, for another year. They continued their social relations together, going out for picnics with the Schmidebergs. Paula asked Melitta, Melanie Klein's daughter, if she minded her going into analysis with her mother and Melitta replied that she had thought that this would happen. Paula said that she hoped it would not spoil their relationship, but she told me later that it had. After visiting her previous analyst, Theodor Reik, in Holland, Paula decided she would accept Melanie Klein's offer and told her so.

In the years between 1933 and 1939 Paula Heimann regularly attended Scientific Meetings but made only a few contributions to the scientific discussions. She was, however, busy and not only learning English. Jones had insisted that she obtain her British medical qualifications, which she finally managed to do at Edinburgh University in 1938. She said that she was later very grateful to Jones for making her do it, but that at the time, as she was very short of money, it was difficult for her.

During this period Walter and Melitta Schmideberg had become increasingly critical of Melanie Klein's point of view and they were supported by Edward Glover and Barbara Low in particular, in the British Society. In 1938 when a number of the Viennese analysts also joined the Society, opposition to Melanie Klein was becoming much more powerful, and a real threat to her. It was in this context in 1939 that Paula Heimann read her membership paper on 'A contribution to the problem of sublimation' (which was later published in an extended form under the title 'A contribution to the problem of sublimation and its relation to the processes of internalization' (Heimann 1942)). She was elected a Full Member in that year, and in 1940 she was recognized as a Control Analyst empowered to undertake the supervision of candidates. It was not, however, until 1944 that she was recognized as a Training Analyst, and in 1945 she had her first training candidate. It should be remembered, however, that it was between 1941 and 1944 that the intensive discussions took place about the validity of Melanie Klein's theories and her contribution to psychoanalysis, and in particular, whether or not those who followed her point of view should take part in the training and teaching of candidates.

When the controversies about Melanie Klein's approach came to a head, it was decided to ask Melanie Klein to present her theories to the Society in a series of papers which could then be commented on in written statements by members. Melanie Klein decided there should be four papers and that Susan Isaacs, Paula Heimann, and herself should write them. Paula objected on the grounds that she

4

was too junior, but was overruled. They met together and Melanie Klein tried to dictate what they should each say, but Susan Isaacs rebelled and said that she did not work like that. Paula Heimann, who was still in analysis with Melanie Klein, was less able to object, although she was allowed later to take her draft home to revise it. Paula found this experience very difficult. However, she said that she felt supported by Susan Isaacs, with whom she wrote one of the four papers. The ten Scientific Meetings that followed are now known as the 'Controversial Discussions' (King and Steiner forthcoming).

After these discussions and the reorganization of the Society's training into courses A and B, Paula Heimann started taking a more active part in training and in the scientific life of the Society. I do not know when she finally stopped going to Melanie Klein for analysis, but I have the impression that it was not continuous and that she went back from time to time for additional help. Paula appreciated her own need for analytic help and was grateful for what she got from her analysis during the difficult period leading up to the war. What made her uncomfortable was that Melanie Klein told her, later on, not to let anyone know that she was still in analysis with her. This meant that she was placed in a position of divided loyalties between Melanie Klein and her own integrity and feeling for truth. It is now easy for us to be aware of the pressures on Melanie Klein, for we know that one of the accusations that Glover and others made of the Kleinians was that, by keeping colleagues in analysis, they influenced how they were behaving in the Society, and at this time Melanie Klein must have felt that she was fighting for the survival of her ideas and contributions to psychoanalysis.

My first encounter with Paula Heimann was when I was a student in the late 1940s. She was taking a seminar on Freud's papers on technique, and she had asked me to summarize the main points in his paper 'Recommendations to physicians practising psychoanalysis'. When I came to the recommendation that analysts should take as a model 'the surgeon, who puts aside all his own feelings, even his human sympathy, and concentrates his mental forces on the single aim of performing the operation as skilfully as possible' (Freud 1912e: 115), Paula Heimann, to my surprise, strongly disagreed with Freud's emphatic recommendation. She formulated her point of view later in her paper entitled 'On counter-transference', which she read in 1949 at the 16th International Psycho-Analytical Congress in Zurich, which I also attended. In this paper she stated, 'My thesis is that the analyst's emotional response to his patient within the analytical situation represents one of the most important tools for his work. The analyst's counter-transference is an instrument of research into the patient's unconscious' (Heimann 1950). She continued, 'This rapport on the deep level, comes to the surface in the form of feelings, which the analyst notices in response to *his* patients, in his counter-transference.'

To those of us who were her students she had given sanction to make use of a whole range of our affective capacities, which we had previously considered should be taboo. It was now possible to draw on these sources of data to help discover not only how our patients were using us and what figures from the past were being projected on to us, but also to explore the subtle distortions which take place in the interplay between phantasy and reality, delusion and despair, as patients attempt to come to terms with both their good and bad experiences with their actual parents, and the psychic elaboration of these experiences. Paula Heimann's point of view is now widely accepted, but when she first formulated it, many psychoanalysts considered it heresy. It was only later that I learned from Paula that Melanie Klein had been angry about this paper and had tried to persuade her to withdraw it, on the grounds that Willi Hoffer disliked it. Ernest Jones, however, congratulated her on it and she refused to rescind her point of view. Indeed, the approach she described in this and other papers has since been an inspiration to many younger analysts, including Kleinians, in their later work.

At this time, we regarded Paula Heimann as Melanie Klein's 'crown princess', and it was often Paula who would get up at Scientific Meetings and put the Kleinian point of view, giving either a blessing, or a rebuke, or a lecture, according to the scientific stance of the presenter. Not that her contributions went unchallenged by others, but whether one agreed with them or not, they always contained food for thought.

During this period, the training activities of the British Psycho-Analytical Society were orchestrated by the Training Secretary, who was elected by the Members and who had a seat on the Council. They had previously been drawn from the Middle Group. In July 1954, it was decided to nominate two Joint Training Secretaries, one from the Kleinian group and one from the 'B' group. Paula Heimann and Hedwig Hoffer agreed to stand together and they were elected. It was not Paula's first experience on the Training Committee; she had been a member of it since 1949. Sylvia Payne was, I believe, the architect of this experiment, and she told me she was pleased with the way they had both worked together. As I was invited, in 1955, to take part in the training scheme, and started my first analysis of a candidate while they were in office, I can vouch for the helpful way they supported me and worked together.

6

In that year a committee was set up to arrange the activities to mark the centenary of Freud's birth, with Sylvia Payne, the President, as chairman, myself as secretary, and which included Paula Heimann and Hedwig Hoffer. I then had to work closely with Paula, and I noticed how she was becoming more at home working in a mixed group setting and not having to put forward or follow a particular point of view; that is, working for the Society as a whole, rather than feeling she had her prestige and authority from only one section of it.

In 1955 at the Geneva Congress Paula read her paper on the 'Dynamics of transference interpretations' (Heimann 1956), which was well received, and to many of us it appeared as a fairly orthodox and useful formulation of a Kleinian approach to the concept of transference. It was also at this congress that Melanie Klein first read her paper 'A study of envy and gratitude', but it was not published along with the other congress papers in 1956. In February 1956 Melanie Klein read an expanded version of her paper to the British Psycho-Analytical Society. The original version has recently been published for the first time in a selection of her papers edited by Juliet Mitchell (Klein 1956).

In the months that followed, it gradually became clear that Paula Heimann was parting company with Melanie Klein and her group. At Melanie Klein's request she resigned from the Melanie Klein Trust in November 1955, and then she made a statement to the Society that she no longer wished to be considered a member of the Klein group. I remember Sylvia Payne telling *me*, in December 1955, while we were clearing up after a life painting class which used to take place in her consulting room in the evenings, that Paula was no longer a Kleinian. It is difficult to convey the sense of shock we younger analysts experienced at this news and its repercussions in the Society. A number of leading analysts had left Melanie Klein's group in the past, including John Rickman, Donald Winnicott, and Clifford Scott (her first candidate), but none had appeared so staunch in her support, at least in our eyes, as Paula Heimann. At the time of the previous defections, the Klein group was only loosely organized and existed as an integral part of Course A (as contrasted with Course B – Miss Freud's group), so that candidates in analysis with these defectors were not called upon to decide to which group they wanted to belong. By the time Paula decided to withdraw, Melanie Klein had managed to delineate her supporters more sharply, so that any candidate in analysis with Paula Heimann would be unacceptable as a member of the Klein group. I understand that Paula herself did not want any of her candidates, who remained with her, to consider themselves as members of the Klein group. This rift was reinforced when, in February 1956, 'the Training Committee agreed to Mrs Klein's suggestion that six seminars be given by Dr Jaques in place of Dr Heimann . . .' and 'that four seminars be given by Dr Segal instead of Dr Heimann', two colleagues who, Mrs Klein thought, would more accurately reflect her views.

Sylvia Payne had suggested that Paula should write a paper giving an account of her differences with Melanie Klein, but Paula told me that she had felt too traumatized to do so, at that point. Paula Heimann became an enthusiastic member of the group of non-aligned analysts of the Society, who are now called, at her original suggestion, I believe, 'Independents', and she continued to play an important role in the Society until her death. However, the rift between her and Melanie Klein never healed, and Psychoanalysis was, I think, the poorer because of it.

When discussing this period with me Paula said that she felt that one of the many reasons why Melanie Klein was so angry about her paper 'On Counter-transference' was that she had written it by herself and had not showed it to Melanie Klein prior to reading it. It was her first gesture of freedom and assertion of her own creativity. She herself gave the date 1949 as the beginning of her split from Melanie Klein.

The final split, which came after the Geneva Congress in 1955, was when Paula realized that she profoundly disagreed with Melanie Klein's theory of inborn envy, although she still agreed with Freud's concept of the death instinct. I think she was enabled to make the final break because she was by then supported by her own experience of being valued by many colleagues for herself and not because she was a member of a group. In describing some of the things that went wrong in her psychoanalysis with Melanie Klein, Paula commented to me that she could not remember Melanie Klein interpreting the transference link between herself – that is Melanie Klein – depressed at the loss of her own child, and Paula Heimann's mother, depressed at the loss of Paula's older sibling. Paula realized later that she had attempted to look after Melanie Klein, as a repetition of the way in which she had behaved towards her own mother, who had so admired Paula's capacity to do so. Perhaps with hindsight we can be aware also of Melanie Klein's need to have a replacement for her own daughter, Melitta, who was also a psychoanalyst, and who had by 1935 become really alienated from her, with someone who would be more satisfactory to her and support and value her theories. Paula herself was very aware of the fact that she was herself a replacement for her mother's own lost elder daughter.

8

After leaving the Klein group, Paula Heimann was much in demand as a Training Analyst and as a Supervisor, and she continued to play an important role in the training of psychoanalysts. She went on to publish twenty-five articles, short communications, and critical reviews, and she read papers in a number of other countries, including Germany, France, and Italy, and in North and South America. Some of these have not previously been published or been available in English, in spite of repeated requests, so that this collection of her papers has been long awaited.

In the course of writing about Paula Heimann, I have come to realize again how courageous was her struggle to achieve her right to her own way of understanding psychoanalysis and her quest for her own identity as a psychoanalyst and a human being. I know that she did realize that many of her colleagues supported her in this difficult task, and I believe that many psychoanalysts have been encouraged by her example to work out their own way of understanding psycho-analysis and their right to their own identity as a psychoanalyst, while being firmly rooted in Freud's classical contributions.

Pearl H. M. King,
January 1989

Editor's introduction

MARGRET TONNESMANN

This collection of Paula Heimann's papers represents the professional development of a clinician, an analyst who in her daily work with patients assessed and reassessed not only her technique but also her theoretical assumptions applied to the clinical work.

Paula Heimann qualified as an analyst (1933) in Berlin after she had received a classical Freudian training. Before she could consolidate her training with her own independent work with patients, she had urgently to emigrate to London to save her life. Here she found to her surprise a very different situation from Berlin. In the British Psycho-Analytical Society there were lively discussions and critical appraisals concerning early infant development stimulated by the work of Melanie Klein. It was a new situation for Paula Heimann, and in the draft introduction for this book written in 1978 she said that in Berlin the emphasis had been on the libido and its vicissitudes whereas in London it was all vicissitudes of the death instinct.

Paula Heimann soon became interested in Melanie Klein's work and she underwent further training with her. In time she became one of her closest associates, and her early papers are clear expositions of some Kleinian conceptualizations applied to subject-matters like sublimation and creativity (1939),[1] the internal object (1948), and the early stages of the Oedipal complex (1952). Other papers like 'Certain functions of introjection and projection in early infancy' (1942/52d) and, in co-authorship with Susan Isaacs, 'Regression' (1942/52e) have not been included in this volume as in 1978 Paula Heimann decided against including them in her book. They were contributions to the 'Controversial Discussions',[2] and as such she regarded them as statements of Melanie Klein's thoughts. We have,

10

however, included the paper on 'Notes on the life and death instincts' (1942/ 52c), which is also based on the Controversial Discussions but was revised and enlarged for its publication. It seems from the draft notes in 1978 that Paula Heimann could identify with that paper as her own writing. It also is important for the reader to have access to this paper, as Paula Heimann presents later in 'Evolutionary leaps and the origin of cruelty' (1964/69a) a new attitude to this concept. Three early technical papers (1949/50; 1952b; 1955/56), which were written within the Kleinian frame of reference, are also included in this book.

The differentiation from Melanie Klein

In 1949, Paula Heimann gave a paper 'On counter-transference' (1949/50) to the 16th International Psycho-Analytical Congress. It was partly stimulated by a discussion with students of what Freud may have meant when comparing the analyst's work to that of a surgeon. This paper, as I have said, is reasoned with Kleinian technique in mind and describes counter-transference as arising from, without using the term, the patient's use of projective identification, when she says that counter-transference is 'the patient's *"creation"*'. But one can also ask whether it shows an early attempt to integrate some of her early classical training in Berlin with Kleinian teaching, to which she was ostensibly committed in 1949. What is of interest here is that her first training analyst was Theodor Reik, who coined in 1948 the term 'listening with the third ear' when investigating the analyst's tasks in the psychoanalytic situation.[3] Whereas Paula Heimann's early contributions show her full commitment to Kleinian early object-relation theory (stressing the conflicts arising from deflected death instinctual impulses from the beginning), she also emphasized right from the beginning the independence of the ego (conceived as the self), its strengthening, its widening, and the enlargement of its perceptive functioning, as the task of psychoanalytic treatment.

In her clinically oriented membership paper (1939/42) she discusses sublimation and creativity, and maintains that it is the patient's unconscious phantasies of hostile impulses towards the internal object which hinder the ego from pursuing its creative urges seen as 'the instinctual drive to creation (procreation)'. Repairing these damaged and damaging internal objects results in the ego's assimilation of them, thus freeing the ego's capabilities.

By 1955, as Paula Heimann herself said in her draft paper in 1978, she had already become critical of Klein's theories and technique for some time but it had remained an internal matter and was known only to the members of the Kleinian group.

Her important and well-known paper 'Dynamics of transference interpretations' (1955/56) which she presented to the 19th International Psycho-Analytical Congress was still mainly reasoned in Kleinian terms (hostile impulses directed towards objects from the beginning) but there were also definite signs that her technical approach as well as her understanding of the aims of psycho-analytic therapy was changing. She saw the analyst's task as becoming the patient's supplementary ego which can temporarily take on those ego functions, particularly perception, which are disturbed by the patient's unconscious hostile impulses towards the internal object. It is within transference communications that the inner world of the patient becomes immediate and alive to him. The last paragraphs of the paper, however, already foreshadow clearly Paula Heimann's change of direction. She described there analytic situations in which the patient is not engaged in transference communications but recounts, deeply emotionally engaged, memories which signify that the patient has recovered the value of the original objects which were hitherto lost to him by virtue of his own hostile impulses towards them. She says that now they are 'alive to him and present, they are felt as an essential part of himself, and his past life even though in fact they may be dead . . . there is some happiness within sadness and remorse'. Such communications, Paula Heimann advised, should not be interpreted as transference communications, as the analyst should remain a listener, a bystander accepted by the patient as being there and sharing his experiences with him. (In modern terminology such occasions may be seen as an indication that only those interpretations which mirror the patient's emotional state should be given, if at all.) Indeed, Paula Heimann saw the *aim* of all transference work as enabling the patient 'to recover the lost *original* object'. Here is the first printed hint that Paula Heimann will in time return to the assumption of an earliest pre-ambivalent stage of development, as K. Abraham (1916) had maintained in contradistinction to Melanie Klein, who conceived of conflicts of the life and death instincts from the beginning.

In 1969 Paula Heimann added a postscript to the French translation of this paper in which she discussed the various changes of her views developed over ten years of further professional work.

It was at the same Congress in 1955 that Melanie Klein introduced her concept of inborn envy seen as an object-related impulse operating in infancy ·as part of the deflected death instinct; she published it in *Envy and Gratitude* (1957). Following the Congress,

Paula Heimann officially left the Kleinian group and was invited by Sylvia Payne to join what is now known as the Independent Group in the British Psycho-Analytical Society. Her criticism of the concept of primary envy was, and is, shared by many non-Kleinian analysts; namely, that envy is a complex emotion which presupposes a more advanced stage of development. Conceiving of it as operative with effective energy from birth, Paula Heimann suggested, places it under the category of the instincts and so replaces Freud's concept of them (1961/62a). But Paula Heimann's critique of Kleinian conceptualization has been far more extensive than simply questioning whether envy can be re-categorized as an inborn part of the death instinct.

In 1957 Paula Heimann read a second paper on sublimation and creativity, 'Some notes on sublimation' (1957/59), at the 20th International Psycho-Analytical Congress, and already here she presented most aspects of the revised orientation which she was to hold throughout the remainder of her professional life. I have already said that in her first paper on sublimation (1939/42) she laid stress on a free-functioning ego ('I') as the ultimate aim of working with the transference-manifestations of mainly hostile internal object relationships as they emerge, damaged and damaging, in unconscious phantasy configurations. In line with Kleinian thinking she used the structural model of the ego (Freud 1923b). The ego is here conceived of as being secondarily derived from the id; it is its surface and becomes modified through the various effects of external and internal stimuli. In Kleinian thought of that time unconscious (id) phantasies in time become ego mechanisms. In her second paper in 1957 Paula Heimann revised the use of what she called Freud's 'first' ego model and introduced Freud's 'second' ego model as presented in his late paper 'Analysis terminable and interminable' (1937c). Freud corrects there what he felt had been misunderstood as 'weakness of the ego', and, as Paula Heimann stressed in a later contribution (1965/66b) again, he states that the ego and the id are both primary and exist at first as an undifferentiated ego/id. Not only the id but also the ego has its own innate characteristics which Paula Heimann conceived of as being subject to its own developmental line. She also takes from this paper Freud's revised classification of the instincts, namely that the somatic instincts in the id have to be differentiated from the primal forces of life and death which are not confined to any one mental province. This allowed her to postulate conflicts in all areas of psychic life and also to postulate, like Hartmann, that the ego has its own energy without having to accept Hartmann's concept of a conflict-free area of the ego.

If one tries to evaluate Paula Heimann's change of orientation one could see it as a return to her first classical Freudian training. But whereas her publications from now on show indeed great emphasis on studying the ego in its functioning and also as the 'I' [she later, 1975, revised it to 'self']⁴ in its theoretical and also technical aspects, namely the patient's and the analyst's dynamic functioning and interpersonal communications within the psychoanalytic situation, she remains committed to early object-relation theory and also instinct theory. Her contributions are attempts to link these three aspects of psychic structure and of dynamic psychic functioning in their conceptually separate yet interlinked developmental lines and also to apply them to the subject-matter of individual papers.

This development of her approach shows indeed 'a changed philosophy to her work', as she pointed out when preparing a draft introduction for her Collected Papers in 1978. Not only did her philosophy in her work change but also her style of writing. Perhaps a comment she made on interpretation can throw some light on it; she said that an interpretation has to add a creative thought, a new dimension, which will advance the patient's thinking and stimulate his own creative ability to work in partnership with the analyst. Paula Heimann's papers are also creative contributions which advance psychoanalytic concepts yet invite further development of thought and reappraisal. In a letter to the editor she wrote in 1978 that she wanted him to know that her papers were 'unconventional' and therefore often not liked in some quarters.

In her paper 'Some notes on sublimation' (1957/59) she postulated a primary urge of the ego to be creative in its widest sense, which manifests itself in sublimatory activity of the ego. She suggested that sublimation has two sources, one which stems from object-love and object-conflicts and serves their mastery, a vicissitude of the instincts and a defence. Here belongs the urge to repair damaged objects and the re-finding of lost original ones. The other equally important source is a spontaneous process, innately rooted in the ego [self] that strives to objectify itself in the sublimatory process and its object. Paula Heimann refers to Marion Milner (1957) who postulated a similar creative process, whereas other authors of that time dealing with creativity and sublimation emphasize the repairing urge in sublimation. In her paper Paula Heimann studied the manifold conflicts, anxieties, and pain but also the enjoyment and satisfaction the ego experiences when engaged in a creative process in its widest sense. She refers to the 'regression in the service of the ego' (Kris 1952) to which artists are usually exposed and experience in their work. In this context she already alluded to her revised concept of early development, which she discussed in her paper 'Notes on early development' (1958) in greater detail, and also already paraphrased the new approach to narcissism which she presented in her paper 'Notes on the anal stage' (1961/62b). In a margin of one of the reprints of the German translation in 1959, she wrote in 1978 'narcissism not mentioned, only paraphrased, why?'.

These three papers (1957/59; 1958; 1961/62b) outline Paula Heimann's revised assumptions, and a critique of Kleinian concepts at that time is inherent in them. Paula Heimann never gave a comprehensive paper stating her views but particularly in her contributions to discussions at International Psycho-Analytical Congresses (in 1961/62a; 1963/64; 1965/66b) does she refer to some of them in response to the topics under discussion. However, in 1965 she seems to have given a seminar aimed at discussing some of the Kleinian concepts at the Psycho-Somatic University Clinic of Heidelberg/Germany, and a very badly typed transcript based on a tape-recording or perhaps shorthand notes by a secretary which is in part unintelligible was found in her literary estate. I will use some of the material when I discuss a few more pronounced reorientations to Kleinian concepts.

Early development

Paula Heimann revised her views on early development and conceived of it as an undifferentiated phase of development under conditions of maximal helplessness, when the mothering care provides in *objective experience* life and death forces, and the 'self' is *experienced subjectively* in somatic sensations which provide the matrix for the earliest psychic experiences and leave memory traces which she calls 'somatic memories'. In subjective experience it is an objectless state as, fused with the mothering environment, everything good is attributed to 'me' and everything painful to 'not-me', as Freud had maintained in his developmental schemata. It is the · original and short-lived form of omnipotence governed by the pleasure principle and the capacity to imagine what is wanted. In other words, Paula Heimann returned to the concept of primary narcissism but also acknowledged the importance of environmental provision and facilitation. In Winnicott's terms, the nursing mother holds the infant's ego. In Paula Heimann's Freudian terms, she holds the life and death forces. She also points out that Freud himself stated in 1911 that the primary narcissistic state governed by the pleasure principle is a 'fiction' which is nevertheless justified, as it can be taken for granted that no infant would survive even for a short time without the nursing mother. In 1965 Paula Heimann enlarged on

15

her conception of earliest development by pointing out that the earliest defences against somatic sensations of unpleasure are either primitive forms of discharge or involve a shift of cathexis from the locus of unpleasure to the locus of pleasure accompanied by positive or negative hallucinations. If, however, these primitive defences become exhausted, then the infant in his objectless state suffers a somatic trauma experienced as annihilation or dying. (Winnicott talks of 'unthinkable' anxiety.) Maximal pleasurable states as well as somatic traumata leave somatic memories which can be reactivated in later life as sensations of bliss, re-birth, or death (Heimann 1975a).

In her paper 'Notes on the anal stage' (1961/62b) Paula Heimann reconsidered instinct development by stressing the various developmental phases with their specific conflicts and traumata influencing the development of object-relating and also the development of the ego and its narcissistic orientation. She criticizes in this context any one-sided emphasis on early orality only. It is also in this paper that she presents her thesis on narcissism, the ego's relationship to itself, which in her opinion undergoes development and becomes in states of primary ego creativity and assertiveness of the self a healthy, mature aspect of the personality. During the anal phase it takes on an object-hostile quality but it also fosters identity formation: 'I against you'. In ego creativity there is often regression in the service of the ego to such early developmental narcissistic configurations. Object-hostile narcissism is different from an ego–object (self–other) relationship governed by destructive impulses. Paula Heimann pointed out that a narcissistic orientation and destructiveness are not the same. 'Go away, I don't want you now' can be motivated by an object-hostile narcissistic impulse in contradistinction to a cruel, sadistic attack aimed at hurting the object and being motivated by a destructive impulse.

From her reassessment of the early phases of development and her thesis of continuously interlinked but conceptually separate developmental lines (instinct development, object relating, and ego/narcissistic development exposed to conflicts and anxieties from the opposing life and death forces, an emphasis on environmental facilitation and with this the importance of the concept of early traumata), it becomes clear that a number of Kleinian assumptions cannot be integrated into this approach.

If there is no ego yet at the undifferentiated beginning, there is also no object, and Paula Heimann states (in the transcribed manuscript 1965) that at the beginning there is 'not me' but 'not me' is not the same as 'object'. 'Not me' can be seen as a discharge of unpleasurable tensions. In her opinion a sign and action need differentiation. For

16

instance, an intended signal of a subject to an object presupposes that the subject understands the difference between subject and object and expects the object to be capable of modifying the subject's unpleasurable state by some action because the object is separate. A discharge, on the other hand, an action, is motivated by sensations of unpleasurable tensions. It simply means 'I don't want it, it should go away'. She goes on to say that she believes that the way Freud expressed himself in 'Negation' (1925h) and 'Instincts and their vicissitudes' (1915c) has led to confusion. She quotes Freud: 'Expressed in the language of the oldest – the oral – instinctual impulses, the judgement is: "I should like to eat this", or "I should like to spit it out". . . . That is to say: "It shall be inside me" or "It shall be outside me". As I have shown elsewhere, the original pleasure-ego wants to introject into itself everything that is good and eject from itself everything that is bad' (Freud, 'Negation' (1925h: 237). Paula Heimann then states that in her opinion

> Freud expressed in the *metaphor* of oral language and in connection with the oral impulses a very early process of wanting, wanting to have and wanting to get rid of. I believe that this had led some to assume that Freud here believed that even the infant sends intended signals. Yet anyone familiar with the bulk of his articles knows that Freud did not in fact imagine an object relationship from the beginning and distinguished between the object of the instinct and an object relationship. The breast, for example, is the object of the oral instinct.
>
> (From the transcribed manuscript 1965)

I should add that the question of Freud's use of metaphor has remained a controversial one and has recently come under discussion again in connection with the English translation of his works.

As Paula Heimann used the second model of the ego, the ego which develops independently and from its innate potentialities, it is natural that she did not accept that early defence mechanisms develop from unconscious phantasies alone as Kleinian teaching had maintained. She believed with Hartmann that ego mechanisms are developed. They can become part of creative ego functioning and can also be used for defence.

Aggression and destruction

In 1964, Paula Heimann gave a contribution to a symposium on 'Aggression and Adaptation' which was held in the Sigmund Freud

Institut at Frankfurt am Main, West Germany, and in which psychoanalysts from various countries took part. In this paper (1964/69a) (chapter 15) she revised her assumptions about the life and death instincts which she had held, as she said, so enthusiastically since her contributions to the Controversial Discussions (1942(43)/52c). She felt that Freud's antithesis had been historically speaking an advance in 1920 as it clarified the earlier assumption that sadism was part of the libido. Pleasure in torture and other cruel impulses could now be conceived of as an expression of the death instinct. However, she said that Freud's later approach (1937c) of a more philosophical orientation towards the life and death forces which govern all human conflict allows for a separate assumption of the life and destructive instincts which is nearer to experiences in our clinical practice. [This view is shared by many psychoanalysts who are unable to accept the duality of the life and death instincts.]

In response to Konrad Lorenz's book *On Aggression* (1963/66) to which all participants of the symposium had been asked to address themselves, Paula Heimann contemplated whether in phylogenetic evolutionary development a new form of aggression had occurred in man which has changed the adaptive evolutionary power-function and aim of animal aggression so that human beings are endowed with two different kinds of aggression: one from phylogenetic sources serving survival and activating assertiveness of healthy narcissism, and another one, specific to human kind – namely, cruelty – the expression of the destructive instincts. The latter she saw as a regular part of ontogenetic development and it signifies normative problems of adaptation to the manifold dimensions of human development.

In line with her reasoning about an undifferentiated early phase of development, Paula Heimann stated that the infant experiences *objectively* the primary forces of life and death through the nursing environment – care or neglect, love or hate – but *subjectively* there is only self-experience in somatic and later somatopsychic sensations at the beginning. When the earliest adaptive defences fail, the infant experiences death-like sensations that leave somatic memory traces which can be reactivated in later life. That is why the destructive instincts, cruelty against the object and the self, manifest themselves in phantasies and images of death, anxiety about dying, and the wish to die without being exposed to death. Even if cruelty towards the outside world is controlled, it stays operative and active in intrapsychic experiences against objects and self in phantasies and dreams. It is from observations in our clinical practice that we know how each developmental phase contributes to the content of those

18

anxieties and phantasies, the psychic manifestations of the destructive instincts. Paula Heimann viewed severe pathological states, like psychotic depressions, as regressions to early death-like somatic traumata with lack of differentiation of self and object and extreme cruelty operative in the patient's inner world. In her above-mentioned paper, 'Notes on the anal stage' (1961/62b), she suggested re-naming the anal-sadistic phase of development the anal-locomotor phase, as sadism and cruelty point to failure in the environmental facilitation during this phase of development.

With this shift of emphasis towards the vicissitudes of the destructive instincts, cruelty being viewed as normative but also dependent on early environmental care of the infant, Paula Heimann moved away from the Kleinian concept of the life and death instincts as operative from birth and the resulting annihilation anxieties motivating projection.

Technique

It appears as a natural consequence of the changes in her theoretical assumptions that Paula Heimann also revised some of her hitherto held views on psychoanalytic technique. As I have already mentioned, in her paper 'Dynamics of transference interpretations' (1955/56) she maintained that work in the transference aims at helping the patient to re-find his lost original objects. These are moments when the analyst should refrain from interpreting the patient's communications in the transference and instead allow the patient space to be with himself. In her paper 'Some notes on sublimation' (1957/59) she again presented case material which led her to similar conclusions. She described how at the beginning of a session the patient related to the analyst in a defensive/conflictual way but once this had been interpreted the patient withdrew from the analyst and in a self-absorbed way recited a poem. Paula Heimann viewed this as an example of primary sublimatory ego activity, when the ego is related to itself. She stressed again here how important it is for the patient at such moments to withdraw from the analyst into creative activity in contrast to having such a withdrawal interpreted in the transference as a hostile turning away from the analyst. The patient's withdrawal is often followed by object-hostile *narcissistic* manifestations, like an omnipotent attitude, and this in time brings the patient back into communication with the analyst. This should not be mistaken for a *destructive* object-directed impulse.

19

In a contribution to a symposium on 'counter-transference' held by the Medical Section of the British Psychological Society in 1959, during which Freudian and Jungian analysts from London presented papers, Paula Heimann warned against the too liberal use of the term 'counter-transference', as not all feelings the analyst has for his patient during a session are a manifestation of counter-transference as she understands it ('Counter-transference', 1959/60). In the above mentioned transcript from 1965 and also in her paper (1965/66b) she explored projective identification and the introjection of bad internal objects, as these concepts have a bearing on counter-transference as she conceived it.

In a discussion of 'so-called' projective identification Paula Heimann objected strongly to its application in *interpersonal* relating signified by the expression projected 'into' [the other person]. For her, projective and introjective identification are phantasies which have *intrapsychic* relevance only. The patient's projection, she said, leads to a disturbance of his ego function but it is also the expression of such a disturbance. For instance, when a patient projects a hateful impulse on to the analyst, then his perception of the analyst is distorted by the very fact of employing the mechanism of projection. Identification, on the other hand, is a concept describing a change in the subject's ego. If projective identification is employed as an *interpersonal* phenomenon it contains what the subject does – projection – and what the object does – identification – combined in such a way as if it does not refer to the psychic actions of two persons but only one. The correct description, Paula Heimann continues, would be that the patient psychically intrudes into the analyst's psyche and the question has then to be asked why the analyst allows such an intrusion to take place. To put it differently: how is it that the patient is conceived of as having the power, via projective identification, to change the analyst's cognitive ego function? If projective identification actually leads to 'the patient changing the analyst's functioning', then this is certainly quite a different conceptualization than its original meaning in which projective and introjective identifications were conceived of as phantasy configurations which have the power of changing *intrapsychic* object representations only. Paula Heimann had always maintained that Melanie Klein herself did change the use of the term 'projective identification' and, according to some notes left with her manuscripts, held this to be Bion's influence. Exactly what Melanie Klein did believe remains controversial to this day (see Bott Spillius 1988: 81–6).

Paula Heimann repeatedly stated that the phenomenon described by the term 'projective identification' ('into') is a familiar one and is an instance of the analyst's counter-transference. In a note on 'Comments on Dr Kernberg's paper . . .' (1965/66b), she defined the problem clearly when she said that 'the analyst fails in his perceptive functions so that instead of recognizing in good time the character of the transference, he on his part unconsciously introjects his patient who at this point acts from an identification with his rejecting and intruding mother figure, re-enacting his own experiences in a reversal of roles' (Heimann 1965/66b: 257). This leads the analyst to perceive an alarming change in his self, which he experiences as foreign. Hence, counter-transference is closely related to the concept of the introjected object and to trauma in Paula Heimann's revised orientation. She stressed that intrapsychic 'good' objects are assimilated by the ego (self) and enrich and stimulate ego-creativity. In subjective experience they are equated with the self. Introjections with a 'negative' valence are either introjected objects which were once felt to be 'good' objects but later assumed 'negative' valence because a bad experience occurred, an experience which is related to disillusionment. Or the infantile ego was helpless against the intrusion of an object and so *passively* had to endure the intrusion. In Paula Heimann's view, such passively suffered introjections lead to a substructure within the structure of the mind which in consequence has a crucial effect on the formation and development of all three structures – id, ego, and superego. Such patients show an absence of healthy narcissism and are often misdiagnosed as showing constitutionally abnormal strength of destructive impulses. Paula Heimann saw it rather as an identification with a corrupt superego which condones the ego's cruelty. In the transcript of 1965 Paula Heimann viewed counter-transference also as a response to deeply regressed patients. There are factors belonging to the early undifferentiated phase which are activated, and the analyst tends to respond with concerned feelings similar to those of the early nursing mother.

Twenty years ago, in 1965, Paula Heimann compared the different understandings of the phenomenon of 'so-called' projective identification, and was critical about those interpretations which assume the patient to have split off an unwanted, often destructive aspect of himself and to have projected it 'into' the analyst. She maintained that such an interpretation shows a superego attitude of the analyst who, in her opinion, is then not operating from the role of the patient's supplementary ego. There is certainly a substantial difference between on the one hand an interpretation based on the assumption that there is conflict from the beginning, the anxieties aroused by it setting into motion the defence mechanisms of splitting and projection, and on the other hand an interpretation which conceives of it as a transference manifestation in a reversal of roles. In the latter, the patient's identification with an aspect of a bad internal object results in the analyst being exposed to feelings similar to those which the patient had when the early mother failed him. In this context, Paula Heimann is near to Winnicott's concepts of early impingement and the development of a false self and even Balint's concept of the basic fault. They all share the belief that the environmental provisions during early infancy are fateful for the development of psychic structure.

It may be of interest to refer to Herbert Rosenfeld, a prominent Kleinian training analyst, here. In his book *Impasse and Interpretation* (1987) he *describes* similar configurations in severely disturbed patients who are so dominated by destructive narcissism that the analyses may reach an impasse. Rosenfeld states that when he interpreted to such patients that there is an 'inner, silent hypnotic influence of the destructive figure, posing as a benevolent figure', the patient 'becomes gradually more aware what is going on inside him'. The patient can then feel less threatened by an internal attack which has been brought into the open, and he has gradually to distinguish between the threat of the murderous inner attack and his own angry, murderous feelings against external objects. Rosenfeld was firmly committed to the Kleinian approach to theory and technique but he also observed clinically an alien destructive introject.

With her revised orientation, Paula Heimann investigated several aspects of the psychoanalytic situation. She maintained that when Freud changed his technique from being the authority figure of the hypnotist to becoming the partner in the analyst–patient relationship, engaged in investigation with the analyst's free hovering attention and the patient's free association, he gave the patient his freedom and respected him as a partner of a working team. This working team Paula Heimann saw as part of the psychoanalytic milieu, by which she meant a suitable, comfortable, quiet consulting room, the couch, the regularity of sessions, and all those aspects which provide the patient with an atmosphere in which unstable stimuli are kept to a minimum and which offers symbolic if unspoken care for the patient. Paula Heimann reasoned that it is this milieu which maintains the early non-verbal communication so that the patient can develop basic trust without having to give it conscious attention. In states of distress and regression, however, the milieu can become the focus of the work when early pre-verbal states and traumata are re-experienced during the analysis. In her papers 1964/66a and also 1969b she discussed this in greater detail.

Her emphasis on fostering the patient's own ego-creativity and giving him space for his own explorations is prominent in her paper on 'The nature and function of interpretation' (1970b) and also the 'Postscript' (1969b). In the papers 'The evaluation of applicants for psycho-analytic training' (1967/68) and also the late paper 'Further observations on the analyst's cognitive process' (1975/77), she explored the analyst's (and future analyst's) ego functions and those characteristics which are necessary to function in the work of prolonged involvement in an intense, one-to-one relationship with patients. She laid stress on a healthy narcissistic structure which she regarded as an essential part of the personality, side by side with the ability to maintain stable adult object relationships. She referred to 'genitality' as a term which has been known to psychoanalysis from the beginning. Whereas she maintained the viewpoint that the analyst should not burden the patient with his personal and private feeling-responses which might have contributed to a counter-transference reaction (in her 'Opening and closing remarks of the moderator to "Discussion of the 'Non-transference relationship in the psychoanalytic situation'"' (1969/70a)), she added an interesting thought in a paper written for a book in honour of Alexander Mitscherlich in 1978, 'On the necessity for the analyst to be natural with his patient' (1978). She discussed in some detail the difference between the analyst clinging obsessionally to what one could call his neutrality and his behaving naturally with his patient without losing the analytic stance. She referred to an incident when she spontaneously gave an opinion in response to a patient's statement, and she reasoned that a direct personal response to a patient's communication may further the analytic process and does not contradict her opinion that the analyst should not burden the patient with his private affairs. This paper marks the long way Paula Heimann had come from her opinion in 1954 that it is seductive to make a point with a joke or a short remark. [The paper 'Problems of the training analysis' (1954) has not been included in this book.]

One could say here that this paper (1978) foreshadows by a few years two controversially received papers, one by Nina Coltart, ' "Slouching towards Bethlehem" . . . or thinking the unthinkable in psycho-analysis' (1986) and one by Neville Symington, 'The analyst's act of freedom as agent of therapeutic change' (1983). Both these analysts from the Independent Group of the British Psycho-Analytical Society discuss similar questions of spontaneous emotional responses.

Her last paper, which she wrote in 1979 for the *Nouvelle Revue de Psychanalyse* by invitation of J-B. Pontalis, is in the nature of an essay. She was asked to say how she sees and relates to children not as their therapist but as a person. She was eighty years old when she wrote it, and her charm and her ability to tell stories came to the fore in it. In the second part of this paper she presents the reader with many thoughts based on observations from forty years of professional life.

Paula Heimann was a clinician and a sought-after teacher. When she left the Kleinian group she did not introduce a new theoretical framework. What she did was to link basic Freudian concepts with new developments from ego psychology and object-relation theory. She maintained that many Freudian concepts were still adequate and should be used, and that new developments be added to and linked with them. As she conceived of early development and also later stages of child development as being significantly influenced by the environmental facilitation of the nursing mother, giving the concept of early trauma a central place in her thinking, so many of the Kleinian concepts became obsolete for her. Instead, she drew on Balint, James, Khan, Milner, Winnicott, and others with whom she shared her views. But she also took from American ego-psychologists ideas which she found helpful when she presented her ideas of the development and functioning of the ego. Her contributions to the development of a healthy narcissism pre-date those of Kohut. She held the view that the relationship of the self to itself in creative pursuits is of equal importance to the relationship of the self to the object and that the one cannot be maintained without the other.

As her papers were read to analysts in various countries prior to their publication, it seems unavoidable that they contain at times nearly verbatim repetitions of one or other statements from previously given papers set in a new context and given to an audience unfamiliar with her revised opinions. This may be a drawback and seems unavoidable when a book of Collected Papers is published posthumously. In her own preparation for her Collected Papers in 1978 she often wrote in the margin of the reprints of them that it needed rewriting or that it could be replaced.

Sometimes one can find mentioned in a paper an interesting idea which was never taken any further. An example is the idea that regressive access to somatic memories may contribute to the symptoms of conversion hysteria.

Paula Heimann's papers bear the stamp of a basic Freudian training, and often ideas are expressed within this frame of reference which Balint presents in a language near the Hungarian language of Ferenczi, or Winnicott presents in a style which is near to that of the Bloomsbury circle. When Paula Heimann talks of the ego's withdrawal into creative activity she describes something which Balint (1968) also perceives in the 'one-person area of creativity' or

Winnicott (1958) in his concept of 'the child being alone in the presence of the mother'. In whatever way these authors and also others from the Independent Group presented their views in a different psychoanalytic language, and though they reasoned with different basic concepts, there was a common theme in the fifties and sixties in the Independent Group. This was the study of the central role which environmental facilitation plays in psychic development from the word go, how early traumata manifest themselves in the psychopathology of adult patients, and what impact this has on psychoanalytic technique.

Paula Heimann became a close associate of Melanie Klein after she had qualified as an analyst of classical orientation. She was one of the few already qualified analysts interested and close to Melanie Klein's work, who actually became a member of the Kleinian group. However, although it was inevitable that she integrated both these approaches in her clinical work with her patients, she also questioned and reassessed her basic assumptions from observations in her clinical work with them. The papers selected for this book bear witness to it.

Notes

1 For reasons of chronological clarity, the dates of the presentation of Paula Heimann's papers are used. In bibliographical references both the date of presentation and the date of publication are quoted.

2 A transcript of the 'Controversial Discussions' will be made available in P. H. King and R. Steiner (forthcoming) *Freud–Klein Controversies – 1941 to 1946*, London: Routledge.

3 A short note was found in a book by T. Reik in Paula Heimann's estate. She wrote that he had the gift of bringing the unconscious to life for her but she found him less able when dealing with the negative transference. And also 'he called me "his winning horse"; fancy that!'.

4 'I found [the concept 'self'] most useful because it is closer to immediate experience and more comprehensive than the terms "subject" or "ego"' (from 'Sacrificial parapraxis – failure or achievement?' 1975a).

A contribution to the problem of sublimation and its relation to processes of internalization (1939/42)

This paper is an expanded version of Paula Heimann's membership paper which she read to the British Psycho-Analytical Society in July 1939. It was published in the *International Journal of Psycho-Analysis* 13(1) (1942), and was her first psychoanalytic publication.

In this paper my aim is to point out and discuss certain aspects of the sublimatory processes which in my opinion have not so far been investigated or perhaps sufficiently described. They involve consideration of unconscious phantasies related to internalized objects.

I am taking the artistic productivity of a painter as an example, although I am well aware that in this type of sublimation there are some specific factors operating which are still obscure. I do not aim at dealing exhaustively with the vast subject of sublimation, and the material will illustrate only those important aspects to which I wish to draw attention.

I start from the psychoanalytical conception that sublimation is a form of discharge of the instinctual drive to creation (procreation). I will recall Freud's original concept of sublimation as an activity in which the sexual impulse is deflected from its direct aim but does not succumb to repression, which leads to achievements serving a social or higher interest and involves an adaptation to reality, that is, the progress from the pleasure principle to the reality principle. Gratification on the part of the ego is also an essential element in sublimation; since the ego does not have recourse to repression, it is not restricted and impoverished but enriched by the sublimatory activity. This last point, the conscious gratification, bound up with the experience of expansion and development of ego, seems to me an important indication that a sublimatory activity is successful, although it may be of short duration only and give way to various forms of discontent, or even to depression and despair. Complete absence of it, however, would suggest to me that there is some serious disturbance in the sublimatory process.

When I use the term 'ego', I am not thinking so much of an organization which is firmly established and demarcated in contrast to other parts of the personality – indeed, Freud has warned us against being dogmatic in this matter – but of the sum total of an individual's feelings, emotions, impulses, wishes, capacities, talents, thoughts, and phantasies – in short, all those psychic forces and formations which a person (assuming that his consciousness reached so far as to embrace so much) would identify as his own and which would make him feel: 'That is I.' Actually most of our patients suffer from not having achieved this experience and I think that it is one of the essential tasks of analysis to help them so to find themselves. This, if successful, goes along with widening the boundaries of the personality and increasing its capacity to tolerate the fight with the inner and outer world.

The patient I am going to describe is a painter in her early thirties, an intelligent and attractive person. She comes of a middle-class family. Her father's profession took him about to sea-port towns and this made a stable home life difficult for the family. The patient has vivid recollections about anxieties in stormy nights on the Scottish coast and of blissful happiness in being beside her mother by a cheerful fireplace. Her one-year-older brother was until puberty her intimate companion and an object of intense feelings of love and hate, domination and jealousy, guilt and envy. Her early sexual games with him, a source of pleasure, guilt and anxiety, proved a lasting influence on her later sexual life. In the analysis her parents were for a long time divided into good and bad objects, in that her father was felt to be entirely good with admirable qualities – intelligence, humour, creativeness – and her mother entirely bad – stupid, dull, and narrow-minded. All happy experiences with her, such as that by the fireside, were denied or at least ignored.[1] Only when the anxieties and feelings of guilt, requiring such an extreme separation of love and hate, and leading by such over-simplifications to great distortions of reality, had become allayed, and when the patient became more capable of maintaining feelings of love even to a not perfectly good person, could she admit faults in her father and good qualities in her mother. She then came to see them in a less obsessionally tabulated way and more as real human beings. It turned out then that even the humour of her father, which she had valued so highly, had a very bad aspect; for he had treated her as a funny little thing and refused to take her seriously, whereas her mother, to whom she had denied any sense of humour and understanding, showed a kindly appreciation of her conflicts.

The family moved about a good deal, but the final blow to security and family unity fell in her early teens when her father left her mother. The standard of the family life changed abruptly. Her mother went to work in a factory to earn a living for herself and the two children. A most painful and dramatic event brought her father back, after he had got into serious trouble from which his wife rescued him. But he was not the same man as before; the relation between the parents was gravely disturbed, and, as it seems, never fully repaired. Her father returned a broken man and became addicted to alcohol, and his death at a comparatively early age appears to have been precipitated by his alcoholism.

The father's desertion of the family led to striking changes in his daughter. She had been a good, though mischievous pupil, but now her achievements in school deteriorated conspicuously, and she became uninterested and restless. After school she attempted various trainings and kinds of work, none of which satisfied or stabilized her. When she came of age she broke away from the family to live independently and lived an unconventional, wild, and unhappy life. By chance she was introduced to Freud's works and she read his books with an eager interest, which resulted in her coming for analytic treatment herself.

When she came to me she was suffering from intense depressions with suicidal tendencies, inhibitions in her work of painting, disturbances in her sexual life and an addiction to morphia, the extent and significance of the symptoms becoming apparent only in the course of analysis.

As a result of analysis all these disturbances have been to a large extent overcome. She has married a man with whom she has a satisfactory relationship in many respects although full sexual gratification has not yet developed. She is infinitely happier than she ever was before; in fact she has learned what it means to be happy. She mixes well with people of different types and has an open and keen interest in actual events. Her capacity for sympathy and helpfulness has developed. She takes a lively part in the world around her, and – what she values most of all – has attained to real creative power in her painting and has made a name for herself in the artistic world.

I shall now describe the course of this analysis with reference only to the connection between her phantasies about internalized objects and her artistic productivity.

The first period of the analysis covered the work of penetrating behind an attitude of dissimulation about the severity of her illness.

28

Above all she tried to gloss over the morphia addiction, and some time was needed before she gained sufficient confidence in me to enable her to show more freely how much she was really suffering. Thus I did not at once realize the psychotic character of her anxieties, since on the whole she did not give the impression of being a psychotic patient. In my opinion it is one of the great gains of the new research by Melanie Klein (1932, 1935, and 1940) and her school into the processes of internalization that we have become able to discover and analyse psychotic traits in people who are classed as neurotic.

After this first phase, the analysis found access to the full depth of her depressions and her persecutory anxieties, which were intimately bound up with her morphia addiction. During this period she was mainly engaged in drawing from the model. These drawings showed strong, but rather gross and coarse lines. Without laying claim to an expert understanding of this matter I would say that they definitely showed talent, but perhaps hardly more than that.

When the analysis proceeded to deeper levels it became clear that her depressions were related to a system of phantasies in which she felt herself possessed and inhabited by devils. These devils – at the beginning of the analysis they were innumerable – persecuted her constantly and in ever-varying ways. They roamed about inside her, caused her physical pain and illnesses, inhibited her in all her activities, especially in painting, and compelled her to do things she did not want to do. When she wanted to get up in the morning they moved about violently in her stomach and made her vomit. When she wanted to paint they interfered. They would roar with laughter when she tried to achieve something. They would force her to go to the lavatory constantly, and during a certain period she had to urinate so frequently that it disturbed her work seriously. They had forks with which they prodded and attacked her in the most cruel ways. They would eat her up from inside and force her to take food for them. But she felt she could not eat because they would poison her with their excrement and thus turn the food into poison. Owing to these persecutions she was in agony, especially when painting.

All these phantasies became fully conscious during analysis, in particular through the analysis of the transference-situation, and were intensely real and vivid to the patient. No doubt the fact that she possesses the talent of a painter accounts for the richness and vividness of her phantasies and for the comparative ease with which they could become conscious. There was often not a very clear distinction between conscious and unconscious phantasies. The great drive to paint, inherent in her, in the processes constituting her talent, proved a powerful ally to the analysis and to the endeavour to reach her as yet unpainted internal scenes and situations.[2]

Against these persecutions by the devils she took morphia. Morphia calmed the devils down or put them to sleep or drugged or paralysed them. Morphia also fed and placated them. But they were only temporarily put out of action and with their renewed tormenting the need to take morphia again arose. Gradually the devils became reduced in number and differentiated in type, for example, 'blue painting devils' and 'morphia devils'. These two types of devils represented her two parents in antagonism to each other carrying out a warlike sexual intercourse inside her, but they were also banded together in a conspiratorial alliance against her. During one period there were three devils of each type.

Phantasies like these which take parental intercourse for a persecutory act arise when the subject stands under the sway of his destructive impulses and his libido is temporarily overpowered. In order to defend himself against the aggressiveness (death instinct) set loose inside himself, the subject directs it outwards, as Freud (1920) has shown, and attributes his own aggressiveness to the object. In this particular situation (that of observing or phantasizing parental intercourse), under the impact of jealousy and anxiety the subject's destructive drives become projected on to the parents, so that they are felt to be the agents of destruction. Since in the subject's own processes the fight between the life and the death instinct, love and hate impulses, has entered a phase in which the hate impulses occupy the stronger position, he is unable to perceive parental intercourse as a sexual situation, but interprets, or rather misinterprets, it as a war – war by each partner against the other and against himself. Impotence and frigidity have an important root in such phantasies.

Actual events and childhood memories were interwoven in these devil phantasies and gigantically distorted; and the transference situation mirrored them. To give one example for many: in her childhood my patient often 'dared' her brother to do something and vice versa. Once he 'dared' her to prick a pin into a workman's buttocks as he bent down, and she did so. In the devil-phantasies this small mischief became magnified and reversed into attacks by the devils' forks upon herself. She dreaded and hated the devils and she wanted to get rid of them, but she also loved them, was proud of them ('Aren't they brainy to be always finding new ways of tormenting me?') and wanted to keep them. Moreover, she needed them to punish herself for her bad impulses and actions.

Throughout this persecution by devils, however, there had also existed in her mind what she called 'the design', and this meant her good parents joined together in harmony with each other and with their children. The design also stood for her own love and creativeness and her capacity to undo the harm she had done to her objects.

Whenever she had some experience of the connection between things – for instance, when the interpretations in analysis joined up various fragments of her associations and made her feel that these associations were not accidental and senseless, but had a deep meaning through which she could appreciate the whole context of the processes in her mind – then she would say: 'That fits into the design.' After an hour, for instance, in which light had been thrown on important factors in her life, she would experience a blissful state of happiness, about which she said: 'I saw my design. It came into me.' This made her love me so much that she wanted to rush to me and to give me all her possessions; on that day she had no need for morphia. The design represented love and creativeness. It was the principle which binds together, and which turns chaos into cosmos. It was an ideal of perfection. When she realized, however, on one occasion that by saying that the design comprises everything, good and bad, she used it to justify her bad feelings to herself and to carry out destructive actions, the design was felt to be destroyed and lost, and a deep depression resulted from this experience. Gradually the design became more and more established, and she developed a firm faith in its existence, and was no longer dependent on getting constant visible proofs of it. The working of her design could be applied more and more to her painting, and her pictures became more and more manifestations of the design.

To return to the devil phantasies. The devils represented the objects of her instinctual drives, both libidinal and aggressive; that is to say, they stood primarily for her parents and her brother, but also for people in her actual surroundings, including myself; and all these objects could be both parts of persons and also whole persons. Moreover, the devils were a cover for her own sadistic and destructive impulses, which she disowned and personified in them.

I will now endeavour to explain how this world full of devils inside her had come about.

The memory-traces of psychical experience, past and present, are not static imprints like photographs, but moving and living dramas, like never-ending scenes on a stage. These inner dramas are composed of the subject and her instinctual impulses towards her original objects (father, mother, brother, and their later substitutes, up to and including the analyst), who are seen as they had been felt and are felt to be under the impact of her impulses; in addition, the objects also display her own impulses. Moreover, all the protagonists in the drama, herself and her objects, her own impulses and their responses, derive some features from the actual setting and events of childhood: her own physical and emotional personality during childhood and that of the persons around her, and the things, places, and events of that life. Features of the world in which and towards which her instinctual impulses were originally directed, dating from the period of time and the actual occasions on which they were originally felt (and were more or less expressed or denied), become woven into the inner drama played out by her impulses and their objects.

In this way the drama of the internal world took shape originally; and it continues a ceaseless activity throughout life, all subsequent experiences after the original ones providing new scenes, mostly on the pattern of the earliest. Conversely also, the drama of the internal world colours the subject's perception of the external world and lends features of internal phantasy and memory to experiences with present-day external objects. The sense of reality often suffers considerably from this admixture.

I said above that in the inner drama the objects also display the subject's own impulses. This phenomenon is essentially a defence mechanism against the subject's own evil impulses – a variety of the mechanism of projection and turning outward of aggressiveness (death instinct) discussed by Freud (1920). The object which has been internalized in hate and greed becomes the internal carrier of these very impulses. This comes about by way of many phantasies, which can be summed up as methods of divesting the subject of his own evil and aggressiveness and transferring them elsewhere, thus relieving the subject of anxiety and also of the guilt resulting from his aggressiveness towards his objects.

At this stage, therefore, the internal drama tells a story of the subject's innocence; its purpose is achieved only when the subject arrives at a point where he no longer feels guilty. My patient's impulses have been projected on to the objects of her internal world: hate and greed actuate them on the stage of her inner drama; *they* are bad, *they* are devils – no blame could be attached to *her*. In thus disowning guilt, however, and denying all responsibility, she is adopting a passive position; she can only feel helpless and persecuted, a victim of all the evil taking place inside her – she has no say in the matter, as it were. Now she has got into a cleft stick, an impasse from which there is no way out; since she disowns responsibility, her own capacities are rendered impotent, she can do nothing. One consequence of this is that since her own efforts, the efforts of a human being, can achieve nothing, magic must be introduced, and a magic means from outside must come to her help – morphia.

Moreover, the feeling of being inhabited by persecuting creatures (people, animals, and things) necessitates energetic defences aimed at destroying these persecutors. But since these defences consist of attacking the persecutors inside the self, they are of no avail as a solution, for they involve the subject at the same time as her objects. The battlefield is in the home country, not on enemy territory. A vicious circle is thus set up and a perpetual warfare ensues which is played out in the subject's internal world – always affecting her external life and often expressed in terms of physical symptoms.[3]

In this way the patient's objects had become devils to her, because she had been a devil to them. A ceaseless war was going on inside her between them and her, or between their allies and hers. Analysis was able to break up this vicious circle by bringing home to the patient her responsibility for her internal objects, their origin in her own impulses which had been active in her relation to her external objects, and the manifold aspects of her motives in regard to external events and her responses to 'real situations', as they are called. Only when the experience of analysis brings home to the patient his own impulses and his responsibility for them (when he is enabled to endure guilt and grief as such and comes to dispense with defending himself against these experiences by persecutory systems) can the internal world become modified, can 'past experiences', 'unconscious memories', be transformed so that they lose their hold over the patient.

Thus a fuller understanding of the internalization processes shows us in detail the facts implied in Freud's early statement (1910a) that 'hysterics suffer from reminiscences'. These memories are not, however, exact replicas in the child's mind of people and events he encountered, but a complicated summation and interweaving of external and internal experiences with live persons in action, as I tried to show above when I described how my patient's world of devils had come about. We must not conceive of the child's mind as if it were a blank photographic film which reflects external scenes exactly and faithfully; it is a film on which the child's instinctual impulses and defences (unconscious and also conscious phantasies) have already taken shape before it is exposed to a given external reality. So that the outcome we call 'memory' is in fact a composite superimposed picture of two worlds in one. What we call a memory-trace would be felt subjectively from one point of view as a situation involving 'internal objects'. A person re-experiences the past in his analysis, because he still carries this past as a living world inside him; and he perceives present reality in a way that is both restricted in quantity and altered in quality by the influence which his 'past' – his internal world – exerts upon him. We find the access to this past – the drama that is perpetually being acted out inside him – through the transference situation, which enables us to evaluate the interplay between the environmental ('objective') and the subjective factors in the composite picture. However, I cannot attempt here to discuss in detail the way in which our technique of analysis operates in enabling us to come to grips with the patient's internal objects. But I can say that analysis cures the illness caused by 'unconscious memories' in that it deals with these memories in the way they are experienced by the patient; namely, as an internal world of intense actual reality.

It was through the analysis of her devil-phantasies that the patient's whole childhood history was recaptured. The multiple aspects in which she had seen and felt her parents and her brother, and the complicated relationship between each of them, and between them and herself, were faithfully acted out by the devils inside her.

I hope I have succeeded in conveying the feeling of absolute reality which the patient experienced in these phantasies about the devils, and in picturing the intense anxiety states into which these devils threw her. Severe depression, the feeling of absolute unworthiness and suicidal states of despair ensued from this situation of having active devils inside her.

With the analysis of her childhood situation and especially of her penis-envy and her earliest oral anxieties relating to breast and penis, which she dreaded to find destroyed by her insatiable greed, the force of these devils inside her diminished. She came to understand that the devils were her parents and her brother whom she had distorted in this extensive manner by investing them with her own greedy, soiling, persecuting impulses and whom she had devoured and incorporated under the impact of her destructive impulses; that she had created these devils to personify the badness which she could not bear to acknowledge as her own, as part of herself. She gradually realized this, as she became more able tolerate feelings of guilt and pain; she then no longer felt inhabited by persecuting devils and this type of phantasy practically ceased to exert any influence over her. Included in this process was the development of a greater tolerance towards aggressiveness, her own and other people's. And the greater tolerance enabled her to react with less anxiety towards aggressive situations and to avoid the vicious circle in which aggressiveness increases anxiety and anxiety increases aggressiveness.

Concurrently with the process of understanding her internal world in childhood and its relation to the external world, the craving for morphia diminished. She arrived at a 'gentleman's agreement' with herself of a monthly allowance of four morphia tablets, usually taking part of them during her intense menstruation pains, the other part a fortnight after the menstruation. I cannot here go into the problems relating to the menstruation pains and the phantasies determining their gravity; they were principally determined by cruel and frightening phantasies connected with her penis-envy. She eventually gave up morphia altogether; the menstrual pains became so much reduced that she could go about as usual and even dance during the period.

During the phase I have just described (when her life was dominated by the devils inside her) she proceeded from drawing to painting. The subjects were at first somewhat coarsely symbolical representations, and she showed the urgency of her need to restore her objects by painting huge fathers and huge penises, huge mothers and mother symbols. The first picture painted without her having to take morphia during her work represented this kind of wholesale and massive attempt at restoring the destroyed internal objects. It was in some ways primitive and clumsy; there were very few objects, and an absence of elaboration, differentiation, and movement.[4]

In the later part of this period, when the devils began to reveal their human origin and when her childhood history was being translated from the 'devil-language', she proceeded to paint Victorian family scenes showing certain of her childhood situations. Here phantasies were worked out more fully; more objects and more events occurred, and details which offered a possibility of variation and differentiation supplied more life and movement.

The painter derived great relief and pleasure from these pictures; she made her name by them in the artistic world, and she even set a fashion. But there was an obsessional element in this form of restoration which interfered with its sublimatory value. She herself became aware of it as an anxiety that she might not be able to paint in any other manner but this, and that if she was compelled to go on with this type of painting her possibilities of self-expression would be gravely restricted; if she had no other function in life but that of restoring her childhood objects, she would not attain the full range of a boundless territory in which to develop herself.

The next phase in her analysis was characterized by the disappearance of persecution by devils and also of her very severe depressions and suicidal impulses. There were still anxieties of a persecutory nature, relating to the doings of people she felt were inside her, but they were people and not devils; there were also milder depressions and fewer obsessional features in her relation to painting.

The significance of her striving to paint, moreover, gradually developed into a desire to express herself and to *improve* her internal objects, as distinguished from a compulsion to save them from unutterable destruction.

Ernest Jones (1937) has pointed out the great significance of the difference between doing something out of love or out of a sense of duty. To my mind the biggest advance in the development of the patient's personality was shown, not only when she became capable of restoring her objects out of love instead of from compulsive necessity, but when she began to struggle to do something for herself at the same time. She could then attempt this not in her old way, in which whatever her mother gained she lost and vice versa, but in such a way that she could – to some extent – rest assured that she was not still devouring and destroying her objects and need not therefore sacrifice herself utterly and completely for them, but could afford to aim also at the widest possible unfolding and expansion of herself. This in turn would then also enlarge her capacity to restore and benefit her objects.

I do not wish to convey the impression that everything was all right with the patient at this time. She was not yet well, and I could enumerate a number of symptoms which showed her neurosis. This holds good also to some degree even for the present phase of analysis. In the phase I am decribing she proceeded from painting pictures of Victorian life to painting life of the present day; and the boundless territory she had sought for her activities was reached in that anything and everything was capable of inspiring her. The pictures of this period show a great advance in colour and composition. During this period her internal objects (previously represented by the devils) appeared frequently in the form of artistic problems. Her interest was thus not only more objective, but far richer and comprehending far more varied details. Her internal conflicts were objectified in terms of aesthetic and technical problems. Instead of suffering from the torments of a devilish father and mother, she struggled with the problems of 'human interest' and 'aesthetic interest' in painting.

I will now refer to a recent session with the patient, though I shall not give a full account of the hour and of the analytic work done in it. To make the situation clear it is necessary for me to describe the setting of the transference which forms the context of the hour. Two recent events had characterized the tone of the transference:

(1) I had surmised correctly from her associations an external factor belonging to a very important event in her past life and she felt

that I had made a discovery. It concerned an exceedingly painful experience of her father's when he had left the family.

(2) She had come into contact with a man whom she connected with me, and she suspected that I used him to spy on her and to relate to me facts in her life which would enable me to deprive her of her pleasures and of all her good internal possessions.

A third point worth mentioning is that in her painting at this time the technical problem of 'joining up' was absorbing her interest. She reacted to my discovery about the very painful incident concerning her father with great relief, which showed itself in an increase of activities and in a liberation of sexual feelings, leading to a sexual intercourse with her husband after many months of complete abstinence. She felt very grateful to me and admired me, but at the same time her persecutory anxieties and suspicions about my finding out about everything in order to take everything away from her were greatly stimulated.

On that particular day she began the hour thus: 'I am fed up. My mouth is full of ulcers.' She then told me a story of what had happened to her car that day. She said: 'A fool of a man drove into it. Would you believe it? All the scratches on my car have been made by other people.' She then proceeded to describe in a very emotional way another unpleasant experience she had had that morning. When she was going along in her car, after all her excitement and anger about the man driving into it, another car exceeding the speed limit drove up on her wrong side. 'Of course', she said, 'it was a woman driver.' In front there was a lorry which gave a sign and turned to the right into a side turning. Immediately after that the woman on her left, without giving any sign, turned to the right also, passing in front of my patient's car, and in order to avoid a collision she herself quickly swerved her own car into the same right-hand turning, although she had intended to go straight on. She was 'livid with anger' (I am trying as far as possible to repeat her own words) and now took her revenge on the woman by getting in front of her and crawling along at five miles an hour and making it impossible for the woman behind to pass. Presently they came to red traffic lights. The woman pulled up and was now on the same level as my patient, who poked her head out of the window and said: 'That was the worst piece of road-hogging I have ever seen. Do you know that by cutting-in in front of me from the wrong side you forced me to turn to the right so as to avoid a collision, though I wanted to go straight on?' The woman, who had a red beery face, gave a shrug and a laugh and said: 'What do I care?' My patient was furious and sat trying to think of a most scathing remark. Finally she found it: 'On second thoughts', she said, 'there is an excuse for you. I can see that you are well beyond your prime. You should leave driving to women who are younger and more intelligent than yourself.' The woman gasped, but before she could reply the traffic lights changed and my patient drove off. She was very pleased with herself.

I omit my interpretations and add only some more of the material pertaining to our problem.

My patient now drove to her art school and started on a sketch to a given theme; this theme had to do with stealing. She started the sketch, but found that there was something wrong with her drawing, both while she was working on it and when she had finished and hung it up on the wall. She could not find out what it was, and she said to me: 'That was the most awful thing about it.' When the artist who criticized the sketches came to hers, he said in surprise: 'Good God, what has happened to you? This looks like a drawing out of a Victorian family album.' My patient now realized what it was she had felt to be wrong with it. She said: 'It looked like a drawing that had been done fifty years ago.' She felt so awful about this that she had to go and have three sherries. Later she noticed the ulcers in her mouth. I may say here that she never drinks when level-headed. In fact, one of her great anxieties is that she might become addicted to alcohol as her father was.

I will now summarize these points. The patient started by mentioning that she was fed up and her mouth was full of ulcers. Then she proceeded to tell me the events of the day preceding the ulcers, that is to say, the history of the ulcers.

(1) A 'fool of a man' had scratched her car.
(2) She had made scathing remarks to a bad woman.
(3) She hurt the woman by a reference to her age and by demanding that she should yield up driving to herself (the younger and more intelligent woman).
(4) The woman had a red 'beery' face (was drunk).
(5) My patient was very pleased with her scathing remark to the woman.
(6) Something was wrong with her drawing, that is to say, a sublimatory activity was impaired. She did not know what was wrong with it and this was 'the most awful thing' in the situation. She had to go to a public house and have three sherries.
(7) Later she found ulcers in her mouth.

It is important to know that the fault of her drawing was that 'it looked as though it was fifty years old', 'out of a Victorian family album'.

It seems to me that the various symptoms,

(1) the unintentionally old-fashioned painting,
(2) the need to drink alcohol,
(3) the appearance of the ulcers,

point clearly to what had been going on in the patient's unconscious. She had carried out her impulse to hurt the woman and was consciously pleased with her success. But unconsciously – as the woman stood for me and her mother, towards whom she had love impulses as well as hostile ones – she could not bear the injuries she had inflicted on her nor could she remain at a distance from her. She had immediately internalized this mother-figure and she had internalized her in the injured condition for which she felt responsible and guilty, namely, as a worn-out, fifty-year-old, decrepit, incompetent, and useless person; and then she herself became changed, for she was necessarily affected by the injuries and faults of the internalized object.

The ulcers corresponded to the feeling that she had treated the woman scathingly by her sneering remarks; the out-of-date, inadequate drawing corresponded to her having deprived the woman of her prime; and the need to drink reflected the red 'beery' face of the woman. There were of course more determinants for the various symptoms, of which I will only mention some. Thus the ulcers expressed the need to punish the organ which was the instrument of the criminal impulse in a manner that fitted the crime; and they were further related to the phantasies which the scratches on her car had aroused. The experience with the 'fool of a man' and the later encounter with the beery-faced woman had stimulated phantasies about her parents in their persecutory intercourse, phantasies of the kind I described earlier. In her unconscious mind her father had injured her (the car with the scratches) at the command of her hostile jealous mother. (Just as I – in her phantasies – had sent the man whom she connected with me to spy on her and report her doings to me.)

The persecution by the woman driver, 'the road-hog', assumed such an intensity, moreover, because the woman with her red 'beery' face also reminded my patient of her father, whom she had often seen in an intoxicated state.

Along with the conscious feeling of triumph at having successfully attacked the bad woman went an unconscious feeling of guilt. This woman who was her rival and who compelled her to follow a way she did not want to go – to the 'right' – is also identified with her mother and me whom she, at the same time, loved and admired. Unconsciously she was admitting that the wrong way the woman made her take was the right and good way which her mother (and analysis) showed her. She had indeed felt a great relief when I had discovered the painful incident in her father's life which had oppressed her so much, and she acknowledged the help analysis had given her, although her admiration for me stimulated her feelings of rivalry, owing to which she turned me again into an interfering and hostile mother. She was able to deny her anxiety and her guilt and to feel only triumph about her scathing remarks because other mechanisms, namely, self-punishment and the restoration of the injured object, were also at work (the ulcers, the old-fashioned drawing, and the urge to drink).

It is important to see that the atonement for guilt is here carried out by internalizing the attacked external object and restoring it after the internalization in a specific manner in which every detail of the crime has to be dealt with and which corresponds to the subject's conception of the object's character and qualities. The patient felt that the mother-figure to whom she had made the scathing remarks, out of whose hands she had torn the driving wheel and the capacity to steer her way through life, was now inside herself; and in order to restore the destroyed mother-figure she had to take on to herself the condition resulting from the scathing treatment (the ulcers) and to yield up to the mother-figure the steering wheel (the crayons) and her own capacity, the artist's skill. The woman inside her had drawn the sketch, while she herself was poisoned and sore; she had become the mother-figure she had attacked.

We can see that the internal object exerted an influence on the patient's sublimation in that the sketch bore the imprint of the internal object and not that of the subject, and that, in this way, the sublimatory activity was impaired. We did not hear that the sketch was badly drawn, or that the design or the technique was faulty, but that it did not reflect the patient's personality, that it was an inadequate expression of her intention (she had not set out to paint in a Victorian fashion), and that it was alien to her understanding. The experience of self-expression and development with its accompanying conscious gratification was completely absent in this impaired sublimation. This is really the point I wish to illustrate, for it is related to those aspects of the problem of sublimation with which I am here concerned and which have so far not found sufficient recognition. I refer to the element of *internal freedom and independence* which I consider to be an essential condition for successful sublimation.

The child who avoids dirtying or does his homework well because

40

he is afraid of being punished by his mother, or because he has to placate her in order to secure her love and good gifts, has not achieved sublimation in the full sense of the word; he is not carrying out an activity which enables him to express his personality, the wishes, impulses, and inclinations he feels to be his own. In a similar manner, the work of an adult who is compulsively dominated by his internal objects has not the character of a full and true sublimation either.

We know that the impulse to restore is a most fundamental factor in sublimation and creative production. But if guilt and anxiety are too strong they interfere with the successful functioning of the impulse to restore, because they lead to the employment of various mechanisms for *magical control* of the internal persecutors. This control, however, in its turn keeps the ego under control and interferes with the independent ego-expanding activities which are implied in successful sublimation.

I referred to the arousing of anxieties in my patient related to phantasies about the combined parental figures – the parents inside engaged in a warlike intercourse. In such a state the subject is compelled to save the parents and himself from their mutually destructive doings; he is bound to separate them in their disastrous union[5] and to do whatever serves this end, and he is therefore hampered in the expression of his own impulses, wishes, and talents.

Fear of persecution and distrust of the internal objects necessitate defence, just as the supreme purpose in a war is to secure and safeguard vital issues, and this pushes all other tasks into the background. The productive capacity becomes overwhelmed by the subject's frantic efforts at saving his life and the lives of his internal objects whom he feels to be one with him. Whilst thus the dangers from the persecutory actions of the combined parents inside him urge the subject to separate them, their separation brings about new dangers, for they are now felt to be in a hopeless state of aphanisis;[6] moreover, the subject becomes impoverished and impotent on account of having only aphanitic parents inside him. Between the Scylla of persecutorily combined parents and the Charybdis of guiltily destroyed parents the subject is caught in hopeless despair.

The acute anxieties attaching to the primitive combined parental figure lead to severe restriction of the subject's activities and inner freedom. When the subject distorts the parent's sexuality into destructiveness, he is thereby inhibited from obtaining gratifications for himself, whether of a direct or of a sublimated nature. My patient could not enjoy the symbolic intercourse with her crayons nor give birth to a child-picture, because her fear and guilt about her ageing and deprived mother were too intense. There is a great difference between wanting to paint Victorian family scenes and being unconsciously compelled (by an internal Victorian mother) to paint in a Victorian fashion. Indeed she had felt it as awful – as the most awful thing – that, certain though she was that something was wrong with the drawing, she did not know what it was. She did not know her own creation.[7]

My experience has convinced me that the kind of restoration in which the injured object is felt to be snatching away the subject's good possessions leads to an impaired sublimation; because this type of restoration has too much the character of revenge and punishment by the objects, a penal servitude, an utter sacrifice on the part of the subject. In it the relation between subject and object is too much on the basis of oral sadism and too far from co-operation and mutual give-and-take.[8]

All these anxiety situations are well known and have often been described. But I contend that the anxieties resulting from a *compulsion* to look after the good internal objects, to preserve them in a good condition, to subordinate all activities to their well-being and to watch them constantly also constitutes a danger to the success of a sublimation. The anxieties relating to bad and good internal objects which interfere with the subject's internal freedom are bound to arise when the internalized parents are felt as foreign bodies embedded in the self.

I think that the independence which is an important factor in successful sublimation and productive activity is achieved through a process which I like to call the 'assimilation' of the internal objects, by which the subject acquires and absorbs those qualities of his internal parents which are suitable and adequate to him.[9] As Goethe says:

Was Du ererbt von Deinen Vätern hast,
Erwirb es, um es zu besitzen.

[What you inherited from your fathers,
You must acquire yourself in order to possess it.]

This process presupposes a diminution of aggressiveness (greed) and anxiety and thus involves a breaking up of the vicious circle. The subject withdraws the extreme features which he has superimposed on his external objects by his own sadism, guilt, and anxiety, when he can accept them as his own. Thus his internal objects become more human, less like monsters, less like saints; and the subject can admit and accept his own bad and good qualities and those of his internalized parents. These assume more the character which the external parents had and the subject in his phantasy feels that he is creating his parents rather than swallowing them – the child is father to the man – and with the diminution of greed he acquires the right to absorb their good qualities.

This process also contributes to the setting free of forces which the subject can employ for his own benefit in a free choice of activity and for the development of his talents. This will result in an increase of productive capacities directed towards actual reality and aiming at a truer expression of the self and in an increase of the gratification experienced through his sublimatory activities.

I do not mean that the assimilation of the internal objects leads to a static condition in which the conflicts cease to exist. As I have said, the inner world is a never-ending drama of life and action. Life is bound up with the dynamic processes set up by aggression, guilt, anxiety, and grief about the internal objects, and by the impulses of love and restoration; love and hate are urging the subject to strive for sublimation. The internal freedom to which I refer is a relative, not an absolute fact; it does not abolish conflicts, but it enables the subject to enlarge and unfold his ego in his sublimations.

Notes

1 It will be seen later that, although this view of the father as good and the mother as bad is part and parcel of the familiar Oedipus attitude, such an exaggerated, uncompromising, and compulsive form of it is no simple and direct expression of Oedipus feelings. It is rather a complicated outcome of phantasies concerning both libidinal and aggressive wishes for and against both parents, and defences against these, that is, the *separation* of the parents was the essential aim in it, as an expression of the patient's necessity to keep her own love for them separate and unaffected by her hate for them in her inner world.

2 I believe that the analysis can count on the patient's support where there exists a more or less definite channel for sublimatory activities, especially when these amount to real creativeness. The ego sets great store by its creative abilities. My impression is that this support is greater in artists than, for instance, in scientists. It may be because the scientist knows that his production will not last in the form he gives it, that his own contribution creates the very means for its being surpassed by the advance of knowledge at which he aims, whereas the artist can feel that his creation is potentially immortal.

3 Cf. (pp. 37–8) the ulcers which she produced on a certain occasion.

4 The primitive character of this first picture painted without morphia, its lack of detail and imagination, expressed the extreme urgency of the danger in which she felt her good objects to be. She had, as it were, to apply every energy to the single attempt to save their existence and rescue them from a condition of most critical extremity. At such a moment no question arises of comforting such almost lifeless persons by minor arrangements having no bearing on the main dangers: just as it would never occur to one to put flowers in the sickroom of someone whose life was at that instant threatened by a haemorrhage. All minor considerations cease to exist when a live-saving operation is a matter of moments.

5 Cf. note 1.

6 Ernest Jones (1927) introduced the term 'aphanisis'. This concept seems to me to constitute a step forward in our understanding of the fear of castration; for it shows that the experience is not simply that of losing an organ which produces gratification, but that a totality of experience is in question, a threat of the loss of all capacities for ever experiencing any gratification of the libido and thus of all capacity for establishing a 'good' relation to an object. This concept to my mind approaches very nearly to that kind of experience in which the main purpose is to acquire and maintain a 'good' object, internal as well as external. Though Ernest Jones himself has not followed up the idea of aphanisis to the point at which it might link on to the problem of anxieties concerning internalized good objects, I feel that nevertheless his thought was tending in this direction and has widened our understanding.

7 Painters often express the feeling that their hands are only the instruments of something within them that directs their activity. But the tone of this feeling varies greatly, and indicates whether this invisible force (their internal objects) is beneficial, in harmony with the artist's personality, or persecutory, as in this example of my patient's.

8 It will be seen that these phenomena are such as are usually described as due to the superego. I have refrained from using this term (as well as the term 'id'), as it has not been possible within the compass of this paper to discuss the relation between the concepts of internalized objects and of the superego (or of the id). I hope to deal with these problems in a future paper, and will remind the reader here of Melanie Klein's work on this subject, notably in *The Psycho-Analysis of Children* (1932).

9 In a paper recently published by Matte-Blanco (1941), he refers explicitly to my present paper and implicitly to its whole subject-matter. In it he criticizes Melanie Klein and her collaborators – among whom he rightly associates myself – on various grounds. It is not my intention to deal here in any detail with the many inaccurate statements in his paper. I shall **restrict myself to one instance only. Among other things he takes Melanie**

Klein to task for having ignored the ways in which the internalized objects become integrated in the ego, a criticism which, as can be seen from the literature concerned, is fallacious. The method used by Matte-Blanco in his polemic is, I think, best illustrated by the fact that he quotes (p. 26) – though inaccurately – the above passage from my present paper and expresses agreement with it, yet nowhere in his paper does he acknowledge that this passage and my whole paper are a contribution towards the solution of the very problem which he accuses Melanie Klein and her school of having failed to understand. In spite of his agreement with this passage, he says (p. 18): 'Attempts at further development are continually made by Melanie Klein and her followers, but the result seems to be nothing more than, to use a graphic French expression, *"piétiner sur place"*, moving incessantly without ever succeeding in going forward.' Further (on p. 24): 'The introjected object, no matter how much divided into small pieces, no matter how many pilgrimages it makes from inside to outside and *vice versa*, will always remain what these conceptions suggest – something immobile, something outside the psyche of the individual, foreign to it, whose ultimate fate can be none other than expulsion.' This may be his opinion, but my case, on the contrary, clearly illustrated the view that internal objects are far from immobile and very much alive, and essentially a part of the subject's personality. The wish to expel them is but one reaction to one aspect of them (the persecutory). Incidentally, the fear of losing them (in their good aspects) is one of the severest anxieties human beings can experience.

2

Notes on the theory of the life and death instincts (1942(3)/1952c)

This paper is an enlarged and expanded version of a contribution Paula Heimann made to the 'Controversial Discussions' (1942(3)) at the British Psycho-Analytical Society. It was published in Melanie Klein, Paula Heimann, Susan Isaacs, and Joan Riviere *Developments in Psycho-Analysis*, London: Hogarth Press and the Institute of Psycho-Analysis (1952).

A new psychological era began with the discovery by Breuer and Freud (1893)[1] that the hysterical symptoms of their patient were caused by unsolved intrapsychic conflicts. Following the observations made in this particular case Freud continued to investigate his patients' emotional life, and his researches into the nature of conflict led him to the discovery of the unconscious. From this point he proceeded to explore the dynamics and structure of the mind and to evolve his theories about mental illness and mental development. One might, therefore, call the systematic investigation of emotional conflict – up till then outside the sphere of medical science – the birth of psychoanalysis.

Freud traced emotional conflicts to the operation of basic forces with opposite aims, that is, antagonistic instincts. Throughout his work he maintained a dualistic approach to psychological processes and stressed the necessity to understand the nature of the instincts. At first, following the generally accepted contrast between hunger and love, he saw the opposing instinctual forces in the self-preservative and sexual instincts; later he differentiated between ego instincts and sexual instincts and thought that this dualism was in keeping with the human being's double role of an individual and a representative of his species. But advances in his work did not corroborate this distinction, and ultimately he arrived at the conclusion that a life instinct and a death instinct are the prime movers of human behaviour.

It is interesting to see how Freud himself hesitated to give full recognition and status, as it were, to his last discovery about the instincts, and yet how he was driven on by its impelling truth to follow his notion of an antithesis as final and cardinal as that between a primary instinct of life and a primary instinct of death. He stressed the hypothetical nature of this theory, never regarded it as a shibboleth of psychoanalysis, and merely confessed to a 'cool goodwill' for it. Yet his writings contain passages like the following which clearly show conviction in his theory: 'They [a group of instincts] are the actual life instincts; the fact that they run counter to the trend of the other instincts which lead towards death indicates a contradiction between them and the rest, one which the theory of the neuroses has recognized as full of significance' (Freud 1920).[2]

Freud (1917a)[3] once explained the hostile reception of his discoveries by the fact that, like those of Copernicus and Darwin, they wound man's narcissism. Copernicus destroyed the cherished belief that man's earth is in the centre of the universe (the 'cosmological blow' to narcissism); from Darwin came the 'biological blow', when he showed that man has no privileged position in the scheme of creation; and psychoanalysis caused the 'psychological blow' by discovering that man is not master in his own inner world since there are unconscious mental processes beyond his control.

I would suggest that Freud's theory of the death instinct has much intensified this psychological blow. The resentment and anxiety roused by interference with man's narcissism are bound to be still greater when to the painful wound is added the fear that the forces of death are active in man himself.[4]

The theory of the death instinct is frowned upon and has been much disputed. One argument denies its legitimate origin from psychological considerations and asserts that Freud arrived at it exclusively by way of speculation and imaginings concerning biological events. In fact this is not so. In *Beyond the Pleasure Principle* Freud (1920g) clearly starts with clinical material, that is, the dreams of patients suffering from traumatic neuroses which, in contrast to the wish-fulfilling function of dreams, repeat the painful traumatic event; also the play of children re-enacting an unpleasant experience over and over again. While it is true that he breaks off the discussion of both these phenomena, it is clear that he does so only after showing the element of repetition which is the essential point. He goes on to describe the observation that patients in psychoanalytic treatment, instead of remembering repressed events, *repeat* them in their current lives, thus causing much pain to themselves. From clinical observations he comes to deduce the existence of the 'repetition-compulsion', a concept which has since fully proved its validity for psychological work, and shows that this compulsion is ubiquitous and not dictated by the pleasure-principle.

The fact is therefore that Freud proceeded from clinical observations when he embarked on the journey which led him to assume the death instinct and that on his way he discovered a most important psychological principle; namely, the repetition-compulsion; moreover, throughout he kept in contact with clinical facts.[5]

His biological speculations suggest that, when by an event which 'baffles conjecture' life was created from the inanimate, the tendency to return to the original condition came into being as well. Together with the life instinct the death instinct began to operate in the animate being. We may leave it to the biologists to judge the value of Freud's biological considerations, but we have the right to use the psychological part – to use it without claiming that it solves all the mysteries of human life.

Psychological work does not show the operation of instinct directly. What we do see is impulses giving rise to emotions, hopes, fears, conflicts, behaviour, and actions. We observe processes like the transformation of unconscious desire into conscious fear, or of unconscious hate into conscious exaggerated love.

Let us distinguish between impulses as clinically observable entities and instincts as the ultimate forces from which these impulses spring. Instinct is then a concept, an abstraction, consistent with a particular psychological approach. We can neither prove nor disprove it by direct observation. What we can do is to present an interpretation of the facts which we observe. Such interpretation will include some speculation, which, naturally, is open to doubt. Science cannot be pursued, however, by the mere collection of observable material. If we never leave the ground of facts, we give up scientific procedure, which arrives by means of abstraction and inference – speculation – at the discovery of the principles of which the observed facts are a manifestation. A non-analytical psychologist[6] said: 'Science extends the range of evidence beyond what is accessible to common sense.' The scientific worker must combine sober observation with imaginative interpretation. There are pitfalls. Imagination may lead astray if it moves too far from the facts observed, but such a flight of fantasy is not more fruitless than the mechanical listing of facts without any imaginative work on the data obtained.[7]

It has been said that Freud's theory of the instincts trespasses outside psychology into physiology and biology – but so does the subject-matter of psychology, the human being. Psychologists, psychiatrists, and psychoanalysts – none of us deals with an isolated psyche. We are daily shown the extension of psychological forces into the physical sphere by processes like conversion symptoms and psychosomatic disorders (and vice versa, the effect of physical processes on a person's psychological condition) and we cannot exclude physiological and biological considerations from our work.

The study of human behaviour compels us to recognize a dualistic source of forces in the depths of the personality. Moreover, our observations show us that there is no sharp cleavage between mind and body. This compels us to introduce a physical factor into our concept of the ultimate dualistic source. These requirements are fulfilled by Freud's concept of primary instincts pursuing the opposite aims of life and death.

According to Freud's theory the two basic instincts are always fused with each other. The nature of this fusion and the events which alter the proportions or the effectiveness of either instinct must be of the greatest significance, but as yet our knowledge does not take us that far. It may well be that it is the character of this instinctual blend which decides whether an attitude or an activity is healthy or morbid.

Though fused, the two basic instincts struggle against each other within the organism. The life instinct aims at union and drives one individual towards others, the death instinct aims at breaking up the organism and the union between individual organisms, or at preventing such union from being formed. The development from the unicellular to the multicellular individual, with its increasing differentiation through the formation of organs with specialized functions, would be the work of the life instinct; at the same time this development constitutes as many targets for the death instinct, since every step in union offers a potential disintegration.

The theory of the two basic instincts led to a new classification. Both the sexual and the self-preservative instincts are now considered the representatives of the life instinct. The former view that the two aims of human life are in conflict has been corrected. In essence they are complementary. Normally a person's feeling of being alive is supremely heightened in the act of procreation, and fulfilment of the individual coincides with that of the species. Psychoanalytic investigation has shown that, where there are conflicts between the two aims, they arise from disturbances in the individual's development, but they cannot be attributed to an inherent antithesis between these aims themselves.

The psychological expression of the life instinct is found in love, in **constructive trends** and co-operative behaviour, all of which essentially spring from the drive for union; the poetic phrase 'Eros as the force that binds' is often quoted in psychoanalytic literature. The death instinct is expressed by hate, destructiveness, and negativistic trends, that is, all those modes of behaviour which are antagonistic towards making or maintaining connections, intrapsychically as well as socially.

Freud suggested that the main technique available to the life instinct in its fight against the death instinct is the deflection outward of the death instinct. He regarded this mechanism as the origin of projection and thought that the death instinct is 'mute' when it operates inside the organism and becomes manifest only in acts subsequent to deflection.

It is, however, a question whether the death instinct is so 'mute' when it attacks the self. There are ample opportunities for watching self-destructive behaviour, from small blunders which people commit obviously against their own interests to serious self-damage ('accident-proneness'), gross masochistic behaviour, and suicide. Moreover, the existence of physical illness and deterioration as well as of difficulties in recovery should be attributed to the operation of the death instinct, which meets the external damaging agencies half-way and facilitates their influence.

The problem of projection of the dangerous forces within is also not simple. Not only destructive impulses are projected, a process which relieves the person from the pain of feeling dangerous urges raging within himself. Good, loving impulses and traits too are projected,[8] and such projection will prove helpful or dangerous according to the character of the object chosen for it, and of the further relations with this object. The danger of projection lies in its obscuring reality; often indeed it leads to serious delusions. To project 'good' loving impulses on to a 'bad' object and thus turn it 'good' may be no less harmful than to project destructive, 'bad' impulses on to a loved object and so to lose it. On the other hand, projection of good impulses will prove beneficial if it strengthens the subject's attachment to a benevolent object and allows the subject to introject goodness from it. (Such introjection includes the subject's receiving again what was originally part of his own ego.)

The statement that love represents the life instinct and hate the death instinct needs some qualification. In sado-masochism love is intricately connected with the wishes to inflict and to suffer pain, tendencies derived from the death instinct. Yet these phenomena do not challenge the theory of the primary instincts. They are evidence for the fusion between them, which is part of the theory. The same consideration holds for hate, if directed against an assailant, and even for the killing of another person in self-defence. Destructive behaviour in the service of self-preservation indicates that the fusion between the basic instincts is in favour of the life instinct. This interpretation is supported by the observation that, when self-defence is the predominant motive, aggression is not deliberately cruel.

These examples, moreover, warn us against any attempt to oversimplify matters. We cannot draw a straight line from an event on the complex higher level of experience to one basic instinct. In the course of development from the latter to the former, manifold vicissitudes of the primary instinctual aim take place, precisely as a result of the influence exerted by the antithetical instinct, the interaction between the basic instincts.

There are, however, certain observations which suggest that the basic instinctual fusion is capable of modification to such a degree as to allow either basic instinct to operate almost unalloyed. A kind of defusion seems to take place with either instinct reigning supreme. I have in mind examples of extreme self-sacrifice and devotion (without a masochistic pleasure-premium) on the one hand, and of wanton and excessive cruelty on the other.

I wish to discuss only the latter, since the former are not usually treated as a controversial psychological problem.

It is unnecessary to give instances. From time to time the world is shocked by reports of savagely cruel, 'bestial' murders committed by an individual or a group. Excessive cruelty is committed, either without any provocation or, if there was some provocation, the cruelty displayed clearly exceeded what could be considered necessary or expedient in response. Moreover, in such cases the cruel acts are so calculated and worked out in detail that nothing but an instinctual urge for savage cruelty can be regarded as the motive and purpose. The murderer needs a victim to satisfy his urge to inflict maximal suffering on someone, and he proceeds obviously without any inhibition arising from empathy, guilt, or horror at what he is doing.

Strangely enough, such behaviour is usually regarded as perverse sexuality, and often such crimes are called 'sexual crimes'. It is true that sadism is a form of sexual perversion, but it is necessary to distinguish between sexual practices in which sadism (and masochism) have some share, and violent assaults in which cruelty is the predominant feature. In a strict sense of the term, sexual perversion should refer to such physical intimacies between adults in which fore-pleasure excels over end-pleasure, oral and excretory activities, voyeuristic and exhibitionistic aims exceed the urge for heterosexual intercourse, and also where bodily pleasure is derived from contact with a person of the same sex. Freud has shown that such perverse sexuality (which usually contains a small admixture of sadistic and masochistic elements) is due to a persistence of infantile sexuality, and represents ways in which a child experiences sexual gratification.

The murdered victim of the so-called sexual crime does not die from a sexual experience, however infantile it may be, but from the infliction of maximally cruel violence. The sexual aspect of the murderer's behaviour may possibly only be introduced in order to deceive the victim and so to provide the opportunity for the aim of the urge to cruelty. Possibly the murderer starts in a state of sexual excitement, which, however, soon subsides and merely serves to open the floodgates to the violent and destructive impulses. It seems that the investigators of these crimes are aware that only the elemental power of an instinct can be their cause, but can only concede to sexuality the character of such an instinctual force. I would suggest that Freud's theory of the two basic instincts in the struggle against one another, and of the deflection outward of the death instinct by the life instinct, gives us an idea of the forces concerned. I think the hypothesis is justified that in cases of wanton cruelty a kind of instinctual disaster takes place, that for some reason the fusion between the two primary instincts is broken up, and the death instinct stirs within the self to an extreme degree without any mitigation by the life instinct, so that the only defence by the latter is the most primitive; that is, the crude deflection of the inner danger of cruel suffering and death on to a victim. I do not suggest that the murderer experiences his own threatening inner catastrophe in any way consciously, or that he acts in a state of conscious panic, but I think that his actions can only be understood by the assumption of his being seized by a frenzied urge to find a victim – as a substitute for himself. This assumption alone seems to me to explain the complete absence of any empathy with the victim's suffering, the need for as many savage details in the act of murdering as possible and the satisfaction obtained (mistakenly thought to be sexual in nature) by the victim's agonies. Owing to some such process at the deepest level, which for want of more certain knowledge I call an instinctual catastrophe, the murderer must feel the raging of the force of death within himself to such an intense degree, because uncontrolled by the life instinct, that nothing but deflection outward could save him from it.

Freud's theory of the instincts of life and death as the ultimate source of motivations represents a most comprehensive co-ordination system for our clinical observations which clearly indicate that emotions and behaviour are the result of the impact of two opposed forces. The much-discussed problem of the origin of anxiety, too, now appears in a clearer light.

In the main, there are three theories concerning the origin of anxiety. The first is Freud's original theory, which regards anxiety as the result of an 'automatic transformation' of repressed libidinal impulses. When a libidinal claim is repressed, anxiety appears in its place. Although Freud (1926d)[9] later qualified this statement and pointed to the observation that anxiety often precedes repression, and even though at times he seemed to discard this theory, he yet did not in fact abandon it. It recurs frequently in his writings.

The second theory was put forward by Ernest Jones (1911)[10], who started by considering what it is that enables human beings to feel fear at all. He concluded that there is an 'innate capacity of fearing', which he classified as the 'fear instinct'.

Melanie Klein (1932, 1948)[11] has produced the third theory. Anxiety arises in a direct line from the destructive impulses; the danger to the organism from the death instinct, the source of the destructive impulses, is the primary cause of anxiety. The libidinal factor, however, enters her theory, in that libidinal frustration by heightening aggression increases or liberates anxiety, whereas libidinal gratification diminishes or keeps anxiety at bay. In operation therefore it is the degree of fusion and the interplay between the primary instincts which are responsible for anxiety.

I think it is possible to define this interaction and to describe the share of either instinct in the production of anxiety. It will then be seen that these three theories, which seem to be greatly at variance between themselves, can be reconciled.

There can be no doubt that the capacity of fearing is innate, as much so as the capacity of loving or hating. It forms part of the individual's psychological equipment. Anxiety may be regarded as the condition in which the capacity of fearing is actuated. It is subjectively felt as a state of painful tension which impels the individual to take steps towards its removal, and these steps imply defences against the danger. In this way anxiety serves a protective function[12] and must be ranged together with the self-preservative instincts. This would mean that it is the life instinct to which the innate capacity of fearing should be attributed, as well as its activation in the experience of anxiety.

The danger, on the other hand, against which the life instinct institutes and mobilizes the capacity of fearing originates in the operations of the death instinct, whose aims are antagonistic to life and health.[13]

Danger arising primarily within the organism provides the stimulus for the human being's innate capacity of fearing. This pattern may be regarded as the intrapsychic disposition for recognizing external dangers and using against them defences learnt originally in the response to internal danger.

These considerations obviously make full use of Melanie Klein's theory and of Ernest Jones's concept of an 'innate capacity of fearing', whilst they make it unnecessary to complicate the theory of the basic instincts by assuming a third primary instinct.

As regards Freud's original theory of an 'automatic transformation' of repressed libido, I would suggest that two factors have to be recognized. First, that the notion of an 'automatic' process in the production of anxiety implies an instinctual element, an event on the instinctual level; second, we have to consider the force which is responsible for the inhibition of a libidinal impulse. As we know, inhibition of a libidinal desire may lead to substitute-gratification – for example, sublimation – and in such a case anxiety does not appear and no unfavourable condition of tension ensues. If the repression of a libidinal desire leads to an intolerable condition, it can be seen in analysis that destructive impulses[14] enter into the libidinal wish, so that the gratification desired (and repressed) would have simultaneously allowed their expression as well (a deflection outwards of the death instinct). In such cases libidinal repression leads to anxiety, in response to the danger from the stirring of the death instinct within the self. The anxiety which is connected with certain types of repression is thus the response to a danger which arises from the activity of the death instinct. The notion of an 'automatic transformation' of repressed libido implies a struggle between the basic instincts in which the life instinct cannot enforce full victory (libidinal gratification or sublimation), but in face of the danger can bring about the anxiety response.

It may be useful to state explicitly that I have been concerned only with the origin of anxiety on the deepest, the instinctual level, and not with the complex processes on higher levels, which, however, are constructed according to the basic pattern.

One word may be added about the many instances in which anxiety fails in bringing about purposeful, protective behaviour. As we know, an excess of anxiety may paralyse the person and thus aggravate the danger against which it should protect. In such cases the struggle between the basic instincts issues in favour of the death instinct which has proved capable of interfering with the very defence, the mobilization of the capacity of fearing, which the life instinct brought about. A similar constellation of forces would account for the undue absence of anxiety and of protective behaviour in the face of danger.

Freud's final theory of primary instincts of life and death, clinically represented by the impulses of love, sexuality, and self-preservation or of destructiveness and cruelty, has not yet been fully worked out and applied. In his work the libido-theory still stands in its original form, in which cruelty is treated as a 'component instinct' of the libido. Psychoanalytical theory has treated the two instincts in an unequal manner: the sexual instinct is the first-born and privileged child, the destructive instinct is the late-comer, the stepchild. The first was recognized from the beginning and distinguished with a name, *libido*; it took much longer to recognize its adversary, which still has not been given a special name. (The term '*destrudo*' suggested by Edoardo Weiss (1935) many years ago has not received civic rights in psychoanalytical terminology.)

One of the foundation-stones of psychoanalysis is the principle that the libido develops anaclitically; that is, in dependence on the physiological functions. Although this principle, discovered by Freud, was readily enough accepted and its usefulness is established beyond doubt, its implications have not been worked out fully. All the familiar phenomena of oral, anal, muscular, and other erotisms, as well as those of the libidinal ties formed with the object which satisfies the physiological needs, exemplify the attachment of the libido to bodily functions. Melanie Klein's work with young children,[15] her discovery of the intensely destructive phantasies connected with bodily functions, produced the data which led to the conclusion that the same principle applies to the operation of the destructive impulses. In the light of her findings it can be seen that Freud, in discovering that libido attaches to the great physiological functions, did more than describe a character of the libido: he stated a special case of a broader principle, which concerns the mode of operation of instinct in general, and which rests upon the fact that the human organism is a mind/body entity. The instincts are the source of the energies on which all the mind/body processes depend. They lie on the borderland between soma and psyche; Janus-faced, they turn one face to the bodily, the other to the mental components of the organism. Both instincts – the libido and the destructive instincts – seek to fulfil their aims in bodily activities, just as, conversely, mental functions derive from them both.[16] Mental experiences are bound to accompany the operation of the instincts in the body, and an emotional relationship must follow in the wake of the bodily activities with the object who satisfies or frustrates them; that is, relations of both a libidinal and a destructive kind are formed with objects, beginning with the first. Conversely, the object's attitude in physical contact involves emotional elements as well. It goes without saying that the mother who feeds her child does not offer him *merely* a physical substance, nor has she herself merely a physical sensation.

Freud's view that the libido develops 'anaclitically' must be expanded to include also the development of relationships in which destructive impulses predominate. Frustration of physical needs paves the way for object-hostility. Early hate no less than early love is closely linked with bodily sensations. The terms 'oral-sadistic' and 'anal-sadistic' in fact describe the attachment of cruelty to bodily functions, although they were coined prior to the discovery that cruelty represents the death instinct, and is not part of the libido but fundamentally opposed to it.

There is another basic contention of the libido theory which is derived from the attachment of the libido to the physiological functions, namely, that of the erotogenicity of virtually all organs. This too must be expanded on the basis of Melanie Klein's work. The organs capable of producing pleasurable sensations involving libidinal phantasies will also be the seat of sensations which accompany destructive instinctual impulses and cruel phantasies.[17]

All bodily and mental activities, based as they are on the primary instincts, are bound to serve two masters, the life instinct and the death instinct.

Does the theory of a death instinct advance our psychological understanding further than the more simple concept of an instinct of destructiveness or of inborn aggressiveness would do? It has been argued that the speculations bound up with the concept of a death instinct are unnecessary, since all clinical data of destructiveness and cruelty can be accounted for by the assumption that there is an instinct of destructiveness.

Against this I would suggest that, by rejecting the postulate of an ultimate source for a destructive instinct (or for inborn aggressiveness), the entire background of our theoretical concepts and the total frame of reference for psychological work would be impoverished. The implications of the concept of a death instinct operating in antithesis to the life instinct are much richer than those of a destructive instinct. We should be in a similar situation to that in which we were with regard to sexual problems before the sexual instinct was recognized as derived from a greater entity, the life instinct. The imperative nature of the sexual impulses and the significance of pleasure for emotional life were only incompletely understood before Freud showed the derivation of the libido from the life instinct. There was an hiatus in the theoretical ordering of facts as long as the self-preservative instincts were seen in opposition to the sexual impulses. Many problems became more accessible when Freud united the sexual and the self-preservative instincts as varying expressions of the one superimposed force, the life instinct.

In a similar way cruelty and the whole system of motivations related to it can only be seen in true perspective if recognized as derived from a source as powerful and ultimate as the death instinct. Without this connection the destructive instinct hangs, so to say, in mid-air; it is like an ambassador without a country to account for his existence and function. Conversely, the theory of the life and death instincts, of an antithesis as final and cardinal as that between inherently conflicting primary instincts, offers us a bridge to the deepest aspects of human nature and simultaneously helps us to find our way through the confusing wealth of meanings (over-determination) and ambiguities of the surface expressions of the psychological processes. Over-determination is caused by the basic dualism and bears witness to the dynamic operations it engenders.

Again, acceptance of the theory of the death instinct changes our assessment of hostility and cruelty; so that since these are elements of the complex and interacting emotional network, our conception of the total personality is influenced. One sees the human mind by its very nature compelled to manipulate constantly between two basically opposed forces, from which all emotions, sensations, desires, and activities derive. It can never escape conflict and can never be static, but must always go on, one way or another, must always employ devices to mediate for an equilibrium between its antithetical drives. It is the successful outcome of such devices which brings states of harmony and oneness, and these states are threatened by endogenous as well as exogenous factors. And since the instincts are inborn, we have to conclude that some form of conflict exists from the beginning of life.

We claim that the orientation towards psychological problems which follows from the acceptance of the primary instincts of life and death is of inestimable value in our work. Our evaluation of the conflicts in *social* relations is notably influenced when we approach them against the dynamic background of a perpetual *intrapsychic* struggle between life and death. We hear a great deal in our work about wrongs done to our patients by their parents, wives, husbands, partners in work, and so on, and their complaints often seem truthful and in line with general observations. Yet analysis shows how much unhappy experiences are actively provoked or exploited by the sufferer. On account of the need to deflect hatred and destructiveness, ultimately the death instinct, from the self on to

57

objects, 'bad' objects are needed and will be created, if not found to hand.

Closely linked with this problem is that of frustration (of bodily needs or of libidinal desires) which also appears in a different light when considered in relation to the operation of the life and death instincts. Since frustration acts as a lever for the deflection of hate and destructiveness from the self, it is sought after because an object which inflicts the pain of frustration may be more justifiably hated and annihilated. Thus frustration has its appointed place in the design of primitive defences. But precisely for this reason a frustrating environment, lack of understanding and love are so dangerous for the child. When the environment meets his primitive needs for the deflection of his destructive impulses half-way by coldness, rejection, and hostility, a vicious circle is created. The child grows up in the expectation of badness and, when he finds his fears confirmed in the world outside, his own cruel and negativistic impulses are perpetuated and increased.

Our understanding of the individual becomes more poignant through our awareness of the deep biological sources from which his destructiveness, his defensive need for unhappiness, and his anxieties spring, and our capacity to deal with such baffling technical problems as sado-masochism, delusions of persecution, or negative therapeutic reactions will be greater through the light gained in our work from Freud's concept of the life and death instincts.

Notes

1 'On the psychical mechanisms of hysterical phenomena' (1893) Sigmund Freud (in collaboration with Joseph Breuer), Collected Papers I, 1924, London: Hogarth Press and the Institute of Psycho-Analysis; also *Studies on Hysteria* (1893–5) I 'On the psychical mechanism of hysterical phenomena: preliminary communication' (1893a) Breuer and Freud, SE 2: 1–17.

2 *Beyond the Pleasure Principle* (1920), p. 50, London and Vienna: International Psycho-Analytical Press (1922); also *Beyond the Pleasure Principle* (1920g) p. 40, SE 18: 7–64.

3 'One of the difficulties of psycho-analysis' (1917), Collected Papers IV, 1925, London: Hogarth Press and the Institute of Psycho-Analysis; also 'A difficulty in the path of psycho-analysis', SE 17: 137–44.

4 We suppose that there are two fundamentally different kinds of instincts, the sexual instincts in the widest sense of the word (Eros, if you prefer that name) and the aggressive instincts whose aim is

destruction. When it is put like that, you will hardly think of it as anything new; it looks as though it were a theoretical glorification of the commonplace opposition between love and hate, which may perhaps coincide with the polarity of attraction and repulsion which physics postulates for the inorganic world. But it is remarkable that this hypothesis was nevertheless felt by many to be an innovation, and indeed a most undesirable one which ought to be got rid of as soon as possible. I think a strong emotional factor was responsible for this rejection. Why have we ourselves taken so long to bring ourselves to recognize the existence of an aggressive instinct? Why was there so much hesitation in using for our theory facts which lay ready to hand and were familiar to everyone? One would probably meet with but little opposition if one were to ascribe to animals an instinct with such an aim as this. But to introduce it into the human constitution seems impious; it contradicts too many religious prejudices and social conventions. No, man must be by nature good, or at least well-disposed. If he occasionally shows himself to be brutal, violent, and cruel, these are only passing disturbances of his emotional life, mostly provoked, and perhaps only the consequence of the ill-adapted social system which he has so far made for himself (Freud, *New Introductory Lectures on Psycho-Analysis*, London: Hogarth Press and the Institute of Psycho-Analysis (1933), p. 134; also *New Introductory Lectures on Psycho-Analysis* (1933[32]) Lecture 32: 'Anxiety and instinctual life', pp. 103–4, SE 22: 81–111).

5 Cf. also: 'for it is not on account of the teaching of history and of our own experience in life that we maintain the hypothesis of a special instinct of aggression and destructiveness in man, but on account of general considerations, to which we were led in trying to estimate the importance of the phenomena of sadism and masochism' (*New Introductory Lectures on Psycho-Analysis*, p. 135, London: Hogarth Press and the Institute of Psycho-Analysis, 1933; also *New Introductory Lectures on Psycho-Analysis* (1933[32]) Lecture 32, p. 104, SE 22: 81–111).

6 Stout, *The Groundwork of Psychology*, p. 26.

7 Both failures, I would think, derive from a narcissistic attitude on the part of the worker, who remains aloof from the object of his research, in the one case by following only his own whims, in the other by withholding any contribution of his own to his observations. Such a narcissistic attitude is essentially uncreative.

8 Cf. Heimann (1952d) 'Certain functions of introjection and projection in early infancy', and Klein (1946) 'Notes on some schizoid mechanisms'.

In his paper 'On narcissism: an introduction' (1914c) Freud discusses various attitudes towards the loved object which can be observed in men and women. He describes it as characteristic for the man to love according to the anaclitic type and to show a sexual overestimation of the loved object. 'Complete object-love of the anaclitic type is, properly speaking, characteristic of the man. It displays the marked sexual overestimation which is doubtless derived from the original narcissism of the child, now transferred to the sexual object. This sexual overestimation is the origin of the peculiar state of being in love, a state suggestive of a neurotic compulsion, which is thus traceable to an impoverishment of the ego in respect of libido in favour of the love-object' (p. 45; Collected Papers IV, London: Hogarth Press and the Institute of Psycho-Analysis, 1925; also: 'On narcissism: an introduction', p. 88, SE 14: 73–102).

Closer investigation of the mechanisms used in what Freud here calls 'transference to the sexual object' has shown that parts of the ego are here split off and projected. Components of the ego-attitudes – traits, etc., and libido – are disowned by the self, split off from the ego and projected on to the object, which subsequently appears to possess highly appreciated qualities rendering it not only supremely lovable, but also exceedingly superior to the subject. (Cf. the concept of projective identification defined in Klein (1946) 'Notes on some schizoid mechanisms'.)

9 *Inhibitions, Symptoms and Anxiety* (1926d), pp. 23, 112, and *passim*, London: Hogarth Press and the Institute of Psycho-Analysis, 1936; also *Inhibitions, Symptoms and Anxiety*, pp. 93, 140, and *passim*, SE 20: 87–174.

10 Jones, 'The pathology of morbid anxiety' (1911: 423): 'Morbid anxiety is commonly described by Freudians as being derived from repressed sexuality. While this is clinically true, it is psychologically perhaps more accurate to describe it as a reaction against repressed sexuality, a reaction derived from the *instinct of fear*.' (My italics.)

11 Cf. Klein (1948) 'A contribution to the theory of anxiety and guilt'; also *The Psycho-Analysis of Children* (1932: 183–4).

12 Jones, loc. cit.

13 Freud, *Beyond the pleasure principle* (1920g).

14 Cf. Heimann and Issacs (1952e) 'Regression'.

15 See *The Psycho-Analysis of Children* (1932).

16 As Freud described in some detail in 'Negation' (1925h).

17 Cf. Joan Riviere's description of the destructive charges of various organs. 'Limbs shall trample . . .', in 'On the genesis of psychical conflict in earliest infancy' (1936).

3

Some notes on the psycho-analytic concept of introjected objects (1948/9)

This paper was a contribution to a symposium on 'Archetypes and Internal Objects' of the Medical Section of the British Psychological Society held in April and June 1948. It was published in the *British Journal of Medical Psychology* 22 (1/2) (1949).

A young man who was sent to me for vague depressive symptoms and work inhibitions opened his analysis by telling me that he felt he had a little white cotton-wool man in his stomach who turned black when the patient did something wrong.

Another patient began with a recollection. When he had been looking at his dead mother, he had felt something cold in his stomach. This patient, a man in the middle thirties, suffered from severe depressive states. His condition had become very acute by the breaking up of a love relation. His mother's death had occurred several years earlier, and whilst he had not been able to experience the emotions of mourning adequately, the memory of this sensation of something cold in his stomach kept on haunting him.

These two patients came into my mind when I started thinking about this paper, because both referred spontaneously to introjection processes; they presented their incorporated objects to me on a plate, so to speak, demonstrating neatly the two main situations which Freud and Abraham discovered as determined by introjection – moral conflicts and mourning.

History of the concept of introjection

Let me give you briefly the history of the concept of introjection. Ferenczi introduced it in his paper 'Transference and introjection' (1909) as the mechanism by which the ego makes contact with the world and expands. Freud specified this concept. In 'Instincts and their vicissitudes' (1915c), he suggested that introjection is used in early infancy under the sway of the pleasure principle so as to include into the self all that is good and useful, a process complementary to the expulsion, or projection, from the self of all that is bad and harmful. Abraham in his paper 'The first pregenital stage' (1916) concluded from his work with depressive patients that the wish to incorporate the sexual object forms part of the oral instinctual impulses and that these cannibalistic wishes underlie definite symptoms of depressive illness. Freud penetrated further in this direction. In 'Mourning and melancholia' (1917e) he worked out the specific connection between introjection and the loss of a loved object. When a person loses a loved object – be it through death or in other circumstances – he introjects this lost object and continues his relation with it in his inner world.

The next important step in our knowledge of introjection occurred in 1923, when Freud showed in *The Ego and the Id* that introjection has a regular place in the development of the mental structure. The introjection of the parents is instrumental in the formation of the superego, the system of moral standards. Freud believed that only the parents, and more explicitly the father, of the Oedipus phase are introjected as superego, and that later introjections merely affect the character of the ego. As you know, he called the superego the 'heir of the Oedipus complex'.

Abraham in his 'Study of the development of the libido' (1924b) presented further important conclusions about the earliest developmental processes and, with clinical material obtained during the treatment of neurotic and psychotic patients, demonstrated the role introjection plays.

Melanie Klein's (1932, 1948) researches have carried our knowledge of early mental life still further, and an important section of her work concerns introjection. This part is often singled out as if the investigation of introjection were exclusively her domain. Such a view is incorrect, considering both the earlier work just mentioned and the wealth of her contributions to other problems in psychoanalysis.

By devising play technique, which facilitates access to the child's unconscious phantasies, she confirmed by direct observation many of the inferences drawn from analytic work with adults. In addition, she made new discoveries which have led to certain modifications and reformulations of existing theory.

Those pertinent to our theme can be summarized as follows:

The superego as discovered by Freud represents the peak of a complex system which starts in early infancy and which develops *pari passu*, and under mutual influence, with the development of the ego and of the Oedipus complex. Moreover, Oedipus complex, superego formation, and ego-development are interacting processes largely by virtue of the operation of introjection and projection.

Use of terms

I have to say a word about terms. You will have noticed that I have spoken of 'incorporating', 'introjecting', 'including into the self', and of 'internal objects'. These and other words, which describe one and the same process, occur in analytic literature, and on and off in discussions a voice has been heard asking for a demarcation of these various terms. Some analysts emphasize the need to differentiate sharply between the mental mechanism and the subjective experience, and recommend the word 'introject' for the mental mechanism. I have come to the conclusion that it is not possible to follow a hard and fast rule. The phantasy of including objects into oneself is a dynamic process, and this dynamic process we call a mental mechanism. I have no intention of developing this line of thought further here. I can only hope that the context will make it clear whether I refer to the subjective experience or to its objective aspect.

Introjected objects

The theme with which I am dealing tonight is one about which divergent views are held amongst psychoanalysts. I shall not discuss these divergences, but I wish you to understand that I do not claim to speak for all psychoanalysts. I am presenting my views. They are shared by a number of colleagues whose work, like mine, is closely connected with the work of Melanie Klein.

The theme, moreover, brings us into the darkest spheres of experience, and the theories evolved cover the range from conjecture and hypothesis to definite conclusion. This is connected with the difficulty of verbalizing psychological events which take place before language has been achieved. It is tempting to speculate here on the psychological aspect of the infant's physiological inability to speak. Might it not be that infantile mental processes are by their nature opposed to articulate and coherent language so that the use of words becomes possible only after these earliest mental processes have undergone important changes? From this aspect the process of verbalization would represent an important step towards the overcoming and mastering of internal chaos. Be this as it may, when we try to describe in words what goes on in the infantile mind we feel that our language is an inadequate instrument. The artist rather than the scientist seems capable of conveying these deepest experiences. His medium, appealing to sensation and feeling instead of to reason, is more appropriate to events which are of the stuff of sensation, phantasy, and primitive feeling. I would like you to know that, though I express infantile phantasies in coherent language, I do not imply that this description portrays the mode of infantile experience.

Introjection operates from the start. From the beginning of his life the infant has instinctual impulses, and the oral impulses have primacy in the earliest phases of development. Oral desires comprise two parts: sucking and swallowing, mouthing and incorporating. These, like all instinctual desires, have a dual source, a libidinal and a destructive one, and the latter we regard as the endogenous cause for anxiety. The infant eats all his objects, and he eats them in love, in hate, in rage, and in fear.

Unconscious phantasy is bound up with sensation,[1] and the phantasies mobilized in the act of eating determine the character of the objects swallowed or incorporated. By virtue of his oral impulses the infant builds up an inner world which contains the doubles of the objects he has contact with in the outer world. But these doubles are not correct portraits; they are the external objects transformed by his impulses and phantasies.

The infant's capacity to perceive objects is to begin with limited by his immediate sensations so that he knows only those parts of his objects with which he experiences direct contact. We call this the stage of 'part-objects'. Since his most vital sensations are connected with his mother's breast (or its substitute), this is the first object he perceives and to which his impulses are directed. It is his first incorporated object.

Moreover, first love and first hate are closely knit with the sensations of gratification and frustration respectively. When his libidinal impulses are satisfied, and pleasure and love are experienced, the infant incorporates a 'good', pleasure-giving, helpful breast. Under the stress of frustration which acts as the lever to his destructive impulses, he incorporates a 'bad', pain-giving, attacking breast. Primitive feelings are massive, intense, absolutistic; good and bad occur in extremes. The infant either idealizes his objects or turns them into persecutors. He is omnipotent and blissful, or completely helpless, and helpless means in the throes of evil figures. According to the view presented here the earliest type of anxiety is paranoid.

64

These feelings extend to both series of objects, external and internal objects.

It is easy enough to understand that the infant incorporates his mother's breast. (He incorporates, as development goes on, more part-objects belonging to his relation with his mother, but her breast occupies first rank.) It is more difficult to account for the infant a few months old incorporating his father's penis. Here we meet one of the obscure points to which I referred earlier.

While we have obvious biological reasons for the infant's incorporating the mother's breast – and we can think in terms of his continuing pre-natal oneness with his mother by such incorporation – none of these factors operates with regard to his father's genital. But *ça n'empêche pas d'exister*. In analysis of adults and children we find phantasies about an incorporated penis which refers to the father in settings so primitive, so much betraying their origins in early infantile life, that it would appear to be prejudiced not to accept the conclusion that such incorporation does occur – and in very early life.

Winnicott (1945) suggested that the infant hallucinates the breast even before his real experience with it. It seems that he regards such hallucination as the prerequisite for the infant's capacity to accept the real breast. Perhaps a similar process gives the infant a notion of his father's penis, and his omnipotent phantasy treats it as if it were accessible to his desires.

Ultimately, I think, we have to put it in terms of instinct and to say that instinct is object seeking. I agree on this point with Fairbairn (1941, 1943, 1944, 1946), who has elaborated this concept of instinct in a series of papers. The situation would then appear as follows. Under the sway of hunger and oral desires the infant in some way conjures up the object which would satisfy these impulses. When this object, the mother's breast, is in reality offered to him, he accepts it and in phantasy incorporates it. His phantasy works here in conjunction with reality, his incorporation desires being supported by contact with the real object and by the sensations of swallowing a physical substance.

It may be that under the sway of genital sensations the infant conjures up or 'hallucinates' the corresponding object, the father's penis, and in incorporating it, follows the channel prepared by his basic experience with his mother's breast. We do not assume that such hallucination is of a visual kind. It will rather be a process on the deep instinctual level, involving bodily sensations and unconscious phantasies of a predominantly oral nature.

How closely this description approaches the facts must be left an open question, but it must also be emphasized that hypotheses of this kind are forced upon us from psychoanalytic observations. When in our work we uncover the primitive unconscious phantasies about the father's genital, this appears as something very similar to the mother's breast, as something to suck, bite, feed from, or attack orally, yet also with other qualities derived from and reflecting the infant's own genital stirrings. That such stirrings occur in early infancy, be it spontaneously or in response to stimulations by the nursing routine, cannot be doubted. It is important to remember that such genital sensations occur first during the period of oral predominance. This fact would account for the phantasies in which the father's penis is orally incorporated.

Whilst many questions which arise here must be left unanswered, one consideration may be put forward. It concerns the effect of reality on the infant's phantasy life. The infant fluctuates between omnipotent phantasy fulfilling all his wishes and helpless frustration. Some wishes are gratified by reality, which thus confirms his phantasies. Some, however, are always frustrated by reality, and the desires towards the father's genital belong to this group. I would think that the persistent real frustration by the father contributes a good deal to the unconscious fears about the father's penis which we find in analysis and to the general tendency in conscious thought of regarding the father as a non-yielding, restrictive figure. (The same argument might be put forward with regard to the mother's genital. It is, indeed, true that this too is unconsciously an object of fear and horror. But, on the other hand, the mother, far more than the father, is in early infancy the source of intense physical and emotional gratification.)

Our difficulties in explaining the incorporation of the father's penis would be greatly diminished if we decided to assume that the origin of this phantasy coincides with the beginning of the Oedipus complex – that is, roughly at the middle of the first year. But I am not at all sure whether we should not be bending facts to suit our need to be rational.

We know that integration is a gradually developing capacity. To begin with the infant knows only part-objects, mother's breast, mother's and father's hands, smile, voice, smell, and so on. Only gradually does he achieve the integration of his multiple impressions and weave them into the recognition of persons. Memory must play a part in this advance from fleeting to more permanent experiences. Such recognition of the parents as persons includes the recognition that there is much more to them than what they express in their dealings with the infant. In other words he also comes to discover that there is an interrelation between his parents. He has reached the triangular setting of an emotional relationship, which, as we know, will forever occupy a special place in his object relations. He has entered the first stage of the Oedipus complex.

Naturally the first stage differs in many respects from the climax, the 'classical' Oedipus phase. Instinctual development at this first stage is still under the predominance of the oral impulses, including incorporation desires. But urethral, anal, and genital stirrings assert themselves, and, although in this orchestra of rivalling instinctual claims the oral impulses play the role of the leader, these other claims are there and colour the infant's relation to his parents.

In addition to part-objects the incorporation phantasies now concern 'whole' objects, the parents as persons, as complex entities with bewildering things going on between them. Amongst the part objects mother's breast and father's penis are most important, and the infant's phantasies about them interact with his feelings towards his parents

This period of development is of the utmost complexity. One would need a multi-dimensional moving model to illustrate the infant's emotional processes. Urges from the various bodily zones with their dual, sexual and destructive, charge operate towards the parents in the outer and inner worlds, leading to a wealth of conflicting and confusing emotions.

It is to this period of instinctual and conceptual confusion that we attribute the origins of the unconscious equations, first pointed out by Freud, between organs and substances – breast/penis, mouth/vagina, penis/faeces/babies, urine/milk, and so on – which we find in every analysis. To mention these unconscious equations is tantamount to referring summarily to a great number of infantile phantasies which we have cause to regard as ubiquitous. In the frame of this paper I cannot attempt to describe these phantasies in detail. But in order to understand the role introjection plays at this point, it is necessary to say a few words about the phantasies and feelings which form part of the infantile Oedipus complex. Parental intercourse is the centre of these phantasies. The infant pictures it in the terms of his own polymorph instinctual desires as an act in which the genital function fuses with eating and excreting, and sexual actions serve cruel aims like robbing, soiling, and castrating. Consequently parental intercourse assumes the character of the 'primal scene', a destructive battle between the partners, and whilst the infant's sexual impulses are roused when he imagines bodily intimacies between his parents, he hates and dreads the sexual parents. Nevertheless, he incorporates them, partly because incorporation is bound up with his sexual

67

urges, partly because it is the executive of his need for control and domination. But this technique does not achieve pleasure and reassurance; on the contrary, it leads to severe anxiety situations, for the infant comes to feel that his parents carry out their destructive activities inside his own body. Persecutory fears of this kind are often manifested in night terrors and similar disturbances.

Another root of the infant's sadistic misinterpretation of his parents' sexuality lies in his jealousy. He does not want them to enjoy each other's company when he feels lonely and frustrated, and in omnipotent hate turns their pleasures into mutual attacks.

In infants of either sex the desire for the father's penis is connected with feelings of envy and rivalry towards the mother who, moreover, is believed to swallow the father's genital in intercourse and to keep it inside her body. This notion gives rise to the impulse of attacking the mother's body in order to get hold of her hidden penis. In another version the penis which the mother acquired from the father is attached to the surface of her body in her genital region. Every analyst is familiar with dreams or day-dreams in which the 'phallic woman' appears, a female figure with a male genital. Not infrequently this male genital is distorted in some way, and the dreamer reacts with very varied feelings including hate and horror at its appearance. On analysis we find that this phallic woman stands for the dreamer's mother and refers to the infantile phantasies just described.

Introjection and ambivalence

The advance to 'whole' objects, to the personal relation with his parents, brings about important changes in the total emotional life of the infant. These can be described under the heading of ambivalence. The conflict of ambivalence comes into full force when the infant realizes that his love and his hate go towards one and the same person. This is really saying again that the infant has progressed in his capacity for integration. Hate implies the wish to injure and annihilate the hated object. It forms the psychological foundation for the experience of losing an object. When the conflict of ambivalence is fully established, the fear of losing the loved person is easily roused. The wish to get rid of the hated object, once this is realized to be also the loved person, blends into the dread of losing by one's own destructiveness the loved and to-be-preserved person.

This dread, this mixture of fear and guilt, was first studied in adults going through the experience of 'loss of the loved object' – that is, in adult patients suffering from depressive illness. In the light of Melanie Klein's researches (1935, 1940, 1945), we are now able to trace the infantile origins of this experience and to locate it in the phase of full ambivalence. The infant who reacts to frustration – inevitable and frequent in view of his contradictory wishes and the shortcomings of his environment – with violent impulses feels that, by attacking the hated frustrating person, he attacks and immediately loses his loved object. He also feels the pain inflicted on this object which in his phantasy exists in his inner world as well as outside, and he grieves for it and feels guilty. He wishes to make reparation, and he despairs of his capacity to do so since hate and greed again and again come to the fore and mobilize fears of retaliation and persecution.

Melanie Klein described these emotional processes as the 'infantile depressive position' and suggested that they represent the fixation point for depressive illness in later life. The 'infantile depressive position' in itself is not an illness; the infant does not suffer from the persistent emotions and fixed symptoms characteristic of the adult's pathological condition. What he suffers can be called normal 'growing pains', and normally in a good environment he overcomes his transitory depressive moods. By and large the healthy infant is content and happy. But this overt picture should not make us overlook the severe depressive feelings which are in the wake of mental and emotional progress. Nor must it be forgotten that, if for external or internal reasons things go wrong, the infant may actually fall ill, either with a depression or in other ways, or that he may be retarded in his development.

The phantasies underlying the 'infantile depressive position' centre round the incorporated loved person(s), harmed and lost by the infant's impulses. I may here remind you of my patient who could not mourn for his dead mother and was haunted by the sensation of something cold in his stomach. Instead of feelings and emotions he produced a physical symptom, a bodily sensation which in turn roused pain and fear. This substitution is the hallmark of regression; the introjection of the lost mother was effected in the pattern of early infantile phantasy. In this case the persecutory element predominates, and the internalized dead mother imparts the coldness of death to her son who feels haunted by this sensation. The introjected object acts as the superego punishing the patient according to the talion principle for his lack of emotional warmth, his lack of love.

Introjection and superego formation

In order to understand how it comes about that a person experiences persecution instead of feeling guilty, we have to go back to the early states of superego development. The primitive superego is represented by the earliest introjected objects and, since these are either supremely benevolent or supremely malevolent, the earliest conflicts with the superego are felt as fear of persecution. In their good aspects the early introjected objects give a sense of security to the ego which allows the infant to venture forth and to expand his interests and activities. Since the ego can assimilate its good objects and become richer and stronger by this assimilation, the benevolent aspect of the superego acts as a stimulus for ego development. The forbiddings and demands of the superego are specific for the given stage of development – that is for the leading instinctual impulses. Abraham (1924 a, b) drew attention to the inhibition of greed in early infancy, and Ferenczi (1925) showed that there is a 'sphincter morality'. Here I come back to my patient with the cotton-wool man in his stomach, who turned black in response to the patient's misdeeds. This internal object is a memorial to the anal stage when the destructive aims are executed predominantly by the excretory act, and the maximal harm the child can do to his object is by messing and dirtying it.

This example of a primitive superego formed in early infancy illustrates also another point. The patient himself was once a little man swathed in soft white clothes which remained white only as long as he was good and which got black as soon as he did the wrong thing by making a mess. Thus we see that the internal object represents also the child himself. The infant introjects objects on to whom he projects his own impulses. Moreover, he animates and personalizes his impulses and treats them as objects. Both processes lead to the chaotic, magic-animistic nature of his inner world.

In the course of development by interacting processes in all parts of the psychic personality, the archaic internal figures are modified and come to lose their monstrous characters. In the instinctual sphere pre-genital impulses and phantasies give way to the increasing power of genitality. The sense of reality grows and affects the child's object relations, so that his parents, while for a long time very grand figures, yet are human beings and not gods or demons. The growth of physical and intellectual capacities is another factor of greatest significance. All these developmental processes have to be considered to account for the changes in the internalized figures which, as they lose more and more of their extravagantly unrealistic nature, become more and more integrated.

The superego, which Freud described as resulting from the introjection of the parents of the fully developed Oedipus complex, when the genital has become the leading zone, is the end-product of this gradual development from archaic beginnings. Tonight I have been chiefly concerned with these beginnings. At the time of the fully developed, the 'classical' Oedipus complex the child has developed all round in the way described, and his most primitive sexual and cruel impulses have lessened. The superego of the genital stage forbids, under threat of castration, genital gratification and rivalry with his parents, and it orders the child to restrict his love to affection and tenderness. It promises love from his parents as reward for obedience. But by demanding that the child should take his parents as models in all other – that is, non-sexual – respects, it gives scope for many pleasures, amongst which increasing independence and sublimatory activities have a specially positive value.

Introjection is not confined to infantile life, but the objects to be introjected change from organs and persons to ideas and abstract formations. We refer to this fact often in our everyday speech. We speak of being 'deeply impressed' or 'influenced'. We 'absorb' a book; we feel something 'in our bones'. We refuse to 'swallow' an idea. We thus use imagery to describe the process of introjection.

Summary

Internal objects are a construct of infantile phantasy and originate in the most primitive phase of life. Unconscious phantasy is a function of the mind operating in close connection with sensation. It flourishes the more powerfully the younger the human being, because then the less developed is his sense of reality. Internal objects are the doubles of the most important figures in the child's life – that is, of his parents and of himself. These doubles are as conceived by the child, and his conceptions differ widely from the originals. In reality parents and child possess limited power of goodness and bad-ness, wisdom and foolishness. The child's phantasy makes gods and demons and all those unearthly creatures of them which folklore and mythology, religious legends, and artistic creation present to us in sublimated, and the imagination of the insane in more unsublimated, form. Moreover, the child places his self-created figures inside his own body and treats them as live entities alien to himself and beyond his control.[2]

Notes

1 Susan Isaacs, 'Nature and function of phantasy', *International Journal of Psycho-Analysis*. [The paper was published in *The International Journal of Psycho-Analysis* 29 (1) (1948).]
2 [In one of the reprints of this paper Paula Heimann wrote in 1978: 'A number of good points – owing to its character as part of a symposium it is not "von einem Guss" ['of one piece']. Yet it is important and would deserve to be re-written and considerably expanded.']

---------------------- 4 ----------------------

On counter-transference (1949/50)

This paper was read at the 16th International Psycho-Analytical Congress, Zurich, 1949, and published in the *International Journal of Psycho-Analysis* 31 (1/2) (1950).

This short note on counter-transference[1] has been stimulated by certain observations I made in seminars and control analyses. I have been struck by the widespread belief amongst candidates that the counter-transference is nothing but a source of trouble. Many candidates are afraid and feel guilty when they become aware of feelings towards their patients and consequently aim at avoiding any emotional response and at becoming completely unfeeling and 'detached'.

When I tried to trace the origin of this ideal of the 'detached' analyst, I found that our literature does indeed contain descriptions of the analytic work which can give rise to the notion that a good analyst does not feel anything beyond a uniform and mild benevolence towards his patients, and that any ripple of emotional waves on this smooth surface represents a disturbance to be overcome. This may possibly derive from a misreading of some of Freud's (1912e) statements, such as his comparison with the surgeon's state of mind during an operation, or his simile of the mirror. At least these have been quoted to me in this connection in discussions on the nature of the counter-transference.

On the other hand, there is an opposite school of thought, like that of Ferenczi, which not only acknowledges that the analyst has a wide variety of feelings towards his patient, but recommends that he should at times express them openly. In her warm-hearted paper 'Handhabung der Übertragung auf Grund der Ferenczischen Versuche' (1936) Alice Balint suggested that such honesty on the part of the

73

analyst is helpful and in keeping with the respect for truth inherent in psychoanalysis. While I admire her attitude, I cannot agree with her conclusions. Other analysts again have claimed that it makes the analyst more 'human' when he expresses his feelings to his patient and that it helps him to build up a 'human' relationship with him.

For the purpose of this paper I am using the term 'counter-transference' to cover all the feelings which the analyst experiences towards his patient.

It may be argued that this use of the term is not correct, and that counter-transference simply means transference on the part of the analyst. However, I would suggest that the prefix 'counter' implies additional factors.

In passing, it is worth while remembering that transference feelings cannot be sharply divided from those which refer to another person in his own right and not as a parent substitute. It is often pointed out that not everything a patient feels about his analyst is due to transference, and that, as the analysis progresses, he becomes increasingly more capable of 'realistic' feelings. This warning itself shows that the differentiation between the two kinds of feelings is not always easy.

My thesis is that the analyst's emotional response to his patient within the analytic situation represents one of the most important tools for his work. The analyst's counter-transference is an instrument of research into the patient's unconscious.

The analytic situation has been investigated and described from many angles, and there is general agreement about its unique character. But my impression is that it has not been sufficiently stressed that it is a *relationship* between two persons. What distinguishes this relationship from others is not the presence of feelings in one partner, the patient, and their absence in the other, the analyst, but above all the degree of the feelings experienced and the use made of them, these factors being interdependent. The aim of the analyst's own analysis, from this point of view, is not to turn him into a mechanical brain which can produce interpretations on the basis of a purely intellectual procedure, but to enable him to *sustain* the feelings which are stirred in him, as opposed to discharging them (as does the patient), in order to *subordinate* them to the analytic task in which he functions as the patient's mirror reflection.

If an analyst tries to work without consulting his feelings, his interpretations are poor. I have often seen this in the work of beginners, who, out of fear, ignored or stifled their feelings.

We know that the analyst needs an evenly hovering attention in order to follow the patient's free associations, and that this enables

74

him to listen simultaneously on many levels. He has to perceive the manifest and the latent meaning of his patient's words, the allusions and implications, the hints to former sessions, the references to childhood situations behind the description of current relationships, and so on. By listening in this manner the analyst avoids the danger of becoming preoccupied with any one theme and remains receptive for the significance of changes in themes and of the sequences and gaps in the patient's associations.

I would suggest that the analyst along with this freely working attention needs a freely roused emotional sensibility so as to follow the patient's emotional movements and unconscious phantasies. Our basic assumption is that the analyst's unconscious understands that of his patient. This rapport on the deep level comes to the surface in the form of feelings which the analyst notices in response to his patient, in his 'counter-transference'. This is the most dynamic way in which his patient's voice reaches him. In the comparison of feelings roused in himself with his patient's associations and behaviour, the analyst possesses a most valuable means of checking whether he has understood or failed to understand his patient.

Since, however, violent emotions of any kind, of love or hate, helpfulness or anger, impel towards action rather than towards contemplation and blur a person's capacity to observe and weigh the evidence correctly, it follows that, if the analyst's emotional response is intense, it will defeat its object.

Therefore the analyst's emotional sensitivity needs to be extensive rather than intensive, differentiating and mobile.

There will be stretches in the analytic work when the analyst who combines free attention with free emotional responses does not register his feelings as a problem, because they are in accord with the meaning he understands. But often the emotions roused in him are much nearer to the heart of the matter than his reasoning, or, to put it in other words, his unconscious perception of the patient's unconscious is more acute and in advance of his conscious conception of the situation.

A recent experience comes to mind. It concerns a patient whom I had taken over from a colleague. The patient was a man in the forties who had originally sought treatment when his marriage broke down. Among his symptoms promiscuity figured prominently. In the third week of his analysis with me he told me, at the beginning of the session, that he was going to marry a woman whom he had met only a short time before.

It was obvious that his wish to get married at this juncture was determined by his resistance against the analysis and his need to act out his transference conflicts. Within a strongly ambivalent attitude the desire for an intimate relation with me had already clearly appeared. I had thus many reasons for doubting the wisdom of his intention and for suspecting his choice. But such an attempt to short-circuit analysis is not infrequent at the beginning of, or at a critical point in, the treatment and usually does not represent too great an obstacle to the work, so that catastrophic conditions need not arise. I was therefore somewhat puzzled to find that I reacted with a sense of apprehension and worry to the patient's remark. I felt that something more was involved in his situation, something beyond the ordinary acting out, which, however, eluded me.

In his further associations which centred round his friend, the patient, describing her, said she had had a 'rough passage'. This phrase again registered particularly and increased my misgivings. It dawned on me that it was precisely because she had had a rough passage that he was drawn to her. But still I felt that I did not see things clearly enough. Presently he came to tell me his dream: he had acquired from abroad a very good second-hand car which was damaged. He wished to repair it, but another person in the dream objected for reasons of caution. The patient had, as he put it, 'to make him confused' in order that he might go ahead with the repair of the car.

With the help of this dream I came to understand what before I had merely felt as a sense of apprehension and worry. There was indeed more at stake than the mere acting out of transference conflicts.

When he gave me the particulars of the car – very good, second-hand, from abroad – the patient spontaneously recognized that it represented myself. The other person in the dream who tried to stop him and whom he confused stood for that part of the patient's ego which aimed at security and happiness and for the analysis as a protective object.

The dream showed that the patient wished me to be damaged (he insisted on my being the refugee to whom applies the expression 'rough passage' which he had used for his new friend). Out of guilt for his sadistic impulses he was compelled to make reparation, but this reparation was of a masochistic nature, since it necessitated blotting out the voice of reason and caution. This element of confusing the protective figure was in itself double-barrelled, expressing both his sadistic and his masochistic impulses: in so far as it aimed at annihilating the analysis, it represented the patient's sadistic tendencies in the pattern of his infantile anal attacks on his mother; in so far as it stood for his ruling out his desire for security and happiness, it expressed his self-destructive trends. Reparation turned into a masochistic act again engenders hatred, and, far from solving the conflict between destructiveness and guilt, leads to a vicious circle.

The patient's intention of marrying his new friend, the injured woman, was fed from both sources, and the acting out of his transference conflicts proved to be determined by this specific and powerful sado-masochistic system.

Unconsciously I had grasped immediately the seriousness of the situation, hence the sense of worry which I experienced. But my conscious understanding lagged behind, so that I could decipher the patient's message and appeal for help only later in the hour, when more material came up.

In giving the gist of an analytic session I hope to illustrate my contention that the analyst's immediate emotional response to his patient is a significant pointer to the patient's unconscious processes and guides him towards fuller understanding. It helps the analyst to focus his attention on the most urgent elements in the patient's associations and serves as a useful criterion for the selection of interpretations from material which, as we know, is always overdetermined.

From the point of view I am stressing, the analyst's counter-transference is not only part and parcel of the analytic relationship, but it is the patient's *creation*, it is a part of the patient's personality. (I am possibly touching here on a point which Dr Clifford Scott would express in terms of his concept of the body-scheme, but to pursue this line would lead me away from my theme.)

The approach to the counter-transference which I have presented is not without danger. It does not represent a screen for the analyst's shortcomings. When the analyst in his own analysis has worked through his infantile conflicts and anxieties (paranoid and depressive), so that he can easily establish contact with his own unconscious, he will not impute to his patient what belongs to himself. He will have achieved a dependable equilibrium which enables him to carry the roles of the patient's id, ego, superego, and external objects which the patient allots to him or – in other words – projects on him, when he dramatizes his conflicts in the analytic relationship. In the instance I have given, the analyst was predominantly in the roles of the patient's good mother to be destroyed and rescued, and of the patient's reality-ego which tried to oppose his sado-masochistic impulses. In my view Freud's demand that the analyst must 'recognize and master' his counter-transference does not lead to the conclusion that the counter-transference is a disturbing factor and that the analyst should become unfeeling and detached, but that he must use his emotional response as a key to the patient's unconscious. This will protect him from entering as a co-actor on the scene which the patient re-enacts in the analytic relationship and from exploiting it for his own needs. At the same time he will find ample stimulus for taking himself to task again and again and for continuing the analysis of his own problems. This, however, is his private affair, and I do not consider it right for the analyst to communicate his feelings to his patient. In my view such honesty is more in the nature of a confession and a burden to the patient. In any case it leads away from the analysis. The emotions roused in the analyst will be of value to his patient, if used as one more source of insight into the patient's unconscious conflicts and defences; and when these are interpreted and worked through, the ensuing changes in the patient's ego include the strengthening of his reality sense so that he sees his analyst as a human being, not a god or demon, and the 'human' relationship in the analytic situation follows without the analyst's having recourse to extra-analytical means.

Psychoanalytic technique came into being when Freud, abandoning hypnosis, discovered resistance and repression. In my view the use of counter-transference as an instrument of research can be recognized in his descriptions of the way by which he arrived at his fundamental discoveries. When he tried to elucidate the hysterical patient's forgotten memories, he felt that a force from the patient opposed his attempts and that he had to overcome this resistance by his own psychic work. He concluded that it was the same force which was responsible for the repression of the crucial memories and for the formation of the hysterical symptom.

The unconscious process in hysterical amnesia can thus be defined by its twin facets, of which one is turned outward and felt by the analyst as resistance, whilst the other works intrapsychically as repression.

Whereas in the case of repression counter-transference is characterized by the sensation of a quantity of energy, an opposing force, other defence mechanisms will rouse other qualities in the analyst's response.

I believe that with more thorough investigation of counter-transference from the angle I have attempted here, we may come to work out more fully the way in which the character of the counter-transference corresponds to the nature of the patient's unconscious impulses and defences operative at the actual time.

Notes

1 After presenting this paper at the Congress my attention was drawn to a paper by Leo Berman: 'Countertransferences and attitudes of the analyst in the therapeutic process', *Psychiatry* 12 (2) May 1949. The fact that the problem of the counter-transference has been put forward for discussion practically simultaneously by different workers indicates that the time is ripe for a more thorough research into the nature and function of the counter-transference. I agree with Berman's basic rejection of emotional coldness on the part of the analyst, but I differ in my conclusions concerning the use to be made of the analyst's feelings towards his patient.

5

A contribution to the re-evaluation of the Oedipus complex – the early stages (1951/2a)

This paper was read before the 17th International Psycho-Analytical Congress, Amsterdam, 1951, as part of the symposium on 'The Re-evaluation of the Oedipus Complex'. The second part of the paper, 'The polymorphous stage of instinctual development', was read before the British Psycho-Analytical Society in January 1952, as an appendix to the Congress paper. It was included in the publication of the Congress paper in a special issue of the *International Journal of Psycho-Analysis* 33 (2) (1952) which was dedicated to Melanie Klein on the occasion of her seventieth birthday. A revised version appeared in M. Klein. P. Heimann, and R. Money-Kyrle (eds) *New Directions in Psycho-Analysis*, London: Tavistock (1955).

Introductory remarks

For the purpose of this paper I have decided to concentrate on the early stages of the Oedipus complex which Melanie Klein has discovered in her analyses of young children. Her contributions naturally influence also the assessment of the later stages, but I think that the most useful way of approaching divergences of opinion lies in discussing the field in which they originate.

Although my presentation seems to emphasize the controversial points in our views on the Oedipus complex, this does not mean that we underrate the amount or the significance of the ground which we share.

Before dealing with my subject-matter I wish to define our

position with regard to some basic concepts and to outline briefly the period preceding the Oedipus complex.

The theory of the instincts

All understanding of psychological phenomena rests on Freud's discovery of the dynamic unconscious. The two primary instincts of life and death, the borderland entities between soma and psyche, from which all instinctual impulses are derived, are the source of mental energy; all mental processes start from an unconscious stage.

Freud's concept of an inherent antithesis in the deepest and the most dynamic levels of the mind is fully born out by Melanie Klein's work. More than this, her work has produced many observations which substantiate his theory, but precisely on this account major divergences between her views and classical theory have arisen.

I am referring to the position which the mental facet of the instinctual urges, which we call 'unconscious phantasy', occupies in Melanie Klein's work.

Unconscious phantasies

By the term 'unconscious phantasies' we mean the most primitive psychic formations, inherent in the operation of the instinctual urges, and because these are inborn, we attribute unconscious phantasies to the infant from the beginning of his life. Unconscious phantasies occur not only in the infant, they are part of the unconscious mind at any time and form the matrix from which the pre-conscious and conscious processes develop. In the earliest stages they are almost the whole of psychical processes, and, of course, they are pre-verbal, or rather non-verbal. The words which we use when we wish to convey their contents and meaning are a foreign element, but we cannot do without it – unless we are artists.

Unconscious phantasies are associated with the infant's experience of pleasure or pain, happiness or anxiety, they involve his relation with his objects. They are dynamic processes, because they are charged with the energy of the instinctual impulses, and they influence the development of ego mechanisms. For example, introjection develops from the infant's unconscious phantasy of incorporating the mother's breast, which accompanies the desire for the breast and the actual sensation of sucking and swallowing when in contact with it.

Conversely, the mechanism of projection develops from the phantasy of expelling an object.

In order to understand the infant's psychic development and many of his physical processes, we must appreciate his unconscious phantasies.

Earliest object relations

The first childhood period is characterized by the infant's maximal dependence on his mother and by the maximal immaturity of his ego. The instinctual urges and the phantasies which they imply reign supreme. Perception of the reality of the self and of objects is poor and phantasy flourishes the more. To obtain satisfaction, the infant needs his object. He wills it, when he experiences his needs. He omnipotently possesses it, when he is satisfied. When he is caressed and gratified, he has the ideally good breast. He loves this breast, he could eat it. He incorporates the gratifying breast and is one with it. He goes to sleep with his loved object. If things go well, he will do the same thing in adult life.

In states of hunger or pain, he does not believe that the pain is part of himself; it is the malicious breast which is responsible, and he hates it. His attempts at introjecting and keeping the good breast, and projecting his pain and the bad breast, have been without avail. He feels persecuted by the bad breast within his own self.

Throughout, in Melanie Klein's work, the focus has been on anxiety as the most dynamic element in frustration and conflict. By consistently analysing the phantasies associated with anxiety, and the defences determined by these phantasies, she discovered that the most primitive type of fear is the fear of persecutory objects (at first the bad breast), and that splitting mechanisms are amongst the earliest ego defences.

She has termed these early processes the paranoid–schizoid position, thus pinpointing the character of the anxiety and of the defences against it, which prevail during the first few months of life, and which underlie later schizophrenic illnesses.

Lack of cohesion in the early ego and the use of splitting mechanisms lead to the infant's living with a good and a bad double of his object, which correspond with his feelings of gratification or frustration.

Love, hate, and fear, the fundamental units of psychological experience, develop in the wake of instinctual urges and physical sensations.

The whole object stage

At this stage, which begins roughly in the second quarter of the first year, the infant's ego is stronger and more coherent. Perception leads to more integrated objects. The infant sees more at the time, and remembers more of the past. He recognizes his parents as whole objects – that is, as persons. He has lost some of his omnipotence and gained more sense of reality. This holds not only for the external world of objects, but also for internal psychic reality.

The conflict of ambivalence begins to play its part in the infant's emotional life. Melanie Klein regards it as the nucleus of the infantile depressive position.

The infant begins to realize that when he loves and hates his mother, it is one and the same person whom he desires and attacks. He feels unhappy and guilty, he suffers from the pain which his destructive impulses inflict on her, and he fears that he will lose her and her love. These feelings concern also his internal mother.

Hatred against the loved object matters so much, because at this stage the belief in the omnipotence of evil outweighs the belief in the power of love. It is *depressive* anxiety which the infant now experiences. The 'infantile depressive position' represents the fixation point for later manic-depressive illness.

Normally the infant's depressive moods pass off quickly. Amongst the defences we distinguish a regressive type, the 'manic defence', which revolves upon denial and flight, and a progressive one, which consists of the drive for reparation and attempts at inhibiting destructive impulses, in particular, greed, in order to spare the mother.

Moreover, other factors which are implied in the many advances at this stage of development help the child.

This leads me to my main theme. When the infant begins to realize that his parents are persons, he also feels that they are not only objects for his needs and wishes, but that they have a life of their own, and with one another. With the widening of his emotional and intellectual orbit, the infant enters upon the triangular stage of his relation with his parents. He does not merely add the whole object to his part objects, it is also the relationship between his mother and his father which becomes a highly significant factor in his life. This first establishment of an emotional triangle with his parents is the beginning of the Oedipus complex. Increasingly the infant's emotions, impulses, and phantasies centre upon the parental couple.

This new focus of interest in his life, which stimulates and exercises his mental energies, operates as another means of defence against the depressive position.

The early stages of the Oedipus complex

The beginning of the Oedipus complex coincides with the poly-morphously perverse condition of the child's instinctual impulses. Excitations from all parts of his body are active, and because the erotogenic zones are also the seat of the destructive impulses, the child fluctuates not only between one erotic desire and another, but also between libidinal and destructive aims. Such movements and fluctuations are characteristic for this phase.

The phantasies which accompany these excitations have specific contents. The child wishes to experience the gratification of each of his manifold urges by specific oral, anal, and genital contacts with his parents.

Under the dominance of the libido the child's phantasies are pleasurable. He imagines the fulfilment of his polymorphous desires. But this holds only up to a point, and polymorphous wishes recur as polymorphous fears, not only because his parents do in fact frustrate many of his desires, but because the destructive components of his wishes, his cruel cravings, are in phantasy experienced as actions and lead to destroyed and destructive objects in his inner and outer world. At the beginning, the oral impulses lead in this orchestra of polymorphous urges, and, together with the urethral and anal zones, overshadow the genital for a time, so that genital excitations are in part linked with pre-genital phantasies. In the second half of the first year, however, genital stirrings gain in strength, and the wish for genital gratification includes the wish to receive and give a child. In our observation a child of eleven months is not only capable of feeling rival hatred and jealousy of a baby brother or sister, as Freud described, but the child *himself* desires the baby and envies his mother. His jealousy is double-edged.

It is to this phase that we attribute the origin of the unconscious equation of breast, penis, faeces, child, and so on, and the infantile sexual theories, which Freud discovered and related to the child aged three to five years. In our view these equations and theories express the infant's phantasies at the polymorphous stage of instinctual development, when the excitations from all bodily zones and libidinal and destructive aims rival one another.

Thus the theory of parental intercourse as a feeding or excretory act, of babies being conceived through the mouth and born through the anus, show the overlapping of oral, excretory, and procreative urges and phantasies. The notions of the 'primal scene', or of the castrating phallic mother, betray the fusion of libidinal and cruel impulses which is characteristic of early infantile genitality.

A three-year-old child is capable of verbalizing some of these phantasies, but the time at which he expresses them does not coincide with the date of their origin. The three-year-old child who has achieved a considerable degree of organization has largely overcome the polymorphous condition of his instinctual impulses.

Our clinical observations in the analysis of children and adults have shown us that the most crucial contents of the Oedipus complex, and the most severe conflicts and anxieties, relate to the primitive impulses and phantasies which form the early stages of the Oedipus complex.

In passing, I would mention that, apart from dreams, we can see the phantasies of this early stage clearly in certain states of both normal and pathological regression. Adolescence normally shows the re-efflorescence of early infantile sexuality. When the adolescent in horror turns away from his impulses, it is not only because he discovers his incestuous object choice, the wish to sleep with his mother, but because he becomes aware that he is attracted and excited by perverse and cruel phantasies.

The regressed schizophrenic often expresses polymorphously perverse phantasies without any disguise, and attributes his bizarre bodily sensations to his internalized parents and their intercourse.

After these general remarks I wish now to consider some features of the early Oedipus complex in more detail.

Melanie Klein holds that the boy and the girl each begin the Oedipus complex in both the direct and the inverted form.

The early Oedipus complex in the boy

The boy's 'feminine position' is due to several factors. The conflicts of the depressive position concern predominantly the mother and acts as an incentive for seeking a new love object. In addition, he is in many ways frustrated by her, and particularly during weaning.

The loss of the external breast intensifies the identification with the mother which has been going on all along. In the triangular relationship with his parents this identification strengthens the homosexual component of the boy's bi-sexuality.

Predominant in his many desires for his father are the impulses for the father's *penis*, which at first is largely equated with the breast.

The boy wants to suck, swallow, and incorporate it orally, as well as through his anus and penis, which he treats as receptive organs. There are also active versions of such phantasies, the boy wants to enter with his own penis the father's body, mouth, anus, and genital, In the latter part of the first year the desire to receive a child from the father plays an important part.

These wishes represent the roots of male homosexuality. In his feminine position the boy is his mother's enemy and rival.

The man's envy of the woman, of her ability to bear and feed children, has been underrated in classical theory. Yet the analyses of fathers give ample evidence of such envy. Whilst the occurrence of the 'couvade' has been acknowledged, the conclusion has not been drawn that this manifestation of the man's desire to be a woman has its origin in the infant's early inverted Oedipus complex.

Envy and hatred of the mother, which accompany the first homosexual impulses in the boy, form an important source of the man's fear of the woman. The familiar notions of the *vagina dentata* and the so-called cloaca theory bear witness to the infant's jealous attacks on the mother's genital, and specifically to those phantasies in which the attacks are carried out by teeth and excrements.

Phantasies of attacking the mother's genital may lead to inhibition of heterosexuality in both the boy and the girl. For the boy, the woman's genital assumes qualities which threaten his penis; the girl, who identifies her own genital with that of her mother, comes to regard it as a dangerous organ which she must not use with the man she loves.

The boy's feminine wishes for his father are in sharp conflict with his masculine desires for his mother.

In our view the infant assumes the existence of the vagina from his own genital sensations. His urge to penetrate is connected with phantasies about a corresponding genital opening in the mother's body. His primary libidinal desires for her are secondarily intensified by reparative tendencies. The drive to make amends to her by giving her genital pleasure and children contributes in the course of development a great deal to the establishment of the boy's heterosexual genitality.

These masculine impulses are associated with rival hatred against the father and with the corresponding fears of the father's retaliation.

In both his feminine and masculine position, the boy's desires are frustrated; and frustration is maximal when the infant witnesses or imagines that his parents are united in intercourse. The 'combined parental figure' is the object of many phantasies in which libidinal and destructive aims are combined and opposed. Almost simultaneously, the infant aims at destroying both parents and at destroying only his rival, while he desires the other parent. These phantasies lead to severe anxiety, the fear being that he destroys the desired object, be this mother or father, in the same attack which is aimed at the other parent, and his anxieties are multiplied because, owing to his incorporation phantasies, he feels that this hated 'primal scene' takes place inside himself as well.

Anxieties of this kind play an important part in the boy's phallic manifestations. Pride in his penis is not only derived from his unconscious knowledge of its creative and reparative function. Such knowledge, we find, is a strong incentive for libidinal phantasies of intercourse with his mother. The narcissistic pleasure he derives from masturbation, urinary games, or exhibitionism is partly used as a defence against his fears of the mother's body which, as a result of his attacks, has become a battleground, full of dangerous objects. And by his contempt for the female genital and denial of the vagina, he tries to escape from all notions about the inside of the body, his own as well as the mother's, because of the fears connected with internal persecutors. The sight of his penis and its functions gives him again and again the reassurance that all is well with him, and that he need not be afraid of persecutory objects in his own body.

In this connection I would remind you of Ernest Jones's lucid exposition of the factors which result in the 'secondary nature of narcissistic phallicism'.

Castration complex

I have already described many of the anxieties which the boy experiences in connection with his early Oedipal impulses; when these anxieties are taken into consideration, Jones's suggestion that it is *aphanisis* which is dreaded, and not merely the loss of the penis, gains in significance. As far as the specific fears for the penis are concerned, in the early stages the boy is afraid of both parents.

In response to his own oral and anal attacks he fears that his penis will be bitten off, soiled and poisoned.

After the establishment of the genital organization, his leading anxiety is castration by his father. This anxiety too has depressive as well as persecutory qualities; it is not only the fear of being deprived of the organ and power for sexual pleasure, but also the fear of losing the means for expressing love, and reparative and creative impulses. This depressive component is evidenced in the well-known equation between being castrated and being completely worthless.

The early Oedipus complex in the girl

To turn now to the girl: her position in the early stages of the Oedipus complex is in many respects similar to that of the boy. She, too, oscillates between hetero- and homosexual positions, and between libidinal and destructive aims and goes through the corresponding anxiety situations. She has the same motives for turning away from her mother, and in her case identification with the mother intensifies the heterosexual impulses.

I shall here consider merely the genital aspects of her early Oedipus phantasies.

Our observations are that vaginal sensations occur at this stage, not only sensations in the clitoris. Moreover, the clitoris has a conductor function and its excitations stimulate the vagina. Oral, urethral, and anal impulses also lead to vaginal sensations and phantasies.

The phantasies associated with vaginal urges have a specific feminine character. The little girl wishes to receive and incorporate the father's penis, and to acquire it as an *internal* possession, and from here she soon arrives at the wish to receive a child from him. These wishes, partly because they meet with frustration, alternate with the desire to possess an external penis.

The masculine component of the sensations and phantasies connected with the clitoris can only be fully assessed if the girl's conflicts and anxieties which follow from her feminine position are taken into account.

When jealousy stimulates phantasies of attacking her mother's body, these attacks recoil upon herself, and she feels that her own genital will be mutilated, soiled, poisoned, annihilated, and so on, and her own internal penis and children stolen from her by her internalized mother. These fears are the graver, because she feels that she lacks the organ – that is, the external penis – which could adequately placate or restore the avenging mother, and because she has no evidence that in reality her genital organs are unharmed. We consider that here there is a psychological consequence of the anatomical difference between the sexes which is of the greatest significance for the development of the girl.

We distinguish several sources for masculine drives in the little girl. Frustration of her feminine desires gives rise to hatred and fear of the father and drives her back to the mother. Anxieties related to her external and internal mother lead her to concentrate on phallic activities and phantasies. Her primary homosexual trends are thus most strongly increased by failure in her feminine position. She then comes to find that her male organ is inferior, that it is not a proper penis, that it cannot rival the father's penis. Because her phallicism is largely a secondary and defensive phenomenon, she comes to develop penis envy at the expense of femininity. She disowns her vagina, attributes genital qualities exclusively to the penis, hopes for her clitoris to grow into one and meets with disappointment. Devaluation of femininity underlies the overvaluation of the penis.

The familiar grievances of the girl against her mother for withholding the penis from her and sending her into the world as an incomplete creature are based on her need to deny her attacks on the mother's body and her rivalry with both parents. With her laments that she has come too short she protests that she never was greedy, never usurped the mother's position with her father, never stole the father's love, penis, and children from her.

To say this does not mean that we underrate the girl's intense admiration for the penis, or her greed which makes her want to have whatever she regards as desirable. Nor do we doubt that penis envy plays an important part in female psychology. My point is that penis envy is a complex fabric of which only certain threads have been generally acknowledged.

The analysis of penis envy in a woman with pronounced rivalry with men shows us so clearly that it is built on the failure to master persecutory and depressive anxieties arising from her early femininity, and that these early anxieties lend the compulsive character to her demand that she must have a penis.

The conclusions from our work which I have here presented differ from Freud's view that there is a long period of a pre-Oedipal mother fixation in the girl. The phenomena which Freud described under this heading in our view represent the inverted form of the girl's Oedipus complex, which alternates with the direct Oedipus complex.

The girl who shows an exclusive attachment to her mother, and hostility against her father, has failed to cope with the frustration of her first feminine wishes.

Our observations also lead us to disagree with the view that the woman's wish for a child takes second place to that for possessing a penis.

The role of introjection

I have endeavoured to show that throughout his development the child internalizes his parents, and that his internal objects have both a good and bad aspect for him. In relation to the good internal object, he experiences a state of well-being, and in the earliest period the good internal object fuses with the self, whereas states of anxiety, of a persecutory or depressive kind, are connected with the bad or destroyed internal objects.

This relation between the child and his parents prevails throughout the early stages of the Oedipus complex, and therefore the development of the Oedipus complex is throughout influenced by his feelings about his internal parents, by fears of being persecuted by them, and by guilt for harming them.

According to Freud, the superego is the result of the child internalizing his parents at the *decline* of the Oedipus complex; the tension between the ego and the superego is experienced as guilt and fear of retaliation.

Melanie Klein holds that all processes of internalization enter into the formation of the superego and that it begins with the first internalized object, the mother's breast. In her view there is throughout an interaction between the development of the ego, the Oedipus complex, and the superego.

Conclusion

In the light of Melanie Klein's work the Oedipus complex, which Freud discovered, appears as the *final* stage of a process which begins in early infancy. Its roots are set in a crucial phase of development. The child makes the first steps towards recognizing the reality of other persons, the first steps towards establishing full emotional relationships; he encounters the conflict of ambivalence; in his first experience of the triangular relationship with his parents his instinctual impulses are polymorphously perverse, and he oscillates between a hetero- and a homosexual object choice.

In the early stages of the Oedipus complex the scales are weighted for the first time. Much of the way in which the child will enter and leave the final stage depends on the interplay of forces at this early period.

The understanding of the child's problems in the early infantile Oedipus complex makes us realize all the more the truth of Freud's discovery that the Oedipus complex is the *nuclear* complex in the individual's life.

Appendix: the polymorphous stage of instinctual development

When I prepared my contribution to the symposium on 'the Re-evaluation of the Oedipus Complex', I was compelled to think again, very thoroughly, about familiar matters. That is always a salutary experience, because it counteracts the tendency to use terms glibly instead of thinking afresh about the conditions and processes to which these terms refer. I then found that certain topics came up in my thoughts, and one of these I wish to bring forward here.

It concerns the problem of the instinctual stages. Melanie Klein's discoveries which have necessitated a re-evaluation of the Oedipus complex lead also to a re-examination of our views on the course of instinctual development.

In his *Three Essays on the Theory of Sexuality* (1905d), which are the foundation of psychoanalytic theories of infantile sexuality, Freud speaks of the polymorphously perverse disposition of infantile sexuality. I shall quote only one passage. In his summary[1] he says: 'Experience further showed that the external influences of seduction are capable of provoking interruptions of the latency period or even its cessation, and that in this connection *the sexual instinct of children proves in fact to be polymorphously perverse.*' (My italics.)

Abraham in his 'development of the libido' (1924b) carried our knowledge of infantile sexuality further, mainly in three ways: (1) by showing the subdivision of the oral and the anal stages; (2) by correlating the differing sexual stages with the development of object love; and (3) by stressing the development of the destructive strivings. As to this third point, I regard it as noteworthy that, although his book appeared four years after *Beyond the Pleasure Principle*, Abraham does not refer to the death instinct. It seems to me possible to conclude that Abraham did not accept or perhaps had not yet accepted the theory of the death instinct, and this to my mind would explain why he maintained the idea that the first oral stage, the sucking stage, is free from destructive impulses, 'pre-ambivalent', although in other connections he described the vampire type – that is, the tendency to kill the object by sucking it to death. In passing I would repeat, what has often been pointed out before, that Melanie Klein's work does not endorse the view of a pre-ambivalent stage as Abraham describes it, but that her findings of the early splitting mechanisms which create an ideal and a persecutory breast represent an important modification of Abraham's concept of the pre-ambivalent stage. But this is only in passing, because my main interest in these short notes concerns the fact that in Abraham's scheme the notion of the polymorphously perverse disposition is not included.

As I have endeavoured to show in my Congress paper, in Melanie Klein's work this notion is of considerable importance. She has often pointed out that the trends from the diverse zones overlap, and that this overlapping characterizes the instinctual climate of the early stages of the Oedipus complex.

We can today define the notion of a 'polymorphously perverse' disposition in more detail. The infant tends to experience in an uncoordinated manner excitations from all parts of his body and to crave for their simultaneous gratification; further, he equally simultaneously experiences and seeks to satisfy libidinal and destructive impulses.

The polymorphously perverse disposition arises thus from the fact that the infant from the beginning of life is under the influence of the two primary instincts of life and death. Their derivatives in the form of self-preservative and libidinal impulses on the one hand and of destructive and cruel cravings on the other are active from the beginning of life.

Both primary instincts operate in the infant's contacts with his first object, and thus begin in the manner which Freud in respect of the libido called 'anaclitic'. Freud attributed erotogenetic qualities to all parts of the body. Melanie Klein's observations in the analyses of young children showed that there were also immensely cruel phantasies related to all parts of the body. It therefore follows from her work that Freud's statement about the way the libido operates has to be expanded to include the operation of the destructive impulses – a point which follows theoretically from the concept of the primary death instinct.

In addition, she has shown that the anxieties roused by the combination and opposition of the libido and the destructive impulses lead from the beginning to the development of ego-mechanisms, defence mechanisms.

The conclusion I wish to put forward here is that the transition from the oral stage to the anal one is not direct, but that there is interpolated a period in which the infant's polymorphously perverse disposition becomes actually manifest and dominant.

This polymorphous period or stage, occupying roughly the second half of the first year, could be regarded as one of the intermediate stations – in Abraham's analogy – which his timetable of the express trains does not mention.

I find it easy to bring the notion of this polymorphous period in line with Abraham's first anal stage, the stage in which the aim is to eject completely and annihilate the object. This tendency would appear as a kind of reaction formation against the turmoil which results from the simultaneous operation of so many inherently conflicting, inherently frustrating impulses with their corresponding anxiety situations. The developmental process which consecutively brings the different zones into a leading position implies a growing mastery by the ego of the instinctual urges and thus serves in part a defensive function. The aim of the first anal stage of 'relieving' the self by the complete evacuation of the internalized parents, equated as persecutors with the infant's own faeces, can be appreciated as a reaction to the overwhelming impact of the first Oedipal strivings (during the polymorphous stage). The experience of eliminating and getting rid of a bodily substance would come to occupy a central position, because in addition to the organ pleasure – libidinal pleasure – there is an *emotional* experience of relief. Many clinical observations suggest strongly that anal interests and gratifications are secondarily heightened for defensive purposes.

As a result of further development in the various spheres of the ego this massive defence by ejection is modified, and Abraham's second anal stage is established in which the predominant aim is to retain the object on the condition that it be dominated and controlled. The stronger the ego, the more can it deal with its sources of conflict intrapsychically and the less does it use the most primitive defence of expelling them.

Whilst I could connect the polymorphous stage easily with the next, the anal stage, I was confronted by difficulties when I tried to see its relation to the oral stage. What troubled me was the notion that if I thought of the polymorphously perverse condition of instinctual life, in which the Oedipus complex starts, as a *stage* extending for a certain time, if I thought that the oral stage does not proceed directly to the anal stage, I could not account for the powerful operation of the anal trends and mechanisms during the first three to four months of life – namely, during the paranoid/schizoid position.

Ejecting – splitting – projecting: these are aims and mechanisms which are to be correlated to the anal function. Their nature is anal, even though there are oral and nasal forms of ejecting, such as spitting or breathing out. This accords with our clinical experience which shows that the phantasies underlying splitting and projecting are predominantly anal: the persecuting object is equated with faeces, the faeces are treated as internal persecuting objects. As long as I thought in terms of a direct transition from the oral to the anal organization I did not see a problem in accounting for the occurrence of anal elements in the stage of oral primacy. The two stages being neighbours, so to say, explained their making loans one from the other. But I then realized that the problem which baffled me was due to a mistake, an omission on my part. I had failed to distinguish between the operation of *trends*, in this case anal trends, and that of an *organization*, in this case the oral organization. This distinction, however, is decisive. And if it is appreciated the question of nearness or distance between organizations becomes irrelevant.

During the first, the oral organization, the oral impulses reign supreme, but, of course, they are not the only ones in existence. Because they are of supreme power, they subordinate the other instinctual trends to their own purpose.

The oral impulses are essentially connected with an *inward* direction, they are receptive. The oral aim is to acquire and incorporate the object on whom the infant depends: the good, feeding, gratifying breast. Ejection and annihilation are derived from the anal organ and function. Under the predominance of the oral organization these anal trends are used as a complementary technique to achieve the oral aim of maintaining the blissful relation with the good breast with whom the self fuses. The *caesura* of birth is, as Freud pointed out, less sharp than superficial impression might suggest. The infant strives to continue or regain his pre-natal oneness with his mother with all the means at his disposal. The oral impules with their inward direction are eminently suitable to achieve it: the good breast is incorporated, loved, and treated as self. But the breast is not alway good, the infant experiences a frustrating and persecuting breast and pain from the self, and against this painful experience the anal trends of ejection and annihilation are marshalled and put into operation. What is bad is split off, projected, eliminated, the predominantly oral aim of oneness with the good mother is preserved.

In an odd way, one might say, this aim of the oral organization – that is, to be one with the mother and to regain the pre-natal condition – is even pursued in the realm of splitting and projecting, because these mechanisms amongst other consequences result in identification, though of a certain kind: projective identification. The mother into whom the infant projects what he does not want to keep within himself by this very process again comes to carry him in her body. By means of using the anal trends and mechanisms in a complementary way the infant pursues the policy of a double insurance against loss and separation.

The fact that he does achieve this aim only to a limited degree and the complex *sequelae* of his oral pursuits are beyond the frame of my present considerations.

The notion then that there is a 'polymorphously perverse' stage interpolated between the oral and the anal organization is not in conflict with the theory of the oral organization of the instinctual impulses. If anything, the acknowledgement of this stage throws into relief how much it takes to undermine oral primacy.

Before I conclude I wish to refer very briefly to certain observations which can be better evaluated by the assumption that there exists a stage in which the polymorphously perverse disposition is manifest and dominant. These observations concern patients whose mothers became pregnant during this stage of their development, whose siblings were thus younger only by fifteen to eighteen months or so. Whilst in many respects these patients differed in their personalities, they seemed to have in common certain inhibitions in their object relations. They had the capacity for empathy and sensitivity, the readiness to help and understand the object, and well-developed intellectual sublimations, and so on – that is, genital character trends. But at the same time there was a very deep underlying resentment and an unforgivingness, an aggrieved attitude of 'I do not expect to be loved and cared for. I know I must consider mother and her baby. Not for me the good things in life – but I understand, that is how it has to be'; that is, they also had character traits derived from the oral and anal stages. Much of this attitude could be traced to the Oedipal conflicts of the polymorphous stage heightened by the mother's pregnancy.

I believe that in the older literature such phenomena were described as a discrepancy between the development of the libido and that of the ego. I find it helpful to think in terms of a too early accentuation of the genital trends during the polymorphous stage when the oral and anal impulses are not yet sufficiently mastered and therefore give rise to particularly strong depressive and persecutory anxieties.

I do not, of course, wish to suggest that a child whose mother is pregnant when he passes through the polymorphous stage of instinctual development must unfailingly develop disturbances in object relationship. I am mentioning my observations because they illustrate the significance of this phase for the formation of character traits and social capacities.

That this stage deserves to be closely studied is also suggested by observations concerning the perversions. But it is not my aim to embark on this vast topic in the frame of these short notes. It is interesting, though, to remember that Freud developed his conclusions about infantile sexuality from the analysis of the sexual aberrations of adults.

Notes

1 *Three Essays on the Theory of Sexuality* London: Imago Publishing Co., 1949, p. 111; also *Three Essays on the Theory of Sexuality*, p. 234, SE 7: 135–243.

6

Preliminary notes on some defence mechanisms in paranoid states (1952b)

This paper was published in the *International Journal of Psycho-Analysis* 33 (2) (1952), which was dedicated to Melanie Klein on the occasion of her seventieth birthday. A revised version of it appeared in M. Klein, P. Heimann, and R. Money-Kyrle (eds) *New Directions in Psycho-Analysis*, London: Tavistock (1955).

In this paper I wish to draw attention to a combination of defence mechanisms which I observed in the analyses of paranoid patients. I do not intend to present a comprehensive study of paranoid conditions, nor do I wish to deal with the important problem of distinguishing between paranoid states in neurotic and psychotic patients.

The analysis of paranoid patients has some characteristic features. The patient is preoccupied with experiences in which a certain person or persons have done and are doing harm to him (or her). He produces abundant material to prove that he is the victim of this person's hostility, and he describes in much detail his own state of suffering, pain, fear, and mental incapacity. The person by whom the patient feels persecuted is one very near to him (wife or husband or child), and often enough the patient is quite certain that his contemporary enemy does exactly the same things to him as an important figure in his earlier life, usually one of his parents. He concludes that he is doomed to suffer in this way and he feels very bitter about it.

The analytic sessions are filled by the patient's reporting ever new incidents in which he has been humiliated, attacked, and in one way or another made to suffer.

He describes intolerable states of panic and agony. He cannot find peace anywhere. Attempts at activity do not relieve his state of mind, but on the contrary infinitely add to his suffering, because he cannot accomplish what he has started; either his mind goes blank, or a turmoil of ideas overwhelms him. He cannot read or converse with people because he cannot follow a train of thought, and a new terror sweeps over him. People will pounce on him, he will be scorned and ridiculed. And so one pain follows another, one persecution and anticipation of persecution leads on to others. When his persecutory fears have become transferred to the analyst, the analytic sessions become devoted to the enumeration of the analyst's wrongdoings. At such a point my patients have accused me of having no human sympathy with the sufferer – indeed I make my living out of him; I have no interest in helping him since that would end my sinecure; I am conceited and dictatorial and intent on putting my stupid theories over, to the patient's detriment; my interpretations are taken from the textbooks which I have learnt by heart and which have no bearing on the patient; analysts think they are God Almighty, but in fact nobody has ever been helped by analysis. The patient is convinced that his condition has deteriorated through the analysis; he never was as ill as now. He feels that the analyst sides with his enemies – is his enemy.

The analytic sessions with Mr X. followed this pattern. He would begin the hour by complaining about his condition and reporting on his sufferings in great detail, each of which he felt to be due to analysis in general and me in particular. Whilst he himself was quite unaware of it, it was obvious to me that the detailed report on his painful experiences offered him the chance of attacking me and gave him a good deal of satisfaction. Consciously he was alarmed and distressed and the victim of my persecution. I used to listen to his complaints for quite a time silently. Then, when he felt he had expressed himself sufficiently, I took up his accusations in detail and made explicit what he had merely implied or hinted at. I found that it was very important to establish the links between his actual feelings of persecution and the incidents or interpretations, which had occurred in recent or earlier analytic sessions, and which had stirred his persecutory fears. I put into words as completely and specifically as possible whatever in his statements had remained only a vague allusion or an innuendo. I did not make any remarks of a reassuring or comforting nature, nor did I assert my sympathy or good will. The rationale of my technique was not that I wished to show how much I understood his feelings or how seriously I took whatever he said explicitly or implicitly, but I felt that only by fully dealing with his conscious and preconscious ideas of persecution could I establish contact with him, and that he was only able to converse with me after he had had a free run of accusations against me. As Freud has stressed, the analyst must start with the material which is on the surface of the patient's mind. When I thus traced his references and allusions to interpretations and incidents in preceding sessions, his tendency to feel insulted and wronged and to distort my interpretations became to some extent obvious to him, and he did come to feel that I understood him. Thus even in this part of the analytic session in which we focused on his complaints, it became possible to interpret his actual motives, feelings, and phantasies. Insight into his tendency to invest my interpretations and behaviour with malicious intentions on my part emerged, so to say, effortlessly, as a by-product.[1] Gradually this feature – that is, ordinary interpretative work – became dominant, and he collaborated by producing relevant associations, dreams, or memories which brought his unsolved conflicts with his original objects more into the open.

In this way, by an exclusively analytic procedure, the patient's initial state of persecutory anxiety was reduced, and he often volunteered the information that he felt better and that his alarm and restlessness had gone, and so on. He would, however, hardly ever give me any thanks for the relief which on his own statement he was actually experiencing, and at a later point he often made this very relief a cause for complaint – namely, that by my 'nice voice and pleasant personality' I seduced him and lulled him into a false sense of security which, he declared, was not founded on any 'real' improvement. Indeed, whenever in his introductory report on his condition during the interval between the sessions he did mention an improvement, he almost unfailingly attributed it to some person having been nice to him and explicitly disavowed any connection with the analytic work.

I have already mentioned that, when listening to my patient's complaints it was obvious that unconsciously he enjoyed attacking me. In general I have found that paranoid patients unconsciously derive a good deal of sadistic gratification in situations which they consciously only register as persecutory. However, I had not been quite certain how this unconscious sadistic gratification was connected with defensive processes. In one particular session with Mr X. this was demonstrated very clearly. As usual, he began with a report on his wretched life, his anxieties and inabilities, the torments caused by his fears and his futile attempts to ward them off. Scornful and mocking references to the analyst were there in plenty. He felt at the end of his tether. His situation was aggravated this time, because he had to make a change in his business. He knew what he wanted to do, yet felt unable to make the decision. He felt maximally persecuted, and the decision he had to make appeared to him to be of a vital order. Analysis, in his view having obviously failed to ameliorate his condition, had at this point to be put aside, and he demanded that I should give him advice about his so pressing 'real' problem and intervene directly in his external situation. I did not obey his order but proceeded in the usual way, and he became less anxious and less persecuted and recognized at some point that in fact his situation was not as urgent as he had at first believed. But his attacks on the analysis and on me, and his pleasure in inflicting insult and accusations seemed a bit stronger perhaps than usual. On leaving, though much relieved and with more insight into the factors related to his actual problem, he stated that I had not helped him at all and that he would be as much tormented after the hour as he had been before it.

The way, however, in which he made this statement did not accord with an anticipation of misery. It was with relish that he flung this parting shot at me. The affect accompanying his remark was triumphant and menacing. Manifestly his words contained two statements, one about my failure to help him and the other about the condition of torment he foresaw for himself. The hostile triumph in his attitude was clearly related to my failure and might be rendered by a phrase like this: 'You should be ashamed for having so blatantly failed in your job.' But this rendering of his thought would only express his triumph at having established my incompetence. There was also, as I said, an unmistakable threat in his attitude, which if put into words would run like this: 'I shall torment *you* after the hour exactly as I did when I came. You cannot escape from my attacks, although (or because) you will not be there to defend yourself.'

The unconscious meaning of the patient's parting remark was that *I* was going to be tormented. He used the pronoun which referred to himself because he was unconscious not only of his cruel impulses towards me, but also of the means by which he anticipated their gratification.

It takes much longer to describe than to perceive a process which takes place in a moment. It seemed to me that I could actually witness the process of introjection in operation, and the fact that such introjection occurred when he was about to leave me, brings to mind Freud's (1923b) suggestion that introjection may be the sole condition on which the ego can give up an object. Throughout the hour the patient had attacked and scorned me and tried to force me to enter his life outside the analysis. At the point of leaving me he introjected me in order to continue his attacks.

Before presenting my conclusions from this observation I wish to relate briefly certain facts of this patient's history which elucidate the transference situation.

The anal-sadistic quality of his conduct in the analytic sessions will have become obvious already. In his sexual life anal-sadistic elements played a significant part.

During a certain period in his life he greatly enjoyed breaking wind in the presence of his mistress who did not like this, but for his sake tolerated it. With his complaints my patient repeated with me this element of his love life. Further he sometimes visited prostitutes and ordered them to beat him and manually excite his penis. It can be seen that his conscious notions of suffering at my hands partly represented a transference from his beating practices.

I can here mention only a few of the phantasies connected with these practices which are relevant to my subject-matter.

(1) He was strongly identified with the prostitute whom he ordered to do the beating. (Identification with the manifestly sadistic partner in masochistic relations has long been established by psychoanalysis.)
(2) It was not so much he who was beaten, but his internal father.
(3) To beat meant further to beat something out, in the way in which Moses by beating the rock forced the water out of it. When the patient was beaten, it was not only that the pain was experienced by his internal father, but he got the persecuting, bad, and hated father out of his system.
(4) The prostitute, who had to be subservient to his will and on his bidding carried out the beating and gave him pleasurable sensations in his genital, was not to have any pleasure herself. In this way he enacted his parents' intercourse as in his Oedipal phantasies he wished it to have been: his mother should not have loved his father, she should have married him only for his money, and she should loathe sexual intercourse with him. The father should feel the humiliation of being rejected and of being impotent to give pleasure to his partner.[2]

Another detail of my patient's history is significant for the understanding of his behaviour in the session which I reported. He often spoke with great love and admiration of his mother and illustrated her kindness and forbearance by various incidents. He remembered, for example, how he took her into his car and drove off with her, and how, when they had gone a good distance from home, he unburdened himself by accusing her of the many wrong things he felt she had done to him. She listened patiently and with her characteristic kindness. When my patient tried to make me leave the sphere of analysis and follow him into his life outside, he re-enacted his relation with his mother in the transference situation. In the past he took the original object of his sadistic love, his mother, into his car and removed her physically from her home. It is not difficult to see that the car was a symbol of himself and that in unconscious phantasy the patient took his mother into himself introjecting her once more as often on earlier occasions. In the transference relationship he introjected the substitute object, the analyst.

When Freud (1921c) introduced the concept of a grade in the ego, the ego ideal, which he later developed into the superego, he envisaged the intrapsychic situation as an internal object relationship. The relevant passage may be quoted:

> Let us reflect that the ego now appears in the relation of an object, to the ego ideal which has been developed out of it, *and that all the interplay between an outer object and the ego as a whole,* with which our study of the neuroses has made us acquainted, may possibly be repeated upon this new scene of action inside the ego.[3]
>
> (My italics)

In his subsequent writings this wide notion of an intrapsychic emotional relationship has not been worked out. It has been superseded by the concept of the ego as one functional unit and the superego as another, entrusted with the enforcement of moral principles on the ego. The structural relation between the ego and the superego has assumed a dominant position in psychoanalytic theory. Melanie Klein's research by widening our knowledge of the development of the superego takes us back to Freud's first notion of an intrapsychic object relation. The introjected object which acts as the judge of the ego, the superego, represents only one aspect, a highly important one, of the relation between the ego and its introjected objects, but it does not exhaust all the emotional experiences which the ego derives as the result of introjection (and projection).[4]

The paranoid type of introjection with which the present paper is concerned establishes an internal object which the ego can treat with the same sadism with which the subject treats or wishes to treat the original object in the outer world. This, it seems to me, is possible because, together with the introjection of the object, a splitting in the ego takes place, and the part of the ego which becomes identified with the introjected object is split off from the rest. In this way a 'new scene of action inside the ego' is arranged in which the ego continues its sadistic love relationships. The sadistic gratifications which the ego obtains from the internal object represent at the same time a discharge of the destructive impulses by which the ego is endangered; in other words, they represent an *intrapsychic* deflection of the death instinct.

I used to think of processes of internal projection when I observed incidents similar to the one I described in some detail; but I did not understand how such intrapsychic projection took place until I came to appreciate the part played by the splitting mechanisms. In the light of Melanie Klein's (1946) concept of the paranoid/schizoid position and through her presentation of the defensive processes of splitting in early infantile life, I realized that intrapsychic projection is preceded by a split in the ego.

This combination of introjection, splitting, and intrapsychic projection seems to me to represent defences which are characteristic of paranoid states, and of very great significance in preventing the patient from breaking down under the stress of his persecutory fears. To put it in an over-simplified manner: the paranoid patient is endangered only to the extent to which he is identified with the internal object which he persecutes. By means of splitting and projection this identification is controlled and limited.[5] It seems that occasionally the protective inner processes of splitting and projection which for the time being end the identification with the internal persecuted/persecuting object reach consciousness. Several of my patients who suffered from paranoid states told me that sometimes, without any accountable reason, the whole torment, panic, whirlpool of incoherent ideas, and so on, would disappear, in a flash, and they would feel free, capable, and even happy.

If the division in the ego is maintained, the success of the defensive splitting appears to depend on how much of the ego remains free and separated from that part which through the introjection of the persecuted/persecuting object is lost, and no longer operates within the organization of the ego. To use a spatial analogy, it must be very important that the dividing line should run between a smaller part, which becomes the introjected object, and the larger part of the ego. This would ensure that a sufficient amount of ego-functions remains comparatively unimpared and available for the subject's needs. An assumption of this kind is in keeping with the fact that all the patients under my observation who suffered from paranoid states were capable of maintaining themselves in an ordinary milieu and of carrying out social and professional activities with a varying degree of competence.

Spatial analogies are not very satisfactory, but they are useful for the description of quantitative factors. A 'broad mind' is not entirely a metaphor. Wealth of ideas and associations and width of the mental orbit are very real facts. An essential part of the therapeutic process of analysis, 'working through', depends, as Freud has shown, on the quantity of the associative links which the patient's ego comes to establish with the formerly dissociated idea. In this process, which undermines the pathogenic power of the particular idea, the ego makes use of introjective techniques.

Analytic therapy follows the patterns of normal development. The child progresses by introjecting his loved and admired parents; his ego assimilates its good internal objects and is at the same time stimulated to develop its own constructive capacities, its social, intellectual, and artistic gifts.

When introjection, however, is determined by the person's destructive impulses, under the pressure of paranoid fears, the introjected object is not assimilated. The ego acquires a dangerous object and, as I suggested above, by means of splitting it is divided into a part which is maintained as ego, whereas another part is identified with the bad internal object and is treated as such. Repeated introjections of this kind lead to repeated splits in the ego. The defensive process is bound to fail, if for various reasons the division in the ego cannot be maintained and the different parts of the ego fuse. On this hypothesis, the moment of integration spells danger; when integration occurs, the ego will be flooded with anxiety, and it will have to marshall other defences. I think that projection outwards will often be used at this point, and for this reason the individual will need objects suitable for such projection (projection of what is felt to be bad and dangerous); in other words, the individual will need a 'bad' object in the external world. A vicious circle may be started in this way, because the subject is both attracted and persecuted by the external object which through projection has become an alter ego (projective identification).

The paranoid type of introjection and splitting seems to impair many ego functions to a certain extent. In a paranoid condition the ego is not coherent and well functioning; it is not merely reduced in quantity owing to the split. I believe that here lies an important difference between the results of splitting and of repression. In the latter case the ego is impoverished. A certain amount of its energy is spent in maintaining repression, and the person has not developed his potential abilities. Within his limits, however, he is fully coherent and capable, and he is largely free from anxiety.

Paranoid patients are practically always in a state of anxiety. They are preoccupied with the theme of their persecutions. As is well known, these patients have a sharpness of observation, but ideas of reference lead to faulty conclusions. Their attention is focused on whatever feeds their suspicion, and they are unable to give due weight to anything else. They are shallow in their thinking, spread over a wide area on the surface, but avoid the depth. (This suggests that the splitting line runs also between depth and surface, horizontally, as it were.) By exaggerating an isolated aspect, hairsplitting, they lose sight of the essence of the matter. They cannot accept a different view of the situation and repeatedly change the issue.

I have found that paranoid patients often are gifted speakers. They find words easily and have a rich and varied vocabulary. They are capable of arguing successfully, but they argue too much and think too little. They prove their own foregone conclusion, which is that they are being wronged. (One of my patients complained that analysis was like a Russian trial in which the outcome is pre-judged.) I believe it is this capacity for verbalization and skill in arguing, which is sometimes mistaken for a high intelligence, whilst in fact the paranoid patient's intellectual achievements are restricted and rather poor. When the ego is predominantly engaged in defensive manoeuvres, it is not free to assimilate ideas and use its creative capacities (Heimann 1942). It is often quite striking to see the extent to which a person, otherwise intelligent and imaginative, can become dull, rigid, and monotonous, in fact stupid, when swayed by paranoid fears.[6]

The triumph which the paranoid patient shows when convicting his object of incompetence, stupidity, cruelty, and so on, links the paranoid with the manic state. Exaltation of the self occurs in the manic and in the paranoid patient alike. Freud and Abraham have shown that the delusion of persecution has a highly narcissistic character and implies delusions of grandeur. The paranoid split in the ego leads to a condition similar to mania, where the ego, as Freud (1917e) described, has mastered the complex or thrust it aside or surmounted the object itself. The manic patient consciously feels cheery, loved, elated, and capable of achieving whatever he likes; the paranoid patient consciously feels persecuted, bitter, wretched, and interfered with in his activities. Behind this impressive difference, however, there are great similarities. The manic person, if contradicted in his amiable, pally expansiveness, easily becomes violently aggressive. Other similarities lie in the impaired thought processes such as shallowness, flight of ideas, change of issues, inability to accept a different view, and so on.[7]

The common denominator of the manic and the paranoid state is the defence against the sense of guilt, unworthiness, and depression;

that is, the emotions which Melanie Klein comprises under the term 'depressive anxiety'. Both states derive from the 'manic defence' which operates when the infant has reached the depressive position, but under the impact of depressive anxieties again and again returns to the former, the paranoid/schizoid position. These regressive movements re-establish the mechanisms of denial and splitting, idealization and omnipotence, and so on.

It is from the conflict of ambivalence and from guilt for attacking the loved and good object that both the manic and the paranoid person take flight.

The paranoid person develops the delusion of persecution and denies that he both loves and attacks the person by whom he feels persecuted. His defences against his conscious fears include the unconscious gratification of his sadism. As a result of combining introjection with splitting and intrapsychic projection he experiences such sadistic gratification also in relation to his introjected object. When the division(s) in his ego cannot be maintained, he is in danger of becoming identified with his persecuted object and of breaking down under the impact of depressive and persecutory anxieties.

Whether or not he can avert this danger depends on his ability to marshal other defences.[8]

Notes

1 Cf. James Strachey: 'Symposium on the theory of the therapeutic results of psychoanalysis', *International Journal of Psycho-Analysis* 18 (April–July 1937), Parts 2 and 3. Strachey shows that it is important to enable the patient to make a 'comparison between his archaic and imaginary objects and his actual and real ones' (p. 142).
2 The homosexual aspects of the beating practices are omitted because I am not concerned with presented a comprehensive case history. For the same reason I also do not mention in which way shame and horror affected the patient and how in certain situations he attempted to make reparation.
3 *Group Psychology and the Analysis of the Ego* (1921c), chap. XI, London: Hogarth Press and the Institute of Psycho-Analysis, 1940; also *Group Psychology and the Analysis of the Ego*, chap. XI, SE 18: 69–143.
4 Cf. Joan Riviere, 'The unconscious phantasy of an inner world reflected in examples from English literature', *International Journal of Psycho-Analysis* 33 (2), 1952: 160–72.
5 To some extent the beating incidents reflect these intrapsychic events. Since the patient employed the prostitute, he could control and limit the amount of pain he wished to experience.

6 In this context I am not dealing with the role which anal obstinacy plays in such 'stupidity'. In passing I would mention that, as is to be expected, all my patients who tended to produce paranoid states showed strong anal features both as part of their sexual (heterosexual) activities and in the form of character traits.

7 Intolerance of an opinion different from his own which occurs in both the paranoid and the manic patient shows that both have regressed to an early infantile phase in which the gratifying mother fuses with the self, whilst the frustrating mother is felt as different from the self and its enemy. The patient from whose analysis I have quoted found it exceedingly frustrating if his sexual partner showed any initiative, and often in the analysis he longed for me to be completely passive, absolutely silent, and not express any opinion of my own, different from his. I found that all my paranoid patients resented interpretations because they 'had not thought of this' themselves. This resentment was not only an expression of a general attitude that whatever comes from an enemy must be dangerous and better rejected; it had the specific quality that something was dangerous because it was different from the person himself.

The manic patient's attitude is illustrated by the German saying: 'Und willst Du nicht mein Bruder sein, so schlag ich Dir den Schädel ein.' ('If my brother you won't be, I shall just slay thee.') The paranoid patient makes the same statement in a less humorous manner.

8 [Paula Heimann wrote in the margin of a reprint of this paper in 1978: 'Very good paper, references to Melanie Klein need critical re-appraisal. "Projective Identification" is clearly treated as an intrapsychic, not as a social phenomenon, i.e. the object feels, phantasizes etc. that object is identified with him, not that object [analyst] in fact has become identified with subject [patient]'.]

7

Dynamics of transference interpretations (1955/6)

This paper was read before the International Psycho-Analytical Congress, Geneva, 1955, and was published in the *International Journal of Psycho-Analysis* 37 (4/5) (1956).

In 1919 Freud wrote: 'We have formulated our therapeutic task as one of bringing to the knowledge of the patient the unconscious repressed impulses existing in his mind and, to this end, of uncovering the resistances that oppose themselves to this extension of his knowledge about himself.'[1]

This definition of psychoanalytic therapy still holds good. Advance in psychoanalytic work has proved the truth of the theories embodied in it. To paraphrase those germane to the present paper: mental illness is caused by unconscious conflicts, the clashes between instinctual impulses and what is opposed to them. Mental recovery depends on conscious work on these conflicts, and this work proceeds through the medium of the patient's emotional relation with his analyst. Psychoanalytic therapy is thus directed towards the patient's *ego*.

Freud's definition of psychoanalytic therapy anticipated his systematic formulations of the nature and functions of the ego and its interaction with the other mental systems (Freud 1923b), but his earlier work (Freud 1900, 1911b) had already presented the basic principles governing mental processes. Perception and motor action are the two poles of the mental apparatus, perception initiating mental activity and controlling physical activity. Between these poles is the realm of attention, the readiness for perception, memory, the store of past perceptions which is used in fresh perceptive acts, and conscious associative thought, leading to correct assessment of inner and outer conditions. It is on such conscious and reasoned judgements that reality-adjusted and purposeful activities are based.

The ego is the system of consciousness and its sequelae. It grows and takes shape through contact with objects. Its root function from which its other functions stem is perception. 'In the ego perception plays the part which in the id devolves upon instinct' (Freud 1923b).[2] Perception is thus the prime and fundamental activity of the ego, as Freud stressed, and not a passive experience. The ego brings something of its own towards the object to be perceived. It cathects the object actively. Cathexis presupposes the existence of a mobile energy, derived from the instinctual reservoir, which can be moved from one place to another, from the subject to an object, from one object to others. Mobility is a primary character of life, and the ultimate motive which makes the ego turn towards an object, perceive, and cathect it lies in its helplessness and in its wish to live. The first perceptions are those of bodily sensations and bodily needs. 'The ego is first and foremost a body-ego' (Freud 1923b).[3] The urge to obtain satisfaction expresses the life instinct. I would suggest that when the ego turns towards an object for satisfaction, what it brings forward of its own for a perception of this object is the expectation that it will be good, gratifying, loving; that is, it sends out some of its own libido towards the object. According to Melanie Klein (1946), such libidinal cathexis includes projection of part of the ego's own love on to the object.[4] Perception furthermore involves introjection (Heimann 1952d). The basic function of the ego, perception, is thus associated with the main structural processes which are responsible for ego development.

The analysis of the factors involved in perception and following upon it bears out Freud's statement of the paramount significance of perception for the whole of ego development. The ego is the sense organ and executive of the total organism. Perception initiates contact; and contact involves the main structural mechanisms of introjection and projection, which then build up and shape the ego. Contact, moreover, initiated by perception, leads on to obtaining both satisfaction and protection (defence). Satisfaction, gratification, gratitude, and love are closely allied experiences. Thus the ego is the seat of the feelings and emotions. It contains the affective responses to perceptions and the emotional charge of memory traces. It is the organ which expresses the total personality. It was in this last wide sense that Freud used the term before he proceeded to his definition of the system ego. Yet this wider meaning still pertains to it, since what we call a person's character 'must be thought of as belonging entirely to the province of the ego' (Freud 1933a).[5] It is in the wake of his gratifying contact with his first object, the mother's breast, that the infant comes to love this object (anaclitic process).

109

The first sense organ to function for the total personality in contact with another human being is the mouth; the basis and model of all later perceptions is feeding, oral intake.

The point I wish to underline here is that it is the life instinct which is operative in perception, the instinct which aims at union and contact, in contrast to the death instinct which aims at avoiding or breaking up contact and union. It is, of course, true that an expression of destructive impulses also needs contact with an object, but this does not invalidate the proposition that contact primarily and ultimately serves the life instinct. If contact is wanted in order to attack and destroy an object, this object is one that rouses fear. Self-preservation requires it to be defeated or annihilated. In contradistinction, negativism, refusal to perceive and cathect the object, turning away from it, denial, are characteristic expressions of the death instinct. (Heimann 1952c).

Libidinal and self-preservative needs drive the subject towards objects and engender perception. When these needs are satisfied, the ego ceases to perceive; the baby after a happy feed, the adult after orgasm, falls asleep.

In its role of root function of the ego perception leads to and establishes healthy life. Conversely, distorted perceptions and hallucinations lead to malformation of the ego and mental illness, with all the sequelae of delusional thinking and acting and failure in social life.

These propositions – namely, that perception is the basis of consciousness, that it is the expression of the life instinct and promotes contact and union, intrapsychically and inter-personally, that it is the foundation of reality-adjusted behaviour – give substance to Freud's definition of the therapeutic task of widening the patient's knowledge about himself through the medium of his emotional relation with the analyst. Perception is the prime mover in the unifying analytic process of reconciling into a whole the disparate, repressed, and conflicting elements of the patient's personality. In this work the transference becomes the battleground on which the patient's conflicts have to be fought out, since it is in the transference that the experiences that originally developed and shaped his ego are repeated. Under the sway of the pleasure principle the patient wishes to repeat only the pleasurable aspects of his past life. He wants the analyst to gratify his libidinal wishes and to comfort and reassure him against his painful feelings of dread and guilt. He fights against the analyst's endeavour to make him conscious of what he excludes from consciousness on account of its painful character. When he is interested in the analytic approach and is willing to learn, it is in the pattern of pleasurable learning as in childhood that he wants to proceed, and thus his intellectual interest becomes a form of resistance. The infant learns pleasurably by introjecting his loving and protective parents. As ordinary observation shows, an infant who first shrank from a new object, say a cat, and took flight into his mother's arms, will venture forth and stroke and explore this object when he has seen his mother do so and so feels encouraged by her. He does not merely emulate her; he has taken this mother inside himself and under her protection can now do what before was too dangerous. Melanie Klein has called the introjection of the mother's breast in its loved and loving aspect the focal point of the developing ego (Klein 1946).

In fact, however, the patient is unable to follow the pleasure principle by repeating only the pleasurable parts of his past object relationship in the transference. He re-experiences his old conflicts with their attendant persecutory and depressive anxieties. But repetition turns into modification, because the analytic relationship provides not merely a stage on which the patient re-enacts his past experiences. This time the patient's emotional object, the analyst, does not react by responding emotionally to his wishes and fears, as his original objects did. In this new emotional setting in which the patient repeats, the analyst contributes, in the form of interpretations, the perception and consciousness of what is happening in this setting. This combination of contact with an object together with conscious insight into what this contact unconsciously signifies distinguishes the transference from the original relationship.

It follows, and this is the main contention of this paper, that the specific instrument of psychoanalytic therapy, in contrast to other forms of psychotherapy, is the *transference interpretation*. Repetition gives way to modification, to dynamic changes in the patient's ego, because the transference interpretation enables the patient's ego to *perceive* its emotional experiences, its impulses, and their vicissitudes, makes them conscious, *at the moment* when they are actively roused in a direct and immediate relationship with their object. The emotional excitation must be followed closely by perception of it, and almost coincide with conscious awareness of it. We know that a person can be profoundly changed by religious experiences, divine revelations, a vision of the divinity. The quality of immediacy characterizes these experiences, and it is this that engenders conviction. But whilst in religious convictions of this kind the ego accepts unquestioningly the divine truth, and submits passively to its deity, the personality changes which follow from the psychoanalytic process are founded on the fullest activity of the ego – that is, on realistic, critically tested perceptions.

111

Unconscious phantasy in the transference

In spite of general agreement amongst analysts that the transference is the battleground – in other words, that the dynamic changes in the patient's ego depend on the working through of his emotional conflicts as they centre upon the analyst – there are great differences in psychoanalytic technique as practised. These have often been defined in terms of the timing of transference interpretations, of interpretations of the negative versus the positive transference, or deep versus superficial interpretations, or the number of interpretations altogether. In the past – perhaps not only in the past – the analyst's efficiency was measured by the amount of his silence.

These definitions, important though they are, do not go to the core of the matter. The essential causes of the differences in psychoanalytic technique are in my view related to the analyst's appreciation of the role played by unconscious phantasy in mental life and in the transference.

It is not sufficient to regard the transference as a manifestation of the repetition compulsion and as a mechanism of displacement of ungratified libidinal impulses and unsolved conflicts. In such repetition and displacement unconscious phantasy itself is operative. The patient is not prompted by realistic perception and rational thought when he treats the analyst as his parents; when interpretations are enjoyed as the sustaining milk from his mother's breast or dreaded as the castrating father's attacks. He is behaving under the domination of his unconscious infantile phantasies, those dynamic psychic processes which Susan Isaacs (1948) defined as 'the mental corollary, the psychic representative of instinct'. 'All impulses, all feelings, all modes of defence are experienced in phantasies which give them *mental* life and show their direction and purpose.' 'A phantasy represents the particular content of the urges or feelings . . . dominating the mind at the moment.'

When Freud (1911b) described that a special mental function, that of phantasizing, remained exempt from the reality principle, he considered defensive and gratifying phantasies. But these are only one particular form or manifestation of that basic mental capacity which Susan Isaacs showed to be inherent in Freud's concept of instincts as borderland entities between mind and soma, and in his derivation of intellectual function from the interplay of the primary instinctual impulses (Freud 1925h). I have mentioned above one example of the wish-fulfilling type of phantasizing in the transference, and one of the opposite, and anxiety-rousing type. Moreover, it is

112

not only in regard to objects that this basic capacity of phantasizing comes into play, thus determining the character of the transference; it is also in regard to parts of the self, body and mind, that this capacity exerts itself. On account of unconscious phantasy the patient treats his own ideas, his memories of past events, his wishes and fears, and so on, as personified entities localized within himself, and he transfers these internal objects as well on to the analyst. In his phantastic evaluation of ideas and memories the patient repeats (or retains) the infantile mode of reaction to bodily sensations and intrapsychic processes, following in part the connection with real external objects, his parents, who first gave him words and ideas (as well as concrete gifts), and whom he internalized together with the ideas and the activity of thinking.

Another aspect of unconscious phantasies is important in psycho-analytic work. The communication of an idea, or a memory, or a dream not only forms part of the patient's emotional relation with his analyst; it is also prompted by it. Here, as so often in our work, we encounter a two-way traffic. The patient tells a dream not because it just happened to come into his mind. It came into his mind because to tell it to his analyst is a suitable way of expressing his impulses towards him, which he then acts upon by telling the dream. The degree to which infantile modes of thinking prevail does, of course, differ with different individuals, but they must never be neglected in any analysis, and they become dominant when the analytic process has stirred early infantile levels of experience.

At times these unconscious phantasies find expression in a dramatic manner, but it is not only at these conspicuous moments that they are operative. (Nor is the drama of life in appearance always dramatic.) They are in existence always, even if hidden and apparently quiescent, and they necessitate a persistent readiness in the analyst to perceive them. On this view unconscious phantasy, the cause of the transference, is not something that occasionally irrupts into the patient's relation with the analyst and then interferes with his reason and co-operation. It is the fertile matrix from which his actual motives spring and which determine his apparently rational behaviour, his reasoned presentation of ideas and co-operative acceptance of the analyst's interpretations no less than his silence, or negativism, or openly defiant resistance.

The therapeutic task of extending the patient's conscious knowledge about himself, about his unconscious impulses and defences against anxiety and pain, makes it necessary to bring his unconscious phantasies to consciousness. This holds for the positive transference no less than for the negative. Whilst the latter more obviously acts as resistance, the former too serves this purpose. The patient's infantile need to deify his parents is repeated with the analyst, at the cost of forgoing independence and objectivity. Moreover, the analyst, at one point raised in unconscious phantasies to the stature of a god, is bound to change into a demon when the patient's expectations that his total life will become blissfully happy through his analysis are thwarted. In any case, even during the apparently smooth period of a predominantly positive transference there are negative undercurrents: the very idealization of the analyst covers hostile feelings, sanctions, greedy and possessive demands and so on, so that we cannot make so very sharp a distinction beween what in fact always occurs in a fusion or in rapid oscillations.

When the analyst expresses these unconscious phantasies in his interpretations, the patient's ego makes contact with them and so discovers something which is in reality its own, although he himself was unable to verbalize these phantasies or can remember only fragmentary flashes of such feelings or ideas flitting through his mind at some former time. Superficial contents of feelings will be nearer to consciousness and easily accessible to interpretation; but underlying them are the infantile and primitive contents, some of which have never been experienced in verbal form. Verbalization of the most primitive and chaotic impulses and of the ego's relationship with its intrapsychic objects renders these unconscious experiences only in approximation. Nevertheless, words are of the greatest significance, because they remove the barriers between the different strata of the ego, they promote clear and critical thinking, and they are the vehicle of conscious, explicit communication between patient and analyst. The interpretations of the character of the patient's relation to his analyst in terms of these primitive impulses and of the transference of intrapsychic object relationships are necessary if analysis is to bring about the patient's fuller understanding of himself.

The analyst as the patient's supplementary ego

Freud has given us the most succinct description of the analyst's function in saying that the analyst acts as a mirror to the patient.

A mirror has no self, so to speak, no independent existence: it is there to reflect the patient. Thus the analytic process is carried out by a team of two persons acting as a functional unit, in which separate roles are accorded to each.

The patient's share is described by the fundamental rule under which he has the right and duty of saying whatever comes into his

114

mind. He initiates the themes of the discussion by words or silent behaviour. He can discard logic, reason, and social conventions in behaviour and language. He can express his emotional demands on his partner, love, trust, seduction, or hate, contempt, rejection; can roam over every place and time of his life; can forget the purpose of the relationship.

The analyst's share is to be the mirror, to record and reflect the patient's mental processes and so to provide his ego with perceptions of these processes.

The analyst assumes the role of a supplementary ego for the patient.

The analyst does not speak spontaneously, but in response only to the patient's associations, verbal or behavioural. He has to follow the themes which the patient has brought up. His remarks need to be clear and to the point. He cannot roam, but must relate himself to what is emotionally and actually relevant for his patient. He has to remember that all that the patient says and does is taking place in the transference situation, and he has to seek the reasons and meanings for the patient's associations. His own emotions are barred from expression; both his hostility and his benevolence have to be sublimated into the readiness to perceive without personal bias, without selecting or rejecting; he has to analyse his counter-transference and extract clues from it for the patient's processes. His first objective is to enable the patient's ego to perceive its intrapsychic and inter-personal processes, as they occur in the *immediate* situations.

The loss of perception with its sequelae which the patient incurred in his attempts to solve his conflicts with his original objects, his defensive acts of denial, repression, isolation, splitting, and so on, become actual and manifest in the transference. His perception is reduced and distorted, his thinking repetitive, rambling, blocked, or irrelevant; awareness of these defects in his ego functions is absent or obscured. Illusion, delusion, or hallucination replace realistic perception and judgement. Thus the analyst is not only or primarily to interpret something that happened in the past; it is happening now.

The question the analyst has to ask himself constantly is: 'Why is the patient now doing what to whom?' The answer to this question constitutes the transference interpretation. It defines the patient's actual motives, arising both from his instinctual impulses and from his defences against pain and anxiety towards the analyst as their object. It defines the character of the analyst and the character of the patient at the actual moment. In the wake of these clarifications of the immediate relationship some picture of his earlier object relations emerges, to which the patient responds with either a general feeling of familiarity or with direct and specific recollections. His immediate emotional experience with his object, rendered conscious by this object's interpretations, taps the depths in him, his phantasies and memories. It is the transference interpretation which fully reinstates the past in the present and makes it accessible to the patient's ego. The patient is not then looking back coolly and intellectually at what he once felt with his parents, but is experiencing his immediate feelings and their phantasy contents towards the analyst as the real and living equivalent of his past life with his original objects who have indeed been intrapsychically preserved.

Although the patient re-enacts his past object relations in the transference, the analyst has to consider the reciprocal fact that his own personality, no matter how much he controls its expression, is perceived and reacted to by the patient. He must be aware of himself, his personal peculiarities, and so on, as prompting responses – both correct and distorted perceptions – in his patient which interact with the patient's spontaneous productions. Therefore the patient's criticisms of his analyst and attempts at analysing him cannot be dismissed as resistance only. The analyst's personality is one part of the analytic situation and of the patient's problems on a realistic as well as a phantasy level. An interesting sideline concerns the patient's unawareness of his analyst – especially, for instance, when the analyst himself has had some distressing experience. Such a lack of perception in patients may spring from tact, or insensitivity, or from the need to deny whatever threatens the use of an object as a source of gratification.

Such incidents reveal important aspects of the patient's personality in his immediate contact with an object; yet in my view it is not possible to interpret them directly. The analyst cannot make his patient aware of his failure of perception, since this would involve expressing something about himself. I have pointed out elsewhere (Heimann 1950) that any confession of personal matters by the analyst is injurious to the analytic process. It amounts to an intrusion and projection by the analyst. It may, though, be possible for the analyst to point to a conspicuous absence, a phobic avoidance concerning himself, in the patient's associations, if indeed this is an observable fact. This may or may not lead to the emergence of the patient's denied, repressed, split-off experience of having noticed something disturbing in the analyst. But in any case it is an important part of the analyst's work to be aware of such incidents. Since they do show something of the patient's way of dealing with inter-personal problems, repetitions in other settings are bound to

116

occur which the analyst can interpret freely. The value of his perception in the incident described lies in his having become sensitized, so that he will detect the same phenomenon the more quickly when it occurs next time.

An important part of the transference interpretations concerns the patient's introjection of his analyst. The theory that introjection of the analyst modifies the patient's archaic superego and, therefore, is part of the analytic therapy needs to be revised. Introjection of any friendly authority represents a therapeutic experience and may modify a strict superego. But it is not the specific characteristic of psychoanalytic therapy; that is the extension of the patient's consciousness and the widening and unifying of his ego. The really valid modifications of the superego result from changes in the ego by the conscious working through of its impulses, conflicts, and anxieties.

The origin of the cruel superego, as Melanie Klein (1932) has shown, lies in the infant's projecting his own sadistic impulses on his parents as external and internal objects. Introjection of the analyst into the patient's superego alone is far from breaking the vicious circle of destructive impulses and dread of the superego. It merely achieves a shift and maintains the dangerous twin formation of idealization and persecution. If the ego's conflicts with its superego are not worked through, the ego continues with its early infantile mode of splitting and doubling its relationships. The patient in fact repeats unconsciously his oscillation from one bad parent, now his real and internalized parents, to the other good parent, now the kind analyst.

What really change the archaic superego and divest it of its demoniacal or godlike character are processes in the ego: its conscious recognition of its impulses, its accepting responsibility for them and withdrawing projection from its external and introjected objects. This process of working through is experienced in the transference with the analyst in the role of the original and internalized objects, and includes the re-experience of infantile conflicts down to the levels which Melanie Klein (1935, 1940) has described as the paranoid and depressive infantile positions. Alongside the modification of the ego, the superego changes its character. It ceases to be a cruel intrapsychic figure which restricts the ego, prohibits libidinal pleasure, and by relentlessly equating impulses with deeds, punishes cruel wishes. It assumes an abstract character; the character of guiding principles which the ego can critically test and accept as valuable. Many of these the patient may consciously remember to have been held by his parents. Closely linked with these processes the ego's capacity for sublimation is freed, and its former rebellion against an intrapsychic devil or submission to an intrapsychic god is replaced by the ego's creative struggle with ideas, with intellectual, or artistic, or practical problems, for whose solution it exercises itself and works hard, often, indeed, painfully (Heimann 1942). An introjection of the analyst as a benevolent, permissive figure bypasses this development of the ego. The interpretation that such introjection is in progress is a vital part of the analyst's work.

The patient's tendency to short-circuit his painful labours by accepting his analyst as a saviour and mentor makes it necessary for the analyst to avoid authoritative attitudes. Giving his opinion on the patient's friends or parents, proffering advice or practical interventions – all this runs counter to the analytic aim and procedure.

It is introjection of a different kind which analytic technique aims at. The analyst acts as the patient's supplementary ego by providing perception and consciousness of the patient's own processes. What the patient introjects, therefore, is something that essentially belongs to his own ego, but which had been in a state of abeyance through various denial techniques, or else had been stifled at the beginning and thus been prevented from pursuing its normal growth. In the course of the analytic work the patient does arrive at new ideas and points of view, at new emotional constellations, but they are a part of his own self, not his analyst's ideas or feelings. He becomes conscious through the interpretative work of what he had forgotten; he also becomes capable of thinking consecutively and finds conclusions where earlier his line of thought was blocked. His integrated ego advances farther. When the patient's consciousness is extended in the hard-won battles against his resistances, he discovers and re-discovers himself; he also grows and his capacities develop; he becomes more creative, and the assimilation of apparently new ideas and feelings is facilitated by the fact that, as the patient sometimes says, he 'actually knew it all the time'.

The functional unit of analyst and patient reproduces the functional units which the patient experienced in the past, first with his mother's body, and later with both parents. The fundamental difference is evident. The parents are supplementary to a physically and emotionally helpless infant and their responsibility is maximal, as is their child's dependence on them. The analyst is not his patient's parents. His responsibility and his means of caring for his patient are limited in extent and different in kind. If his patient is incapacitated to a major degree and in need of parental care, it is not for the analyst to take on that function. Freud (1923b) warned the analyst against the temptation to act as his patient's saviour and defined his function as the patient's mirror. This limitation signifies an acceptance of reality by the analyst and constitutes a safeguard against his own weaknesses and faults. Moreover, it protects the patient from an interference with his personality arising from another person's opinion that he ought to be different. To believe that analysis is compatible with influencing the patient's life is to fall in with the patient's wish for an omnipotent solution of his problems – that is, his wish to retreat into babyhood.

Conversely, the patient's tendency to regress is lessened and his adult ego strengthened when the analyst steadfastly refrains from encouraging the acting out of infantile experiences by participating in them.

The transference interpretation is the real tool of analytic technique. It is not always instantly available. Often the analyst is baffled. To expect that he should always understand what is going on would be tantamount to claiming that his own ego functions to perfection. But the fact that he is bewildered is a reality in the immediate situation and needs to be clearly perceived as such by the analyst. He will then avoid blurring the issue further by irrelevant or misleading comments. Moreover, he will discover, if only gradually, the specific meaning and significance of such occurrences. His own contribution to such situations he will find from the analysis of his counter-transference which, as I have suggested, forms part of the analyst's work. Often what has happened is that the patient has succeeded in projecting his fears and defensive dissociation into the analyst's ego, or that he has re-enacted a primal scene with anal attacks on his parents and effectively confused the analyst, or that he has taken flight by a special form of narcissistic withdrawal.

If the dynamic transference interpretation remains in abeyance for too long and the analyst merely supplies preparatory clarifications, the patient either finds more fuel for his intellectual defences or he experiences just another emotional upset, as so often in his outside life, without gaining from it. Repetition has not been turned into modification, and often this will lead to more repetition by the patient – that is, acting out in his social life.

Whether the patient talks about a dream or a current incident or a childhood episode, the analyst's task is to perceive the dynamic line which links this with the patient's actual motives, preconscious or unconscious, towards the analyst.

The emotional centre, the centre of growth, lies in the transference relationship and is kept there against the patient's resistance by the interpretations.

119

My contention that it is the transference interpretation only which achieves dynamic changes in the patient's ego does not mean that the analyst speaks only about himself and denies the importance of the persons with whom the patient is consciously concerned. Nor do I overlook that often a patient takes flight into the transference from a current conflict in his life. My contention is that the relevant meaning, the true understanding of the patient's conscious problems can only be discovered if the dynamic line is perceived and followed out linking these problems with the emotional motives governing the patient in the immediate, the transference situation. The patient's unsolved problems can only be recognized and made accessible by the understanding of the transference.

There are moments in the analysis when the patient recovers his lost original objects. He then dwells on memories of incidents and feelings, speaks with deep and genuine concern about them, works out what a certain episode meant to him and must have meant to his mother or father, how he misunderstood them or they misunderstood him at the time, whilst he now realizes that he falsely attributed to them motives of indifference or hostility. In these thoughts and feelings there is sadness, remorse, and quiet love, not paranoid hatred or self-pity. The experience is immensely meaningful and important to the patient; it is truly an experience with his original objects, they are alive to him and present, they are felt as an essential part of himself and his present life even though in fact they may be dead. (Joan Riviere (1952) has shown that such free and direct contact with past love objects acts as a creative source.) His ego is an integrated whole and functions optimally. There is some happiness within the sadness and remorse. The analyst is also felt to be there; he is admitted to the relationship, and incidents with him interweave with the recollections of incidents with the parents.

Such moments are the reward for the work done; transference interpretations have led to contact with the object from whom the conflicts had been transferred. During these passages the analyst remains a listener, a bystander; nevertheless, vigilance is needed to perceive a sometimes insidious transition to disturbances in the patient's ego, to resistance, denial of emotions and withdrawal from them and from the actual object, the analyst. Recovery of lost love is succeeded by the emergence of hostility and new problems. The patient swings into a different mood and experience: the affect of love and contact in relation to his original objects has become exhausted. Again conflict is operative in the transference relation and has to be discovered and made conscious. The analyst's activity is called for in order to recognize and interpret the changes in the patient's condition and in his relation to the analyst.

Unusual events in the patient's life outside the analysis (for example, bereavement or threat of bereavement) may stir the depths of his emotional life, so that at this point his ego does not take the detour via the transference relationship to arrive at a dynamic contact with his original objects. (This does not mean that the patient is not then in an emotionally significant relation with his analyst, but that the latter is *additional* to what he is re-living from his past.) These, however, are exceptions, and exceptions are rare. As a rule the patient employs the medium of the transference and the analyst has to take everything he presents as a *parable*, that is, to quote the *Oxford English Dictionary* as 'a narration in which something is expressed in terms of something else'.[6]

Notes

1 'Turnings in the way of psycho-analytic therapy', p. 392, *Collected Papers II*, London: Hogarth Press and the Institute of Psycho-Analysis, 1924 pp. 392–402; also: 'Lines of advance in psycho-analytic therapy' (1919a), p. 159, SE 17: 159–68.

2 *The Ego and the Id*, London: Hogarth Press and Institute of Psycho-Analysis, 1927; also *The Ego and the Id* (1923b), p. 25, SE 19: 3–62.

3 *The Ego and the Id*, p. 26, SE 19: 3–62.

4 Freud described an extreme example of such projection in the condition of infatuation. When the lover endows his beloved with all the virtues, his own ego becomes depleted (*Group Psychology and the Analysis of the Ego*, 1921c; SE 18: 113).

5 *New Introductory Lectures on Psycho-Analysis*, London: Hogarth Press and the Institute of Psycho-Analysis, 1933; also *New Introductory Lectures on Psycho-Analysis*, Lecture 32, 'Anxiety and instinctual life', p. 91, SE 22: 81–111.

6 [In 1978 Paula Heimann wrote in the margin of a reprint of this paper: 'I find it a good paper. The influence from Melanie Klein is in quotations, not substance!' Paula Heimann wrote a 'Postscript' to this paper when it was translated into French in 1969. It is published in this book on pp. 252–61.]

8

Some notes on sublimation (1957/9)

This paper was read to the British Psycho-Analytical Society in January 1958, as an enlarged version of a paper presented at the 20th International Psycho-Analytical Congress, Paris, 1957. It was accepted for publication by the *International Journal of Psycho-Analysis* in 1959, in vol. 40 (5/6). However, Paula Heimann withdrew the paper for reasons unknown. A German translation though appeared in *Psyche* in 1959, vol. 13 (7), and a revised version of it in *Psychologie des Ich*, Darmstadt, Wissenschaftliche Buchgesellschaft (1974) pp. 239–61. We have taken from the latter notes which were added in 1974.

I

The concept of sublimation has met with considerable criticism for a long time. It has recently again come under review in the wake of the research into ego psychology based on Freud's last theories of the mind (1937–8), research which has done much to clarify his highly condensed formulations in those papers.

In the framework of the present paper it is impossible to discuss adequately the considerations put forward in recent literature. I shall only – somewhat brusquely and arbitrarily – mention those conclusions which are significant for my own views on the nature of sublimation.

In his historical and critical survey of the development of the concept of sublimation Hartmann (1955) rescues it from the inhibiting notion that it is a capacity of 'the few' only. Leaving room in his own theory of sublimation for temporary increases or decreases of sublimatory activities, he presents sublimation as a continuous process rather than an occasional happening.

Although I am largely in agreement with these formulations, I consider that 'occasional happening', the shaped and definite single production, is of very special and high significance. It may well be regarded as a climax of a more or less continuous unconscious process.

Hartmann indicates two sources of energy for sublimation: the neutralization of both the libidinal and the aggressive drives and a 'primary ego energy', his very apt term for the innate, non-instinctual energy in the ego which Freud postulates in his last work and attributes to heredity.

Hartmann is, however, very cautious about this latter source of energy and describes Freud's idea as a hypothesis, attractive but not proved, although stating that his own work on the primary autonomy of the ego has been developed from it. Essentially he subsumes sublimation under the wider notion of neutralization.

Lantos (1955) arrives at the conclusion that sublimation should be regarded as a 'special blending of sexuality and ego instincts'. Thus, like Hartmann, she assumes a dual derivation of sublimation, one from the primary instinctual urges and the other from within the ego itself.

Here is the meeting ground with my own views. I am, however, laying more stress on the original contributions made by the ego which need conceptually to be distinguished from the contributions made by the vicissitudes of the primitive instinctual impulses, vicissitudes, which of course are themselves a result of influences by the ego and arise from its relation with objects.

My aim in this paper is to present some of the observations and theoretical considerations which may have led me to discern two areas of processes involved in the sublimatory activity: one which concerns the ego's relationship with objects, based on the instinctual impulses, which emanate from the id, and another area which concerns the ego's relationship to itself, its innate endowments, interests, tendencies, and so on.

In an earlier paper on sublimation (Heimann 1942) in which I focused on the ego's relation to its introjected objects, I recorded an incident of impaired sublimation by an artist, and concluded that successful sublimation depends on a state of intrapsychic freedom, which enables the ego to be self-seeking and self-fulfilling with regard to its own capacities. In its introjections, it is selective and assimilates only those aspects of its internalized objects which are congenial to itself and promote its talents and interests. The ego fulfils itself, expresses its dispositions and capacities, and gratifies itself in its sublimations, as distinct from, though additional to, serving, and restoring its objects.

The freedom, however, to be selective and discriminating in introjection and assimilation in turn depends on the ego's mastering its cruel and greedy impulses towards its objects and acknowledging their rights and individuality – setting them free as well. This may be a simplified statement, and it is possible that inner constellations occur in which there is no cathexis of objects at all, neither love nor hate, neither dependence nor power wishes.[1] I have suggested as the hallmark of successful sublimation a conscious sense of achievement and pleasure, though this may be only short-lived and may give way to dissatisfaction, to depression, even to despair of one's own capacities.

In the incident from the analysis of an artist to which I have just referred, the artist produced a drawing which she felt to be a failure although it was technically correct: it was utterly alien to herself and it looked 'too old'. She also developed painful ulcers in her mouth. Preceding her defective sublimatory activity, the patient had attacked a strange woman with scathing remarks about her age and incompetence. Consciously she felt very pleased with her success in hurting this woman, but the analysis revealed that unconsciously, owing to the particular character of the transference situation in which the patient re-lived certain very poignant childhood experiences with her parents, she was overwhelmed by guilt. The strange woman represented her mother, and in its sublimation the patient's ego had been compelled to surrender its capacities and functions to the attacked object after introjecting it.[2] Significantly, too, the organ which had carried out the attack – the mouth which had made the scathing remarks – was punished in talion fashion by the ulcers (which disappeared in the course of the analytic session). Sublimation is impaired when the ego is consumed by conflicts with its internalized objects. The combination of failure in sublimation with a somatic symptom rather neatly, I think, illustrates the deep involvement of the ego in the sublimatory process: we are reminded of Freud's definition of the ego as being first and foremost a body-ego. This somatic symptom, moreover, hints at processes preceding awareness of and concern for objects: bodily sensations occur before concern for an object has developed.

There are thus two areas of problems to be considered in sublimation, one concerning the ego's relationship with objects, the other its relation to itself, its interests, endowments, talents, and so forth.

II

While problems concerning sublimation are conspicuous in the analyses of artists, who, indeed, often seek analysis on account of such problems, they are of no less significance in every analysis, and, as has been stated by others, particularly deserve the analyst's attention in the analyses of future analysts. There is a tendency to set the 'creative' person's sublimatory problems apart from those of the ordinary person. However the criteria of value on which this tendency is based are, as Hartmann pointed out, extraneous to the process of sublimation itself. Moreover, they are unreliable since, as we all know, the same achievement can be hailed by some as a masterpiece whilst others decry it as degeneration. We have cause to regard the removal of these criteria as an important scientific step.

Analysis deals with sublimation not only because the patient reports his sublimatory activities, but also because they occur in the analysis itself as an immediately observable phenomenon. Accepting Rycroft's (1956) description of the analytic situation as a trial object relationship, I would add that it is also a setting for trial sublimations.

This aspect of the analytic situation has not been sufficiently appreciated nor, so far as I know, has it been brought into systematic connection with theories of technique. Obviously, any new evaluation of psychic processes calls for an examination of psychoanalytic technique with regard to its adaptation to these processes. However, it is not my intention to attempt such an investigation in this paper and I shall confine myself to a few observations only.

I am here suggesting that many 'quite ordinary' associations have in fact a sublimatory quality. I am thinking of the patient's interest in the analytic process as distinct from his wish for relief or for libidinal gratification from his analyst, of his attempts to find new meanings in habitual thoughts and actions; of incidents where a patient, contrary to his usual muddled manner, expressed his ideas clearly and where he worked something out by having his data available at the crucial moment. It does not matter what the actual issue is, it is the functioning of the ego, the use and exercise of its capacities of which I am speaking here as constituting sublimation.

Here is an example of sublimation emerging in the course of an analytic session. A few introductory remarks about the patient need to be given. She was a young woman from a gifted family, whose various members excelled in artistic and scientific activities. The patient herself was a gifted speaker, very sensitive to words, and strongly attracted to poetry, plays, acting, and so on. Her own communications usually were rich and vividly descriptive with an easy mastery of words. What I might call a negative use of her talent, artificiality, represented a major form of resistance during a certain period of her analysis.

From an early age onwards she was preoccupied by ideas of dying which, with a wealth of phantasy, centred on a sibling who had died several years before her own birth. In passing I would mention that in my experience a dead, never-known sibling exerts a most profound influence on a person's life: love with profound guilt and fear of retaliation, reproaches against the parents for the death, suspicion that the living child is not really loved and wanted as himself, but merely as a replacement for the one they lost, are typical components of the complex feelings which constitute an intense tie to the dead sibling, causing deep depression and severely restricting the total personality.

One day this patient entered the consulting room with the air of a 'bright young thing'. She made some remarks about how carefree and well she was. Her insincere play-acting and the anxiety behind it were transparent, and I interpreted that for fear of rejection she was masking feelings of affection and concern for me. The patient confirmed my interpretation with relief and went on to talk about her parents, showing her love and concern for them and interest in their personalities more freely than was usual. Dwelling on certain instances, she ended by speaking with great admiration of her father's positive attitude to life. When interpreting this material I used at some point the words 'avidity for life' and the patient liked the phrase. She repeated it tenderly, hugged it, so to say, and said it was good. She became thoughtful for some moments, then asked whether I knew a certain poet, and proceeded to recite one of his poems which is a protest against death. She spoke freely and with deep emotion. As she went on she moved away from me, not in hostility or fear, but towards herself, living and creating an important experience for and with herself: a successful sublimation was achieved and her sense of achievement was obvious.

I wish now to review briefly the essential points in this rich and over-determined experience. Under the impact of conflicts with fear and guilt towards an actual object, the analyst, the patient made an attempt at sublimation, acting the part of a carefree, happy young girl. The choice of the role she attempted to act was historically determined, a condensed presentation of intense conflicts with her original objects. She failed. The analytic work resulted in a resolution of her fears, sufficient to make her abandon the defence of acting, to accept the transference object as good and helpful and to express

126

what really had been on her mind, important matters concerning her parents. There followed a moment of direct gratification by the (transference) object: certain words were experienced as a love gift because they specifically suited the ego's own interests and capacities. They were selected in fair acknowledgement and gratitude, assimilated by the patient's ego, and used as a stimulus for highly cherished ego capacities. *En route*, a return gift was made to the object which was now no longer needed: it was invited to share in the ego's important and gratifying experience. But more and more as the ego proceeded in its activity, it became concerned with creative functioning and fulfilling its own urge. The experience of reciting was the essential thing, while the object's significance as companion or audience receded more and more. Sham acting had given way to genuine reciting.

In my brief biographical remarks about this patient I have indicated the significance of the death theme in her life. Although I cannot present more material to show the meaningfulness of this incident, or to explain why from the beginning my attention was directed to its sublimatory aspect, I wish to underline what I have described: when the patient became able to claim 'avidity for life' herself and to express her protest against death both of her loved objects and of herself, she actually became more intensely alive, real, and creative.

The design of the analytic situation is such as to confine our patient's sublimatory activities essentially to the verbal medium and to the production of thoughts, memories, and dreams.[3] I shall omit consideration of dreams for a variety of reasons, but this should not be taken to mean that I am discarding their possible connection with sublimation.

As regards thoughts, I would suggest that a single idea or hunch does not represent sublimatory activity, although it may well prove its starting point. Memories also need to be distinguished. There are those which merely confirm conclusions already arrived at from the work on the transference. There are, however, other memories which can emerge only as a result of unconscious creative work in the patient. His ego, stimulated by contact with the analyst, withdraws to some hitherto lost and forgotten area and produces experiences either in relation to objects or to himself. I would attribute a strong sublimatory quality to these fertile recollections. They liberate and highlight unconscious ego processes, contain a direction for the further work, and turn out to be highly germane to important problems.

Usually these recollections belong to the latency or late toddler period, but notwithstanding their possibly screening an earlier experience, their value is still very great. I have often felt regret about the tendency to treat them only as screen memories and to deny their significance on the grounds that they belong to a relatively late period of development. The theoretical basis of this tendency is not in accordance with the principle of the fundamental dualism of psychic processes which psychoanalytic research has established, for it does not acknowledge the primary character of new steps in maturation and development and regards them as elaborations or modifications of early infantile processes.

The experience of remembering spontaneously and freely irrespective of the time to which the remembered event belongs is an important psychic process. In the present context I am focusing on the creative use of ego functions which lead to the production of certain memories. Therefore analytic procedure should give the patient ample room for remembering, while symbolic interpretations, particularly about earliest processes which the patient cannot recollect, should be offered judiciously. Symbolic interpretations fulfil their purpose of opening new dimensions to the patient's understanding of himself and of bridging gaps in his ego, if they can be assimilated and integrated into a living structure of self-images based on his own remembering. Without this foundation, they appeal to the patient's suggestibility, which can hardly be taken too seriously and often is not taken seriously enough, and encourage intellectual defences (analytic 'jargon').

I do not think we can safely measure the proportion of independent insight achieved by the patient and of suggestion – that is to say, improvement through emotional gratification from the parent substitute. Whether we shall in future be able to do this must remain an open question and a consideration. Meanwhile we can only again and again take this factor into account and be aware of the danger of turning the analytic situation from one of fact-finding into one of creating facts. In my view, as I have presented elsewhere, the best safeguard against such pitfalls lies in the analyst's accepting the function of a supplementary ego for the patient, essentially proceeding from perception of what is actually going on in the analytic situation, and when offering speculations which neither can nor need be avoided, leaving no doubt as to their character as a speculation.

It is my impression that the early stages of an analysis are usually mostly devoted to instinctual and emotional problems, whereas in later stages problems related to the use of ego capacities tend to predominate. A., whose analysis had proceeded for only a short time, dreamed that his analyst saved him from disgrace by covering

128

up the traces of his sexual activities. B., who had been in analysis for a much longer time, dreamed that the analyst prevented her from sinking into unconsciousness.

If this impression is correct, it would bear out Freud's statement about the way psychoanalytic theory has gone: that the problems of the transference neuroses obscured the problems of the nature of the ego. Through focusing on the object-related transference problems, psychoanalytic research was directed towards the ego's conflicts with its objects and their origin in early infancy. Today we are no longer in danger of underrating the significance of early infantile life or our need to know more about it, but I think we are in danger of proceeding in a one-sided manner and of underrating the significance of later phases and of adult life. One-sided orientation towards certain aspects cannot lead to a true picture, and overemphasis of the infantile and primitive leads to neglect of the singular and specific individual personality.

Clinical observations have led me increasingly to recognize the importance of the analyst's keeping in close contact with the patient's contemporary conscious and unconscious ego.

Among the gains derived from this orientation in the analytic situation is a clearer recognition of sublimatory activities within the analysis and greater independence generally, which beneficially affects the patient's capacity for sublimation.

I may here briefly mention some observations of the analytic work on successful sublimations which seemed more pronounced in male patients. These observations concern feelings of omnipotence. However, with different patients omnipotence had different qualities, either manic and aggressive or depressive. Thus one patient, after resolution of inhibitions in sublimations, showed a manic and hostile omnipotence: he dwelt with great satisfaction on his various successful activities and on his pleasure in functioning freely. The idea that the analyst's work had contributed to this new cherished condition occurred to him, but was arrogantly, imperiously dismissed. This manic and aggressive omnipotence went together with belief in magic and clamour for magic. Another patient, when enjoying progress in his sublimatory activities inside and outside the analytic situation, showed extreme difficulties in admitting the operation of his own capacities and tried to attribute everything to some object, the mother's breast or the analyst. It was obvious, however, that this was not what he really felt. When he could not maintain his denial any longer, he felt omnipotent, but with sadness and fear of isolation. The pleasure of achievement through his own capacities turned into the fear of becoming utterly lonely and losing all his love objects.

Although I cannot describe here how the analytic work on such occasions moves back and forth from the area of ego capacities to that of object relations, I wish to refer again to considerations put forward in my paper 'Dynamics of transference interpretations' (1956). I mentioned there poignant situations in the analytic work, when the analyst's position is that of a vigilant bystander, and gave as an instance part of the mourning work, when the patient is in full emotional contact with his original love object.

In the present context, I wish to stress that the role of a bystander, of a non-interfering presence, is further called for when the patient moves towards a sublimatory activity and while he is actively engaged in it.

This leads me back to the patient's withdrawal from me, which I described earlier. Her withdrawal, as I said, was not motivated by hostility or fear, but by her urge to engage in a creative ego activity. She withdrew towards her own depth. This calls to mind Winnicott's (1958) paper on the ability to be alone. He spoke of the 'paradoxical fact' that the ability to be alone depends on the child's experience of having been alone in the presence of an object, the mother, who is actively tuned in to the infant, but refrains from bringing herself into a relationship with him. This is an important example of the mother's adaptation to her child's needs. My own observations of young children confirm Winnicott's view; they have shown me that it is hard to say which is the greater evil: a child's being neglected and left without response to his needs and wishes, or his being intruded upon by an object when needing and wishing to be with himself. The dangers of the latter situation for the development of the child have often been described in terms of a libidinal over-stimulation. I wish to underline that this includes an attack on the child's ego, an enforced identification with the object, and therefore an interference with the natural growth of the ego and with its independence. In the transference situation the same dangers occur. Winnicott concentrated on the conditions which lead to the ability to be alone; a related problem of great importance for sublimation is that of the need and wish to be alone. Man is not only a social creature, he is also a lone rider, and creative activities need freedom from objects. In my view it would be insufficient to explain Winnicott's paradoxical fact only in terms of the ego's relation to an internal good object. It represents an important experience of *self*.

It would be equally insufficient to describe infantile auto-erotism exclusively as an activity conditioned by a relation to an object. Freud has shown that the thumb-sucking infant makes use of the memory of sucking at his mother's breast, and that by memory or hallucination he reproduces a real gratification with an object. Melanie Klein, connecting actual feeding with phantasies of incorporating the breast, has added phantasies about the internal breast to the experience of remembering it in the auto-erotic sucking. However, to acknowledge memories, hallucinations, and phantasies about the breast does not exhaust the components of auto-erotic sucking. There is also a primary libidinal experience which results from the infant using and manipulating his own body and discovering with pleasure many things that happen when mouth and thumb make contact with each other. Freud fully acknowledged this and stressed the quality of independence in this experience.

Moreover, we have to consider the observation that some neonates suck their fingers before they have been put to their mother's breast. In these cases we cannot speak of an object-related experience which is preserved and reproduced by means of memory and introjection. We may deduce the theory that in the instinctual impulse itself the phantasy of the gratifying object is contained, but even on the basis of this theory we cannot maintain that the infant's own finger is merely a substitute for his mother's breast, nor can we preclude phantasies revolving upon his own body. In fact, we may be tempted to reverse the direction of the movements between finger and breast. Perhaps this links with Winnicott's notion that the infant creates the breast. Ethological concepts also may be considered which lately have aroused justified interest among psychoanalysts. However, we can also explain the phenomenon under discussion with Freud's concept of phylogenetic memories, which is not rendered unnecessary by more modern researches and which seems particularly apposite for psychological research. It forms, moreover, a bridge to the theory of inherited capacities in the id as well as in the ego.

My remarks about auto-erotism are not incidental. I wish to stress the auto-erotic pleasure the person experiences – and seeks to experience – from the libido involved in sublimation. (Some artists describe that they feel they are using their genitals in their creative activity.) This aspect, it seems, is not sufficiently acknowledged, among other reasons probably because analysts have ample opportunity for tracing failure in sublimation to an unconscious equation of sublimation and masturbation.

The acknowledgement of auto-erotism, when focusing on the libido, and of pleasure of self-experience and self-fulfilment, when using a wider term of reference, is indeed only compatible with an approach which does not assign to sublimation primarily and essentially the function of defence, whether this is defined as aim-inhibition of primitive drives (Freud, Abraham) or as a defence against the fear of death, mental disintegration, and so on (Lee), or as the overcoming of the 'infantile depressive position' (Segal 1955).

The fact itself that the creative process yields enjoyment has indeed not escaped analytic observation, but in the evaluation of this enjoyment the tendency predominates to restrict it to object-relatedness. Barbara Lantos (1955), who mentions pleasure of the highest intensity, 'ecstatic' pleasure, takes the connection with auto-erotism into consideration, but decides after a lengthy discussion that auto-erotism itself is an object-related phenomenon. Ella Sharpe (1930, 1935, 1940) certainly gave great importance to the pleasure of the self in the creative process, but even in her analysis the motive of repairing the injured love object overshadows the self-related motivations. Thus Marion Milner (1957) is rather in an exceptional position when she emphatically expresses the view that the creative process originates in primary sources, aims at giving the artist fulfilment and joy, and that the product of the creative activity is so important for the artist because it gives permanence to the supreme moment of the creative experience. Although she does not omit the relation to internalized objects, she puts it in a different perspective by stressing here too the involvement of the self. I find myself in full agreement with her evaluation of the creative process.

As I mentioned earlier, the emergence of a single idea does not amount to sublimation, though it may prove its starting point. The process of sublimation presupposes a number and variety of ideas on which characteristic ego functions engage in work. These include perceptions which I believe to be the root function of the ego (Freud 1915c), from which all its other functions stem, and which, therefore, I believe to partake significantly in all ego activities. Further, a most important part in sublimation is played by the ego's 'synthetic function' (Nunberg 1931). Perception undertakes reality-testing and reality-accepting. I find myself here in full agreement with Hanna Segal when she points out that no matter how neurotic an artist may be, he possesses a strong sense of reality with regard to his material. The work of the ego's synthetic function results in the arranging and shaping of the ideas, giving them *Gestalt* and structure, with perception of reality contributing the recognition of some inherent necessity of sequence and interrelationship which the arrangement must follow. Only when at least these ego functions are active does the process amount to sublimation.

The sublimatory product owes its appeal to objects largely through its inherent relation to reality. It is this relation to reality which makes it transcend the realm of subjective meaningfulness and gratification.

Thus an intellectual sublimation results in a scientific conception of more or less wide applicability to various phenomena which are accessible to observation by other people too. Artistic sublimation expresses an emotional truth which also holds for other people as well as for the artist. In addition, of course, the product of sublimation appeals to objects on account of the sensual pleasure which it evokes and which results from the participation of the senses in the sublimatory process.

These considerations lead on to the recognition that sublimation expresses the life instinct, the functions of perception (Heimann 1956), and synthesis, expressing the force that drives towards union and integration specifically and directly. It is not difficult to recognize the ultimate reason for the appeal which sublimation exerts.

In the literature much stress is laid on the ego as a system of functions, and my impression is that function and capacity are not clearly distinguished. These terms, according to the *Oxford English Dictionary*, are partly synonyms, but not entirely so. 'Function' derives from the Latin word 'to perform', whereas 'capacity' is originally related to holding something, and from there has acquired the meaning of 'receiving mental power' and, further, that of 'the power, ability or faculty for anything in particular'. Both are concerned in sublimation. I shall return to this point.

Throughout his work Freud operated with dualistic concepts, and from the beginning he was concerned with an ego/object antithesis. In his last papers, to use a phrase from Hartmann's centenary paper (1956), he added a 'new dimension' to the ego. This new dimension of the ego emerges from the greater weight Freud there gives to heredity by stressing the ego's inborn dispositions and tendencies which from the beginning of the individual's life determine his future. These inherited aspects of the ego are to be distinguished from those it acquires as it develops from the id, in response to external stimuli and through contact with human beings. It might be said that Freud started by discovering pseudo-heredity, which is largely identification, and ended by defining heredity.

When accounting for the original formation of these inherited deposits of phylogenetic life, we follow observations of ontogenetic life and imagine that they came into being in the fight for gratification and self-preservation (survival). Meeting with obstacles from external forces, animate and inanimate primitive impulses came to grief, and had to be renounced or modified; or alternatively,

133

inventive processes were developed which again made other activities desirable, gratifying, and safe. Adaptation to reality does not simply mean giving up certain modes of pleasure; it equally means the finding of new ones. These evolutionary changes endured at the behest of the life instinct are what the individual's ego holds and contains from the beginning – its 'mental receiving power' – its 'power, ability or faculty for anything in particular', in other words, its highly individual and specific talents.

On account of their origin these innate capacities of the ego are charged with energy, Hartmann's 'primary ego energy' (1955). In my view the existence of this energy cannot be thought of as divorced from primary ego capacity and primary ego function – that is, performance of these capacities – nor, I wish to stress, from that peculiar quality, the style of functioning and living which makes a human being a distinct and singular personality. Sublimation, the ego's creative activity, represents *par excellence* these inborn precipitates of phylogenetic experiences. From its innate capacities, its original endowments, the ego derives primary and original urges and aims which make sublimatory activities a condition for the survival and health of the ego. Capacities and functions which are not used atrophy, and such atrophy amounts to a partial death which not only quantitatively restricts the ego but also qualitatively affects its totality, including its relation to objects. In the living ego the processes of growth bring to the fore more and more of its innate qualities (as well as an increase of acquired capacities) with the urge to perform, to give expression to them.

However, again on account of their history, the exercise of the ego's innate capacities is registered as danger and fraught with anxiety.[4] When the ego's innate capacities are stirred into activity, they can result in a creative product, but there is also a stirring of fears which may inhibit the activity or spoil its result. This is one reason among many for the frequent gap between potential capacity and actual performance. For this reason, too, when the ego overcomes its fears, does not take flight, but persists successfully with its creative activity, it may react with a sense of omnipotence – as if it had triumphed over superhuman forces.

Archaic anxieties are a legacy with which the infant starts life. They are evoked and increased by the fears he experiences in the wake of physical pain and somatic illness. With these he has to cope alone, on his own, no matter how much his loving parents endeavour to soothe and succour him.[5]

In the sublimatory activity, in the exercise and performance of its innate singular endowments, the individual again is alone, has to cope on his own and take the responsibility for his self. His archaic and somatic memories[6] of danger are reactivated, as well as his pre-Oedipal and Oedipal fears and also feelings of guilt.

Freud certainly took the existence of inherited capacities and inherited fears seriously. As instances I will recall to you symbolism, castration, fear, and shame of wetting. In his last works, he stressed the inherited 'independent' aspects of the ego and attributed a non-instinctual source of energy to the ego. In addition he provided a new classification of the instincts by distinguishing 'organic instincts operating in the id' from the 'primal forces of life and death which cannot be thought of as confined to any province of the mind, but reign throughout its totality'. Thus every province of the mind experiences the antithesis, the clash between primal forces, which is the ultimate cause of fear. I would suggest that the antithesis of the primal forces of life and death is manifested in specific ways in every province of the mind. With regard to the ego's specific capacities, the urge to exercise them is countered by the opposite force which aims at stifling them, and anxieties arise, as I tried to describe, when the ego engages in its specific and highly personal creative effort.

In subjective experience, these anxieties are explained as not-me and attributed to some object or objects. Animism, which recently Augusta Bonnard (1958) demonstrated so clearly, and real persecution by his objects, which no person is spared, support this subjective explanation of anxiety.

Moreover, here is another 'paradoxical fact'. Whereas the exercise and expression of its innate capacities is primarily a subjective urge and aim, it results in something that affects objects, invites and establishes object relationships, and that itself assumes the character of an object; the product of the subjective urge is an objectivation of the self which continues to exist and be an entity, for good or evil. All the emotions encompassed in human relationships, love, hate, fear, guilt, depression, remorse, as well as joyful expectations, elation, triumph, and so on, are aroused in the sublimatory process and towards its product.

So far in accounting for the anxieties attending sublimation, we have used concepts belonging to the ego–object area, and they serve us well and we need them. I am not underrating their importance when suggesting that we also need concepts belonging specifically to an area in the ego that is primarily not object-related. We may confine our investigations to the problems of the ego–object area, but we must know that when we are doing this, we have omitted investigation of the other area of processes operative in sublimation, the problems related to the activation of the ego's inborn inherited specific talents, the problems within the ego itself.

Recent research into the nature of the ego points in this direction, and so far as I understand these new ideas I can only accept them in part. Hartmann, also in collaboration with Kris and Loewenstein, has presented the concept of an autonomous ego with a conflict-free area. My view of the nature of the inherited aspects of the ego and my acceptance of the theory of the death instinct are not compatible with the notion of an area in the ego which by its nature could be free from conflict.

Observations of the sublimatory process as it occurs within the analytic session is an important area of research into the nature of the ego and the total personality.

For the purpose of this paper I have attempted to focus on the ego's innate and primary urge for sublimation, as distinct from the interpersonal determinants of sublimation which, among many aims, include reparation and re-creation of injured and lost love objects. I have tried to distinguish conceptually between an original, primary process and a defence mechanism.

I have also attempted to indicate something about the analyst's position *vis-à-vis* the occurrence of sublimation in the analytic setting, laying stress on an attitude informed by the appreciation of the patient's need for sublimation and withdrawal into himself rather than suggesting any new technical device.

It would simplify our communications if we used two terms for the two different components of the sublimatory process.[7] Following the history of theory formation, we might reserve the term 'sublimation' for its original meaning – namely, a secondary process, a special type of instinct vicissitude; and to use a term like 'primary ego creativity' to designate the contribution by the innate, primary ego capacities. The usefulness of such a terminology, however, would depend on our resolutely and consistently divesting the word 'creativity' from its habitual connection with greatness.

Notes

1 Michael Balint recently suggested that there is a creative area in the ego which operates in a 'one-body-relationship' that is outside object relationships.
2 I am giving here a very condensed summary and am omitting certain features which linked this strange woman significantly with the patient's

father as well. The attack on her was thus an attack on both parents, hence the severity of the patient's guilt feelings.

3 It will be obvious that I am considering the problem of sublimation in adults and therefore refraining from dealing with child analysis.

The following notes were added in 1974 and have been translated by the editor.

4 I do not consider here those anxieties which specifically arise from the vicissitudes of object relationships nor those problems which result from the interactions of both these sources of anxieties.

5 I certainly do not disregard the consequences of privation in the earliest relationship to the mother, but they are not my subject-matter here.

6 I am aware that I introduce the concept of somatic memories without substantiating it; I hope to do so on another occasion.

The following note appeared already in 1959 and seems to refer to the discussion at the International Psycho-Analytic Congress in 1957.

7 Dr F. J. Hacker drew attention to it in a discussion remark.

[In 1974 Paula Heimann added a postscript in which she stated that she had revised her agreement with the theory of the primary life and death instincts. She then quotes from her paper 'The evaluation of applicants for psycho-analytic training', *International Journal of Psycho-Analysis* 49 (4): 535 (1968).]

9

Notes on early development (1958)

This paper was read before the 2nd Latin-American Congress in Sao Paulo, Brazil, in 1958. It remained unpublished and two copies of it were found in Paula Heimann's literary estate. One of them was a slightly edited, re-typed version as if the paper had been made ready for publication. It is not known why this paper was never published and whether Paula Heimann intended it for publication in a collection of her papers when she prepared for it in 1978.

Our interest, the interest of psychoanalysts in early development, has its origins in an accident, a chance, an unintended and unexpected event in the treatment of a hysterical patient: the observation that her hysterical symptoms disappeared when she remembered with strong affects certain relevant childhood experiences. From this point, thanks to Freud's genius, a vast body of knowledge and of speculation has grown and continues to grow. We all work with theories which have been well established through trial and error, checking, modifying, re-checking, established because a number of workers have found them indispensable for the understanding of clinical phenomena. We equally use a number of hypotheses, again because we find them operationally valuable, though we maintain some doubt about their ultimate correctness, and while we do use them we are ready to give them up or accept some modification. If we are truly scientific, we shall also be ready to give up or accept modifications in respect of what I have called the established theories. But I think it is true to say that in fact we do distinguish our working tools as regards our readiness to change them. With my initial remark I have stated again what has been stated repeatedly; psychoanalysis is an empirical science. The clinical situation is its fertile matrix. Moreover – and this point needs to be stressed – it is also its *raison d'être* for the psychoanalytic clinician. The practising

138

psychoanalyst wants the scientific concepts because and in so far as they serve his practical purpose and serve as tools.

At this point, we are confronted with limitations and complications. The infinite variety of psychological phenomena leads to variety in the clinical situations: each patient and each analyst have their own uniqueness. Although the fundamental elements of human nature recur in each individual, their constellation differs. The way in which two analysts use the apparently identical tool renders it in fact different. There is no need for me to labour this point. Equally, if two patients do accept the same interpretation, this does by no means prove its correctness, because the motives which determine the phenomenologically identical behaviour may be utterly different.

Thus in our theoretical evaluations the greatest caution is necessary. Among the limiting factors, I want further to mention the analyst's conviction. This may cause a variety of entirely different reactions in the patient; all the gradations between the opposite poles of suggestibility and rebelliousness, wish to please and wish to destroy, and so on. In passing, I may here repeat what I have tried to show elsewhere (Heimann 1956): namely, that the analyst's procedure demands the use of unbiased perception of what is actually happening in the immediate situation.

I have mentioned a historical fact as the origin of the psychoanalyst's interest in early development. I wish now to state a dynamic factor based essentially on two far-reaching discoveries of Freud:

1 that mental illness always involves regression; the patient's past life is not over and done with;
2 that the analytic situation represents a stage on which the patient re-enacts his past life.

The 'psychoanalytic infant'

Regression is never complete, not even in severely regressed psychotic patients. Advanced ego functions, including those of the patient's contemporary stage, are also in existence and operative. Therefore, we find in the analytic situation not only alternations between regressed and age-adequate processes but also, I would suggest, a qualitative change of the regressed aspects of the ego; not only a succession, but a blending of the two.

The infant whom we meet in the analytic session – the 'psychoanalytic infant', to give it a short name – is not identical with the original infant. We cannot make direct translation from the one

139

to the other, if we pursue a scientific purpose (though in our operational procedure we can, and perhaps need not avoid what is called 'loose talking').

To list a few factors:

Not all regression is spontaneous. We, the analysts, arbitrarily induce it by the arrangement of the analytic situation: recumbent position, fundamental rule, encouragement by our behaviour and interpretations to the patient to discard secondary process procedure and to approach primary process procedure.

On the other hand, we limit regression by expecting of the patient to be his adult self, rational, reality-adjusted, tolerant of delay, and so on, when the fifty minutes are over. (Some patients apologize for rudeness the moment they get off the couch.)

The 'psychoanalytic infant' further is not identical with the original one because the analytic environment is not identical with the original one. The analyst is not the patient's parent, and the patient registers this fact. Side by side with the operation of unconscious phantasy in the patient which makes him identify the analyst with his original objects, including his mother's breast, there is his perception of the analyst as different from his original objects, and his perception of various real individual features of the analyst's personality.

The recognition of such limitations and complications which beset the analyst's discovering early infantile processes accounts for the increasing demand in many quarters for direct observation of infants. For example, the late Ernst Kris's project of longitudinal studies, presented at the Paris Congress 1957, may here be mentioned. Also, many analysts feel that research by non-analytic workers, psychologists, paediatricians, neuro-physiologists, ethologists, and others has important contributions to make. Many years ago Susan Isaacs stressed the need for knowledge from non-analytic sources, when she investigated the criteria for interpretation. Like many other analysts, I myself draw on medical and social experiences with infants, and more recently I have had the opportunity of observing closely two children from the neonate stage to the ages of three and four years respectively.

I hope I shall not be misunderstood as belittling the contributions to the knowledge of early development which we as psychoanalysts can make, when I am giving significance to non-analytic researches. I believe that, on the contrary, our use of the data in the psychoanalytic situation will only be furthered by including those other sources of knowledge. And it is with caution and tentatively that I am presenting here certain hypotheses at which I have arrived.

Somatic memories

The earlier the phase we are considering, the more the speculation. Science proceeds through speculation; imaginative evaluations which transcend the factual data – but need checking.

My present hypothesis regards the concept of somatic memories as indispensable. My observations with the psychoanalytic infant and my social contact with babies and children have led me increasingly to give supreme significance to bodily sensations, and my theoretical model here is that presented by Freud when he declared that the ego is first and foremost a body-ego.

To begin with, all communications with the infant proceed through physical means, and I believe that the way the infant is handled by its mother (or her substitute) is of the greatest significance. I know of a mother who, urged by the medical staff to breast-feed, when feeding her new-born muttered, 'Oh, you pig. You wait till we are home, and you'll get the bottle.' This infant's experience with the feeding breast will be different from that of a baby who was held in loving arms of a mother who herself experienced her contact with her infant and her sensations in the feeding relationship as a pleasure.

I know of a maternity nurse who said of a new-born's crying: 'Listen to this. He is wicked.' Now one might marvel at this woman's profound perceptions which enable her to discern the neonate's character in his screaming – or one might shudder at the thought of his being handled and nursed by her and taken by her to his mother's breast for his feed. I myself shudder.

Such examples could be multiplied. You have all met with such incidents, as well as those of the opposite order: the delighted and gratified mother, nurse, father, and so on.

In his recent paper 'Premature ego development: some observations upon disturbances in the first three months of life' (1960), Martin James presented material of an infant whose mother was mourning the death of her brother and who was unable to turn her libido to her child and take delight in her. This infant cried almost incessantly, could not relax, and showed a hypersensitivity to noises and a hypercathexis of her environment. James emphasized the mother's failure to act as the barrier against stimuli, the most fundamental security measure which normally is provided for the infant in his symbiotic oneness with his mother. This infant's ego had precociously to exert functions which it was not mature enough to carry out.

James related later developmental disturbances to this earliest failure in maternal care.

Again, I think that all analysts can supply observations of this kind. Winnicott has repeatedly drawn attention to the important effects on a person's development which are caused by a mother depressed at early stages in the child's life. Other factors equally impairing the condition of the early ego which I have observed lie in over-stimulation when too many persons deal generally with the infant, so that it has too many mothers, so to say, or more specifically when the mother is doubled by a wet nurse.

Further, early physical illnesses have to be considered in this connection which, though the infant survives and proceeds to health, leave their mark as somatic memories. With regard to physical illness and recovery, the somatic memories are of a double order: they store both the experience of what Freud called the 'traumatic situation' in which the ego is actually overwhelmed and flooded with uncontrollable stimuli, and the experience of having surmounted annihilation and gained and regained well-being. In the latter I see a profound source for trust in the self, in the capacity for achievement, which will manifest itself in a variety of ways in the further course of development.

I have mentioned some grossly pathological variations in the circumstances of early life: severe interferences with the conditions of natural growth, originating either in the infant's symbiotic partner or in its body self. However, even in optimal infant care the infant is exposed to upsetting stimuli: delays in the satisfaction of its needs and desires, or painful bodily processes (wind, colicky pains, irritation by wet nappies, urine and faeces, pressure by folds in the sheets and garments, and so on), thus acquiring a store of painful somatic memories. Moreover, no infant escapes the experience of being born.

The birth trauma

According to Freud (1926d) birth is a traumatic situation which gives rise to the anxiety response. As a traumatic situation he defined the condition in which total destruction is experienced as immanent, and no defensive, protective action is undertaken by the ego. You will remember also his distinction between the traumatic and the danger situation, in the latter anxiety serving as a signal to mobilize ego functions of anticipation and protective action. Following changes in the embryo's intra-uterine environment conditioned by the details of the birth process, the embryo is expelled from his mother's body into an unfamiliar world which impinges on him by numerous stimuli: thermal, postural, touch, light, noise, and so on. Among his reactions there are shock, dazedness, unsuccessful flight movements, a scream of pain.

Freud spoke of repudiation of the world, whence came the stimuli, as the infant's primary attitude. There is a common consent in the appreciation of birth as a trauma and of the new-born's repudiatory reaction. As regards the first, when taking a case history we pay much attention to the individual circumstances of the patient's birth: maturity of the embryo – length of the birth process – natural or instrumental delivery – characters of his environment – physical and emotional condition of his mother – attitude of the father – parental relations with each other (including whether the child was wanted or not), and so on. We are by such enquiries at the same time paying attention to the emotional climate into which the infant was born and to the environment's capacity to provide the necessary symbiotic relationship between infant and mother, and to the details of the somatic events which have impinged upon the new-born.

By common consent too – at least in our civilization – infant care acknowledges and respects the new-born's repudiation of the change in his milieu. By providing quietness, mild light, warmth, comfortable position, soft clothing, and so forth, infant care endeavours to act as a barrier against stimuli and to re-establish the familiar environment. The notion of compensating for the trauma is expressed when the new-born is, soon after birth, put to his mother's breast.

I am suggesting that these measures do not only take into account the new-born's actual condition, but appreciate that his actual experiences affect his future development, that they leave a memory trace.

Thus we do take somatic memories very seriously, and indeed it is implicit in Freud's work. I have searched for the explicit mention of this term, but could not find it. I wonder whether I have overlooked it. As I said earlier, in my own work I have found it indispensable.

Do we as psychoanalysts observe birth analogues with our 'psychoanalytic infants'? I think we do. I have found them characteristically related to the experience of a new insight, if this is of profound importance and if it comes about unexpectedly and suddenly. I am here not concerned with the causes for such suddenness (patient's resistance or analyst's clumsiness) which show the limitation of the analogy.

When a patient accepts an interpretation which crucially changes his habitual and therefore comfortable outlook on himself and his objects, for example, when this interpretation runs counter to his idealized self and/or idealized objects, he experiences a total change of his emotional milieu. It is this element that leads to the idea that the patient re-experiences something of his birth trauma. In common parlance we find the phrase 'having lived in a fool's paradise'. I may quote here a passage from *Beyond the Pleasure Principle*, where Freud speculates on the creation of life and connects it with that of consciousness. What he says has in my view a sound foundation in clinical facts:

> The attributes of life were at some time evoked in inanimate matter by the action of a force of whose nature we can form no conception. It may perhaps have been a process similar in type to that which later caused the development of consciousness in a particular stratum of living matter.
>
> (Freud 1920g: 38)

The expressions which patients use in the situation I have mentioned are revealing. They speak of feeling shocked or dazed, or of being about to be exploded, of feeling shot right through the head. Near to such 'birth analogues', highly significant infantile memories emerge, or dreams which unmistakably depict the patient's phantasies of the birth situation, or transient physical illnesses, to be followed by progress in the analytic work and by a heightened sense of being alive and of functioning with pleasure.

In my considerations of birth and the neonate stage, I have stressed the lasting effect of the physical experiences. They are stored as somatic memories which are stirred into operation in certain specific situations in the further course of life.

The crucial questions concerning these earliest experiences revolve upon phantasy and object relationship. Our answers will depend on the impact of our observations in accordance with which we adopt certain theoretical frameworks and meta-psychological systems.

How do we picture the mental apparatus at these earliest phases?

In the course of his work Freud has presented several models of the mind, two of which I wish to discuss briefly.

According to the earlier one (Freud 1923b) the ego develops from the id through contact with the external world. The id is operative from the beginning of life, and it contains the instinctual impulses which originate in the soma. It is the borderland entity in which somatic events find psychical representation. Susan Isaacs (1948) elaborated this concept of the id by integrating into it Melanie Klein's findings. She concluded that unconscious phantasy is the mental correlate of the instinctual impulse. According to this model, the individual's instinctual impulses as part of his mental apparatus are operative from the beginning of life and the conclusion follows that the infant has from the beginning a relationship to his most important external source of stimuli – that is, his mother's breast.

Desirable though a thorough review and discussion of this model of the mind would be, here is not the place to do it. Nor can I even attempt to list summarily the great gains obtained from it for understanding and research. But I may single out one point of specific relevance to the present topic, namely, Freud's discovery of pseudo-heredity, which led to the appreciation that the ego is shaped through identifications. To this model also can be referred Melanie Klein's theories of early infantile object relations, of the early infantile beginning of the Oedipus complex and its interaction with superego formation which were based on her direct work with young children.

However, this conceptualization of psychic processes allots only a secondary role to the ego: it is only 'the record of past object choices' in Freud's formulation or in Melanie Klein's work the container of 'internal objects'. Observations concerning primary narcissism (in itself an unfortunate and contradictory term) cannot be easily correlated with it. You are all familiar with the controversies concerning narcissism. Another extremely important process suffered from it, or rather our understanding of it: namely, sublimation. Sublimation, too, in the framework of this first model of mental processes is merely a secondary phenomenon, a vicissitude of primitive instinctual impulses which occurs under the impact of external and internalized object relationships.

In 1937, however, Freud presented another model of the mind, and although his formulations are brief and intensely condensed, they clearly attribute primary character to the ego. Hartmann, partly alone and partly in collaboration with Kris and Loewenstein, amplifying Freud's statements, developed new researches into Ego Psychology. In parenthesis, I must say that it has taken me a long time to understand his statements. Freud speaks of the ego's 'own etiology' and of its own inherent source of energy. He puts heredity properly into the picture and gives it its due when stating that the ego's inborn and inherited dispositions from the beginning exert their influence on the individual's development. These theoretical formulations accommodate many clinical observations better than Freud's earlier model, in particular problems related to primary 'ego creativity', which has its origin in the ego's inherited capacities and talents, and, as I tried to show elsewhere (Heimann 1957) [chapter 8], needs to be distinguished from sublimation as a defence mechanism.

145

Corresponding with the heightened significance of the ego, there is some reduction of the power attributed to the id. It is not only the id that determines ego development, it is also the ego that influences id processes. The basic dualism of psychic processes is at work here too. This leads me back to the question of the beginning of object relationships and of unconscious phantasies revolving upon objects.

I wish to distinguish between the germinal and the actually operative mental apparatus. During the earliest phases of life mental functions are germinal, whilst the infant's symbiotic partner provides mature mental functions as well as her mature body. According to my present hypothesis, there is a phase during which the infant lives entirely through his body, storing in it what will later act as psychological facts. The ego's root function of perception and, with it, distinction between self and object do as yet not exist. The infant fuses with his mother. As Freud said, the caesura of birth is more apparent than real. The mother's mental apparatus is actually operative, while the neonate's is germinal.

I would compare the situation to that of surgical narcosis at the stage of the developed, organized, and operative mental apparatus. During the surgical intervention which takes place under narcosis, psychological functions are put out of action by pharmacological means. When their effect is over, the experience of the operation becomes a psychological fact and needs to be mastered psychically by the individual. I am, of course, aware that this comparison does not hold completely, since the patient would have known of the operation before it actually took place, but I am speaking of the narcotic state.

I assume that in the phases under consideration, a similar state exists because of the immaturity of the mental apparatus.

All the infantile phantasies revolving upon ideal or persecutory internal objects with which we have become familiar belong to a phase in which the ego's root function of perception has become operative. I shall return to this later.

Here I wish to refer very briefly to Dr Rascovsky's theories.[1] I shall have to study them more carefully than I have so far been able to do. Essentially, the difference in our views derives from our concepts of the condition of the ego. Dr Rascovsky assumes a highly organized ego during the embryonic stage, and of course during birth and the neonate stage. Consequently he considers phantasy formations and object relationships indeed from the beginning of life, and already in the intra-uterine milieu.

I cannot help thinking that for this most primitive stage we should need concepts of an order which is entirely different from those we use for the infant of, say, the oral stage. I do not think that the embryo or the neonate is simply the later infant in miniature. Perhaps Dr Rascovsky has shot a Sputnik into the inter-stellar space of the embryonic existence, but so far I do not want to be the dog in it!

To repeat: in my view the earliest experiences are physical ones and of the pleasure/pain order, paying tribute to the grand biological factors of the life and death instincts. They are stored as somatic memories which at the operative stage of the mental apparatus assume the significance of psychological data. May I again use an analogy? We sometimes buy inconspicuous little bits of apparently colourless and shapeless paper. When thrown into water, they unfold into delightful, richly coloured and definite shapes. They are called Chinese Flowers.

The capacity of the human organism to form somatic memories which at a later time become actual psychological problems appears as the counterpart of the capacity to convert a psychological problem into a physical condition – conversion hysteria. If this hypothesis is correct, the latter process would traverse a pathway formed in early life in the opposite direction.

A few remarks about the infant during the oral stage: during this stage the infant continues to live by virtue of his symbiotic relationship with his mother (or her substitute). She fulfils many of the functions of living which the infant's immature organism as yet cannot carry out for himself. In the establishment of this symbiotic relationship, both partners have to go through a learning process until they find and keep to an optimal mode. The mother contributes all the capacities of the adult being: a wide differentiated ego with discerning perceptions and carefully directed actions. She uses all her capacities in the service of her profound emotional relatedness to her object, the infant. The infant contributes by using predominantly one organ, his mouth, to indicate his wishes and needs and to achieve contact with his object. On account of this fact, this phase has been termed the oral stage. Yet we do not mean that the infant at this stage registers only oral stimuli. As Marjorie Brierley (1951) said: 'Oral primacy is not oral monopoly.' But from whatever part of his body stimuli are emanating, whatever libidinal and aggressive impulses and fears the infant experiences, the mouth functions as the essential organ to express them and as the essential receptor for comfort and satisfaction. During his wakeful periods his most important perceptions are brought about through his mouth, lips, gums, and tongue.

Now I would suggest that whereas the most important experience of perception (the root function of the ego from which all other functions stem) is connected with and proceeds through sensations in the mouth, self and object are not experienced as two different entities. During his earliest contacts with his object, when sucking from the nipple and swallowing the milk, the infant cannot differentiate between what is self and what is object. His experience, I suggest, must be described as fusion. Gradually, this experience of undifferentiation, fusion, gives way to the recognition of self (that is, oral bodily parts) and object (namely, oral object) when, through the advance of ego functions, perceptions of a non-oral kind occur when attention is given to other aspects of the mother, her face, smile, eyes, hands, and so on, and when these become connected with and added to the feeding contact. On account of the primacy of the oral impulses, the first object concept, then, is the concept of an oral object, and to this more advanced phase I would attribute the infantile phantasies of the good/gratifying or the bad/attacking breast.

At this point, too, advance in development can be defined in terms of the change of the quality of anxiety. Preceding this step, anxiety is of the order of the traumatic situation; massive and totally overwhelming. (In later life people speak of blind, unspecified, and unspecifiable fears when· describing a condition of total over-whelmedness and total helplessness.) I consider that both archaic, pre-historic memories, a legacy inherited by ancestors, and the somatic memories mentioned earlier account for this earlier type of anxiety. In the anxieties focusing on the breast we have already the effect of a mental organization, a less primitive state.

Freud described that primitive mental functioning is determined by the pleasure principle. All that is pleasurable and only that which is pleasurable is attributed to the 'me', while all that is painful is attributed to the 'not-me'. I think that in the past, following the first model of the mind in Freud's system, I have too readily equated the 'not-me' with 'object'. I have come to modify my view, and I would now regard this first primitive notion of 'not-me' not as identical with an object-concept, but as the repudiation of pain during the most primitive period. The length of this period certainly varies with different infants and infant-care situations. When mental functions start operating, the 'not-me' assumes object character (thus the first 'not-me' might be described as its forerunner).

If we omit the first days, we can speak of object relationship from the beginning. But we lose something for our understanding, we fail to appreciate the primitive mode of life, the elemental impact of the biological struggle between life and death, and the use of archaic

148

inherited faculties of magic omnipotence and animism in the service of the life instinct.

In this connection also we need to distinguish between active introjection of an object and passive acceptance of, or ineffective resistance to, the object's intrusion. In the first case the establishment of an internal object is based on positive and libidinal impulses: this object is good, I want to take it into me, I love it, I want to have it for ever, as close as possible, to be like it, and so on, and the introjected object fuses with the ego and becomes an integral part of the self. In the second case internalization is experienced as a violent intrusion by a hated and feared object to which the subject submits with helpless rage. Such an internal object remains an internal enemy, alien and persecuting, and engenders a condition which is utterly different from the sequelae of intentional libidinal introjection.

To describe in more detail the difference between these two modes of internalization, however, would lead away from the framework of this paper. What I have said will suffice to substantiate my view that differentiation is necessary.

Here again, infant care is to be considered. Details like intruding into the infant's bodily openings (cleaning of the nose, or the ears or eyes, enemas) and restriction of movement by garments amount to attacks, as the struggling against these measures clearly shows.

When ego functions of perception, recognition, and qualitative discernment of objects have been established, active introjection of objects takes place, which is normally an expression of the libido and anaclitically leads to the development of love – the steps being: gratification by the object, gratitude and love towards the object, pleasure in loving. On this basis identification with the loved object ensues and leads to successful growing up.

Projection and introjection with loving desires for the mother occur as a double insurance for achieving oneness with her. Such projection motivated by the libido does not constitute a loss to the infantile ego – it expresses the symbiotic relationship in terms of his own activity: he is mother/mother is he, both by taking her into himself or by entering into her.

Both mechanisms, however, may not further ego development, but impede and impair it, by bringing about surrender to the object. Sigmund Freud (1910h) described depletion of the ego in the state of adult infatuation: Anna Freud (1936) described 'altruistic surrender'. In relation to the introjected object, surrender leads to ego–dystonic identification, imitation, 'as if' modes of life. In relation to the external object, the renouncing of ego functions out of fear and guilt results in placatory activities rather than in constructive restitution.

Severe failures in the symbiotic relationship deflect the infant's ego not only from its normal pace, but also from its natural course as regards its innate dispositions so that, to use Winnicott's term (1960b), a false self may develop.

In my view, appreciation of the overriding importance of physical experiences laid down as somatic memories will contribute towards establishing the sound symbiotic milieu at the actual time, and the helpful working through in the analytic transference milieu.

Notes

1 Dr Rascovsky was obviously present when Paula Heimann presented her paper. He was a training analyst of the Argentine Psychoanalytic Association.

10

Counter-transference (1959/60)

This paper was presented in a symposium on 'Counter-transference' held by the Medical Section of the British Psychological Society, London, 1959. The contributions from Freudian and Jungian analysts were published in the *British Journal of Medical Psychology* 33 (9) (1960).

I gladly accepted the invitation to partake in this symposium, and I think that the memory of the earlier occasion on which Dr Fordham and I exchanged views had its positive share in this readiness.

In addition, I welcomed the opportunity for thinking again about a problem that so fundamentally enters into our daily work and for revising my earlier paper on counter-transference to which Dr Fordham has referred, comparing my views expressed then (Heimann 1950) with my present views and those of other workers. I like to think that my paper did stimulate discussion. A number of papers have appeared afterwards making important contributions.

My short paper was prompted by a number of observations which led me to pay much attention to counter-transference problems.

In supervision I could see how many candidates, misunderstanding Freud's recommendations (Freud 1910–19) and particularly his comparing the analyst's attitude with that of the surgeon, endeavoured to become inhuman. They were so frightened and guilty when emotions towards their patients came up, that they warded them off by repression and various denial techniques, to the detriment of their work. But it was not only that they lost sensitivity in the perception of events in the analytic situation, because they were so preoccupied and in a fight with themselves; they also used defences against the patient, by taking flight into theory or the patient's remote past, and presenting clever intellectual interpretations. Further, they tended to overlook or omit comments on the positive transference with its attendant sexual fantasies, and to select arbitrarily elements of the negative transference, because they then felt safer in reaching the goal of 'cool detachedness'. That much of the hostility on which they focused was the patient's reaction to being rejected and misunderstood, escaped them.

Often when a candidate's interpretations appeared to be quite outside any *rapport* with his patient, I asked him what he had really felt. It frequently emerged that in his feelings he had appropriately registered the essential point. We could then see that, had he *sustained* his feelings and treated them as the response to a process in his patient, he would have had a good chance of discovering what it was to which he had responded. Naturally, on such occasions the candidate also became aware of his unsolved personal problems which produced his transference to his patient, which he could then take back into his own analysis – one useful aspect of the supervision experience.

However, it would be a mistake to regard counter-transference problems merely as the growing pains of the beginner. I have encountered them in my own work, and even very experienced analysts senior to myself have mentioned such difficulties.

I should like to recapitulate, briefly, the essential points I put forward in my earlier paper.

The analytic situation is a relationship between two persons. What distinguishes this relationship from others is not the presence of feelings in one partner, the patient, and their absence in the other, the analyst, but the *degree* of feeling the analyst experiences and the *use* he makes of his feelings, these factors being interdependent. The aim of the analyst's own analysis is not to turn him into a mechanical brain which can produce interpretations on the basis of a purely intellectual procedure, but to enable him to *sustain* his feelings as opposed to discharging them like the patient.

Along with his freely and evenly hovering attention which enables the analyst to listen simultaneously on many levels, he needs a freely roused emotional sensibility so as to perceive and follow closely his patient's emotional movements and unconscious phantasies. By comparing the feelings roused in himself with the content of his patient's associations and the qualities of his mood and behaviour, the analyst has the means for checking whether he has understood or failed to understand his patient.

Since, however, violent emotions of any kind blur the capacity to think clearly and impel towards action, it follows that if the analyst's emotional response is too intense, it will defeat its objective.

For most aspects of his work the experienced analyst has an

emotional sensitivity which is extensive rather than intensive, differentiating and mobile, and his feelings are not experienced as a problem. His tools are in good working order. But situations occur in which he notices that he is puzzled in a disturbing way with somewhat intense feelings of anxiety or worry which appear inappropriate to his assessment of the events in the analytic situation. As he waits – which he must do in order not to interfere with an ongoing process in his patient, and in order not to obscure the already puzzling situation still more by irrelevant and distracting interpretations – the moment occurs when he understands what has been happening. The moment he understands his patient, he can understand his own feelings, the emotional disturbance disappears and he can verbalize the patient's crucial process meaningfully for the patient.

I gave an instance of this kind which could be readily described. I could have given others, which would, however, have neeeded a far more lengthy report. I have noticed that Dr Fordham is also familiar with the problem of choosing clinical examples.

My earlier conclusion was that the counter-transference represents an instrument of research into the patient's unconscious processes, and that the disturbance in my own feelings was due to a time lag between unconscious and conscious understanding. I did not then attempt to investigate the reasons for this time lag, nor did I attempt to tease out the contributions from the transference to the disturbed feelings, as my main objectives were to lay the ghost of the 'unfeeling', inhuman, analyst, and to show the operational signifiance of the counter-transference.

In passing, I may mention that I have had occasion to see that my paper also caused some misunderstanding in that some candidates, who referring to my paper for justification, uncritically, based their interpretations on their feelings. They said in reply to any query 'my counter-transference', and seemed disinclined to check their interpretations against the actual data in the analytic situation.

In view of the interdependence of the concepts of transference and counter-transference, I would like to take you back for a moment to the pre-analytic era, to the period before Freud discovered the transference. The therapist was in the role of a friendly helper, who encouraged the patient to remember everything that related to her suffering, her hysterical symptoms, and who by hypnosis made such recollecting easier. The violent emotions accompanying the patient's remembering were directed against her past objects, and after discharging them the patient felt considerably better. This relief, manifest and often highly dramatic, was obviously due to the doctor's procedure, and proved his usefulness. Patient and doctor were united in their purpose, on the same side, so to speak, against the patient's past objects, who came up in her memories and to whom she directed the full strength of her affect and impulses.

Freud's revolutionary discovery of the transference fundamentally changed the treatment situation. This is the point I wish to emphasize: with the recognition of the transference the demands which his work puts on the analyst have been *immeasurably increased*.

Hence, as Dr Fordham reminded us, the institution of the training analysis, for which Freud gave explicit recognition to the 'Swiss school of analysts'. In passing, I wish to point out Jung's mistake in thinking that Freud did not acknowledge the universality of the transference. What he did stress was the fact that in other forms of therapy the transference was not recognized.

As long as the therapist was merely administering a particular therapeutic agency to his patient – namely, the encouragement to let memories come to the fore and to discharge pent-up affects directed towards her past objects – his ordinary psychiatric training sufficed. But when the patient–doctor relationship became the stage on which the patient *acted* his violent impulses, *unconsciously* convinced of their originating actually and really from the activities and behaviour of the analyst, the therapist himself became the therapeutic agency and needed a special training to protect himself and his patient against emotional involvement and reaction to his patient's acting.

The concept of the counter-transference was presented by Freud very briefly. He described it as a 'result of the patient's influence on the analyst's unconscious feelings' and demanded that it should be recognized and overcome. Many analysts regard counter-transference as nothing else than transference on the part of the analyst, and I believe that they feel supported by the fact that Freud referred to it without any definition and coupled with it a warning that was already familiar in respect of transference.

I hold, as I have mentioned, that as the prefix 'counter' would imply, there is a factor additional to transference which is of specific operational significance.

In the literature, more recently, some attempts have been made to define counter-transference. Time does not allow a thorough review, but I would like to mention in some detail Gitelson's paper (1952). He distinguishes between *reactions to the patient as a whole* and *reactions to partial aspects of the patient*. The first occur right at the beginning of the analyst's contact with a patient and persist during the initial stages of the analysis. Gitelson speaks of the 'trial analysis'. These reactions, he says, 'derive their interfering quality from the fact that

154

they emanate from a surviving neurotic "transference potential" ' (in the analyst). If this is so strong that the analyst cannot resolve it, and if in the trial analysis the patient shows no progressive movements,[1] the analyst must conclude that he is unsuitable for this particular patient and refer him to another analyst.

The second type, the reactions to partial aspects of the patient, appear later within an established analytic situation. They constitute actual counter-transferences. 'They comprise the analyst's reaction to: (1) the patient's transference, (2) the material the patient brings in, and (3) the reactions of the patient to the analyst as a person.'

The fact that an analyst is potentially capable of producing the reactions mentioned indicates that he himself is not 'finally and perfectly analysed'. As Freud has shown, analysis is interminable. But the result of the analyst's analysis is that he is capable of continuing his analysis. Gitelson uses the expression 'a spontaneous state of continuing self-analysis'. Every analytic situation presents to the analyst the task 'to integrate himself rationally in the face of difficulties'. The counter-transference, as defined by Gitelson, represents the activation of unanalysed and unintegrated aspects of the analyst. Since this, however, occurs only episodically, in a recognized specific connection with the patient's material, and since, moreover, some of the manifestations are grossly symptomatic, there is little danger of the analyst's overlooking them and failing to analyse his attitudes in himself. Through the analysis of his counter-transference, then, the analyst 'can re-integrate his position as an analyst and . . . utilize the interfering factor . . . for the purpose of analysing the patient's exploitations of it'.

I have given these points from Gitelson's paper because of the many valuable clarifications which it presents, and because there is a good deal of common ground between his views and mine. There are also some important differences.

For those analysts like myself who do not adopt the procedure of starting off with a trial analysis, the first diagnostic interview has to decide not only the patient's psychiatric diagnosis, but also to answer the two questions: (1) can the patient be helped by analysis?; (2) can he be helped by my analysing him? It may happen that the first question can be answered with a Yes, and the second with a No. In such cases the patient must be referred to another analyst.

Gitelson's concept of the 'surviving neurotic "transference potential" ' in the analyst offers a valid distinction between transference and counter-transference. But, since in the counter-transference, on Gitelson's showing too, neurotic elements in the analyst are active, I wonder whether the essential factor which makes the difference is a *qualitative* one. In my view what is crucial is the *quantitative* aspect. If there is a greater inclination and ability in the analyst to do the necessary self-analysis in the one case rather than in the other, it is because in that particular case his underlying anxieties and the defences engendered against them are less strong.

This brings me back to points I made in my earlier paper, where, instead of defining transference and counter-transference in the analyst's feelings, I focused on their potential usefulness, the criterion lying in their intensity. In other words, from the patient's point of view it is not of decisive significance from which source the analyst's feelings arise provided that the analyst does not use defences which would impair his perception. Sustaining his feelings forms part of the process of reintegration (Gitelson 1952) and of understanding his patient (Heimann 1950).

Although a conceptual distinction between transference and counter-transference is possible, in the actual experience the two components are *fused*. It is true that the transference potential shows up very strikingly at the first meetings with a patient or during the trial analysis, as instanced by Gitelson. But I think it is also at work in the later episodes in an established analysis. In my experience, when I have afterwards (with proverbially easy hindsight) scrutinized incidents of counter-transference, successfully used as indication of processes in the patient, I concluded that the time lag between my unconscious and my conscious understanding was due in part to transference factors which I had not recognized at the time.

Several authors have raised the question of whether or not to tell the patient when counter-transference has affected the analyst's attitude.

I have expressed the view that a communication of this kind represents a confession of personal matters pertaining to the analyst, and would mean a burden to the patient and lead away from the analysis. Therefore it should not occur.

Gitelson (1952) and Margaret Little (1951) both hold that such communication must be made. Rejecting the notion of confession, Gitelson says: 'In such a situation one can reveal as much of oneself as is needed to foster and support the patient's discovery of the reality of the actual inter-personal situation as contrasted with the transference-counter-transference situation.' Dr Little compares such matters with errors by the analyst about times or accounts. She recommends that the 'origin in unconscious counter-transference' should be explicitly mentioned. Further, she deliberates on the possibility that the analysis of the counter-transference might carry the analysis to greater depths, in the same way as the analysis of the transference did. Both authors recommend great caution and are aware of possible abuses and warn against 'acting out in the counter-transference'.

That errors the analyst has made need to be stated is hardly a problem. Nor is there a difficulty, except if the analyst's subjective need to be honest plays, unconsciously, an undue part in it. The error may concern the account, or times or an interpretation.

How this is done, however, is determined by a deeper and fundamental problem: the role attributed to the *analyst as a real person.*

Here I wish also to take up Dr Fordham's remarks concerning the analyst's personality and its contribution to the therapeutic process.

He has spoken of the ' "stage of transformation" during which the whole personality of patient and analyst become engaged'. In his analysis of an instance of 'syntonic counter-transference' he defines the appropriate interpretation or part of it like this: 'Now I see why I don't answer your questions, it is like it was with your father. You made me like your father by the very persistence of your questions to which you did not expect an answer.' In view of Dr Fordham's earlier theoretical remarks, I take it that the bit 'why I don't answer your questions' is not accidental, but intentionally meaningful. I should also say that I am probably not able to appreciate the full implications, as I am not familiar with Jung's work.

Now the type of interpretation I would give would focus on the patient's putting the question. Why does she ask, and *not* why do I not answer. Similarly, as regards a mistake I have made, I would state clearly that I had made a mistake and that, as I now realize, the point is different, and I would then present the correct interpretation. If it is an error of time causing inconvenience, I would say, 'I am sorry', and offer the practical remedy. A patient has many opportunities in life where a person apologizing for a mistake will give reasons for it. He has only the analytic situation in which it is *exclusively and consistently his prerogative* to be the object of research into reasons and meanings.

My contention is that as the real person the analyst is as useful to the patient as any Tom, Dick, or Harry. What makes him of *unique* use to the patient is his *skill*, which he came to develop through that special training of which I earlier reminded you. Owing to this skill he is able to discover the reasons and meanings in his patient's life, his sources of motivation, the complex network of his personality, *including* the interactions or oscillations between primitive unconscious phantasies and realistic perceptions and judgements. He can discover **and present these discoveries in an** *emotionally* **significant and**

157

therefore dynamically *effective* manner to the patient. This skill, which the analyst possesses and Tom, Dick, or Harry do not possess, puts him in a unique position *vis-à-vis* his patient which is necessary and worth preserving.

To avoid misunderstandings: the analyst's personality is important, since his skill (or should we rather say art?) is in most intricate and complex ways conditioned by it. That is why I said that the analyst's skill is *developed* by his training, not acquired. But only through his art is the analyst's personality to be expressed.

Much of his personality is revealed naturally and inevitably by his appearance, movements, voice, phraseology, furniture in his room, and so on. All of this offers pegs for the patient on which to hang his speculations, phantasies, and recollections. So do the analyst's mistakes. Analysts do not explain why they have this or that piece of furniture, even when a patient finds it in bad taste and thus a gross mistake. I can see no reason why the analyst should become inconsistent when the mistake occurs in a particular episode. On occasion he may not be able to help it so that he does in fact reveal something personal. But this is an unfortunate accident, which, even if it had no bad effects, does not *alter the principle*.

Here is an example. Immediately before a session with a young analyst, I learned of the death of an analyst and was profoundly affected. I considered whether I should cancel the session, but it was too late. The analysand began her session as usual. Twice I could not follow her and asked what she had said. When this happened the second time, she apologized, and said she must be very unclear today and something must be wrong with her. I then said that the fault was mine, and mentioned that I had just heard of the analyst's death. The young analyst, who had not had any personal contact with him, expressed regrets, adding that she knew how much this must mean to me. The analysis which followed dealt with the theme of my mourning, which had specific and high relevance in view of the patient's history. She had lost her father when she was a child, and her mother's widowed state had been an object of long, varied, and intense conflict. The analysis further dealt with the theme of her taking the responsibility for an object's (that is my) fault. As I later examined the situation, I saw possibilities of dealing with the situation without making such a personal communication as I did make. I acted as I did because I was disturbed. Incidentally, my self-revelation did not in fact give away more information than she would acquire on her own. She would have learned about the event soon after the session, and that I, belonging to the older generation of analysts, would be mourning this analyst's death. As far as I could

158

see, my disturbance and my personal communication had not done any harm to the patient. Neveretheless, I regard it as a deviation from sound analytic procedure.

In spite of the manifold unavoidable revelations of the analyst's 'real' personality, the analyst is yet *self-less*. He is the mirror who reflects the patient. Owing to the transference, the patient *repeats* his past life, his complex emotional experiences with his objects and with his own self. Even if the patient's assessment of the analyst is correct, the analyst remains a figure in the patient's inner life and something that he must be left to manipulate according to the dynamics of his own inner processes, determined by unconscious and past experiences. The analyst's reserve concerning his private life does not aim at mystification. Stimuli which have their source in the patient's outside life, or in the analytic situation, will result in the production of specific configurations, and in part of these the analyst may be portrayed *correctly*, in part so fantastically distorted that the fact that the analyst is the patient's transference-object is obvious.

Could it be, I wonder, that we can tolerate it with greater equanimity if this transference-object is *different* from the way in which we see ourselves? Is it an uncanny experience when the patient shows us that it is our real self he possesses and manipulates, so that we then want to invoke the reality of the ordinary 'inter-personal relationship' to get our real selves back to ourselves?

Dr Fordham rightly recommended that analysts take notice of their irrational experiences. As we all acknowledge, no analyst is finally and perfectly analysed, and neurotic residuals remain. What is the clue to the operation of our neurotic residuals? I think there is a simple answer: whenever we feel the tendency to get away from the analytic situation to a situation of an ordinary inter-personal relationship. Dr Little speaks of counter-transference resistance, though in a different context. Here the dangers of the training analysis must be mentioned. It is easy for the training analyst to become concerned with teaching as opposed to analysing; and the contacts between training analyst and candidate in the society or in teaching situations are repeated intrusions which can be exploited by unconscious factors in both analyst and candidate.

Both Dr Fordham and I have traced the analyst's disturbed feelings in the counter-transference to a time lag between unconscious and conscious understanding. This would mean that something the analyst perceived passed without conscious awareness out of the realms of the conscious ego, and therefore became inaccessible. Are there methods of countering such an event? Trespassing beyond the frame of our symposium, I will mention my view (1956) that the

159

analyst's continued self-analysis and self-training can lead him to improve the sensitivity of his *conscious* ego functions, to which I summarily refer as 'perception'. I have suggested that he can and should adopt a multi-dimensional approach by meeting the analytic situation with the questions: What? Why? Who? To whom? What is the patient doing at this very moment? Why is he doing it? Whom does the analyst represent at this moment? Which past self of the patient is dominant? In what manner does this represent a response to a former interpretation (or another incident)? What, according to the patient's feelings, did this interpretation mean to the patient? And so on.

By following closely the patient's verbal and behavioural expressions, the analyst then finds the dynamic transference interpretation which reflects the patient to the patient. The analyst thus, acting as his patient's mirror, acts as a supplementary ego to the patient. This is the factor which, in my view, makes repetition change into modification. Again this is a matter of the analyst's skill.

In conclusion, Freud's injunction that the counter-transference must be recognized and overcome is as valid today as it was fifty years ago. When it occurs, it must be turned to some useful purpose. Continued self-analysis and self-training will help to decrease incidents of counter-transference.[2]

Notes

1 Gitelson makes a very interesting point when describing instances of this kind. One indication for the fact that such an analysis is not a going concern lies in the patient's dreams which depict the analyst without any disguise, engaged in an activity obviously injurious to the patient.

2 [Paula Heimann wrote in the margins of a reprint of this paper that she felt doubtful about including it in her Collected Papers. She said that it needed more explanations concerning the dialogue with Jungian analysts, some re-formulations, general editing, and, particularly, 'the admixture of counter-transference with transference' would need further comment.]

Contribution to discussion of 'The curative factors in psycho-analysis' (1961/2a)

This short paper was a contribution to a symposium on 'The Curative Factors in Psycho-analysis' held at the 22nd International Psycho-Analytical Congress, Edinburgh, 1961. Maxwell Gitelson, Sacha Nacht, and Hanna Segal read papers, and these, together with contributions to discussion, were published in the *International Journal of Psycho-Analysis* 43 (4/5) (1962).

My interest in this symposium that deals with matters close to our daily concern is heightened by the different approaches chosen by the three contributors. Thus Gitelson casts his net very widely. He integrates a variety of concepts used in the literature and presents a profile of his own theories. Nacht focuses on one fundamental factor, itself a composite of many elements, and Segal uses the one-way screen method by giving records from three analytic situations, connected by expositions of Melanie Klein's theories.

Nacht starts with a commendably brief definition of mental health as 'essentially the ability to live in a permanent state of harmony with oneself and with other people'. The precondition for this is a strong ego, and therefore the therapeutic endeavour must be directed towards the ego. Comparing the factors which interfere with the development of a strong ego at the time at which Freud developed his theories on technique with present conditions, Nacht concludes that in our present world it is the *aggressive* energies which represent the severe test on man, in contrast to the Victorian era which demanded repression of sexual impulses. He gives illustrative figures from the patient population coming to the Paris Institute for analysis; only a small percentage is supplied by obsessional and phobic neuroses. I believe that other psychoanalytic clinics too experience the difficulty of finding the, as they are sometimes called, normal neuroses for their candidates. Nacht emphasizes the need to adapt our technique to the changes in the type of the disturbances from which our patients suffer, and he maintains that *interpretation alone* does not suffice. Nacht quotes Glover's formulations concerning 'the humane relation in the transference' and his postulating that 'a prerequisite of the efficiency of interpretation is the attitude, the *true unconscious attitude*, of the analyst'. This emphasis on the humane analyst as the 'common denominator' of all the different and numerous factors which constitute analytic technique is the cardinal point in Nacht's paper. Only if the analyst's benevolence is deeply rooted, and not an artificially assumed attitude, can the patient feel the *security* which he needs to work through and overcome his anxieties. Nacht objects to 'strict neutrality' and 'complete frustration' in the analytic situation. Moreover, since he holds that the transference is not a spontaneous phenomenon, but a result of the analyst's technique, he concludes that the analyst cannot be the 'mirror' on which the patient projects his phantasy world. The person the analyst really is becomes discernible behind his technique, and a good transference can only arise if he possesses the necessary humanity. 'It is of more value', says Nacht, 'to have a mediocre interpretation supported by a good transference than the reverse.' Further, Nacht demands that the analyst should give positive evidence of his benevolence. Such a 'reparative gift' represents a most important curative factor which the patient needs in order to recover from lack of love on the part of his parents in the past, a harsh superego, and traumatic qualities in his current life, to become able to love and be loved. When investigating the reasons for the failure of a first analysis and subsequent success of a second analysis with a different analyst, Nacht found that the first analyst had failed in respect of this basic factor – humanity.

I should have found it helpful if Nacht had given some instances to illustrate what he means by gratification or by the positive evidence of the analyst's benevolence towards his patient. In one of his own papers which he quotes he mentioned matters like time and money. I wonder whether adaptation to the patient's needs in these respects is really something that demands such emphasis. Are there many analysts who would not give an extra hour to a profoundly upset and endangered patient? Would an analyst present his account just during or after a session in which the patient has gone through the pains of bereavement or intense stress of another kind? If this is what Nacht understands by positive evidences, I feel he is storming open doors. I am also in agreement with him if he holds that the analyst should admit mistakes, not claim to be infallible, and acknowledge that if his patient's view differs from his own this need not inevitably be due to

162

resistance. Equally I would agree with Nacht's emphasis on truth and a real devotion to his work in the analyst as a precondition for the success of the analysis. Yet my impression is that Nacht means more than faults in analytic tact or rather gross disturbances in the analyst such as pretence and dishonesty. But tact, honesty, and kindness are not enough. We should not flatter ourselves that we are the only persons with such qualities. The patient finds them outside his analysis. On the other hand he has nobody but his analyst who can put at his disposal the skill and art to carry out the analysis. Taking interpretation as one expression of the analyst's skill, I should not be inclined to put it in opposition to the transference, which equally depends on the analyst's skill. Perhaps what Nacht means is that within a fundamentally sound transference an *occasional* wrong interpretation will not be harmful.

Gitelson's paper can be seen to comprise two not sharply divided parts: a review of the literature and his own original contributions. He maintains that much that is presented as newly discovered therapeutic factors is in fact intrinsic to classical analytic technique. Among the motives for the search for new procedures Gitelson lays stress on the anxieties of our time to which we analysts are as much subjected as other people – thus concurring with a point adduced by Nacht, without, however, being led to Nacht's conclusion.

In his own contributions Gitelson focuses on the opening phase of analysis, which he compares with that early infantile phase in which the 'original tendency of libido to move from its deepest narcissistic attachments to the investment of objects' first took place. As this development depends on an environmental matrix provided by the more or less effective mother, Gitelson postulates as therapeutic factors in the first phase of analysis procedures that recall the principles of early mothering. The quintessence of his comments lies in his emphasis on the 'developmental drive' which the patient brings to his analysis, and which the analyst must both respect and foster. Gitelson defines the view, which I share, that the analyst's interventions aim at supporting and fostering an inner psychic *process* in the patient which started before he entered analysis. Gitelson accepts Spitz's term of the analyst's diatrophic function, integrating with it very neatly and succinctly Annie Reich's view that counter-transference in its affirmative sense is essential, and without it there is no analytic interest or talent. As I myself have made some contributions to the problem of the counter-transference, I may be excused for grinding my own axe a bit. I have been criticized for distinguishing transference by the analyst from counter-transference and for not distinguishing between the latter and empathy. As regards the first criticism, I feel that if Freud had meant that counter-transference is nothing else than transference, he would not have introduced a new term. From my observations both concerning my own work and that of others I consider that the two processes, transference and counter-transference, can and should be *conceptually* differentiated although they are combined in operation.

As regards my confusing the positive aspects of counter-transference which I have called 'instruments for research into the patient's unconscious' with empathy I should have little objection – except the widespread tendency to see nothing but good qualities in empathy, while I would maintain that empathy too needs careful watching. Otherwise all the dangers attending the transference and counter-transference will arise or, in Gitelson's terms, the analyst will in fact offer himself as a 'good object' exclusively to his patient.

I shall conclude my comments on Gitelson's paper by selecting from his remarks some of the factors inherent in the analyst's diatrophic position. Gitelson himself is fully aware of the possibility that the language which he has used can be misunderstood. It will be helpful for many of us if Gitelson further clarifies his views. To save time I shall group the concepts which Gitelson presents in this respect together, although in his own exposition they occur interspersed in highly important theoretical considerations of the nature of the first phase of analysis. The notions with which I am concerned are:

(1) the 'measured gratifications' which the analyst provides for the patient's irrupting instincts. They lead to identification with the analyst as a step in establishing the 'therapeutic alliance' between the patient's autonomous ego functions and the analyst.

(2) the analyst's instructive, advisory, and 'persuasive interventions'. Gitelson strongly deprecates the notion that such interventions can be regarded as 'suggestion' in the banal sense.

Unfortunately, as Gitelson has not given instances of the kind he has in mind, I have not found it easy to distinguish between suggestion and the measures mentioned by Gitelson. Thus, I see here great dangers. First, in my view, the analogy with the infant at the object-finding stage can be carried too far. As I have said elsewhere, the analyst is not the patient's mother, nor is the patient the original infant of long ago. Of this Gitelson no doubt is fully aware, hence his comments on the actual operation of autonomous ego functions in the patient and his stress (common to all three contributors) that it is the ego to which analytic therapy is directed. Gitelson explicitly describes the analyst as the patient's auxiliary ego, a point of view I myself have maintained, using the term 'complementary ego'. However, if the analyst's technical repertoire includes the measures I have just quoted, the analyst is, in my view, likely to play the role of the good object – an attitude rightly deprecated by Gitelson, as not conducive to strengthening the patient's ego. Also if the analyst's technique changes decisively in the course of the analysis, I fear that this is bound to introduce an element of *inconsistency* into the analytic situation which is only too reminiscent of experiences which the patient as a child inevitably had with his parents, and which is not compatible with the atmosphere of steadiness and stability which the analytic situation aims at creating.

Having expressed my misgivings, I must qualify them by quoting Freud, who stressed in his recommendations that technique cannot be streamlined to suit all analysts in every detail. For myself, however, I can only say that I should not feel on safe ground were I to adopt 'measured gratifications of the patient's irrupting instincts'.

I do agree with Gitelson (and Nacht, for that matter) that something other than interpretations happens in analysis which can also be important for *clarification*. A very brief question such as 'Is it?' in response to a patient's conclusion is often more telling than a detailed interpretation, and stimulates the patient to reconsider on his own what he at first stated with absolute conviction. In many situations a preparatory clarification has to precede an effective interpretation, effective because the patient himself has made all but the last small step – which is fully in keeping with Freud's recommendation. For instance, to the analyst's comment, 'You have again told me a dream in which you feel homeless', the patient confirms and elaborates. The analyst then adds, 'This happened again when you were away from the analysis', and lastly the interpretation follows about the patient's having felt homesick for the analyst and the analytic situation – which to begin with the patient had not known.

I turn now to Segal's paper which is very rich in ideas and represents a very clear exposition of Klein's theories. I believe that the design of her paper invites discussion of the clinical material, and I shall restrict myself to a few comments on the session in which the patient brought a dream.

Segal starts the report on her interpretations as follows: 'In the dream the analyst is split into an external ideal object out of his reach, and the internal greedy, dirty smokers, who invade and weaken his ego, represented by his flat.' Now what strikes me most forcibly about this dream and the fact emphasized by Segal that in a wealth of associations to it the patient glaringly omitted a reference to his analyst, who is a heavy smoker, is this: What does it mean that the patient has to use a *dream* to tell his analyst how much he feels persecuted by her smoking, and that he experiences it as a dirty and overwhelming intrusion? I cannot believe that Segal did not pay attention to this exceedingly important transference content, yet in her interpretations she has not mentioned this part of the work at all. Further, with all respect for the vast over-determination of dreams, I do not see that the dream shows a splitting of the analyst into two figures, one of which is persecuting, whilst the other is idealized, but kept out of reach. The only direct and explicit reference to the analyst in the dream itself is in the detail of his wife's informing the dreamer that she had been to the analytic session instead of him, and nothing in the dream itself suggests that the analyst is an ideal figure. The person who is split obviously – in the manifest dream – is the dreamer: he occurs as himself persecuted by the smokers, and as his wife who attended the session instead of him, in his place. Thus to me the dream expresses in the transference the patient's fears of an oral, anal, and phallic mother, from whom he must keep away his masculinity in order to protect his penis; it is only safe to present his feminine self to her. The glaring omission in his associations of any reference to the analyst's smoking suggests that in so presenting himself as feminine, he is to some extent pretending. Obviously Segal's interpretations are based on more material than the time allowed her to put before. us – and this diminishes the gain from bringing a fragment of a session. Inevitably clinical material incites the listener to questions and speculations, possibly of the 'red herring' variety. I feel, however, that Segal's choice of interpretations which she has presented is meant to highlight her theoretical position, with the overemphasis on earlier phases and certain defence mechanisms. It goes beyond the framework of my remarks to enter fully into this realm. No doubt, discussants will take up Klein's theory of inborn envy and gratitude which is crucial for Segal's exposition. It does appear that Klein's last theories about the inborn nature of envy and gratitude have far-reaching implications which go indeed beyond mere dating. It is not only that according to these theories complex emotions which are generally held to belong to a somewhat advanced stage of development are antedated and allocated to the most immature phase of life, in fact birth itself. By assuming that envy and gratitude are inborn and operative with effective energy from the beginning of life, and call into being the ego mechanisms of splitting and projection which in turn lead to complex and sophisticated psychic processes, these emotions are placed in the category of *instinctual drives* and replace Freud's concept of instinctual drives, libido and the destructive instinct, originating in some somatic event, and thus representing borderline entities. Appreciation of the instinctual forces, related to somatic events, as prime movers of psychic processes, brings consideration of the infant's body feelings, of the importance of maternal care or, as Gitelson calls it, of the 'environmental matrix' provided by the mother into the orbit of the analytic situation. According to these basic assumptions a crucial part of the analyst's task consists in following closely his patient's material as it refers to the analyst himself, the analyst's personal traits, behaviour, and activities. On Segal's presentation changes in the theoretical position, conditioned by Klein's last theories, also bring a shift in technique, in that the patient's actual fears and phantasies, based on his observations of the analyst, appear not to be very important for interpretation, while the analyst focuses on the patient's envy, splitting, and projection.

I have been guided in my remarks by the idea that the task of the opener of a discussion lies in his selecting and commenting on some essential points presented by the contributors to the symposium. My own views as distinct from their link with the main speakers can find but little space. I wish to stress that Freud's basic discovery, which has changed the concept of cure in a revolutionary sense, is that the patient is to assume an active role in his cure, and this remains as true as it was in Freud's time. Hence his final formulations are in terms of ego psychology. As already stated, I am in full agreement with the stress put by all contributors on the patient's ego – that is, on their defining as curative factors all those which are designed to free and strengthen the patient's ego; and since, on Freud's showing, perception is the ego's root function, perception in the sense of the Delphic injunction is the alpha and the omega of the curative process. Perception, however, is itself an active function of the ego, and therefore the analyst's interpretations or interventions aim to stimulate the patient's own endeavour to know himself, to see himself. Such seeing himself – insight – will be effective only if the experience includes the emotional change and *cathexis* that pertains to the immediate situation. Otherwise what he learns about himself will merely be added to the store of resistance which has made his self-knowledge before he sought analysis a wasteful and expensive running around in a cul-de-sac. All emotionally significant insight needs the stamp of present immediate reality, and this makes the analyst an important curative factor. He is in the dual roles of the patient's *transference-object* and *transference-self*. I have elsewhere described my view that the analyst's interpretations proceed from a number of questions. Put briefly, though in bad grammar, they are: 'Why is the patient as who doing what to the analyst as whom?' 'And why just now?'. The analyst can never answer these questions in *one* interpretation, nor should he try to do so. It is not his task to present explanations or solutions to his patient on a platter, but to make contact with the patient's actual point of growth, and if he succeeds in doing this, the patient's ego itself will reach out towards the depth of experience and be active in a creative manner.

12

Notes on the anal stage (1961/2b)

This paper was published in the *International Journal of Psycho-Analysis* 43 (6) (1962b). In July 1961, Paula Heimann presented a paper, 'The anal stage', to the Pre-Congress of the British Psycho-Analytical Society, but there is no indication that the published paper is an enlarged version of the paper read at the Congress.

In a discussion held recently in the British Society it became clear that the anal stage has been somewhat neglected in the psychoanalytic literature of the last two decades. What is the reason for this neglect? Is it that Freud and the generation of workers closely related to him, such as Abraham, Ferenczi, Jones, and a few others, have already found and said all there is to say about anality? But analysts have not generally refrained from reviewing, repeating, and reconsidering problems whose essence was discovered and presented by Freud. The reason, I believe, lies somewhere else. Psychoanalytic research has increasingly turned to the earliest phases of infantile life, and the interest in the oral stage and earliest processes, even the prenatal condition, has overshadowed the interest in later phases.

In my view this shift of analytic research and speculation has been at some not inconsiderable cost to our understanding of the psychology of the child and the adult, and of the process of development as such. The impact of maturationally determined new events on the growing child – in fact, the problem of adaptation to new positions and roles throughout life – is a problem that is certainly worth the analyst's curiosity and research. Life is a continuous process, in which the individual is continually exposed to the occurrence of something new. And there is more at stake than merely a modification of what has already been happening. In this connection I would mention some recent unpublished discussion remarks by Dr Payne on the problems of adaptation to growing old.

To return to the anal stage: clearly, as it follows the oral stage, orality will make its contribution, and in unconscious phantasy the anus can be equated with the mouth and the faeces with food, but the anus and the faeces are also, or rather primarily, themselves the subject-matter of unconscious phantasy, and the advance to the new phase brings something entirely new *sui generis* into the infant's life.

The material on which I am basing my considerations is essentially from analytic work, but I also draw from my direct observation of infants. Here my material is limited both by the number of children concerned and by the position taken by myself, being emotionally related to them. However, even the observations obtained from a large number of children and as part of a systematic project are not without drawbacks. In fact, when reading the reports of such sysematic observations made by a non-participant and emotionally uninvolved worker I wonder whether there is such a thing as a non-participating observer. From the child's point of view non-participation represents rejection, and this may influence the material observed. What does a child at the anal stage, for example, feel about a person who appears regularly for a certain time and does certain things, but does not enter into a relation with him? On the other hand: how much did Freud discover from considering the game invented by *one* eighteen-month-old infant to whom he was emotionally related?

Thus I do not apologize overmuch for offering occasionally some snippets and episodes which have an anecdotal ring compared with the material derived from systematic behavioural studies of a large number of children, as for example the findings presented by Spitz from which I shall quote.

For another source of material specifically related to habit training I am indebted to Miss Freud, who kindly put the records made in the Hampstead Nurseries at my disposal. I have found these fascinating and revealing, particularly in regard to the role anality plays in a community of children of the same age group, and to the differences in behaviour displayed by the children towards their peers and towards the grown-ups.

Brief survey of the literature

A thorough review of the literature is out of place, but I shall recall briefly the essential steps leading to our present knowledge of the anal stage. They start with Freud's revolutionary discovery that sexuality is a process which begins by virtue of the inborn drives and follows a biologically prescribed course. Turning the twin beams of his exploring torch on simultaneously the sexual aberrations of adults which, though known to exist, were an unsolved riddle, and on the manifestations of infantile sexuality which were denied, Freud unmasked the former as persistent infantilisms and exposed the characteristics of the latter.

He revealed the existence of the pre-genital zones, which in the course of development assume the character of organizations. Any part of the body can be used as an erotic zone, and sexual aims are further pursued by the component instinct such as voyeurism and exhibitionism, sadism and masochism. Freud presented the concept of *psycho-sexuality*. The repertoire of infantile sexuality includes the 'unconscious equations' and those phantasies which Freud called 'infantile sexual theories'.

To the second pre-genital phase Freud attributed certain features which highlight its importance for the whole future development. The infant knows no disgust or shame, and with narcissistic grandiosity highly values his faeces as a part of his own body. He keeps them back for his own pleasure and, in yielding them to his mother, confers on her the first present that he can produce from his own resources.

In contradistinction to the oral organization, the sadistic-anal organization is particularly connected with the instinct of mastery and sadism. It is distinguished by ambivalence in regard to active and passive, male and female aims, and to pleasure from retention as well as from expulsion. It can persist throughout life.

In his paper 'Character and anal erotism' (1908b) Freud substantiated his view of the permanent effect of the anal organization. The triad of orderliness, parsimony, and stubbornness results from three interacting processes. The original impulses continue directly in an unaltered manner, or lead to reaction formations and sublimations. Many of his later papers, case histories, and theoretical studies have taken up the threads from the *Three Essays* and the anal character, weaving them into new fabrics of discovery, explanation, and incentive for research into human psychology and psychopathology. I mention only in passing the aetiological connections between anality and obsessional neurosis, paranoia and homosexuality. Consideration of these, however, lies outside the boundaries of this paper. In Freud's grand work on the evolution of civilization, anality, and the fate to which it is doomed, came again under close scrutiny. The processes leading to our civilization can be compared with the development of the child.

Abraham, Ferenczi, Jones, and other workers made important

contributions to the problems of infantile sexuality and of the anal character. A study tracing the interest in money from infantile roots in anality was presented by Ferenczi, in addition to other contributions. Jones stressed the need to distinguish between the excretory act and its product in the effect on the psychology of the child and later developments, a point of view which Abraham confirmed. Both presented many clinical examples illustrating Freud's contentions, and correlated adult ambivalence with that pertaining to the anal stage. Thus pleasure in retention leads to procrastination and its manifold manifestations in object relationships and activities in general; expulsion pleasure to perseverance and ferocious activity which brooks no interruption and rouses hostility against the interruptor. Both trends are expressed in the tendency to start an activity, but to break off almost immediately and to repeat such starting and stopping. Anal perseverance, though, is usually un-productive, and relates particularly to unpleasant activities, 'chores' and duties, but makes the person feel that he possesses a particularly highly developed moral sense.

Infantile narcissism in anality leads to perfectionism and the feeling that nobody can do a thing as well as oneself, and to inability to delegate work to others. Self-will, used to impose authority over others, also affects the person's attitude to gifts. Abraham mentions the example of a husband opposing his wife's wish for a certain expenditure, but later forcing considerably more money on her than she had wanted for her own purpose.

In many ways anal sadism is directly expressed by the anal character. Thus Abraham instanced the tendency to rouse desire and expectations and to give only small and insufficient gratification. He gave several examples from dreams. In one the dreamer destroyed her whole family by means of urine, faeces, and flatus as well as by the act of defecation. An eleven-year-old boy dreamed that he had to expel the whole universe from his anus. This dream represented his response to witnessing parental intercourse. New vistas were opened by Abraham's great work in 1924. He connected Freud's libido theory with general psychiatric experiences which employed the symptom of loss of sphincter control as a differential diagnostic criterion in favour of a psychotic condition, and suggested that each pre-genital stage comprises two significantly differing sub-stages. The first anal sub-stage is characterized by the aim of expulsion, and expresses the wish to annihilate the object, whereas in the second anal sub-stage with the aim of retention a change in object relationships appears as the wish to preserve the object on condition that it be totally under the subject's control. Regression below the second anal sub-stage leads to psychosis. Thus a further inroad into the field of psychosis was made by psychoanalysis.

A wealth of observations concerning the sadistic propensities of the excrements was presented by Klein, based on her analyses of children, stressing at the same time the importance of infantile phantasies in general.

To select now some works of the last twenty years, I would mention William Menninger's (1943) study of the anal stage and its sequelae. So far as I know this is the last comprehensive presentation of anality in the English language. Menninger includes a table that relates very clearly the events in infancy with the interaction between the anal and the other instinctual drives and shows how they relate to later conditions. The categories under which he comprises his observations are: direct carry-overs, socially acceptable and unacceptable character traits, reaction formations, and symptoms and signs. His view of the age span of the anal phase differs from general assumptions, since he co-dates its beginning with the oral phase, underlining, however, the accentuations of anal interest in response to weaning and to habit training. As the maximal period of anality he gives the age between two and three years.

A clinical paper by Arlow (1949) neatly confirms the earlier findings by van Ophuijsen (1920) and Stärcke (1920), who independently of each other had found that the prototype of the persecutor in paranoid patients is the patient's own scybalum.

More recently Grunberger (1959) made a thorough investigation into the origin and nature of the anal object. He makes the onset of the anal stage contemporary with that of the oral-biting stage, and defines anality as the sequence of capturing, digesting, and absorbing the object. In contrast to the oral–narcissistic universe, which is open and unlimited, the anal system is closed.

Lastly I would mention a paper based on a behaviouristic project by Spitz with the collaboration of Katherine Wolf (1949). The authors observed a great number of children in different environments from birth to fifteen months of age, and arrived at the conclusion that the child's choice of auto-erotic activities is determined by the relationship their objects offer them. I shall quote two passages relevant to my present considerations.

It came as a surprise to find that the bulk of the psychoses which came to our attention in this environment was concentrated in the group of those mothers whose *children manifested faecal play*.

A surprisingly large number of the coprophagic children had suffered injury at the hands of their mothers. They suffered burns;

they were scalded; one swallowed an open safety-pin; one was dropped on his head; one was nearly drowned during bathing. We got the impression that without the attentive supervision of the staff few of these children would survive.

Narcissism versus object relations at the anal stage

My point of departure for this paper is the hypothesis that the significance of the anal phase lies in the fact that in this period the infant experiences the major clash between his narcissism and his object-relatedness.

Although the strong operation of narcissistic elements in anality has been shown and stressed by Freud and all analysts following him, this crucial fact has not been stated *explicitly*. As a result we have missed a chance for research into the *vicissitudes of narcissism*, by which its original and primitive manifestations are changed into forms that are compatible with later stages of development and with ego-creativity and object relations. I wish to underline the word *explicitly* in the sentence I have just written. Implicitly Freud has in fact shown that the major clash between narcissism and object relatedness occurs during the anal stage in his exposition of the development of civilization. The essence of his statements is that civilization is built upon, and continues to demand, the individual's renouncing a narcissistic pursuit of his instinctual drives. When dealing in detail with the drives that need to be curbed, he instanced anal erotism to illustrate his contention. This, in my view, is only in part on account of the sadism inherent in anality, which makes anal erotism a useful starting point for Freud's penetrating exploration of the destructive drives, their derivation from the death instinct (later re-classified as the 'primal force of death'), and the complex conditions caused by the sense of guilt. I would suggest that his choice is determined in part by the problems of the narcissism inherent in anality. Freud's statement that narcissism is to some extent retained throughout life can be understood as a comment on the imperfections of human nature. It can also, however, be understood to refer to narcissism as something other than a mere manifestation of primitive asocial selfishness. Here there is food for thought.

174

Some remarks on the nature of anality

The anatomical position of the anal zone is dorsal, distal, and hidden. It therefore lies outside the infant's social contact with his mother, which no less than adult social encounters essentially depends on the confrontation of the partakers.

Anal excitations begin and take their course independently of any help on the part of the mother, and both the somatic function and the libidinal pleasures derived from it are regulated by the infant in an autonomous manner. In respect of both aspects of the anal experience, the principle of the anaclitic development of the libido and of object love does not apply to the anal function, as it does to the oral function. Primarily anal urges are not suitable for the establishment or the cementing of object relationship. For anality the object is redundant, if not worse, and we know from direct and from analytic observation that interventions with or rather intrusions into the anal function are registered as attacks. One patient's description was particularly telling. He remembered vividly the rage, savage excitation, and abject dread of being exploded and fragmented by the enema. In many patients with marked sado-masochistic problems such intrusions by physical means or by intense curiosity and fear on the part of the parents, correctly understood by the child to express the parents' own anal sexuality, prove to be important sources of their illness. Since the anal sequence of urge, relief, and pleasure proceeds without the mother's help or participation, the *phantasies* involved in the anal sensations must be thought of as intrinsically devoid of object notions, fully narcissistic, and incommunicable. They need to lean on objects; that is to say, to borrow from the other drives and sensations, oral, genital, tactile, and so on, which by their nature contain object-directed elements in order to become communicable. 'If we look at the attitude of fond parents towards their children', said Freud (1914c),[1] 'we cannot but perceive it as a revival and reproduction of their own long since abandoned narcissism.' One patient early in her analysis devoted the larger part of a session to a description in rhapsodic terms of her baby daughter's play with faeces. She agreed that she was talking about her own anal pleasures. Anal phantasies which are communicated later by actions and words involve objects. In fact we find in analysis that all the constituents of object relationship, including the Oedipus complex, can occur in an anal version. But this is not a primary formation. It has its origin in the admixture with anality of elements belonging to the other zones and the component instincts, which are intrinsically object-related.

Love, hate, rivalry, jealousy, envy, fear, shame, and guilt recur in the anal world, and the contributions made by the instinct of mastery, so closely linked with anality, can be discerned in the violent character of such phantasies.

I expect that objections will be raised to my assertion that the infant does not need his mother's help for his anal function, and that he experiences primarily no relations with her through his anal zone. There are innumerable details of child care in which such contacts do occur. The mother washes, soaps, dries, puts powder and cream on the anal region, and it can be seen that the infant enjoys this. She wraps napkins around his buttocks, he sits on her lap, and so on. But these incidents bring the anal region into *a community with* the rest of his body and allow the whole repertoire of impulses and emotions of the face-to-face relationship, including the activity of arms, hands, and legs, to come into play. Being in the bath offers 'oceanic' sensations of the whole body surface, the ecstasy of nakedness and freedom for vigorous movements in a pleasant medium. Episodes in which the mother elicits pleasurable sensations by handling the anal region clearly affect the neighbouring genital region also. And as regards napkin changes my impression is that the child, particularly once he can stand, frequently reacts with protest and resentment. One toddler would agree to this procedure only if I put him back in the erect position, and preferably let him play at the basin at the same time, while the mirror above the basin moreover allowed for a visual relationship between us.

In contrast to other bodily zones the infant's anal zone does not provide him with an organ to impart information about positive feelings towards the object or about wishes and events other than those related to the anal function. Anal noises may indicate that the function is about to start or is in progress. But they are not inevitable concomitants of this function, and in fact the infant's face makes this communication in a better manner. He gets pink as he presses, his eyes assume an inward gaze, his interest is clearly withdrawn from his objects. Spitz has timed the period of withdrawal as lasting half a minute. The mouth, however, is an organ of intelligence, even before the infant has learnt to speak. Certain gurglings and gruntings tell that he feels happy. Before forming words he tends to produce some specific sound of command that nobody in his environment can fail to understand. An added gesture with his hands defines his wish. Or he may indicate that he is tired when starting to suck his finger. By putting his thumb into his mouth he tells us that he wants to be put into his bed.

Thus, as Grunberger suggests, the oral universe is open and

unlimited, whereas the anal system is closed. Yet this needs qualification. Owing to the intimate association between the anal zone and the instinct of mastery which expresses itself through the muscular apparatus, the latter should be included in the concept of the anal *system*. We indicate this fact by the double meaning of the word 'motion'. Increase in the violence of the infant's motor activities, in throwing, pushing, hurling things with violence, in the obvious pleasure of aggressive self-assertion and contrariness in behaviour without anger, even with the proverbially angelic expression on his face, should be taken as indications that he has advanced to the stage of anal primacy. No toddler I have known has missed out the phase of walking in the opposite direction, opening other people's gates and intruding into their garden, particularly when he sees that the grown-up does not do this or like it.

Owing to the anatomy of the region, we know from direct observation very little of the infant's attitude to his anal processes, before habit training has begun. Here the clash between his will and the mother's becomes obvious, as also the fact that the object relation to his mother, which he has already formed during the oral phase and which continues to develop in accordance with his growing ego, induces him to comply with her wishes. Out of love for her, out of fear of losing her love, out of pleasure, when she praises him, he adapts his function and produces his excrement, when and where she wants it. On the other hand, in the wish to dominate her, to rejoice in his power and her helplessness, to revenge himself for her frustrations, to express his jealousy for her unfaithfulness with his rivals, he defies her, keeps her waiting, makes and breaks the promise to produce.

At this point I wish to express the heretical idea that the infant does not extend his narcissistic pride and overvaluation to the excrements themselves. From direct as well as analytic observations. I believe that the child does not regard his *faeces as such* as good and valuable.[2] That there is a need to distinguish between the act and the product has been accepted since Jones's time by all other analysts, yet neither he nor other authors have applied this distinction when considering the narcissistic quality of anality. Freud originally used a qualifying phrase. He stated that the infant to begin with does not know disgust or shame about his faeces, and values them 'as a part of his own body'. But the stool ceases to be part of his body when it ceases to be a pleasant, warm, and soft substance which fuses with his body sclf. What is unpleasant is in early life not part of the self, as Freud has shown. At this point too, when the faeces have become a source of **displeasure, the infant does want his mother's help. Equally the** faeces in the pot are not part of his body. What we can see clearly is that the child looks down with interest and curiosity, but often also with some fear and disgust. One child placed himself astride in the standing position over the pot and bent over double to look. What did he see in this position? First of all and all the time his penis, and for a moment something that dropped down. He made no attempt at touching the stool, and I do not believe that this was due to obedience. He may have been told on earlier occasions not to touch his stool. But he has been told on innumerable occasions not to get hold of the biggest hammer, not to poke the fire, not to squeeze the kittens, and so on, without the slightest effect. He does not touch the faeces because he does not like them. From my own limited experience I would confirm Spitz's conclusion that faecal play is much rarer than other forms of auto-erotism, and indicates some pathological factor in the infant's life. In my view what the infant is proud of is his *productive capacity as distinct from its result*. Nor do I think that he believes the grown-up who tells him that his stool is a wonderful present. At the time of habit-training his reality-testing has advanced sufficiently to result in his knowledge that nice presents are kept and not thrown away. He probably treats such an assertion with the tolerance towards the oddness of grown-up people which he certainly has to practise quite often in his childhood, a tolerance made easier by his understanding that the grown-up is pleased and well-meaning. Some of the records from the Hampstead Nurseries describe a negative attitude to the faeces which cannot be attributed merely to fear of the grown-up, and expressions of misery, disgust, and fear by some children, when confronted with faeces. I may also remind you of Freud's view that it is not only education that leads to the renouncing of anal pleasure; he considered that this involved an inherited factor also. In other words, from sources within himself the infant has a negative attitude to his excrements.

In analysis we see much of the negative side of infantile narcissism, namely hypochondria, in relation to the whole function, but particularly to the excrements themselves. I have quoted some of the authors who have reported observations to this effect. Of course I may be suspected of forgetting that the psychoanalytic infant, the adult on the analytic couch, is not identical with the original infant. I hope that I shall clear myself of such suspicion in the next section of my paper.

Some remarks on anal work patterns

There are phases in many analyses when it looks as if we were dealing with an anal character, and we wonder why we have overlooked this diagnosis. In fact, however, the patient is not an anal character. It is merely that his work problems have come fully and emphatically into the focus of the analysis. I am restricting myself to inhibition concerning writing, both so-called creative writing and writing that forms part of routine work. In fact, of course, any writing, except copying a text, has some creative and original aspect.

I can best remind the reader of his own experiences by quoting some clinical instances of a familiar kind. One patient cannot start because he feels 'overwhelmed by the mess on his table'. He would have to 'clear the decks and to pay off the debts which he has accumulated'. He does not mind any work that can be done by talking, but in order to write, he has to 'isolate' himself from people, and he is afraid of 'loneliness and depression'. Another patient is terrified that anything he might write would be attacked. People will say that it is all old stuff, other authors had said it before him, and much better. He will be accused of plagiarism. If, however, his ideas were seen to be new, people would reject them as worthless. Confronted with the task of writing, he would go off into a 'brown study' reverie, which depicted with a great wealth of gratifying details that he had finished his writing and produced a work of outstanding quality. Another patient reported daily on his writing problems. The project with which he was concerned underwent considerable changes during this period. He discovered of himself many reasons for the disturbances in his writing. Thus in one hour he told me that he knew now why it was so difficult to write. He could not *sit* for any length of time. After a quarter of an hour he had to get up, move about, and do something else. These other activities turned out to be of an oral nature: either directly so, as making himself something to drink, or displaced on intake by listening, as by playing records. Of the time available he could use for writing only a small fraction. Another discovery concerned place as well as time. When away from home he got a strong urge to write, but it was not appropriate to write there and then. He looked forward eagerly to getting home, but when he did, the urge was gone. A period in the analysis followed in which other problems dominated, and he did not mention his writing at all. This phase ended with two days on which he was intent on provoking a quarrel. He was exasperated with me, my analysis was wrong in a variety of ways, he upbraided me for my interpretations, and so on. On the second day his exasperation was still greater, and he stated this with emphasis. He gave me a lecture on the scientific approach to a given problem, exemplified by an episode in the analytic situation. He demanded that I should state my attitude to his exposition and forbade me to interpret. Although his accusations were clearly transference repetitions of past conflicts and hurts, the lecture itself was very well done, with clear formulations and original ideas, and I concluded that his writing had progressed. On the following day he started by saying 'I want you to share a joy with me'. He said that this was exceedingly difficult for him, and that he was very hesitant. He spoke indeed with an unusual hesitancy. It turned out that the joy concerned progress in his writing. He had found out that he could treat writing as having a dialogue, and this discovery had led to a change in his technique and to enjoying the act of writing. At a still later phase, however, writing went badly again, because, as he said, no book can be a baby. Only a baby is a baby.

My aim in presenting these episodes from an analysis of writing inhibitions is that they show clearly the activation of infantile sexual problems, with a particular stress on the revival of the anal stage. Guilt for retention and procrastination and for making a mess – depression with lonely repentance – fear of punishment for stealing and producing worthless stuff – need for oral comforts – arrogance about the productive capacity – a move towards genitality, foundering on the inability to produce a baby, all these elements reproduce feelings, impulses, and contents of the anal stage. The material quoted shows also the difference between the oral and the anal prototypes of work. The patient who does not mind any work that can be done by talking, and the attempt to turn writing into a dialogue, recall the earliest situation in which work is done. A dialogue represents a co-operative community of two participants. The earliest pattern of such a community is represented by the sucking infant with the suckling mother. That the sucking infant in his blissful experience at the breast is also *working* for his living seems little acknowledged in the literature. I have found a statement to this effect only in Hendrick's paper 'Work and the pleasure principle' (1943). In contrast to the pattern of work laid down by the feeding experience at the mother's breast, and later continued when the child learns to speak, the work pattern derived from the anal stage demands withdrawal from the community and loneliness and full autonomy in the productive act.

Not only writing, every form of creativeness draws from the earliest independent creative activity the individual ever performed.

180

But writing appears particularly endangered by the unconscious recollections that a creative endeavour resulted in something bad, only worthy to be thrown away and in fact thrown away.

Or communication begins in an early phase of development and depends on the help from the partner of the dialogue. The acquisition of words, a decisive factor in the development of secondary process thinking, is derived from the child's relationship to his parents and draws from auditory memories (Freud 1915e). Speaking is close to physical oral contact with an object, and evokes the somatic memories when mouth, lips, and tongue were used in sucking at the mother's breast. Words and phrases are mouthed, come easily off one's tongue, or are tongue twisters. The spoken word is ephemeral and allows for withdrawal and correction on the spot. It therefore limits the speaker's responsibility and committal. The written word, however, extends beyond the immediate present and locale. It conquers time and space, it creates a new dimension of existence. For the same reason, however, it imposes severe responsibility on its author. A part of his self continues to exist, whether he likes it or not, whether he continues to feel identified with it or whether he has outgrown it and moved beyond it.

The prototype of the written communciation occurs during anal primacy, and unconscious memories evoked are bound to lead to the fear of attack and rejection. Anal ambivalence is reflected in the well-known feelings of the writer about his work, his swings from creative absorption to stale inertia, from elation to despair. The first occasion in the individual's life when he becomes aware of his autonomous powers is in the anal stage. He then experiences for the first time his creative capacity to follow an urge and master its sequence by himself, not as part of a dialogue with a co-operative partner who shares his responsibility and immediately responds with reward and pleasure. But before this phase the infant has been creative: I refer to his phantasy formations. These, however, remain inside himself, do not leave his body, and are not subject to his and his objects' reality testing.

I wish now to carry my speculations further. I am emphasizing anality as the prototype for creative ego activities. This leads me to consider the technique which the ego has available to carry out its intentions. This technique employs mechanisms. During the period of Freud's first model of the mind these ego-mechanisms were regarded as serving the purpose of defence against pain originating from the conflicting demands from the id on the one hand and the external world and the superego on the other. The concept of unconscious defensive processes as an aetiological factor is one of the most important of those psychoanalytic discoveries which gave rise to a scientific and specific concept of mental therapy, and its position in psychoanalysis is secure. But already during the (so to say) official predominance of the first model of the mind, which in contrast to the id as the oldest system allocated only a secondary position to the system ego (the crust of the id, formed by the impact of external stimuli, the record of past object-choices, and so on), did Freud in fact also use a different concept of the ego which he explicitly presented in his 'Introduction to narcissism' (1914c) although he then encountered certain theoretical difficulties.

With Freud's second model of the psychic apparatus (1937c) these theoretical difficulties were removed. The position of the ego as a primary formation was explicitly formulated, and ego psychology and ego autonomy have come into the focus of psychoanalytic research, allowing for a conceptual orientation that better fits clinical observation.

Whereas in the earlier phase ego-mechanism was synonymous with defence, we now appreciate fully the constructive and executive function of these mechanisms. In the following mechanisms roots from the anal function can be discerned. *Suppression and repression* (they are used together by Freud in *Civilization*) are measures to prevent an ongoing process from being completed and emerging from the depth (anal retention). *Reversal* consists in the change of the original direction into its opposite. Akin to reversal are the mechanisms of *turning upon the self* and *undoing*. They too reverse the direction of a process and extinguish or counteract the urge that was originally operative.

Lastly I would recall the mechanisms of *splitting and projection*, of which nowadays we hear so much. We can easily recognize them as describing in other words the process of anal evacuation.

Now all these mechanisms can be used defensively, and for the gain of avoiding pain the ego pays a heavy price in suffering a reduction of its range, interruptions of its coherence, loss of perception and its sequelae. But they can also be used for constructive purposes in the service of the ego's creative capacities. When engaged in work, concentration on the problem is necessary, and is furthered by the suppression of distracting ideas and impulses. In thought processes such as discerning and differentiating, a mechanism akin to splitting is used, but it heightens perception and concept formation. Reversal and turning upon the self have an important function in reflective thinking. Constructive projection outward of an inner process helps us to gain more clarity about it; as the ego maintains its awareness that it is concerned with something of its own inner world, projection in this case does not lead to loss, denial, and delusion.

I have attempted elsewhere (1959) to distinguish between the process of sublimation and the process set going by primary ego-creativity which urges the individual to manifest and objectify his innate ego-capacities. During large parts of his creative work the individual is narcissistic. He withdraws from the community, and is absorbed in his own processes. (It is not only toothache that enforces narcissistic withdrawal!) In my view narcissism is not simply the earliest infantile position of the libido or a quasi-physiological state. It is an experiential orientation which draws on innate capacities of the ego. As a broad source of qualities that direct behaviour and contribute to experiences, including those with objects, narcissism is as much a primary endowment as are the instinctual drives, and like these is subject to the laws of maturation and development. Moreover, owing to the primary forces of love and destructiveness, it is also subject to the persistent dualism that governs human life and psychic processes.

Since this narcissistic orientation occurs originally during the period of maximal helplessness, its original form is that of omnipotence expressed by the capacity of the immature psychic apparatus 'simply to imagine what is wanted'. This capacity is supported by the original undifferentiation between infant and mother which allows for fusion with her and for attributing all that is pleasant to the self. When we consider the highlight of early infantile experience during the wakeful state – namely, feeding at the mother's breast – can we assume that the infant at the beginning of his career as a suckling distinguishes between self and object, between his own mouth and the mother's nipple, between his own saliva and her milk? We have to assume a certain degree of ego development allowing for the concept of 'now' and 'before now' and of distance, 'Mother coming nearer', in other words of the active use of memory in perception, of spatial and temporal concepts in order to give the distinction between self and object a place in the infant's mental world. Even then, during the act of feeding itself, such distinction is bound to give way to fusion, since cathexis shifts to the sensations of the feeding experience. What is from the observer's point of view a twosome, is subjectively oneness. During the later months of oral predominance, the infant's identification with his mother can be seen in many of his activities.

The oral experience reinstates the original oneness of mother and infant, wheres the anal experience denotes withdrawal from the mother and autonomy. In this stage of ambivalence narcissism is expressed by aggressive self-assertion, contrariness, and sadism, and the sense of identity depends largely on the opposition: I against you.

It takes a long and hazardous road until in genitality the sense of identity becomes stable and secure and leads the individual to seek other persons with a different identity – that is, to a full object relationship in which self and object interact and mutually intensify the partners' self-experience.

Fusion with identification, aggressive self-assertion with contrariness, identity with mutuality, are the milestones on the road to a civilized form of living.

Notes

1 [A slightly changed translation can be found in *SE* 14: 90–1.]
2 Compare L. Kubie's (1937) view of the body as a factory for dirt.

13

Comment on Dr Katan's and Dr Meltzer's papers on 'Fetishism – somatic delusions – hypochondria' (1963/4)

This paper is an expanded version of opening remarks to discussion of Dr Katan's paper on 'Fetishism, splitting of the ego and denial' and Dr Meltzer's paper on 'The differentiation of somatic delusions from hypochondria', read at the 23th International Psycho-Analytical Congress, Stockholm, 1963. All three papers were published in the *International Journal of Psycho-Analysis* 45 (2/3) (1964).

Both Dr Katan and Dr Meltzer have taken a symptom as the point of departure for the presentation of the conceptual tools they use in their clinical work. It is obvious that their psychoanalytical theories differ greatly, Katan's thinking being based on Freud's work, and Meltzer's on Klein's, particularly on her latest theories. I shall be able to select here only a few points from a rich offering.

In one of my patients, fetishism formed part of a polymorphous sexual condition which included the urge and capacity for normal heterosexual intercourse. This is in keeping with Katan's remarks about the importance of pre-Oedipal conflicts for fetish formation. The fetish in my patient was women's stockings, and particularly their seams which not only symbolized the female phallus but also stated – emphatically, one might say – that the parental couple had identical genitals. Many instances in the analysis revealed the patient's confusion about the sexual character of his parents: in looks, manner, and work his mother appeared to him as masculine and on the same counts his father as feminine. At the same time, as a piece of clothing this fetish suggests the 'pre-traumatic fixation' elaborated by Katan.

My patient's history was reflected in an unconcious phantasy structure which acted as a 'leitmotif-phantasy', determining his unconscious self-image and thus large areas of his attitude to life. It revolved upon being deprived of security and love, upon having come too short of the need-fulfilling presence (rather than person). His private saga, built on information and memory, started with the very beginning: precipitate birth, short breast-feeding from inverted nipples (in many dreams odd mountains figured with a dent at the top instead of a peak), weaning coinciding with the loss of the mother's presence, since she resumed her work outside the house, a number of nurses who, according to their reappearance in the transference, were lacking in sympathy, intense homesickness at boarding school, which started in early latency. At the Oedipal stage a girl of his own age was adopted by his parents, depriving him of his privileged position as the only child and rousing severe jealousy and rival hatred of the intruder. He had a clear memory of feeling digust and horror at the sight of her genital.

The additional cathexis of the fetish, which Katan postulates, emerged significantly, when the patient produced an image of himself, sitting in the staff's sitting-room, located in the basement, and looking out of the window, seeing only the legs of the passers-by. The context strongly suggested a lovelorn little boy, yearning for his parents and unable to turn to substitutes. The leitmotif phantasy became dominant for a long time in the analysis every Friday, the last session of the week. He used to produce an unending chain of associations. Most of these were meaningful, but none of them intended as the communication of just that meaning. I came to understand that the relevant communication was just what my designation 'chain of associations' says: under the threat of separation he became a child clinging to a familiar presence. There were times, particularly at the beginning, when I did not feel that his behaviour had the character of an object relationship in which the ego uses the mechanisms of introjection and projection, in the service of distinct libidinal and destructive aims. Nor was he 'split' in the sense in which Meltzer uses this notion. His associations were coherent and consecutive. In fact, it might be said that he had a 'one-track mind', pursuing one aim only: that of holding on to the source of security. But one could also argue that such an intense fear of separation was only possible on account of the repression of all the pleasurable memories connected with his weekends (and indeed of the repression of many experiences), and in so far one could speak of 'splits' in his ego.

Also, as regards his sexual life, a specific split in this patient's ego is suggested by the fact that he maintained a permanent relationship with one woman with whom he had normal sexual intercourse, while from time to time he was compelled to find different women for perverse sexual activities. These two trends each pursued their own course independently.

In his analysis of the process of fetish formation Katan suggests that the split in the ego is more apparent than real. The perception of the absent penis rouses fear of imminent castration only when the boy is actually in a state of intense excitement, with sensations in his penis (and probably with erection). Only in this condition is the perception denied; later, in a calmer state, it is acknowledged. Katan concludes that this alteration from denial to acceptance represents two successive steps. But, I think, he also considers a repetition of these steps. If so, then there is a failure of integration in the ego, and its mode of operation amounts to a split in its organization. Altogether, a discussion of splits in the ego, invited by these two papers, will hardly deal with the question of whether they occur, but rather how they come about.

The fact that the ego suffers ruptures in its organization was established at the very beginning of psychoanalysis with the discovery of repression which leads to 'separate psychical groups'. Freud repeatedly stated that the ego is 'split, rent and torn' by its conflicts, and returning to fetishism in the *Outline* declared that such splits in the ego occur not only in fetishism or in the psychoses, but also in the neuroses. In other words, they are part of ubiquitous psychopathology. Trauma, either when sudden and massive, or when, though not sudden, the ego is too weak to master the particular demand; introjections, when too numerous or incompatible with essential ego-trends; indeed, many experiences which damage the ego and its synthetic function result in dissociation and rupture. The controversy thus revolves upon the assumption of a special splitting mechanism other than repression, isolation, displacement, shifts of cathexis, and so on. In Meltzer's paper such a mechanism is of crucial importance. I shall make some comments about this later.

Meltzer's suggestion that we should differentiate between hypochondria and somatic delusions by attributing the first to internal and the second to external object relations is tempting. A cancer inside the body is an internal and invisible object, whilst acne or the stump of an amputated leg is external and visible. If, however, acne and other fears about one's appearance are typical examples of somatic delusions, then we cannot forget how typical both are for adolescence, whereas fear of cancer is rare at this phase. This should warn us that somatic delusions may be phase-specific and we should turn our attention to the typical and cardinal problem of adolescence.

A patient's hypochondria revolves upon being 'fatigued'. He tends to start his session with a bulletin on his health, in particular on his state of fatigue. His mother had suffered from a heart disease, and among many memories a very poignant one shows him walking with her and assuring her that this day she walked much farther than the time before. Now, clearly, identification with his mother (shown, of course, by many other factors as well) determines his hypochondria, and this would confirm Meltzer's view that hypochondria originates in internal object relations. But his fear extends to external objects. If he is tired he will not satisfy the persons for whom he has to work, and they will attack him. Does this now make it a somatic delusion?

A sharp distinction between internal and external object relations, as I have tried to show elsewhere, is a linguistic artefact. We simply cannot describe both at once. In fact, phantasies about internal and external objects are interdependent, and, in terms of structure, the superego, itself the result of an external relationship, controls and is influenced by the relation with external objects.

Both hypochondriacal fears and somatic delusions are very frequent, although the role they play in different individuals varies greatly. Moreover, each can form part of a 'pair of opposites'. The hypochondriacal patient often has also a firm belief in his health, immunity from infections, and so on, and, as Meltzer mentioned, his patient, side by side with the delusional fears that his flatus rendered him repellant to objects, also maintained an extremely lovable self-image.

According to my experience, the difference between hypochrondria and somatic delusions revolves upon the sense of shame. The individual reacts with intense, in fact over-intense, feelings of shame in the matter of his delusion (blemishes in appearance, acne, bad breath, body odour, and so on), whereas this is not the case with hypochondria. This explains why hypochondriacal fears are mentioned so much more easily, while somatic delusions are withheld for a long time, as Meltzer pointed out.

This sense of shame, rather than guilt, tells a tale of deeply wounded narcissism and fear of helplessness. Moreover, like all hypertrophied psychic formations, this exaggerated shame has a true and a false component. The former relates to the individual's own defects and destructive impulses, and in respect of his destructive impulses there is an overlap with guilt. The false component arises from 'primary' identification and belongs to the not-recognized object of the original indifferentiation between the infant and the mothering figure. 'Primary' identification is not based on active choice, but on a passively suffered intrusion which the infant during the phases of helplessness cannot resist.

Thus, in my view, the somatic delusion contains deeply unconscious somatic memories of painful sensations that did not originate in the infant but were reactions to passive experiences, of being touched, for example, handled, moved about, and so on. Hypochondria, on the other hand, seems to be based on active introjections. The introject around which the hypochondriacal fears revolve is an ambivalently loved and hated object. Narcissistic problems are also involved, but relate to a later phase of development than somatic delusions. Naturally, these two types of fears can overlap. The difference beween my evaluation of somatic delusions and Meltzer's derives from our different concepts of early life and development. Meltzer proceeds from Klein's theories of a differentiated id and ego literally from the beginning of life, conflict about destructive envy towards the mother's breast and the defence of a special mechanism of splitting with projective identification.

I have come to find the theory of the infantile paranoid–schizoid and depressive positions untenable. There is great value in Klein's elaboration of these emotional conditions, if taken as clinical syndromes encountered in states of regression. But a clinical syndrome in the patient on the couch cannot be transposed directly to the infant in the cot, since regression is not identical with the original condition. The continuation of some phase-adequate modes of thought and feeling, while some advanced ego-functions are destroyed, the sense of illness and the total life situation of the regressed patient constitute decisive differences from the original infantile state.

As regards early infantile life, passively suffered intrusions need to be distinguished from active introjections and primitive discharge from projection. In the notion of projective identification a number of different processes are confounded. Projection is a mechanism that removes something from the ego into the external world. Like every mechanism its result depends on the motive that sets it going. The ego can use it in defence against conflicts or in the interest of its creative capacities. In the first case it leads to delusion; in the second, that is by consciously projecting internal imagery and thought (the technique of the film projector), for the purpose of obtaining greater clarity, reality testing and the creative process are enhanced, and there is no delusion or distortion of inner and outer reality. But projection does not lead to identification. Identification denotes a specific and qualitative change in the ego – one ego becoming like another ego, and this is brought about by the mechanism of introjection. The phrase 'projection *into* an object' describes a phantasy, not a mechanism. There are indeed numerous phantasies of entering into an object, ranging from the 'return to the womb' type to oral, anal, phallic, and genital types with varying proportions of libidinal and destructive aims.

Development can be described as progress towards differentiation and independence. In adolescence the individual is faced with the task of establishing his own individuality and that of other persons on a realistic basis and achieving a milieu that will accept him on his merits in contrast to the acceptance of his first natural milieu, his family. This 'formative' crisis means a hard struggle which needs no elaboration in the present context. What is relevant for the present considerations is the role of the skin and the appearance altogether which are the nub of the somatic delusions, as defined by Meltzer. Being the frontier organ that delineates the individual from the external world, being the seat of the sense organs and the orifices for taking and giving with memories and associations of the modalities of the past, the skin lends itself particularly to being cathected with wishes and fears. Thus acne and other blemishes of appearance lend themselves to forming the matter of somatic delusions.

----------------------- 14 -----------------------

Comments on the psychoanalytic concept of work (1964/6a)

This paper is a revised version of a paper given in German to the 1st Psycho-Analytical Congress in Frankfurt am Main, 1964, on the occasion of the opening of the Sigmund Freud Institut. It was published in German in *Psyche* 20 (5) (1966), and has been translated into English for this book.

I shall attempt in this paper to pursue one particular aspect of psychoanalysis; namely, the role that our theory and practice assign the concept of psychic work. Yet since this one aspect affects so many areas, my comments cannot be comprehensive. My interests are primarily clinical in nature, and I intend to present more an examination of our tools than a description of new ideas.

First I will briefly refer to a few specific kinds of psychic work that, thanks to Freud's research, form the main foundation of psychoanalysis. They are dream-work, joke-work, creative work, and the work of mourning. I will limit myself to the important elements of Freud's descriptions, and not refer to the rich literature on this topic. Finally I will view the analytic situation from the perspective of the concept of work.

Psychic work and therapy

It was apparent even with the pre-analytic, hypnotic cathartic method that the therapeutic process demanded work on the part of the patient. The work in that method involved remembering each experience associated with the symptom of hysteria. It was difficult and painful, and the patient required much help, which the doctor provided by hypnosis, talk, encouragement, sympathetic words, questions, and so forth. Inferred from these memories were the genesis of the symptoms of hysteria, the psychic trauma, the strangulated affect, and pathological forgetting, which actively expels the pathological experiences from consciousness and thus removes them from the thought process. Our attention was directed especially at the difference between normal and pathological forgetting since the interest in mental work proceeds from the clinical observation that the remembering of the pathogenic experiences and the discharge of the affect lead to a cathartic liberation. Thus research was initially on the function of mental work in providing relief; the goal of this work was the disappearance of ideas. 'Normal forgetting' is a consequence of the associative connection made between experiences and ideas that are distressing and frightening and their opposites, while 'pathological forgetting' leads to the formation of 'separate psychic groups' that act like foreign bodies in the organism.

Here we can recognize the starting point for many of Freud's later discoveries, especially his theories of homeostasis, the pleasure principle, and the attempt to reduce the sum of excitation to a level that can be tolerated subjectively. This is analogous to the fact that we can recognize the early definition of psychic conflict as a struggle between unbearable instinctual demands, on the one hand, and the aesthetic and ethical demands raised by the ego, on the other, to be the predecessor of structural theory.

The omission of hypnosis led to new types of work in therapy and extended the patient's sphere of work. Now the patient had to overcome his resistance, which Freud called the most significant function of analysis, and working through supplemented the work of remembering.

The fundamental rule

Freud's discovery of transference and the twin processes of repression and resistance signified the foundation of psychoanalysis as a new science of psychology. The formulation of the fundamental rule made it a new type of therapeutic technique. It is essential to keep the mutual influence of these two factors in mind when looking at the development of psychoanalysis and theoretically distinguishing psychoanalysis from other forms of psychotherapy.

The fundamental rule removed not only the doctor's dependence on hypnosis, but also the factor restricting both the patient's and analyst's attention to a limited area. The patient's free association and the analyst's evenly hovering attention freed analysis from concentrating on the symptom – you could even say, from the dominance of the symptom. Thus the analytic situation came to embrace the patient's entire life and personality. Proceeding from the observation of clinical details that he attributed to a hidden regularity, Freud came to study these regularities themselves. His discovery that psychopathological phenomena occur not only in patients but also in 'normal' people overcame the rigid distinction beween the presence and absence of psychic illness that was then predominant, and replaced it by new concepts that opened the way to further research.

In the two-way street of inferring the general or normal from the specific or pathological and vice versa, Freud studied the nature of psychic work with regard to lived experiences that were generally well known but whose unconscious parts and signs only became accessible in analysis. The activity of remembering was familiar, but the link between psychic illness and past experience was new. To varying degrees in different individuals, spontaneous psychic life also includes dreaming, making jokes, creative work, and mourning. That these psychic acts follow specific modes and unconsciously have a therapeutic function was first made clear by Freud's systematic research.

The patient comes to the analyst because he cannot cope with the tasks of life, in whatever form this manifests itself, and because he suffers as a result. He expects help, consolation, and relief, but with the fundamental rule the analyst gives him new tasks. Freud's (1913c) formulation of the fundamental rule ('and say it although or precisely because you feel an aversion to it') made it clear to his patients from the very beginning that fulfilling these tasks required hard and often painful work.

Dream-work

The manifest content of a dream (Freud 1900), whose features are often meaningless and absurd, was shown to be the final product of dream-work and the latent dream thoughts. The latter, in contrast, are meaningful and comprehensible, and are part of a normal context. Repressed infantile desires join the day's residues of conscious ideas. The desire to sleep, with its turning away from the external world, initiates the return of psychic processes, and in the regression towards narcissism the primary process becomes predominant and pursues the goals of wish fulfilment and avoiding unpleasure.

In the present context I would like to emphasize that the individual techniques in the primary process eliminate the unpleasurable effort of mental work in various but specific ways. Thus, in condensation elements are united regardless of whether they belong together or are even mutually exclusive. Displacement avoids the effort of arranging the individual dream thoughts in a meaningful way. Images serve, similar to templates in waking thinking, as pre-existing concepts the use of which avoids the work involved in independent formulation. For multi-faceted symbols, no specific meaning is selected, and in the visual representation, remembering is replaced by hallucination.

We also recognize a common element in these techniques of dream-work – namely, that gaining pleasure and avoiding unpleasure are attained by refusing to do the work involved in differentiated thinking. The primary process tells us that it is not possible or necessary to distinguish between opposing elements, that we do not need to distinguish between past and present, between wanted and existing, between self and objects. This means that the wish fulfilment in the dream includes being freed from responsibility. This unconscious attitude is reflected in the expression that dreams are froth.[1]

The dream does not only serve infantile wishes. In dreams inspired 'from above' the dreamer can even experience the solution to scientific problems that evaded solution in waking life. Yet, the solutions of intellectual tasks disappear in the light of waking awareness, just as we are tricked into believing that our dreams fulfil primitive impulses.

Freud's description of the dream as a transitory, hallucinatory psychosis has been proved in a marvellous way by Charles Fisher (1965) in modern dream experiments. A 'normal' person who has been kept from dreaming enters a condition of psychotic confusion in waking life, which disappears when the dream deficit is overcome.

Dream-work thus has an exceptionally high value as spontaneous therapy. However, it is linked to a temporary disregard for the reality principle. Freud's study of other forms of spontaneous work showed that they too fulfil therapeutic functions. Psychoanalysis, in linking convalescence and psychic work, follows the example of spontaneous psychic life. Yet, because it replaces the primary process by the secondary process, it cannot relieve the patient of the arduous and unpleasurable mental work and is thus in direct opposition to the spontaneous therapy of dream-work.

Joke-work

When Freud (1905) turned his attention to jokes he also showed how productive the conceptual distinction between primary and secondary processes is. He traced several well-known but uncomprehended features of jokes back to the effect of the primary process. Joke-work also employs condensation and displacement, and overcomes repression. Yet, in contrast to dreams, which are primarily a narcissistic activity and require the distancing from real objects provided by sleep, jokes are told to such objects. Freud called jokes 'the most social of all the psychic activities aimed at providing pleasure'.

Three persons are involved: the joke teller, who does the joke-work, the person who is the butt of the joke, and the person to whom the joke is told. The listener becomes an ally of the joke teller against the victim; the pleasure that is his reward results from decreased repression. The joke teller himself cannot laugh and be rewarded for his work until the listener laughs, proving that he has accepted his role. The laughing links the experience of liberation with an exceptional degree of pleasure. The joke, it can be said, creates psychic luxury.

Joke-work thus is of very great value as spontaneous therapy. By focusing on the three participants we can recognize a similarity between the therapy of joke-work and that of the hypnotic-cathartic approach. The hypnotist, whose authority sanctioned the discharge of the affects toward the original object in the remembered scene, accepted the role of the patient's ally and was never confused with the remembered object, as we know from Freud. The sense of relief resulting from the listener's laughing also depends on the joke teller not confusing him with the butt of the joke. The therapeutic effect of the joke, just like that of the cathartic cure, is only transitory but can be easily repeated.

Another aspect of Freud's study of jokes is especially important for my present comments. Although Freud points out that the joke teller possesses a special ability – namely, that of making a joke – he seems unsure whether we should attribute to him a really creative talent because the joke is not really created by the teller but only enters his mind. With regard to the joke's therapeutic effect, this suggests a comparison with analytic therapy because in analysis, too, associations simply enter the patient's mind. In my opinion both situations contain a creative element. Both the joke and the free association originate in the depth of the ego and represent a sudden extension of the ego. The joke teller leaves it at that while analytic work pursues it further.

Creative work

Freud's comments on creative work ('Creative writers and day-dreaming' 1908e) are a nodal point of his research on sexuality, dreams, and jokes. He recognized the instinctual nature of day-dreams, their similarity to dreams with regard to wish fulfilment (the assumption that the two phenomena are similar is even expressed by ordinary language), and their dependence on objects.

The poet served as an example. Like other day-dreamers, the poet is also unsatisfied with reality and his real experiences with others, and thus turns away from them. He instead seeks refuge in phantasies that fulfil his wishes. For the same reason, his day-dreams have the same primitive narcissistic character of all day-dreams, so that they are not suited for communication. Freud points out that relating a day-dream is repulsive. Yet the poet, in contrast to ordinary day-dreamers, finds his way back to reality because he can utilize his private narcissistic phantasies in his creative work thanks to his special talent. It is the resulting aesthetic form that provides others with pleasure. Freud calls this pleasure 'fore-pleasure', but adds that it provides an access to pleasure at deeper psychic layers.

Thus the poet treats his phantasies as the raw material and starting point for a creative process that modifies the content of the original primitive narcissistic phantasies; at the same time it gives his phantasies an aesthetic form that appeals to deeper layers in others. That which is purely private is eliminated and replaced by something of general validity. When the poet therefore creates something out of his day-dreams that is beyond the creative capacity of the ordinary day-dreamer, then it is because he finds other contents in his ego. He is simply gifted. Content and form coincide and are interdependent. Thus some form of an acknowledgement of reality is a precondition for creative work. The reality referred to here is above all the law according to which only a specific form, sequence, and composition of the individual elements can provide an adequate expression for the artist's thoughts and visions (or the creative scientist's discoveries). The techniques of dream-work or day-dreaming serving wish fulfilment have no use or role in creative work because the latter combines what actually belongs together, separates what is different, and repeats or varies something according to its importance or richness when this increases both the meaning and aesthetic effect. The artist's talent impels him to do this work, and his subjective need to do this work coincides with the product's mediated nature.

In contrast to the authors who trace the roots of creative work back to object-related motives – for example, compensation for infantile attacks on the mother – in my opinion the primary motive of a creative person lies in his talent, which is independent of his object relationships. The creative person thus primarily pursues his narcissism. A consequence of this is, however, the view that narcissism should not merely be considered as the earliest form of erotic pleasure. As I have previously tried to show (1959, 1962b), narcissism should not only be considered the earliest position of the libido, but also an orientation towards lived experiences that, like all psychic phenomena, is subject to the developmental process. I believe we can distinguish three forms of narcissism. At the beginning there is primary, primitive narcissism, a component of the undifferentiated phase in which the child is only aware of itself and does not yet know that, for example, the feelings of pleasure it experiences as a result of its mother's care do not come from itself, as the child assumes. After recognizing the self–object antithesis (at first the self–mother antithesis), a form of narcissism appears that is antagonistic to objects and that results from frustrations in object relationships, frustrations both of libidinous and aggressive impulses and of ego interests. It is this secondary narcissism hostile to objects that manifests itself in other guises in dreams and day-dreams. In the creative process a form of narcissism is active that is compatible with complete acceptance of the reality principle. It can also be found in social life as the condition for the complete, reciprocal object relationship of a mature personality, in which the experience of gratification is so strongly based on the acknowledgement of the partner's individuality. In the framework of libido theory this fact was at first described as the attainment of full genitality.

A few ideas from the development of ego psychology support the assumption that there is a kind of narcissism whose goal is the fulfilment and objectification of the individual's innate talents. In artistic creativity there are also elements of the satisfaction of primitive impulses – for example, in the sensual, libidinous-aggressive treatment of the material being used as a means of expression. Elements of the form of narcissim hostile to objects also come into play when the drive to creative work conflicts with being considerate of others and is given priority over the latter.

It is unfortunate that the term 'narcissism' is so strongly linked with associations that bring to mind either psychic immaturity or defects in object relationships. It would be useful if we employed the appropriate qualifier when using this term.

These considerations lead to another definition of that dissatisfaction in reality which leads to day-dreaming – namely, the failure of a person to develop his innate ego capacities – which of course need by no means be as exceptional in nature as in 'creative' individuals.

Making the creative product public leads to additional satisfactions within object relationships that are of great importance; for example, in the social echo, in external success, and in a new basis for having experiences with others. The drive to objectify the creative potential, however, is primary and superior.

The therapeutic effect of creative work lies in the extension of the ego, in the channels and connections between deeper layers and the surface, and in the richness of the emotional and intellectual processes that it initiates. With regard to the last point, it could be said that the creative individual is occasionally psychotic; he experiences states of mania and depression and of paranoia, as well as extreme forms of love and hate towards himself, his objects, and what he must create. These processes are therapeutic inasmuch as they overcome repression and other techniques of denial, but this spontaneous therapy is largely limited to the creative activity and does not eliminate the person's neurosis or psychosis. The inter- and intra-structural conflicts are only partly or temporarily overcome. But it is possible to say that his illness could become more serious and a manifest collapse occur sooner if he could not accomplish this work.

Work of mourning

Before turning to the work of mourning, it is advisable to first remind ourselves of Freud's 'Formulations regarding the two principles in mental functioning' (1911b). This short, concise paper is both a survey and a programme that Freud carried out in his later research.

The cardinal point that prepares us for understanding the work of mourning concerns the connections between mental growth and the experience of a loss.

In the course of development the pleasure principle loses its primacy and thinking is made subordinate to the reality principle. This loss is exceptionally painful. Living according to the pleasure principle – narcissistic omnipotence – is made possible by maternal care, the source of satisfaction and security. In the language of later theories, to which I will return, this means that the feeling of well-being in infancy depends on the lack of psychic differentiation between infant and mother. The progress in development to thinking according to the reality principle – according to the method of the secondary process – means the loss of the undifferentiated state. The recognition of reality means acknowledging the fact that mother and self are not the same but rather two separate individuals. Thus the loss of narcissistic omnipotence is tied to the experience of differentiation, and differentiation is less an enrichment than a loss –

the separation from the mother's care and body, which the child had treated as its own – and thus the experience of helplessness and dependence. This is also the explanation for the connection between the effort caused by pain, which I have already mentioned, and that caused by differentiation, which is required by reality-oriented thinking. In the article mentioned above, Freud defined the individual mental acts as perception, attention, taking note, remembering, and judging. The unpleasure connected with the secondary process can find expression as a refusal to continue the process by interrupting the mental work at any arbitrary point and reverting to the primary process.

The work of mourning is the most conspicuous example of the pain connected with the work of remembering. Such pain had already been recognized in pre-analytic treatment, which replaced dream-work by hallucinations of gratification. Step by step the person in mourning remembers his lived experiences with the love object according to the dictate of reality that he has lost this object and that these experiences belong to the past. Remembering thus becomes a piecewise and continuous severance of the connections to the loved object and the experience of the tears and wounds within the self of the mourner. The pain of all previous losses is repeated in the work of mourning. Two early concepts of analysis, which have been significantly expanded and deepened by later theories, should be mentioned here: the trauma of birth and the depression of weaning. A healthy trait of narcissism sets a high value on staying alive and recovering, which are the reward for the work of mourning.

Successful mourning includes the process of working through, for each item that is remembered is part of a whole – that is, of an entire network of experiences that the ego integrates and that deepen and strengthen the ego. A therapy based on the processes of remembering and integrating thus reaches lasting modifications of the ego and personality in contrast to methods whose goal consists in cathartic discharge.

Two models of the psychic apparatus

Freud conducted his studies of these specific concepts of work in the period of time I have elsewhere called the period of his first model of the psychic apparatus. This period culminated in his *The Ego and the Id* (1923b). In this model the id is the oldest system, existing since birth, and the bearer of the genetic material. The ego, the psychic system to which the secondary process belongs, represents in

199

contrast only the surface of the id, and all of its functions are dependent on this position. It is simply a secondary structure – the id as modified by external influences – that is a servant plagued by three strict masters.

Fourteen years later Freud constructed his second model in 'Analysis terminable and interminable' (1937c), acknowledging the ego to be just as primary a formation as the id. The specific nature of the original state is not that the id is at first alone, but that the capacity to differentiate does not yet exist and the essence of development is the increasing capacity to differentiate. At the beginning of life ego and id are the undifferentiated ego/id and correspond to the lack of differentiation between infant and mother (Freud 1911b). Both the ego and the id possess inherited qualities. The character of the ego is thus not exclusively determined by identifications with objects ('pseudo-heredity') or by instinctual fate (reaction formations). The significance of both of these processes is put in a new light. Furthermore, the ego has a source of energy of its own.

Since in this publication Freud handles the reasons for the failures of analytic therapy, he primarily discusses pathological ego modifications, but we find the clear statement 'that the individual ego is endowed from the beginning with individual dispositions and tendencies'.

The productiveness of this new concept of the ego can hardly be overestimated. The entire subject of ego psychology, which had in fact played a role in Freud's earliest studies, took on new dimensions, as did psychoanalysis as a whole, of course. Analysis underwent an exceptional refining, as an instrument of both clinical and theoretical research. The undifferentiated phase of development, ego autonomy, autistic and symbiotic childhood psychoses, new concepts of trauma, the different consequences of internalization depending on whether it is based on active introjection of objects or on passively accepted incorporation, research on preventive measures, the role of family pathology in schizophrenia and indeed in all forms of psychic illness – these are a few of the fields made accessible by the improved understanding of the ego.

The literature is too rich for me to name the authors who have developed and extended the second model. I am indebted to many of them for the development of my own ideas.

Perhaps I am exaggerating the differences between the two models. Freud's work was directed towards ego psychology from the beginning, and he had defined psychic conflict as the clash between instinctual impulses on the one hand and ethical and aesthetic demands on the other, long before he described the structural system of the ego as separate from other psychic structures. His article on narcissism made ego psychology a major topic of analytic discussion. The idea of the original lack of differentiation also appeared as early as 1911, the same year in which Freud conducted his detailed examination of the problems of schizophrenia in the Schreber case. I nevertheless believe that the explicit description of the psychic apparatus in the study 'Analysis terminable and interminable' has the significance of a new psychic model. It is connected with a new classification of the instincts – namely, their classification as somatic instincts in the id and as the primary powers of the life and death instincts – which are not limited to a specific psychic structure. It is true that earlier concepts are used, but when earlier phenomena return at a higher stage of development, to quote the modern biologist Teilhard de Chardin (1959), they are not only something different but something new. In my opinion this principle applies not only to biological evolution, but also to the development of concepts.

The psychoanalytic situation: milieu and working team

Since the introduction of the psychoanalytic situation stood at the beginning of Freud's research, the question is sometimes raised whether it today still possesses its validity in view of the development that analysis has undergone. A number of analysts have in fact suggested technical modifications that seem to modify the original character of the analytic situation. Kurt Eissler (1953), who coined the expression 'parameter' of the psychoanalytic technique, examined the problem in detail and pointed out that Freud himself acknowledged the necessity of some deviations in technique. Freud did in fact reject the idea that the psychoanalytic technique could be standardized, and spoke of modifications appropriate to the individual analyst and the patient's illness.

(1) Milieu

It is worth while to take a close look at the psychoanalytic situation. We can recognize two components, one largely constant in character and the other highly variable. The constant component is the location, frequency, and the length of time patient and analyst are together, the analyst's uninterrupted presence, and his undivided attention. In this way the analytic situation takes on the character of a milieu for the patient that is relatively free of stimuli and that becomes customary and natural. The analytic work takes place within this milieu, which belongs to the patient without question or reservations.

The significance of the constant milieu to the patient is shown by his strong reactions to interruptions. To give just one example, after I had rearranged the room where I conduct analysis, one patient said, 'I admit that it is more comfortable, but you know that I hate *every* change.' He could have been a spokesman for all the patients with only one exception. This was a patient whose fundamental problems were expressed in his compulsive searching for something different and new. He was immediately enthusiastic, consciously for aesthetic reasons, unconsciously because the room ('I') was new and therefore good, at least at first.

On the other hand, the analytic situation has a character that is highly variable, inconstant, rich in stimuli, and dynamic. This character is based on the fundamental rule, consists in the verbal exchange of thoughts, and forms the working team made up of patient and analyst. If the patient is silent after relating his associations or reacts with silence to an interpretation, then this is an action and an event that must be examined and that ultimately must be put into words. Whatever the patient says or does not say has a *specific* meaning, one that is different in each instance. Occasionally his thoughts are about the milieu, but we do not expect him to have something to say about it every hour.

The growth in our knowledge has not lessened but increased the validity of the arrangement of the analytic situation. Today we have a much better understanding of the importance of the milieu, the working team, and the combination of both. The milieu repeats the original situation – an undifferentiated state with few stimuli – between infant and maternal care (as well as between id and ego) and allows the patient to re-experience the narcissistic illusion and consequently the original form of trust on which favourable development depends and that both the child and the patient (in the experience of transference) require to overcome the pain and anxiety that accompany growth and differentiation.

The last points, the experiences of the loss of naïve narcissism and of the unquestioned monopoly of possessing the mother, are repeated in the working team and are connected with the verbal intercourse between patient and analyst. In the working team the processes of individuation and of being different, which suffered in the patient's original development, take place and are corrected by analysis.

202

Each patient has moments or phases in which speaking itself represents an unbearable frustration – namely, the frustration of the wish for symbiotic unity. The articulated word then represents a painful acknowledgement of separation and distance and not the pleasurable acquisition of a new medium offering more varied opportunities for contact.

The insight that leads to alterations in the patient's ego is tied to the process of becoming conscious that is initiated by interpretation. Yet in judging the effect of the interpretation we should not underestimate the patient's interaction with the milieu. The constant features of the analytic situation are a source of positive transference, which is different in nature from the moments of acute libidinous intensity caused by specific interpretations. Milieu and oral contact supplement each other. By remaining aware of the dualistic nature of the analytic situation the analyst will protect himself and the patient from a dogmatic or magical exaggeration of each individual factor, of the milieu or of the interpretation.

(2) The working team

As in other kinds of working teams that pursue a common goal, the tasks and procedures of the members of the analytic team are not identical but supplement each other. The common final goal of patient and analyst often seems to disappear, and opposition replaces co-operation. Each partner has duties and rights. The patient experiences the painful side of the fundamental rule as well as the liberation from conventional considerations for others and the inherent permission to regress to narcissism and the primary process. The patient also has the privilege of beginning the session and to some extent of setting the topic. The analyst is not required to take the initiative, but this right often turns out to be a difficult task requiring much control. The patient distances himself from the analyst when he follows his own thoughts, but the analyst stays in a deep relationship with the patient while he waits and listens to the patient's associations. His evenly suspended attention is focused on the patient and helps him to perceive, note, and remember. At the same time, he has to be ready to forget, may not stay glued to any individual detail, and must drop interpretations that enter his mind if the patient's process has taken a turn to something else. He moves with the patient, following him actively and passively, so that his impressions converge to create an empathic understanding. In this way the analyst finally comes to be able to act; this act is the interpretation.

The problem of selecting the right time for an interpretation has been discussed frequently. We can say that the right time coincides with an urgent need on the part of the patient, although the patient often denies his signals that he is in need, for reasons that are fundamental in his illness and of current relevance to his ambivalence in the transference.

It is generally accepted that the 'mutative' interpretation (Strachey, 1934) is a transference interpretation: Freud made the point repeatedly without using this term. I have elsewhere suggested that the analyst finds the dynamic transference interpretation by asking himself a series of questions such as, 'Who is the patient and who is the analyst for the patient at this moment?' and 'What is he doing and why?' In other words, the analyst has to recognize his patient's affects and motivations and the specific transference experiences that they have triggered, and to repeat the patient's real and phantasized conflicts with his objects and with himself. The patient's words are the equivalents of actions and reactions. Dreams and waking experiences are not only repeated, they are also re-enacted in the analytic situation.

It is obvious that the analyst will not find every answer and that a complete interpretation of associations is therefore just as impossible as is that of a dream. Yet, by maintaining such an inquisitive attitude, the analyst experiences at some point in his empathic relationship to the patient that the multiplicity of impressions, messages, signals, or signs have taken on a definite meaning, enabling him to formulate a valid and necessary interpretation for the patient. (Fritz Schmidl [1955] speaks of such impressions taking on a definite *Gestalt*.) Students often ask in supervisory discussions what the ultimate meaning of an association is, and I can only reply that I am more modest than they are; I only want the meaning that is momentarily decisive in a specific situation.

Freud repeatedly modified his definition of interpretation in the course of his work. I would say that the interpretation is largely a tool for exploration. What the analyst offers his patient in an interpretation is the starting point for such exploration, and since this must start from perception, interpretation is concerned with perceiving the process that is momentarily of concern to the patient. It is not the analyst's task to give his patient the solution to his problems. At the same time, the interpretation must add something to what the patient already knows. In other words, an interpretation relates the verbalization of the problem to a statement that in part acts as an explanation, but that also contains a question and a request or stimulus for the patient's ego to go further – namely, to proceed from an advanced level thanks to the explanatory (better, clarifying) element of the interpretation. Without such an element the patient would only go around in a circle and feel tormented and rejected. However, too much explanation would 'solve' the problem without the patient having profited from his own constructive psychic work. His own creative ego capacities would simply have been passed over and turned off, and in reality the problem would not have been solved. From the perspective of the patient's anxiety, the interpretation must achieve a reduction in anxiety but leave enough to trigger a thought process. Too much anxiety paralyses the ego or keeps it chained to the accustomed defence mechanisms. The analyst aims at loosening the rigid connection between anxiety and defence in order to liberate the patient from the fixation which comprises the flight from psychic and external reality into phantasy. Helping the patient to transform his thinking according to the primary process into thinking according to the secondary process means helping him stop exhausting his potentially constructive and creative ego functions in his defence functions. This process offers additional pleasure: in addition to the general experience of psychic liberation and growth there is the specific functional pleasure that goes with the performance of specific ego activities. These forms of gratification should replace the previously dominant tendency to hold on to narcissistic omnipotence, which condemns the patient to helplessness and denies him the creative use of both rational thought and phantasy.

I have one more comment regarding the analyst's contribution to the working team in analysis. What is the optimal distance between his understanding and the patient's? It is obviously necessary for the analyst to understand more than the patient, otherwise he could not add anything to the patient's knowledge. Yet knowing too much can tempt the analyst to interpret more than the patient can accept as a helpful stimulus. An interpretation that is 'too clever' can destroy the working team.

Translated by Michael Wilson, Ph.D., Heidelberg, West Germany

Notes

1 [In the German original: 'Traeume sind Schaeume'.]

15

Evolutionary leaps and the origin of cruelty (1964/9a)

This paper is an enlarged version of a contribution made to a symposium on 'Aggression and Adaptation' at the Sigmund Freud Institut, Frankfurt am Main, West Germany, in 1964. It was published in German in A. Mitscherlich (ed.) *Bis hierher und nicht weiter. Ist die menschliche Aggression unbefriedbar?* Munich: Piper, 1969a, and has been translated for this book.

I

I would like to discuss the questions of how the experience of the psychoanalyst is similar to that of the ethologist, and how they differ. These questions raise for me, however, a number of problems and difficulties that stem from the different nature of the objects studied by these sciences. I would like to point out this restriction at the beginning of my paper.

I have reservations about what those who study animals and those who study man have in common. I find it striking, even stunning, how frequently animal watchers use concepts from human psychology to interpret and describe animal behaviour. They speak of love, hate, anger, courage, fear, triumph, and so on, and in this way lead us to view animals in human terms (as one of Lorenz's colleagues once said in the fire of a heated discussion, 'But geese are also only human'). Yet, viewing animals in this way is beset by dangers, especially that of anthropomorphism, as Konrad Lorenz himself has observed. He gives an illustrative example of a misinterpretation that he made. Although he made the necessary corrections in his study, the person who reads his descriptions without having participated in the study itself can still mistake analogies for identities.

II

The title of the German edition of Konrad Lorenz's book (1963) has two parts: *Zur Naturgeschichte der Aggression* (literally, 'the natural history of aggression') and *Das sogenannte Böse* ('the so-called or purported evil'). We have learned from Freud that a sequence of two thoughts implies a third. Thus, these two titles imply that the knowledge of ethology which Lorenz wants to convey leads us to the realization that *aggression is not the real evil*.

Lorenz does not disappoint us. Referring to numerous careful studies, which he describes in a fascinatingly beautiful way, he shows that animal aggression fulfils elementary, life-maintaining functions. Of special interest is the aggression directed against animals of the same species. It promotes the preservation of the species, preconditions of which are territoriality, food, mating, and caring for the young, and is limited by instincts. Thus, the animal that is attacked is not seriously injured, let alone killed.

In the course of evolution new instincts, or motivations functioning like instincts, such as ritualization, have appeared that work further to reduce aggression. Their strength can be seen in the fact that they, although more recent, can override the 'big' instincts.

This course of evolution, as discovered in animals, is the foundation on which Lorenz bases his hopes with regard to man. He points out that our language acknowledges that aggression is not the real evil in that aggression stems from 'aggredi', and going towards someone else must not necessarily be based on evil motives. You also have to go towards someone to be nice to him. Love at a distance is usually less good.

Lorenz describes the 'principle of the destruction of life' as the real evil. I agree, but I prefer to define this principle as cruelty, as finding pleasure in inflicting destruction, agony, and suffering. Animal aggression, which does not follow this principle, then differs in nature from cruelty.

We also learn from Lorenz's book, however, that there are exceptions and peculiarities in the animal kingdom, some of which seem to prefigure perversions that we know from man. They include killing an animal from the same species. The male aquarium fish, for example, kills its mate if no rival is available. This fact is often explained by the claim that aggression builds up in a creature in an unnatural environment, resulting in a malfunction of aggression. Here, as an analyst, I see a difficulty. Accumulated aggression seems like something borrowed from psychoanalysis. Isn't it identical with the notion of 'strangulated affect'? And with regard to malfunction, I think of the parapraxes, which Freud disclosed to be the successful performance of definitive (unconscious) intentions. Even more problematic for the thesis that animal aggression serves the perservation of the species is the behaviour of the praying mantis, the females of which consume their partners during intercourse. This occurs in their natural environment and thus cannot be considered a malfunction as in the example of the aquarium fish. I assume that the natural and given reservoir of instincts in these animals includes extreme sadism in the case of the females and extreme masochism in that of the males; that is, murder and suicide. I am not an ethologist and can only guess and question.

In connection with the origin of new instinctual motivations in the process of evolution, the question arises whether a new form of aggression may not have been formed as well, in which restrictive tendencies were not only not strengthened but, on the contrary, were weakened or even suspended. This new form of aggression or the change in the object and function of animal aggression would be cruelty, whose goal is not physiological self-preservation (as aggression against a predator from another species) or species preservation (as aggression against animals from the same species), but gaining pleasure in inflicting agony or destruction *per se*.

What appears to be only an exception to the rule in animals may have become in the course of man's evolution a regular part of his instinctual constitution, and for man we would then have to distinguish two types of aggression, one that he has inherited from his animal ancestors and another one (namely, cruelty) that is lacking in animals according to Lorenz. Even without the microscope of psychoanalysis it is impossible to overlook cruelty in man's psychology. Our memories of the concept of *Lebensraum* as applied to man, with which the floodgates to unlimited and calculated cruelty were opened, are still fresh. What a perversion of an animal's territorial instinct, which never involves serious injury or killing! We could contrast ritualization in animal evolution, which represents progress in limiting aggression, to human rationalization and projection, which sanction unbridled cruelty. One element of man's psychic repertoire is that he invents noble goals with whose help he hides and carries out his pleasure in destruction.

III

The concept of adaptation is the opposite of that of satisfaction and refers to the psychic act initiated by an experience of frustration. The frustration may have either internal or external causes, usually a combination of the two, and results in unpleasure. Adaptation also presupposes the loss of an original source of satisfaction, so that the act of adaptation must create a substitute, an alternative gratification. It is successful if the substitute gratification is subjectively satisfying, does not injure the individual in any objective way (neither directly nor indirectly by damaging its objects), and does not block the path to the original source of satisfaction should it be better than the substitute. In the most favourable case the act of adaptation also promotes the individual's ego by helping him/her experience independence, initiative, ingenuity, and so on.

I would like to describe two examples of adaptation, one taken from the observation of an infant, the other from psychoanalytic experience.

A ten-day-old baby woke up crying. It continued crying and started kicking and waving its arms when a nurse picked it up. The way it moved its head with its mouth open had a searching quality. Its body was tense and agitated. At one point its thumb happened to go into its mouth. Then the child became quiet, kept its thumb in its mouth – and began to suck. The baby's body relaxed, its features softened, the unpleasurable excitement disappeared, and it looked satisfied and concentrated on its calm and rhythmic sucking. When its mother put it to her breast – only a few minutes having elapsed since the baby had woken – it let its thumb go, accepted her breast easily and immediately, sucked as before, and swallowed with increasing satisfaction. After it had drunk enough, it fell asleep.

A grown-up man returned to analysis after his vacation. Separation anxiety played a prominent role among his problems, and each interruption of his analysis was a severe frustration for him. After such interruptions he usually displayed anger at the analyst and an especially greedy desire for analysis. This time, however, his rejection was exceptionally strong and he announced his decision to terminate his analysis. He said that he did not need it, it had never helped anyway, and he could spend his money and time in better ways. He had felt better without analysis while on vacation.

After a few hours he became more accessible. He spoke spontaneously of how helpful analysis had been, especially emphasizing his liberation from epilepsy-like attacks. He said he should be thankful for that, and that he in fact was. But he continued to insist on terminating the analysis. At this point he finally mentioned the reason: during his vacation he had succumbed to his old symptom, perversion with prostitutes.

Both the young child and the adult experienced the unpleasure of frustration. The child, woken by its hunger, did not find any food, and the patient was without his analysis. Each looked for and found substitute gratifications. The child's was successful; as described above, its unpleasurable excitement disappeared when it began to suck its thumb. When it later felt contact with the breast, it did not hesitate to exchange its thumb for the nipple and added the activity of swallowing milk to that of sucking. Nourished and satisfied, it went back to sleep, as it had done before its need for nourishment had interrupted it. During the phase of acute unpleasure, during the search for satisfaction, it discovered pleasurable sensations from the contact between thumb and mouth, which it maintained and increased by actively sucking.

Observations of this kind agree with the theories of infantile psychic processes gained from analytic work. At the beginning of psychic life the pleasure-unpleasure principle predominates in the framework of primary narcissism, which is maintained on the one hand by hallucinatory wish fulfilment and on the other by maternal care. The motor activities (screaming, kicking), together with negative hallucinations, serve the discharge of unpleasure, while positive hallucinations are tied to the auto-erotic sucking. The gratification from sucking can thus drown out the unpleasure of being hungry and feign a feeling of being satisfied. We speak of hallucinatory gratification from the auto-erotic sucking because the child does experience a 'real' gratification even though its hunger is not really satisfied. The instinct to suck appears as an alternative to the nutritional instinct.

Yet the word 'alternative' is not quite correct. It is better to view it as a companion of the nutritional instinct or as an instinct associated with it. The infant's activity in quieting its hunger consists of two components, sucking at the source of nutrition and swallowing the milk. Thumb sucking uses one of these components and thus moves in the same direction as sucking on the nipple. This factor surely plays a role in the child's readiness to go from auto-erotic sucking to sucking at the breast. Freud said that the libido attaches itself to the major physiological needs. We would like to add a counterpart; namely, that the physiological needs attach themselves to the libido.

The infant in this example discovered, invented, and produced a substitute gratification similar in nature to the original gratification. Its awakening ego functions of remembering and perceiving led it to prefer the sensations from the nipple to those from its thumb, without recognizing that the former is an object separate from itself. Because both thumb and nipple provide pleasure and thus belong to

210

its narcissistic self, there is no transition from the one to the other – hence the smooth exchange without any hesitation.

The adult's adaptation was frustrated by denial. His substitute gratification was, in contrast to the child's, a failure in every respect. Subjectively, it was not gratifying and served as a source of intense conflicts. It was inappropriate for his stage of development and did not promote his ego. It was different in nature from the original experience of gratification and blocked a return to the latter when this became available again.

What the patient himself said, after his initial complete rejection of analysis had passed, concerned the phenomena of regression in his behaviour. At a conscious level, his conflicts and feelings of shame and guilt revolved around the fact that he had played infantile sexual games. What became clearly evident, however, in the course of his analysis, especially of his dreams, was that he did not view his perversions as sexual at all, but as cruel. In his phantasies he tormented his objects, his wife, his parents, his analyst, and it was his thoughts about how he made his objects suffer and how he destroyed them that gave him pleasure and that he carried out in his perversions. His feelings of being hurt and taking revenge for the cruelty he felt he had inflicted on himself played a role, of course, in the complicated network of his phantasies. I will be brief, because we are not concerned with this patient's case history, and presumably all analysts are familiar with cases of this kind. My reference to his epilepsy-like attacks, which he had overcome in the course of analysis, made it clear to the patient that he had severe problems with his destructive impulses. The situation I have described was in fact not the first in which these problems appeared in the analysis. The despair he felt because of his cruelty was the reason for his decision to terminate the analysis, and in his despair his cruelty was directed primarily against himself. The reason why his ego was ready to subordinate itself at this point to his cruel superego are beyond the present discussion. What I am trying to illustrate is the role that the cruel impulses played in his failure to adapt.

The objection might be raised that my examples of a successful and an unsuccessful adaptation are not comparable. The one case is of a very young child with primitive psychic processes, while the other is of an adult whose highly complicated psychic organization is subject to serious inter- and intra-structural conflicts. The child was healthy, the adult ill. Yet for my purposes precisely these factors are essential. I have compared the behaviour of a ten-day-old child with that of a forty-year-old man in order to emphasize that even the process of ontogenetic development over a period of forty years creates tremendous differences. How much larger must be the differences over the periods separating the species!

IV

Pierre Teilhard de Chardin conceptualized in an extremely profound way the scientific discovery that evolution produces something entirely new, and this discovery received the express endorsement of Julian Huxley. Chardin acknowledged that man's psychological processes have an independent point of their own within biological activity. According to him, the step (or jump) to mankind signified a new world determined by a new kind of consciousness. This new consciousness is reflection, the knowledge that we know, the turning inward of consciousness. Animals also have consciousness; and it is not the invention of tools that distinguishes man from the animals, even those most similar to man (the Hominidae), but self-reflection. Yet this is more than a simple difference. 'Because we are reflective, we are not only different but quite other. It is not merely a matter of change of degree but a change of nature' (1959). Chardin derives the activities of the human spirit from this transformation: 'Abstraction, logic, reasoned choice and inventions, mathematics, art, calculation of space and time, anxieties, and dreams of love' (1959).

His thoughts are so similar to those of psychoanalysis that it would be possible at many points to insert Freud's descriptions of psychic development and especially of the ego and superego. What Chardin describes as 'inner life' is very similar to Freud's concept of 'psychic reality', even though Chardin does not consider the dimension of unconscious processes or the fact that man *inevitably* reaches the borders of the unconscious in his self-reflection and thus knows that he does not know everything that goes on in him.

Psychoanalytic experience is in full agreement with Chardin's express reference that the course of evolution not only creates differences of degree but also at some point a difference in quality, for which a new kind of consciousness and thought is decisive. The principle of genetic continuity should not be exaggerated and reduced to absurdity. The child undergoes a change and experiences itself and the world in a different way when it goes from the phase of undifferentiation to that of knowledge of the duality of self and its mother, or advances from the two-person world to the Oedipus complex. Or think of the progress from sign language to articulated language, consisting of words and sentences. The child does not simply increase its repertoire of signs in order to signal its primitive needs; it acquires a different kind of thinking, the secondary process, and thus the need to exchange thoughts with its objects and the need for help, and stimulus for conceptual, abstract thought. The child acquires, with the language of the secondary process, the means to express, share, and communicate this new kind of desire. In the same way, acquiring the ability to move on its own is not an extension of kicking, but leads to previously unexperienced discoveries and reflections about itself and its objects. This is truly a new world both internally and externally, not just tools improved in some way, but something different. I hope these examples are sufficient.

In the analytic situation we see development in the sense both of differences of degree and of differences in kind, of turning points to something completely new. When a patient establishes contact with his unconscious and insight into his inner self, he feels a new world developing that fundamentally changes his external world and his relationship to others. He and his objects change. One patient used the following words in reflecting on his analytic experience: 'I am no longer the person I used to be.' He described a fact and not just a wish. New conflicts arise at such turning points, requiring new adaptation. Erikson coined the phrase 'normative crisis' to describe adolescence. I believe that this concept applies to all the steps in a child's development that are not just a difference in degree but which are a sign of a fundamental difference.

I have referred to the ethologist's view that the human species began when consciousness turned inward because this aspect – particularly its reference to a specifically human biopsychological factor – appears more rewarding for our subject than the study of animal behaviour. Reflective consciousness is just *one* such factor, however, and is related in numerous and complex ways to other factors whose significance and modes of action were made accessible by Freud's studies. I am referring to the uniquely protracted length of a child's dependence on its parents, the Oedipus complex, and the internalization of object relationships leading to the identification of subject and object and to the formation of psychic structures.

The child's dependence differs in kind from that in animal breeding because it develops the passionate impulses of an adult although lacking the internal and external possibilities of gratification. In the Oedipus complex the child experiences the powerful and ambivalent conflict of incest impulses to each of its parents – namely, sexual desire and the murderous hate of a rival – and thus experiences that its feelings are confused in a manner lacking a phylogenetic predecessor. In the rekindling of the Oedipus complex in adolescence, physical sexual maturity coexists with psychic immaturity. It may well be that animals do not experience a desire to be cruel because incest is not a problem for them and their rivalry does not extend to their most important and most deeply loved objects.

Conscious and, especially, unconscious phantasies provide fulfilment denied by external reality, and these are definitely not merely dreams of love. Due to identification and the formation of superego and ego ideal structures, dreams of cruelty and of the destruction of objects lead the individual to experience cruel attacks on his self and to the vicious circle of anxiety, horror, shame, guilt, and further cruel impulses towards objects. The fact that phantasies are psychically real often leads to a confusion between outer and inner reality, to delusional misinterpretations of the behaviour of real objects, and to destructive actions.

What I am trying to show is that the problems of human adaptation are not limited, because of man's highly complicated psychic structure, to the kind of aggression that objectively serves the preservation of the species, but rather that cruelty constitutes a problem of adaptation that is specifically human.

V

Lorenz's short discussion of Freud's theory of the death instinct is without consequence for the thesis he proposes in his book; namely, that aggression is not the real evil. I have referred to it, however, in order to reconsider this theory.

Freud's hypothesis that the origin of life signified the creation of two opposing dynamic processes is a grand, integrating idea that provides a complete classification of the phenomena of human conflict as part of the universe. His analogy between the origin of life and that of consciousness has been given additional meaning by Chardin's research.

Let us recall Freud's description:

> The attributes of life were at some time evoked in inanimate matter by the action of a force of whose nature we can form no conception. It may perhaps have been a process similar in type to that which later caused the development of consciousness in a particular stratum of living matter.
>
> (Freud 1920g, SE 18: 38)

Many psychoanalysts as well as other scientists reject Freud's hypothesis. Those studying nature, including ethology, have not been able to find any evidence of the origin of a life instinct and of a death instinct. Furthermore, they trace the phenomenon of death back to coincidence (a weaker animal accidentally enters the territory of a stronger one) and to the wear-and-tear principle (the organs vital to the preservation of life gradually wear out). Freud himself never considered his theory an integral part of psychoanalysis, and later modified it by introducing the concept of the primary powers of life and death and distinguished them from the somatic instincts.

Viewed historically, his original version of this theory, positing the antithesis of life and death instincts as the ultimate source of human conflict, was an advance. It corrected his earlier and inconsistent opinion that cruelty is a component of the libido. Finding pleasure in torment and destruction differs in kind from the pleasure in loving. The earlier mixture of concepts was replaced by the clear conception of a mixture of opposing instincts: cruelty was derived from the death instinct, love from the life instinct. Although these instincts are opposed to each other with regard to origin and goals, they operate by means of fusion.

As far as my view is concerned, I was an enthusiastic supporter of this theory for a long time and believed that phenomena as adverse to life as cruelty, the desire to kill, and suicide required an explanation as final and universal as that provided by Freud's theory. I also tried to substantiate this view (1952c). After re-reading this article, I find it necessary to criticize a number of points.

My present point of view does not require a reference to life and death instincts to explain destructive impulses or libido, whose existence is beyond doubt. On the contrary, it seems to me that searching for the ultimate causes of a clinical phenomenon exposes us to the danger of overlooking its real dynamic.

Freud's cosmological hypothesis has not been refuted simply because ethologists have found no confirmation for it. It is important for psychoanalysts to extract the psychological essence of it that can be verified in our work. This does not mean that it should only be viewed as a metaphor.

The psychoanalytic theories that are closer to our work and have proved their fruitfulness for many problems are concerned with the period preceding consciousness, with the earliest somatopsychic processes. I am referring to Freud's theories of primary narcissism and of the initial lack of differentiation between ego and id, and to their far-reaching extension in Hartmann's view that the undifferentiated phase constitutes the basis of psychic development.

Viewed objectively, the child experiences the primary powers of life or death through its mother (or her representative), depending on the care or lack of care, attention or neglect, love or hate she shows it. Viewed subjectively, however, at the beginning of extra-uterine existence there is only the self, and psychic experience (whose beginning can hardly be equated with the actual birth) is initially bound to somatic sensations. In the phase of narcissistic omnipotence, pleasurable sensations are attributed to the self, and unpleasurable ones are hallucinated away. Yet even in the positive case, as can be seen in the example of the ten–day–old infant, there are moments in which the unpleasure is experienced within the self. If the unpleasure stemming from unsatisfied needs is repeated periodically and in an unfavourable environment, it exceeds the effectiveness of the defensive hallucinations and thus of narcissistic omnipotence. The traumatized child must, in my opinion, experience sensations approaching those of death.

Early somatopsychic (and later, psychosomatic) sensations of this kind of the inner powers of life and death leave behind traces that are activated in the course of life. In situations of extreme well-being we speak of a feeling of new life and of being born again, and in situations of anxiety of being near death, of dying, and so forth.

Due to man's specifically human capacities of reflection and self-reflection and to the 'psychic reality' of his phantasies, he experiences mortal agony without being objectively exposed to a mortal danger in such moments. This is by no means merely abstract thinking about the phenomena of living and dying. In analysis, it is possible to recognize a series of meanings behind conscious mortal agony, such as anxiety about the loss of a love object or an object of love, about becoming impotent, about being maimed, castrated, and so on. Every phase of development contributes, as we know, its own specific feature to the substance of mortal agony. Cruel impulses awaken anxiety, anxiety awakens cruel impulses.

In subjective experience the destructive impulse and the powerful motivation to inflict cruelty on the self and on objects appear in connection with the idea of death, fear of dying, and desire to die. We can see the overpowering intensity of these phenomena when there is a maximal disturbance of adaptation – for example, in psychotic depression – and in analysis we find the above-mentioned phantasies and much more. The wish to die is above all an expression of the longing for an unbearable suffering to stop, for peace and quiet, and appears as the phantasy of returning to the womb and of being reborn in a blissful existence. We find cruelty to objects, which goes back to cruelty to the mother as the first hated love-object, and phantasies of revenge, which are linked with the magic belief that everything will be fine after their fulfilment. The danger of suicide is real, and the patient is really as helpless as the infant and needs the equivalent of maternal care in the full sense of the word, only that it is more difficult to give it to him because his behaviour is that of an adult.

He has regressed to the pathological variant of the undifferentiated phase, and thus none of his ideas possesses the quality of their individual identity, neither his idea of his self, nor that of his objects, nor even that of his actions. The process of regression has led to a loss of conceptual differentiation.

I have referred to familiar observations in which we can hardly resist the impression that man is driven to death by inner bio-psychological processes. I have also attempted to show that psycho-analytic theories offer us some understanding of these processes and are thus a precondition for therapy. In doing so, I omitted the other familiar fact, that the analysis of such patients uncovers material pointing to severe disturbances in early maternal care; that is, to a substantial psychopathology on the part of the mother and/or of the mother–father relationship, or to physical illness of the mother or child. This material points, in other words, to an early disturbance of the relationship between infant and mother that was not corrected in the further course of the patient's development. Common to all these disturbances is the influence they exert on the roots of the ego and all of those ego functions that ultimately lead to the creation of individual ego identity. We confront problems that are accessible to research with psychological means, independent of the theory of life and death instincts.

Freud himself gave us the concepts – extended by a number of analysts – of the undifferentiated ego/id and of a naïve narcissism that is in a recriprocal relationship to maternal care. They make the process of differentiation and of the formation of ego and object identity, which repeatedly confront the individual with tasks of adaptation, accessible to psychoanalytic research. The transformation of anxiety about the loss of love or a love-object into finding pleasure in cruelty is of great significance to this problem. The patient is dominated by the death wish when there is a maximal disturbance of adaptation; for example, in psychotic depressions. In analysis we find the unconscious phantasies, and they strive for things other than death, such as cruelty to the hated love-object that takes the guise of revenge and that is tied to the magical belief that everything will be good after the phantasies have been fulfilled; also suicide because of guilt that is both cruelty directed inward and murder of the object, or the desire to return to the mother's womb, to be reborn, and so forth. This results from a far-reaching loss of differentiation in which neither the self, nor the object, nor even any idea has its own individual identity. We see the return of the original infantile lack of differentiation in the pathological form it assumes in regression.

Translated by Michael Wilson, Ph.D., Heidelberg, West Germany

16

Comment on Dr Kernberg's paper on 'Structural derivatives of object relationships' (1965/6b)

This paper is a modified version of discussion remarks made in response to the paper 'Structural derivatives of object relationships' by Otto Kernberg, read at the 24th International Psycho-Analytical Congress, Amsterdam, 1965. Both the paper and Paula Heimann's 'Comment' were published in the *International Journal of Psycho-Analysis* 47 (2/3) (1966).

In his present paper Kernberg, when talking about an 'id-derived oral metabolic principle' (p. 240), expresses agreement with myself. Continuing my discussion with him I shall first repeat the substance of my comments on his original paper and then discuss his view that splitting is a mechanism characteristic for early infantile life.

Structural models

I traced the source of the differences between Kernberg's and my views on early defences to the structural models underlying our theoretical approaches, and pointed out that the first of the two models of psychic structure which Freud (1923b, 1937c) presented can be described, without too gross simplification, as being based on the *oral metabolic principle*. According to this model, the id exists from the beginning and the ego is only secondarily derived from the id and is its surface that becomes modified through the intake of the external stimuli and their effects. Intake of the useful and output of the useless, introjection and projection, appear as the architects of structure. When barring the entry of dangerous stimuli, a sample introjection takes place first to allow testing their nature. Only the id is the carrier of inheritance and the reservoir of energy. The forces of the ego are borrowed from the id, its character is determined by

218

identifications and represents a precipitate of abandoned object cathexes. At the Oedipus complex, the height of infantile sexual development, the third structure, the superego, becomes established; again introjection (of some aspects of the parents) and projection (of others) are the instruments which form this 'grade in the ego', repeating thus the pattern of the formation of the ego from the id.

Although from the very beginning of his work Freud was concerned with ego psychology – namely, his first definition of conflict as the clash between the instinctual impulses on the one hand and the aesthetic and ethical standards on the other, and although he had devoted a paper to narcissism – in this first model the ego is only a secondary formation. One might say the interest in the problems of his preceding two great works, the two classes of drives and identification, stole the limelight from the ego as an original and dynamic entity.

Freud's second model appears in 'Analysis terminable and interminable'. Freud there stated explicitly that his views concerning the ego had been misunderstood, and corrected the notion of its weakness *vis-à-vis* the id by describing both as primary entities which at first exist as undifferentiated ego/id. The ego too is the carrier of inheritance and thus has its own innate characteristics as distinct from those which it acquires from the vicissitudes of the drives and from its objects (identification, 'pseudo-heredity'). It also has its own source of energy, which Hartmann has designated as 'primary ego energy'.

As regards the drives, there is a new classification, which distinguishes the somatic drives, localized in the id, from the 'primal forces of life and death', which are not confined to any 'mental province', and, one might add, not confined to human psychology. This second model is *not* of an id-derived oral-metabolic order. It complements and enriches the first model by new dimensions and puts ego psychology emphatically on the map. Research based on this model has produced new concepts for the understanding of psychological and psychopathological development. In the present context it will suffice to mention the undifferentiated phase, a concept complementary to that of primary narcissism, and ego autonomy, since they are key concepts for primitivity and maturity.

Melanie Klein, whose theories on early development Kernberg accepts, albeit with some reservations, never proceeded to Freud's second structural model and accentuated the oral-metabolic principle of the first model by placing all decisive developmental processes in the reign of oral primacy. Finally she produced her own original system, according to which the three structures are active from the beginning and Freud's somatic drives are replaced by inborn envy and gratitude which are also operative from birth and probably during the late pre-natal phase.

Early infantile defences

Although in his present paper Kernberg does not describe splitting as the earliest defence mechanism, but allocates it to the third or fourth month of life (p. 245), I believe that we still differ in respect of the defensive processes during the undifferentiated phase. I opposed the concept of splitting by that of shift of cathexis, and illustrated my view by an observation concerning a ten-day-old infant, exemplifying '*Unlust*' and its resolution. It may also be regarded as an example of adaptation to frustration. I am using the wide term '*Unlust*', which is unfortunately not rendered fully by 'unpleasure', 'discomfort', or 'pain', in order not to prejudge the question of differentiated emotional contents in the condition of *Unlust* at this early age.

The infant woke screaming, and was picked up, held, caressed, and talked to soothingly by a person sharing in his care. He continued to scream, moved his head with the mouth open, and kicked violently with arms and legs. His body felt tense and agitated. At one point his movements resulted in the meeting of thumb and mouth. The thumb was now held in the mouth (the first time that this was observed), and the infant began to suck his thumb. His body became relaxed, his facial features tranquil, and his arm and mouth movements ceased. He sucked with absorption, quietly, regularly, and contentedly. Meanwhile his mother was ready to feed him and put him to her breast. The infant let go his thumb and took the nipple easily and immediately, and sucked and swallowed with the same rhythmical movements and satisfaction. From the moment of waking to the moment of sucking at the breast a few minutes had passed.

When evaluating this incident, inferences and hypotheses related to theories formed on the basis of psychoanalytic work inevitably play a part, and some interpretations of the infant's behaviour keep more closely to the details actually seen than others. However, in every perception and description of the perceived, experiences from other sources are used; hence different observers will arrive at different interpretations of the data which they see.

I shall attempt to state explicitly when I use theories which may be regarded as going beyond the range of the actual observation. I would distinguish three phases.

First phase: This started with the interruption of sleep. The infant appeared to be in a condition of intense *Unlust*, and to give expression to this by violent movements and screaming. My interpretation is that hunger terminated his narcissistic well-being in the sleeping state, and that his muscular movements including screaming represented the use of the defence mechanism of discharge. The assumption that it was hunger that woke the infant seems sufficiently justified by the fact that he consumed a full meal, after which he fell asleep again. I did not have the impression that he intended to give a signal to his mother, nor that he was seeking the breast when he moved his head with the open mouth. He did give the impression that he was wanting, seeking something for his mouth, but this does not necessarily mean that his need for food was associated with an image of the nipple or a notion of an object. In any case it is impossible to scream without opening the mouth.

Second phase: This began with the chance meeting of thumb and mouth. Following this the infant actively discovered, and went on to reproduce, a pleasurable sensation, which obviously soothed him. It now appeared that his whole being was absorbed in his rhythmical and calm sucking movements. When we ask what happened to his unpleasurable hunger sensation my answer is that the attempt to expel it was accompanied by negative hallucination, while the pleasurable thumb-sucking activity was associated with positive hallucination. There could be no doubt that well-being superseded the former turmoil. Thus there was a shift of total cathexis from the locus of dis-pleasure to the locus of pleasure. To my thinking, the infant's behaviour was in keeping with the theory of primary narcissism and narcissistic omnipotence, in which pleasurable sensations are of overriding power and the mouth–thumb contact as well as the rhythmical sucking movements yielded sufficient pleasure to maintain the positive hallucination of need satisfaction in libidinal gratification. As Freud put it, in primitive psychic life, what is desired is there and 'me', what is painful is not-there and 'not-me'. As regards the latter, we may consider that vigorous discharge movements yield sensations of power. Even in adult life, we work something 'out of our system' by vigorous muscular or locomotor activities. At the infant's age the range of the budding ego functions of perception and memory and discernment is limited. Once pleasure from an activity was experienced, this consumed all exertion of his psychic apparatus. In the first phase all of the infant's being was painful upset, now all was contentment in activity. There was no 'splitting' himself in different parts at either stage.

Third phase: Sucking at the mother's breast and swallowing, until satiation was reached and sleep ensued. The observation that the transition from thumb to nipple occurred so smoothly and without hesitation, and that swallowing was added so easily to rhythmical sucking suggests that the infant had no experience of otherness, did not differentiate between himself and the breast, between his saliva and the milk, or between auto-erotic gratification and need satiation. What he experienced was satisfaction. What was achieved before by means of a narcissistic hallucination was now achieved by objective, real need fulfilment and libidinal pleasure, which within the narcissistic organization of psychic experiences confirms narcissistic omnipotence (Freud 1911b). We might say that at the point of real gratification the former narcissistic hallucination is superseded by a narcissistic illusion; gratification and satiation are real, the source of need fulfilment is an object, but in psychic evaluation attributed to the self. In the exchange of thumb for nipple there was no hesitation, no difficulty of transition from one to the other. The preference for the nipple suggests the operation of memory of past feeding satisfactions, but it would mean attributing advanced modes of ego functions to their incipient mode if we equated this preference with the recognition of the nipple as an object. I would refer here to the familiar observation that even at later stages, for example, the toddler stage, the child uses his loved and trusted objects as extensions of himself and treats their organs as his own tools.

Internalization

Kernberg's paper is devoted to the exploration of the development and sequelae of the process of internalization. I shall take up only a few points. Despite the thoroughness of his deliberations, I find some lack of clarity concerning his concept of the internalization of object relationships. Object relationship involves, as he says, drive derivatives, affects, emotions, wishes, fears, images, phantasies, and so on. But all these psychic phenomena cannot be said to be 'internalized' since as part of the psyche they are internal by their very nature from the outset. In my view, Kernberg sometimes uses the expression 'internalization of object relationships' when he seems to refer to the organization of the complex elements constituting object relationships, sometimes when he seems to define the establishing of object constancy and its effects, and sometimes when he is concerned with a person's conscious or unconscious phantasies that there are objects residing within his mind or body.

It will suffice to quote from many passages the following:

222

'Introjections, identifications, and ego identity are three levels of the process of internalization of object relationships in the psychic apparatus' (p. 239).

Here, to my thinking, the organization of experiences with objects is meant, taking place after the establishment of object constancy.

In the following passage the description of the formation of object constancy seems to overlap with that of subjective phantasies concerning the existence of objects within the self: 'Thus, introjections taking place under the *positive valence* of libidinal instinctual gratification, as in loving mother–child contact, tend to fuse and become organized in what has been called loosely, but pregnantly, "the good internal object"' (p. 241).

As regards Kernberg's comment on the aptness of the term 'the good internal object' and, I would add, also the 'bad internal object', this touches on the problem of the language of interpretations, which he also discusses, when he deals with splitting versus repression, isolation, denial, and so on. It is indeed a most important problem, to which I shall return later.

And this point I wish to make a few remarks about the so-called internal good and bad objects. The introjection of good objects takes place as part of a pleasurable experience with an object, as Kernberg points out. Now, a pleasurable experience, in contrast to a painful one, has no impelling quality, as Freud has shown, and does not set a task to the ego. Therefore, in my view, introjections with 'positive valence' are assimilated by the infantile ego, stimulate and further the innate autonomous ego functions and creative ego capacities, and are in subjective experience equated with them. These introjections do not give rise to thoughts concerning the self/object antithesis. At advanced levels, what is introjected and consciously felt as such are abstract data, and the person distinguishes between, say, an idea which he has accepted from another person and his own ideas, and he is also conscious of the effect of the idea originating in an object on his own thinking.

As regards the introjections with 'negative valence', this is a more complex situation than Kernberg shows. Here the question must be asked why the infantile ego should introject a bad object in the first place. Kernberg rejects Fairbairn's view that only bad objects are introjected, and I am in agreement with Kernberg. but I seem to differ from him as regards the following two points: (1) I do not think that the infantile ego originally and actively introjects a bad object. Thus in my view what happens is that originally the introjected object was felt to be good, so that introjection took place 'under the positive valence'. Later a 'bad', frustrating, frightening, and so on experience occurred, and the image of this object assumed a 'negative valence'. Experiences of this kind are related to disillusionment, indeed a frequent and very important factor in the child's life. (2) The experience with the object was bad, as it occurred. The infantile ego did not actively introject it, but was helpless against its intrusion, because the barrier function was not yet effective.

I have become attentive to the existence of 'bad internal objects' which could be traced to serious deviations from the average in maternal care, beginning in the earliest phase and extending throughout childhood. Khan's concept of the 'cumulative trauma' is very relevant for such cases. For a variety of reasons – in some cases there was widespread psychopathology in the family – the mother was unable to love her infant, and the child was unwanted in the first place and remained so. Its care was left to the domestic staff, and not necessarily to the same person. In some cases the infant was fed with mother's milk, but this was pumped off, and if the mother occasionally did put the baby to her breast this occurred in some kind of emergency without the mother being able to enjoy her close contact with her infant. She remained incapable of loving adaptation and continued to be rejecting and at the same time rigidly intrusive, moulding the child to her notions. In the analysis, at crucial points transference and counter-transference revolve on this quality, rejection and intrusion, and many instances of so-called 'projective identification' should be defined as the reactivation in the patient of his infantile experiences with his rejecting and intruding mother.[1]

On the basis of such observations I am suggesting that in the first place the bad internal objects do not arise as a result of *active introjection* by the infant, but as the result of *passively endured intrusions* of an unloving mother, beginning during the undifferentiated stage when the infant is maximally helpless, and my conclusion, further, is that such experiences lead to the establishment of a *sub-structure* in the budding psychic apparatus, which exerts crucial effects on the subsequent formation of all three structures. This sub-structure would, I think, correspond to Kernberg's identification system on the lowest level of his hierarchical system.

The patients I have in mind belong to the vast and vaguely defined group of borderline cases with varying proximity to the psychotic pole of the spectrum, and they are familiar from various descriptions in our literature. (Dr Ritvo's patient is fresh in our minds.) I also mention here Gitelson's example of 'narcissistic personality disorder', where he described that his patient's mother tried to 'get into the analysis' with him, and that her intrusiveness was combined with rejection. As a key concept for the resulting disturbances I shall point to the absence of healthy narcissism in these patients. In order, for example, to ensure their self-esteem they need to compare themselves with 'bad' and particularly contemptible objects, and they succeed in finding or creating them through projection leading to delusions, as well as through active destructive provocation leading to 'real' bad experiences.

I have suggested that this early established sub-structure of identification system affects the subsequent formation of all three structures. Therefore, in many instances, destructive behaviour is condoned by the superego. In a sense, this sub-structure is used by the ego as an *alibi* for the destructive drives, a kind of 'secondary gain from illness'. My impression is that such a sub-structure can be distinguished from a constitutionally abnormal strength of destructive impulses if we proceed with our customary caution, when reconstructing early experiences. In any case, we should not invoke constitutional factors before evaluating carefully the child's experiences in his environment. As an identification system it represents an enforced identification with an ill mother (and ill parents) that is dystonic to the potential ego capacities of the patient. In keeping with this view is the observation that these patients practically exhaust their ego capacities and functions in offensive defensiveness at the cost of creativity.

Splitting versus repression

Before discussing the concept of a mechanism of splitting *sui generis* it will be helpful to recall some well-known facts about ego mechanisms in general.

We know that the same mechanism may enhance or reduce ego functions and capacities. Whether an ego mechanism is constructive or defensive depends on the motive that prompts the ego to use it, and this motive is found by considering the situation as a whole, in which an action by the ego is called for, including the condition of the ego, its developmental stage, and so on. Although certain mechanisms are called defence mechanisms, we might list many more in accordance with the unlisted repertoire of ego mechanisms. For this reason, not infrequently new defence mechanisms are suggested in psychoanalytic case histories.

The defensive process uses more than one mechanism. Thus repression occurs in combination with one or several of the following mechanisms: counter-cathexis, reaction formation, isolation, phobic avoidance, somatic conversion, and so forth, and specific combinations result in specific pathognomic syndromes.[2]

Since we do consider the situation as a whole, we use a variety of descriptive terms, which sometimes differ only slightly from one another; for example, internalization, incorporation, introjection, or isolation, compartmentalization, and so on. In this way we stress one particular aspect among many, and this is in keeping with analytic procedure that aims at studying in detail the constituents of a complex whole. We have to be careful, though, lest we miss the wood for the trees, lose sight of the essential for the sake of giving due significance to one particular feature.

One important difference between a defensive and a constructive mechanism concerns the factor of consciousness, when it is actually being used. When in the pursuit of a creative activity attention is focused on a particular issue, the repression of diverting perceptions and thoughts serves to converge psychic energy and exertion to the chosen activity, and repression thus acts predominantly as a constructive ego mechanism. True, there is also an element of defence involved – that is, against the anxiety lest the work will not be achieved if energy and time are deflected – but this defence is of a different order from that related to avoiding the conscious awareness of guilty or forbidden impulses. In the case of repression serving a constructive ego aim, the person is conscious of the fact that he pushes certain things out of his mind, and he is later free to attempt to recover them. By contrast, the use of mechanisms for the purpose of defence occurs without consciousness, indeed they would fail in their purpose if consciousness were admitted.

Let us now consider the essentials of repression as a defence mechanism. Historically, the first discovery concerned the pathological 'forgetting' of a complex experience, the 'traumatic scene', with the intolerable conflict that occurred at the time and on account of which the experience acted like a trauma (1895d). Freud's definition of the conflict as the clash between instinctual impulses and the aesthetic and ethical standards foreshadowed structural concepts, as we now know. Twenty years later Freud explored repression more closely and devoted a paper to it. From this paper Kernberg quotes a passage and adds a comment (p. 248) by Anna Freud on repression. Again, looking back at Freud's paper, we realize the limitation, made good later, when psychoanalytic theory formation advanced to the definition of psychic structure, as Anna Freud's statement makes very clear.

However, in the same (1915d) paper Freud presented more facts concerning repression. He stated that remote or distorted derivatives of the originally repressed have free access to consciousness; and further we find the following passage:

> But . . . I will say in advance that . . . the mechanisms of repression have at least this one thing in common: *a withdrawal of the cathexis* of energy (or of *libido*, where we are dealing with sexual instincts).

Clearly then, Freud envisaged variants of repression, a number of mechanisms of repression, or possibly the fact to which I referred earlier, that repression accompanies the use of other defence mechanisms, this leading to specific syndromes. What he emphasized as the common element is the withdrawal of cathexis, according it a particularly important part in the dynamics of repression.

As already stated, Freud's presentations of repression in 1895 and 1915 preceded his later structural concepts. What was earlier the antithesis between conscious and unconscious has later been subsumed under concepts concerning inter- and intra-structural processes. The aim of repression is the removal or forestalling of a painful consciousness, and what constitutes pain depends on the stage of psychic development. The painful consciousness may be that of a memory or of an actual perception of a conflict or of a defence against such conflict or of an external fact that would engender conflict.

The question concerning defensive operations before there exists ego/id differentiation may well start with the question of earliest perceptions giving rise to pain. There is good reason for considering that earliest perceptions are of the order of bodily sensations. It is in keeping with this view that Freud described the ego as 'first and foremost a body ego' and regarded the pleasure/pain principle to be of overriding power at the primitive stage of psychic life. As Kernberg states, perception and memory are autonomous ego functions, but it is necessary to distinguish between the potential and the actually operative ego function as well as between the incipient and the more advanced modes of ego functioning.

The precondition for repression to come into operation is that development must have advanced towards structure formation, and such advance includes steps towards reality testing – that is, thinking in accordance with the secondary process. Preceding these progressive moves within the narcissistic orientation, other defences are used like shift of cathexis and hallucination, hallucination itself resulting from the total shift of cathexis from the memory system to the perceptual system (Freud 1923b). I tried to show these defences in my discussion of the behaviour of the ten-day-old hungry infant.

Kernberg presents several patients with sharply contrasting behaviour, which he calls 'alternating ego states', and suggests that the concepts of defence by isolation and denial (and implicitly, repression) are not appropriate to account for such conditions. He concludes that the defence mechanism at stake is that of splitting. In my view the defensive process consists of repression combined with other mechanisms, and above all a shift of energic cathexis. His clinical observations are familiar, and reading his descriptions I am also reminded of the patient, mentioned by Freud (1922b), who regularly produced a state of paranoid delusional jealousy of his wife after having had a mutually satisfying sexual intercourse with her. Freud explained this phenomenon on the grounds that homosexual impulses became dominant whenever the heterosexual ones became dormant after being satisfied. The shift of energic cathexis is obvious in this case, which would qualify for Kernberg's description of 'alternating ego states'.

All these patients can be said to show a failure of several ego functions, like impulse control, synthesis, integration, reality-testing, identity formation, and so on, which are bound to have many causes which only careful analysis will reveal. Obviously, within the framework of his paper Kernberg could not present case material in greater detail, although with regard to the problem of the defence mechanisms employed this would have allowed a more thorough discussion.

To return to repression. Throughout his writings Freud described amongst the sequelae of repression 'rents, rifts, tears, splits' in the ego and the formation of 'separate psychical groups'. In his discussion of fetishism he spoke of a 'rupture' in the ego and related such a rupture to many psychopathological conditions. To my reading, these expositions convey the view that the ego *suffers* a split in the defensive process, similar to the 'rifts, tears' and so forth, described earlier as sequelae of repression; it does not use a mechanism of splitting *per se*.[3]

Katan's (1964) analysis of the processes involved in fetishism are highly relevant here. He makes the important point that the boy's alternation between disavowal and admission of his observation of the female genital is determined by the degree of sexual excitement. The sight of the penis-lacking female genital amounts to a trauma only when the boy is in a state of excitement, probably accompanied by an erection. When in this state the threat of castration is highly cathected, castration is feared as imminent. The defence, not called for in a calm condition, consists of a fixation to the pretraumatic condition, when the boy still believed in the universal existence of a penis, and disavowal of his perception. It is significant that Katan too considers a combination of defensive mechanisms. According to Katan there is no split in the ego, let alone the use of a mechanism of splitting. The theory that a mechanism of splitting represents the forerunner of repression makes sense within Melanie Klein's theory of early development as starting with the schizoid/paranoid infantile position and moving to the depressive infantile position. As stated elsewhere (1964), I have come to regard these positions as repressive syndromes and not as original early infantile conditions. In my view they are not compatible with original undifferentiation, whilst Kernberg sees a possibility of combining these different theories concerning early psychic life.

Kernberg discusses the relation between splitting and 'keeping apart', and develops the notion that introjections occurring under the positive valence are kept apart from those with negative valence. He also states that the use of splitting is helped by this mechanism of keeping apart contradictory experiences. At the same time he presents an explanation for the fact that dissimilar experiences are kept apart, which seems to me of very great significance. Originally, he says, the introjections with positive or negative valence did in fact occur at different times, thus the factor involved in keeping apart would be the function of association. It seems indeed highly convincing that experiences of a similar kind are associated with one another more easily than those of a different nature. Should we not think that a person is confused if at the point of a satisfactory experience with an object he is concerned with memories of former bad experiences? As regards the infant at the stage of incipient ego functions this factor of associability of experiences has to be given due significance in view of the small orbit of his perception and the short time-span of his attention, characteristic for early life.

My last comments concern the problem of the evidential value of interpretations. Kernberg adduces his observation that interpretations about splitting brought about changes in his patients as further evidence for the existence of such a mechanism. He touches on a vast and important problem which would deserve full discussion, impossible in this context. There are so many factors involved in a successful, or apparently successful, interpretation that we can hardly ever be sure that the decisive process is that of full affective insight. As regards verbalizations of mechanisms it is my impression that very often their appeal lies in their descriptive concreteness appropriate to the patient's regressive condition and phantasies. Obviously too, the language of the consulting room differs from that of scientific investigation. In an investigation of thought processes, terms like association or dissociation and other terms related to the psychology of cognitive processes are appropriate, but they would hardly be meaningful for a regressed patient.

Notes

1 'Projective identification' occurs as a counter-transference phenomenon, when the analyst fails in his perceptive functions, so that, instead of recognizing in good time the character of the transference, he on his part unconsciously introjects his patient who at this point acts from an identification with his rejecting and intruding mother, re-enacting his own experiences in a reversal of roles. I have suggested elsewhere (Heimann 1950, 1960) that counter-transference disturbances usually result from a time-lag in the analyst's thought processes.
2 In a panel discussion of the American Psychoanalytic Association Schlesinger (1965) expressed his belief 'that repression was present in all defences and should not be regarded as a defence mechanism *per se*'. I am in agreement with the first part of this statement, but, in my view, the fact that repression operates together with other mechanisms does not detract from its nature as a defence mechanism *per se*.
3 Strachey's translation of Freud's phrase 'die Ichspaltung im Abwehrvorgang' is to my thinking not felicitous. His word 'splitting' of the ego rather than the noun 'split' in the ego tends to suggest the ego's activity rather than its state.

The evaluation of applicants for psycho-analytic training (1967/8)

This paper was presented to the 2nd Pre-Congress Conference on Training, Copenhagen, 1967. It was published in the *International Journal of Psycho-Analysis* 49 (6) (1968), with the sub-heading 'The goals of psychoanalytic education and the criteria for the evaluation of applicants'.

Introduction

When I was pondering about Dr Kohut's invitation to prepare this paper, my task appeared to me in three images: if the paper was to facilitate and stimulate discussion, it should have the characters of a *basis* and a *framework* and a *backcloth*. As a *basis*, the paper would provide a solid communication with the work already done on these problems and so secure coherence with the past; as a *framework*, it would protect discussion from spilling over the necessary boundaries – a risk with which we are all familiar since we have been trained to free association. The image of the *back-cloth* is taken from the theatre, the 'boards that represent the world', and what it expresses is the opposite of the former concept of boundary. The back-cloth on the stage suggests the continuation of the events depicted in the foreground, a continuation that extends far beyond our actual range of vision and ends in the infinite. In other words, I saw the functions of this paper as starting off with information about the already existing views and definitions of the goals of psychoanalytic education and the correlated criteria for evaluation – hence the bibliography which Kohut added to his letters before the Pre-Congress. Such information should be factually correct, well-ordered, systematic, and integrative. We have a model of such information in Greenacre's admirable digest (1961). Unfortunately, to follow this model is beyond my abilities, and I shall make no attempt to present a critical digest of the relevant literature since 1961. Instead I shall discuss some works related to our topic and select certain concepts that I find important or that formed the starting point for significant developments, or that recur frequently without having found the necessary critical reappraisal. Obviously my choice has been determined by subjective factors, and other members of this Pre-Congress will have made a different choice; but that is hardly a disadvantage.

On the one hand, then, my comments on the preceding works will be incomplete and will not make full use of the offers made in Kohut's bibliography. On the other hand, when preparing this paper I found myself unexpectedly, but forcibly, propelled into a different direction, which made me turn to other works in our literature.

Some comments on the bibliography

The papers of the bibliography can be divided broadly into three categories:

(1) Several works are surveys: of the relevant literature (Greenacre 1961); of the problems and procedure of psychoanalytic institutes in the United States (Lewin and Ross 1960); of reports of discussions (Bird 1962; Console 1963); of systematic investigations in selection (Holt and Luborsky 1955, 1958; Fox *et al.* 1964).

(2) Papers which present definitions or part-definitions of the goals and criteria, based on the very concrete and direct experiences of the training analyst in his various functions as interviewer of applicants, member of a training committee in which such interviews are discussed, analyst and supervisor of students, teacher in the curriculum. In these papers the authors proceed from an empirical point of view. However different the titles of these papers, to which belong also the contributions to the two symposia at international psychoanalytical congresses ('Problems of psychoanalytic training' 1953, and 'Selection criteria for the training of psychoanalytic students' 1961), they could well have adopted Sachs's title: 'Observations of a training analyst' (Sachs 1947; Gitelson 1948; Heimann 1954; Balint 1954; Bibring 1954; Gitelson 1954; Lampl-De Groot 1954; Langer 1962; Waelder 1962).

(3) Studies which approached the problem from a theoretical, systematic point of view (Fliess 1942; Fleming 1961).

It is obvious that whoever is concerned with the problem of psychoanalytic training is inevitably concerned with the future of psychoanalysis, whether or not the author mentions this explicitly. Two works in the bibliography occupy a special place with regard to the considerations of the future of psychoanalysis: one is a weighty volume, the other a thin little paper of barely nine pages – I am referring to Eissler's book, *Medical Orthodoxy and the Future of Psychoanalysis* (1965) and to Anna Freud's paper, 'Some thoughts about the place of psychoanalytic theory in the training of psychiatrists' (1966). Eissler's book pursues the problem of the future of psychoanalysis in a most erudite, multi-dimensional, and thorough manner. I shall not be expected to present an appropriate review of this book, which I have deliberately called 'weighty', in more senses than one. Following the development of Freud's own conception of psychoanalysis, between 1913 and 1923, Eissler quotes the triad of meanings of the term 'psychoanalysis', at which Freud had arrived in 1923:

(1) 'a procedure for the investigation of mental processes';
(2) 'a method . . . for the treatment of neurotic disorder';
(3) 'a collection of psychological information leading toward a new scientific discipline' (Freud, 1923b, p. 235).

On account of this triadic concept of psychoanalysis, a variety of applications are possible and have indeed come into being, but workers in a variety of disciplines are needed in order to further psychoanalysis and secure its future as a 'system psychology'. Among these workers people trained and experienced in the anthropic sciences are particularly promising. Psychoanalysis should not be confined to psychiatrists. Therapy is only one of the applications. Anna Freud, on the other hand, turns to psychiatry and shows how the psychiatric trainee gains in his understanding of his patients by learning psychoanalytic metapsychology. That psychiatrists want the help of psychoanalysts, that psychiatric hospitals employ analysts for teaching and supervision is not new; but, so far as I know, the presentation of the psychiatrist's need to learn, not isolated aspects of psychoanalysis, useful for some *ad hoc* therapeutic procedure, but to learn the whole 'language of psychoanalysis', is unprecedented.

A study of the bibliography shows that there is a considerable overlap between the different papers dealing with the problem under discussion, albeit under different names, and as I said earlier, a number of contributions could have taken the title of Sachs's paper (published posthumously in 1947), 'Observations of a training analyst'. Three works proceed from a different angle: Fliess (1942), Holt and Luborsky (1955, 1958), and Fleming (1961). Fleming expresses her discontent with the 'impressionistic "sizing up" so often used as the basis for accepting or rejecting an applicant'. In her article 'What analytic work requires of an analyst: a job analysis', she attempts to analyse the work process. I wish she had not used the sub-title; not only because a procedure that may be of value in business cannot be transplanted without further ado into the intricate texture[1] of the science and profession of psychoanalysis, but also because of the omission to follow up the obvious allusions to anality. I have elsewhere attempted to show that the decisive clash between primitive narcissism and object-relatedness occurs during the anal stage and that in this phase of development anal work patterns are laid down which make their contributions to all later creative ego activities. To pursue the contributions from anality to the analytic work would be a worth-while task.

I am selecting for further discussion one notion of the analyst's work that Fliess introduced and Fleming, with slight modification, accepts. It is the notion that the analyst, when listening with his freely hovering attention, is in a stae of day-dreaming. Fliess calls it 'conditioned' day-dreaming to distinguish it from spontaneous day-dreaming, in which 'the stimuli come largely from within', whereas the analyst's day-dreaming (within the psychoanalytic situation) is almost entirely stimulated from without, and by one particular source: 'the patient's reactions'. Fleming says, 'controlled daydreaming might be a better term'. I remember in this connection that Bion speaks of 'reverie' as the analyst's state or activity when listening to his patient. My view differs profoundly from the notion that the analyst's free-floating attention amounts to day-dreaming, whether we call it conditioned, or controlled, or reverie. The dominant characteristic of the dream, day-dream or sleep-dream, is the dreamer's narcissism. He himself is the hero of the dream events. The hero in the analytic situation, the person for whose sake this situation has been created, is the patient, not the analyist. In his free associations the patient may wander away from his relationship with the analyst and from awareness of being in the psychoanalytic situation. He may go off in a day-dream; he may actually fall asleep, but the analyst's freely hovering attention hovers around the patient, and he remains profoundly related to him. If his attention wanders off, if he falls asleep, or into a day-dream, something has happened to interfere with his function. It may be that he has unconsciously introjected the patient and, therefore, in his identification, behaves like him, as in a dream. He may afterwards be able to recoup what he has lost in this way, similar to the possibility of learning from other types of error that he made. The analyst's relaxed condition when listening to his patient is yet combined with alertness, paradoxical though this sounds (cf. Greenson 1966). Paradoxes, antinomies, dualism, pairs of opposites – these are phenomena which psycho-analysis discovered as characteristic for human psychology, and the ability to be aware of them, tolerate and use them creatively, represents one of the goals of psychoanalytic education. When, to use Freud's description, the analyst listens as a sensitive receiver of his patient's unconscious communications, be these unconsciously intended or be they unintentional clues, this is an active part of his cognitive work process.

A number of concepts recur frequently, indicating partly an area of common thought among the authors, partly the power of habit rather than critical reappraisal. One of these concepts is empathy. From Fliess (1942) onwards, empathy is described as a most important factor in the analyst's capacity for understanding his patient. Fliess states 'mental health, psychiatric training, and psycho-pathological aptitude' as the 'ingredients of the educational recipe' that held for the selection process twenty-five years ago. While the first two factors have meanwhile, through closer examination, been deprived of their dominant position at the time of Fliess's paper, the third factor, psychological aptitude, has maintained, albeit under varying names, a crucial position in psychoanalytic thinking. Acknowledging that 'we expect nature and possibly infancy to do the better part of the work in creating (psychological aptitude)', Fliess proceeds to present the metapsychology of the psychoanalyst with the focus on this particular quality. It consists in the subject's putting himself in the object's place, stepping into his shoes, and so obtaining an inside knowledge of the object that is almost first-hand.[2] The common name for such a procedure is empathy. In psycho-analytic nomenclature Fliess suggests calling it 'trial identification'. Correcting the popular description of identification, 'stepping into another person's shoes', Fliess stresses that all takes place in the subject's mind, and analyses in detail the process of identification, suggesting four phases:

(1) the analyst is the object of the patient's striving;
(2) the analyst identifies with this striving and thus becomes the patient;
(3) in this way he obtains inside knowledge of his patient;
(4) he now possesses material for a relevant interpretation.

Fliess stresses that the identification must be partial and temporary only, and he points to the dangers specific to the various steps in the process of identification.

Another careful study of empathy has been presented by Greenson (1960). It is interesting that both Fliess and Greenson, who allot to empathy a crucial function in the analyst's work, arrive at significant operational concepts. Fliess develops the notion of a 'work ego' that the analyst acquires and thanks to which the analyst achieves something that seems impossible 'because it is actually impossible for the average person'. I wish to underline the notion of limitation that comes through here, as it did earlier, when Fliess referred to the work nature and infancy have to do. I shall come back to this point later. Fliess connects this work ego with a special temporary displacement of cathexis between ego and superego, and presents a number of interesting suggestions which I cannot follow up. Greenson develops the concept of a 'working model of the patient' that the analyst builds up within himself. As so often in psychoanalytic research, the normal process comes to be recognized after observation and analysis of its pathological version. Thus, Greenson presents the formation of a 'working model of the patient' as a phenomenon that occurs naturally in the analyst's contact with his patient, after giving an instance of failure in his empathy. Puzzled, he scrutinized his working model and carried out certain manipulations with it: 'The events, words, and actions the patient described were now permitted to permeate the working model. The model reacted with feelings, ideas, memories, associations, etc.' As a result, the failure in his empathy was removed.

This anthropomorphic description of the model as an active agency may be merely a stylistic device to bring home the significance of this part of the analyst's working process; yet it lends a rather magical quality to the concept of empathy. I hasten to add that I am far from underrrating Greenson's ability for sharp intellectual, un-magical clarity.

I have mentioned earlier that empathy occurs in the literature with a high positive valuation. I wish to add now that there is one dissenting voice; this is Waelder's (1962). Defining empathy as 'a particularly high ability to see, to sense, or to guess, on the basis of infinitesimal clues, what is going on in another person – a kind of immediate insight into the unconscious of others', Waelder describes it as a rather dangerous quality. It may be of advantage initially, and on account of such quick results empathy is more use for a practitioner of short psychotherapies than for an analyst. Waelder says that while it is always impressive, it is not always correct, and 'those favoured by the gods with this gift are sometimes slow in revising their early views where necessary'. I very much agree with Waelder's warnings, which, I think, paraphrase the tendency towards omnipotence in an analyst who is capable of such quick insight into the unconscious of another person. Empathy and intuition will be of benefit for the patient only if these qualities are checked by a particularly high degree of self-criticism on the part of the analyst and awareness of how easily his quick perceptions may lead to cruel interpretations.

Greenson has also described negative forms and vicissitudes of empathy, which 'lead not to understanding but to a counter-transference reaction'. It is obvious that Greenson uses the concept of counter-transference as synonymous with transference by the analyst on to his patient, as do indeed many analysts. I have elsewhere given my reasons for distinguishing counter-transference from transference on the part of the analyst. The incident of failing to understand his patient, which Greenson used to present his concept of the working model of his patient, is, in my conceptual framework, a disturbance in the counter-transference; and the counter-transference, in contrast to transference, serves as an instrument of research into the patient's unconscious processes. Elasticity in the analyst's mental position *vis-à-vis* his patient, his moving between positions of involvement and detachment, between observing and participating, which Greenson so well describes, are, in my view, not so much a matter of empathy, but of counter-transference. When, for stretches, the analyst acts without difficulty as the sensitive receiver of his patient's unconscious communications, or when he presents valid interpretations, his counter-transference functions smoothly, and he is hardly aware of it. But he does become aware of it when there has been a failure in its functioning. Whilst Fliess replaces 'empathy' as a term of ordinary language with the metapsychological term 'trial identification', I wish to replace it to some degree with the specific psychoanalytic concept of counter-transference.

I shall later return to the problem of semantic difficulties between psychoanalysts. In the present connection I wish to reduce the importance attached to identification, if it is treated as the only or the main instrument for understanding another person. Identification means a change in the subject's ego which is brought about through the introjection of the object's ego – Fliess emphasizes that this should happen only partially and temporarily – but, in my view, so far as it happens, it does not lead to an understanding of the patient, unless it is *at once* combined with a number of other processes. If I become like my patient then there are two of the same kind in the room. (Gitelson reported an amusing and telling experience when the supervising analyst pointed out that his identification with his frightened patient could not be helpful.) I am perhaps more critical of the dangers of introjection, just because I believed for a time that introjection and projection were the only valid mechanisms in object relationships. I also wish to draw attention to a frequent confusion between introjection as a mechanism, which leads to structural changes, and the perception of intrapsychic processes, such as thinking, feeling, imagining, and so on. The term 'cognition', according to Holt (1964), has acquired a considerable broadening in its recent renaissance so that it comprises 'perception, judging, forming concepts, learning (especially that of a meaningful, verbal kind), imagining, fantasying, imaging, creating, and solving problems'. Each of these events represents a psychic event, and as such it is by necessity an internal process, but it is not by necessity the result of introjection. By means of such cognition an object becomes represented internally (Sandler and Rosenblatt 1962). Only the young child who is under the dominance of his oral impulses forms his perceptions and conceptions to a large extent with the help of oral tasting. In later development, when the inherent ego capacity of perception has become operative, the contribution of oral mechanisms in perception recedes. One of the unfortunate effects of the greater attention given in recent years to early infantile processes has been the attribution of a near-monopolistic dominance to orality.

When studying the literature, particularly when reading descriptions of the psychoanalytic process, or of the interaction between analyst and patient, or of the qualities expected of the applicant, I encountered a feeling of unease, which is in fact an old acquaintance and has assailed me at times about my own writings, but this time, concerned with the goals of psychoanalytic education, I read with sharpened sensitivity and came to define this sense of unease. Briefly, it is the reaction to descriptions which have a subtle, yet unmistakable, flavour of illusions about psychoanalysis, with idealizations of the analyst as a person. It would need rather full quotations from several papers to substantiate my point, and to do this is obviously beyond the framework of my paper. I am thus aware of the risk of being misunderstood when I am singling out a few phrases from a few papers. For example, Lampl-De Groot, in the first symposium (1954) and van der Leeuw in the second (1962) mention 'integrity' as a necessary requirement for the analyst. To my mind 'integrity of character', Lampl-De Groot's phrase, is a very rare quality; it occurs only in a few persons, for whom 'nature and infancy' have combined to produce such exquisite intrapsychic relations that they are able to conduct their whole social lives in accordance with the highest ethical principles. True, Lampl-De Groot then turns to medical ethics and demands that the analyst should honour them. These remarks considerably reduce the first impression which her phrase has caused. Similarly, van der Leeuw goes on to endorse Freud's demand for 'Zuverlässigkeit des Charakters' in the analyst. Medical ethics and professional reliability are part and parcel of ordinary human decencies. The demand for 'integrity', however, is bound to evoke the notion that psychoanalysts are persons of exceptional qualities.

The same claim is made by Fleming (1961) and Langer (1962), although these authors do it in different ways. Fleming repeatedly mentions 'special endowments' and 'high level of integration' as qualities of the analyst. When discussing the therapeutic goal of developing the patient's capacity for communication with himself and others, she concludes 'that an analyst must already possess a high level of capacity for this kind of communication', a point to which she refers back repeatedly. Another example is her statement that 'the main instrument (for reaching therapeutic goals) is the personality of the analyst'.

It is true that Freud's discovery of the transference so fundamentally changed the position of the analyst because it amounted to nothing less than the discovery that the analyst himself becomes the therapeutic agency, but that refers to his position as *worker* in the analytic situation. I want to remind you of Fliess's description, which clearly distinguishes between the analyst as a person and the analyst as a worker. I wish to quote him again:

> The analyst must make possible what rightly seems impossible, because it is actually impossible for the average person, and must do so by becoming a very exceptional person *during his work with the patient* [my italics]. To this end he will have to acquire a 'work ego'.

Greenson, who in several papers (1960, 1965, 1966) has added significantly to our understanding of the analytic process, and the more so since he clearly describes shortcomings in himself or other analysts, depicts them as 'persons of unusual sensitivity, personality and character' and only later corrects the balance by acknowledging the analyst's need, after office hours, to be a very ordinary person, bad-tempered, uncontrolled, and in need of being surrounded with love and understanding.

Marie Langer, quoting from the Chicago Institute's 'The capacity for communication' and from my contribution to the first symposium, 'the wish to help . . . combined with respect for other person's individuality', accepts these notions but declares that more is needed.

She regards as necessary for the analyst a *passion* [my italics] derived from his need to repair damaged internal objects and parts of the ego. Such need expresses the 'feeling of being summoned by an internal voice (the superego)' and forms the basis of any vocation. It is this concept of a profession as a call from the superego, the one-sided stress on reparation/sublimation to the exclusion of ego creativity and healthy narcissism from the motivational sources in the analyst that lend to Langer's picture of the analyst a quality of idealization, and even mysticism. (By contrast, compare her paper, written in conjunction with Puget and Teper 1964.) Now I am quite sure that if the analysts from whom I have quoted were asked whether they regard analysts as wonderful persons they would say 'No'.

Am I exaggerating and misinterpreting what is only a semantic matter? But are there 'only semantic' differences, or do we find other more serious and uncorrected attitudes of illusion and idealization in psychoanalytic societies?

Syncretism

The useful term 'syncretism', introduced (Lewin and Ross 1960) to epitomize the headaches of the American training institutes (and of those of other countries as well), is a valid concept also for the criteria derived from the goals of psychoanalytic education. It refers in fact to what is part and parcel of the human condition: the precarious balance between opposite views, impulses, aims. Its recurrence in the training situation is merely a special manifestation of this general phenomenon. If we take evaluation as not confined to the interviews with the applicant, but related to the whole course of the training, as indeed we must do (in the Training Prospectus of the British Psycho-Analytical Society this is specifically stated), we meet syncretism as a severe problem that threatens, and sometimes succeeds in breaking, the analysis only in those cases in which, to use Fliess's description, nature and infancy have done much less than we should wish. In other words, in my experience, it is only for cases on the borderline that syncretism does represent such a severe obstacle to psychoanalytic education. This is in keeping with the observation, mentioned by several authors dealing with the problem of evaluation, that difficulties arise only with borderline applicants. Those that appear clearly as gifted or as unsuitable do not present problems for the training institutes, although the question has been raised whether those rejected as unsuitable might not have turned out to be capable of favourable changes had they been accepted for training.

240

Several authors have referred to measures taken to exclude the troubles of syncretism in the training analysis, but I agree with those who pointed out that this is not really possible.

Among those who emphasize syncretism as a very grave phenomenon I wish to mention Waelder (1962), who speaks of the novel element that the training requirements introduced into the psychoanalytic situation. He makes a comparison with political totalitarianism, and maintains that any combination of power, however small, over a person's physical condition with spiritual authority is necessarily a demoralizing influence. He leaves no doubt about the severity of the problem and his inability to offer a solution, but he prefers to see an 'occasional ill-suited candidate being graduated' rather than see the basic climate of the psychoanalytic situation (that is of the analyst's secrecy and acting as his patient's 'agent' (p. 286)) changed. He is, however, fully aware that the phrase 'occasional ill-suited candidate being graduated' does not in fact describe the problem appropriately.

In my view, we are in need of finding a new approach to syncretism, and I would suggest that there is a tendency amongst analysts to deny the difference between a therapeutic analysis and an analysis undertaken for the sake of acquiring a new profession. It is a *reality* that the applicant for psychoanalytic training chooses his analyst with different aims and objectives than does the person who only wants therapeutic help from his analyst. Bibring, in her contribution to the first Symposium, probably has this in mind when she says 'We introduce into the training analysis the waning reality principle for which the analyst stands' (p. 171).

I believe that the emphasis on syncretism is based on a displaced sense of guilt on the part of the training analyst. This sense of guilt does not really arise from his contact with the future analyst, but has its source in his contact with his colleagues – that is, in the conditions pertaining to his psychoanalytic society. I shall present some ideas about this point in the next section of this paper. Here I would like to add that I have stopped feeling guilty towards my candidate when the problem of his suitability becomes actual, and I have also found that my frank admission of difficulties in deciding on the next step in his training helps to carry the analysis deeper. I do not agree with Waelder that this position of the analyst has a totalitarian flavour. It appears like this only to that candidate whose early childhood deviates significantly from the 'averagely expectable' so that in phases of intense dependency he did not experience the love, support, and understanding which he needed.

Psychoanalysis and its discontents

It is obvious that there are widespread discontents with psychoanalysis, psychoanalysts, and the results of psychoanalytic education. The very institution of this Pre-Congress on Training bears witness to this fact. At the same time, this addition to our scientific congresses indicates that the problems of psychoanalytic education represent a research area of the first order.

I shall in this section trespass beyond my brief, since Kohut's instruction is 'strictly speaking, not research *in* psychoanalysis but research *about* it' (p. 4 of his letter of 1 October 1966). Yet I feel that I am serving my task.

The goals of psychoanalytic education cannot be considered by focusing on the applicants only, and the problems of evaluation do not end when the applicant becomes a student; they continue throughout his training. When applying for training, the applicant makes his first step on a road that will not only lead to his acquiring a new profession, but also to his becoming a member of a certain cultural community, the psychoanalytical society, which affects him during his whole training directly through its representatives involved in the training, and indirectly in a multitude of ways.

In her paper for the last Pre-Congress on Training, Greenacre (1966) has dealt with the unsatisfactory features of this cultural community: strife, rivalries, formations of hostile cliques, and so on among psychoanalysts are a general phenomenon, once the psychoanalytic society has reached a certain size. I suggested that one reason may be the 'turning inwards of aggression' when external attacks are diminished (or when their effect is diminished owing to the increased strength of psychoanalytical societies) – a phenomenon with which we are familiar in the analyses of individuals. This idea is in keeping with Gitelson's view of an 'identity crisis' amongst psychoanalysts (not only in the United States) since such a crisis is specific for a developmental phase.

It is the phase of adolescence for which an identity crisis is characteristic, this bewilderment being due to the clash between progressive and regressive strivings. Side by side, or rather inter-mingling, a mature and gifted individual coexists with an infantile, babyish one yearning for fusion with mother. Highly idealistic trends go together with strong cruel impulses; intellectual grasp of many problems suddenly changes into religious mysticism; and submissive hero worship alternates with rebelliousness.

I am returning to my earlier question. There are indeed more serious manifestations of illusion and idealization among analysts than the examples I have quoted earlier. There is a 'return of the repressed' (Gitelson 1964) of religious attitudes. Psychoanalysis is not free of the *Zeitgeist* of our period of history with religio–political tendencies, personality cult, and the formations of cliques, ritualistic incantations of phrases coined by the leaders in contrast to rational discussion of semantic differences.

Intrusion of religious attitudes into psychoanalysis has been noted by other analysts. Eissler brings a religious term into the title of his book in which he pleads for opening psychoanalysis to the anthropic scientists – Balint (1954) speaks of 'supertherapy' and ends with a motto taken from the attempts at reform recommended by a certain church – Kohut pointed to the degenerating of discussion into contemptuous attacks on colleagues holding different views and connects this phenomenon with religious tendencies (1964).

Lampl-De Groot is right to stress medical ethics (whatever aspects she has in mind) but they are bound to count for nothing when it is a question of saving an erring soul and converting it to the only right faith, an analyst of his own clique.

These conditions in psychoanalytic societies breed syncretism in psychoanalytic education.

At this point in my deliberations I turned to Freud's books, *The Future of an Illusion* and *Civilization and its Discontents*. The latter appears at first as a sequel to the former, but on careful study I find that with *Beyond the Pleasure Principle* these three works form a trilogy. Notwithstanding his magnificent excursions into ethnology and anthropology when tracing the origin of civilization, it becomes clear that Freud's main concern is to establish his concept of a 'primary instinct of destruction or death instinct' on a firmer basis by showing how many phenomena of extreme importance for human life radiate from and to this instinct. In fact, thus, his excursions are means by which he pursues this aim. They illustrate the wealth of his scientific ideas and power of his art as a writer. Moreover, he invites scientists in other fields like ethnology, anthropology, physiology, and so on to join forces with psychoanalysis – with the warning, though, that concepts, like human beings, cannot be torn crudely from the area in which they originated, but need careful handling.

Freud starts by linking *Civilization and its Discontents* with *The Future of an Illusion* by taking up Romain Rolland's criticism that he had neglected the 'oceanic' feeling as the true source of the religious sentiments which are used by the various churches and religious systems. Freud, however, traces this 'limitless' feeling, this 'sensation of eternity' to that early ego state which knows no boundary, in other words, to the primary narcissism of the undifferentiated stage, whereas he derives religious needs from the infant's helplessness and the longing for the father aroused by it. He leaves room for the possibility that there may be something behind this, and also for the possibility that later the oceanic feeling may become connected with religion, and these hints may imply states of helplessness occurring before the infant has advanced to a relationship with the father. Helplessness in earlier phases due to breaks in maternal care which maintains primitive omnipotent narcissism would represent the deeper sources of religious needs (and possibly of matriarchal religious systems).

The religion with which Freud is concerned is the system of doctrines and promises attributed to an 'enormously exalted father' (p. 74). From this religious man derives guidance and comfort which he needs so badly, because life in accordance with the demands of civilization is too hard. How did this civilization come into being? I may recall briefly Freud's conjectures. Civilization started with man's adopting the upright posture and its fateful chain of consequences. These include the devaluation of the olfactory stimuli – loss of the periodicity of sexual excitation – dominance of the visual stimuli – fear and shame related to the genitals now exposed – permanence of psychical sexual excitations associated with stronger motives for the founding of permanent families – recognition that common work and common fight against the forces of nature are more successful than the efforts of the single individual with the help only of his family. This extension of family to the greater community of civilization fails to lead to happiness because nature has not been mastered sufficiently: 'when we consider how unsuccessful we have been in precisely this field of suffering, a suspicion dawns upon us that here, too, a piece of unconquerable nature may lie behind – this time a piece of our own psychical constitution' (p. 86).

This statement at an early point in *Civilization* foreshadows the presentation of the primary instinct of death or destruction and its clash with Eros, the life instinct. In the further course of the book Freud constructs a multifaceted ideational structure revolving around this concept, and deals with one facet after the other.

Starting with the demonstration that anal erotism succumbs to 'primal repression', Freud moves to the 'cultural frustration' which forbids the egoistic/narcissistic pursuit of instinctual gratification in general, distinguishes between the sadistic component of erotic relationships and a primary destructive drive which serves no other aim than its own. Against this, religion raises the demand, impossible to fulfil, of extreme altruism, the demand to love thy

244

neighbour as thyself, and even to love thine enemy. Further, the most important method used by civilization analogous to the development of the individual against the destructive drive is internalization – in fact it is 'sent back to where it came from – that is, it is directed toward his own ego' (p. 123).

I have now arrived at the two problem areas to which I wished to draw attention by reminding you of *Civilization and its Discontents*. The two crucial concepts that need discussion in connection with our topic are narcissism and the destructive drive.

In *Civilization*, Freud operates with primary narcissism in the 'oceanic' feeling and with object-hostile narcissism, thus tying narcissism up with the destructive drive. It is this narcissism which the many authors have in mind when they treat narcissism as a disqualifying factor in the evaluation of applicants.

However, many voices have been raised for the defence of narcissism and acknowledged a healthy narcissism which does not need disguised gratification by forming groups of mutual idealization and creating gods and demons and similar illusions. To refer to my own ideas, I have suggested that we have stuck too closely to the concept of infantile narcissism, and presented an alternative view, that is, to regard narcissism as an experiential orientation which is subject to development as much as any other aspect of psychic life (Heimann 1962b). We should distinguish at least three types of narcissism: first, the naïve primary narcissism as a component of the undifferentiated stage; second, after recognition of the self-object antithesis, the secondary object-hostile narcissism makes its appearance, largely based on frustrations by the object, not only of the child's drives but also of his ego interests; the third type of narcissism, which belongs to maturity, is instrumental for creative work (which is not identical with sublimation), and it is fully compatible with the recognition of the reality principle. It is moreover a condition for full mutuality in mature object relationships (Heimann 1966).

Kohut described the exploitation of scientific controversy for the discharge of destructive impulses as an illness and suggested that further exploration of narcissism might solve the problems posed by it (Kohut 1964). This task he meanwhile carried out (1966), so that we have rich material available for discussion.

I equally feel that we need to discuss the views held about the destructive drive, since the quasi-religious position given to the death instinct contributes a great deal to syncretism.

Freud's concept of a primary destructive drive ended the theoretical confusion which treated cruelty as part of the libido. The notion of a fundamental antithesis between an instinct of life and an instinct of death, both of which came into existence with evolution to living substance, is grandiose and fascinating. But I have come to recognize that my enthusiasm for a concept that links the human being with cosmic processes, with attraction and repulsion, the expanding and the shrinking universe, is by nature 'oceanic' rather than scientific. Natural scientists do not confirm Freud's theory. What is perhaps more important for us, clinical work does not demand such a derivation nor can it prove or refute it. What, however, clinical exploration does show, is that narcissism and destructiveness are not necessarily bound up with each other.

Whither psychoanalysis?

Praxiteles has not become obsolete through Henry Moore, but in the realm of science and technology progress involves relinquishing the position from which the newer steps occurred.

The scientist must be prepared for this development. It is precisely his discovery that will lead others to leave him behind.

Is this what is happening to psychoanalysis as a science and a technique?

It is a fact that a great number of new therapeutic and exploratory techniques have come into being. They are based on psychoanalytic concepts, and many of them are indeed carried out by psychoanalysts who clearly say that the particular method is rooted in Freud's discoveries. Often also it can only be carried out by somebody trained and well versed in psychoanalysis. To list a few of these new methods: group therapy, family therapy, the treatment of families with an acute problem, like the return of a member of the family from a hospital or from prison, the treatment of a married couple, of a mother and child, parents and child, short-term focal therapy (initiated by Balint), G.P. seminars (also originated by Balint) and other forms of what might be called therapeutic instruction given to groups of professional and industrial workers.

Gitelson (in his Presidential Address in Stockholm, 1963, 'On the present scientific and social position of psychoanalysis') referred to psychoanalysts engaged in such kinds of work 'which have undoubted ethical appeal but are not psychoanalysis'. He attributed this development in the interests and activities of psychoanalysts to anxiety, which he connected with the period of history in which we are living and the totalitarian trends affecting us from several sides. Added to these social sources of anxiety is the intrapsychic one of what he calls 'exposed isolation'. Compare also Eissler's statement (1965: 101–2):

> The ease with which some analysts forsake part of their analytic practice in favour of applications stems in part from the demands that the community puts upon them; but it also stems from the burden of the psychoanalytic situation itself. It is my belief that to conduct an analysis in such a way as to conform with the spirit pervading Freud's work, is one of the most difficult of tasks, and that most of the techniques with which innovators try to replace Freud's, offer as their chief advantage the fact that they are very much easier to handle.

When we look at the therapeutic or exploratory methods which I have mentioned earlier, one factor is common to all of them, and that is that in these kinds of work the analyst does not find himself alone with just one other person in the psychoanalytic situation which, by imposing the obligations of discretion, maintains the analyst's position of isolation and loneliness even beyond the actual psycho-analytic session. Either the work itself proceeds with a number of patients or quasi-patients, or the therapist proceeds from and returns to a group of colleagues who share his problems and from whom he obtains help. It does then appear as if flight from contact with only one person to be faced alone forms one motive for this development. By relinquishing the psychoanalytic situation which by its very nature mobilizes the most primitive forces in the patient and demands contact with them over long periods, the analyst removes himself and his patient from the dangers of the unconscious operating in a dyadic relationship. Neither patient nor analyst are exposed to the anxieties of being sole target or sole source of the most unbridled demands and attacks.

It is true that workers in groups state that very severe anxieties are caused by the dynamics of the group; nevertheless it seems to me that there is a kind of belief that there is 'safety in numbers'.

In the article mentioned, and in his later one, 'On the identity crisis in American psychoanalysis' (1964), Gitelson examined the relationship between the need of psychoanalysts to go outside the psychoanalytic situation and what might perhaps be called a craving to obtain for psychoanalysis full recognition of his science and conformity with other acknowledged and respected sciences. He suggests that a 'fantasy of merging' lies behind this. Turning to the problem of the scientific position of psychoanalysis, he demonstrates that the definitions of science as given by highly respected scientists do in fact apply to psychoanalysis. (Compare also the interesting point made by Lagache (1966) that ' "the appearance of inexactitude [of psycho-analysis] derives principally from the enormity of the material to be treated" '.)

Clearly, Gitelson is concerned with the future of psychoanalysis, and I share his anxieties. Like Gitelson, I am fully aware of the great value of the work done by analysts in these various other therapeutic activities, and I also agree with those analysts who point to the needs in the community and demand that the benefit of psychoanalysis should be made available to a greater number of people than those few who can be fully analysed as individuals. But we must be aware of the differences between psychoanalysis and social psychiatry, and exert the greatest caution before allowing a feed-back from these fields into the psychoanalytic situation. Moreover, I believe that some scepticism is in place *vis-à-vis* the enthusiasm often found in the attitude of workers in these new therapies. Time is still too short to allow judgement about their efficacy and the duration of their apparent successes. Perhaps they are still in the 'honeymoon phase' and thus free from objective assessment, let alone disillusionment.

I am not suggesting that psychoanalysis has nothing to learn from other disciplines, or that it has to continue in isolation, as was the case at its beginning, but I am pointing to the need for careful appraisal of what is being taken from other sciences. Eissler pleads to make use of the anthropic sciences, and some analysts have shown that ethological research can make valuable contributions to our understanding of human nature. Thus, for example, Bowlby's (1960) ethological researches have produced significant observations for the understanding of the processes involved in the young child's separation from his mother, and that these form the basis for all later experiences of mourning. He has removed a great deal of the mythology attending the concept of instinct at Freud's time (and Freud complained about this), and by disentangling oral need (hunger) from the need for protection and security (clinging) in the child's tie to his mother, he has contributed to the undermining of the breast mystique which obfuscates some current theories of development.

The goals of psychoanalytic education and the criteria derived from them

I have avoided attempting any definition of the goals of psychoanalytic education, and perhaps for that reason I feel also hesitant about the criteria derived from the goals. It would be perfectly easy to say that the goals of psychoanalytic education lie in attracting and accepting those applicants who appear to possess, if only as potentials, those qualities, or, in Greenson's terms (1966), those skills, traits, and motivations which promise that the training analysis and the other ingredients of psychoanalytic education will make these potentials actual and manifest. These persons, therefore, would appear to secure the future of psychoanalysis, and, since survival can never follow the maintaining of a status quo, a definition of the goals of psychoanalytic education would necessarily include the category of scientific creativity. However, I do not feel that such a formulation would really be of value. It is so facile. I therefore leave it to the discussion to produce and test explicit definitions or to agree that at this juncture no suitable definition is forthcoming. I would like to recall here Bird's report (1962) of a discussion in a meeting held in Toronto, in which he says:

> For reasons not entirely clear, the meeting turned out rather well. It was not that anything startling or even new came up. In fact, little was discussed that had not already been far more fully dealt with in published papers. Yet much of what was said did seem new, or at least fresh. And perhaps in a way it really was.

I am quite sure that something new really did emerge and affect the discussants – as happened at the Pre-Congress in Amsterdam, because frank verbalization and communication, and sharing of problems, follow the principles operative in the psychoanalytic situation. Psychoanalysis does not aim at bringing about a 'cure' in the naïve sense of the term, as just meaning disappearance of symptoms. What it aims at, and brings about, is the process of psychic growth which also has an effect on symptoms. This is achieved to a large extent by the 'psychoanalytic working team' (Heimann 1966), the free admission of problems, primarily by the patient's associations and secondarily by the analyst's communications, provided he does not feel he has to act as omnipotent and omniscient, but fulfils his function as his patient's working partner (or partner in the 'therapeutic alliance'). To do this he does not need to be an extraordinary personality, and we need not attribute to his character more than the ordinary human decencies. I like to mention in this connection a remark by Solms, which impressed me so much because of its simplicity. At the end of our function as members of the Advisory Committee to the A.P.F. we were waiting for transport to the air terminal. In a desultory talk about nothing in particular, Solms suddenly said: 'After all, no matter how sophisticated our concepts of ego psychology have become, what we really expect in a psychoanalytic candidate is that he should have a good heart and that he should have gone through some suffering without denying it.' It is obvious that what Solms meant with the phrase 'a good heart' is not a wishy-washy sentimental goodiness, the kind of thing, which, to quote from another conversation about psychoanalysis, Sutherland recently called 'the mush of love'.

Freud's discovery of the unconscious psychic world and of the tools by means of which its existence may be made accessible and beneficial to individuals and groups of individuals represents an event to which the status of an *evolutionary step* must be allocated. Teilhard de Chardin (1959) describes the step (or leap) from the hominids to the human being as the last and highest event on the evolutionary spiral, and defines this advance as a change in the direction of consciousness. Only *Homo sapiens* knows that he knows; with him consciousness folds inwards as in earlier phases geological folding occurred. The capacity for *reflection* appears and with it a new world ('noösphere'). His descriptions read like a paraphrasing of Freud's presentation of mental development.

Reflection, reflection on the self, includes knowledge of the past and anticipation of the future. For evolutionary changes to be firmly established, the time span of analysis is still very short. Indeed analysts have not become better persons than those who have not experienced analysis. What they have achieved as a result of undergoing the process of being analysed is that they have acquired a new dimension in their thinking. Thus, despite the fights and hostilities among psychoanalysts, we do possess a special common ground; the civilization we share allows of possibilities for understanding and clarification.

Fleming attributed to psychoanalysis the acquisition of new ego functions and refers in this connection to Kramer (1959) who states this view on the basis of her continued self-analysis. From my own experience, I have come to the conclusion that self-analysis at some point regularly transcends into the tackling of an objective problem. Kramer, at any rate, has enriched our knowlege by describing her conflict between the wish to contribute to an important problem and the resistance which used the fear of giving away too much private material. She has found an elegant solution.

Works of this kind may well be regarded as giving tangible evidence of an essential criterion of the goals of psychoanalytic education; that is, continued self-analysis which goes together with continued self-training. The scientific exploration of such an evidence would lead to questions about the nature of the preceding training analysis, for example, in respect of transference and counter-transference, and of the other constituents of the preceding training, including a checking of the criteria used at the original evaluation.

I have earlier suggested, without any enthusiasm, a possible definition of the goals of psychoanalytic education and the criteria derived from them. After emphasizing that the aim of psychoanalysis is psychic growth and the acquisition of new ego functions, we may arrive at a definition in accordance with the measure of Freud's discoveries. Such a definition would revolve upon the creative use of the new world opened by psychoanalysis.

Notes

1 I believe that in my reading I have encountered a criticism to this effect and I apologize for not being able to remember the author.
2 In view of the great significance given to the concept of projective identification introduced by Melanie Klein in 1946, which meanwhile has assumed the status of an omnibus concept, it is noteworthy that Fliess anticipated this concept – and corrected it.

18

Postscript (1969b) to 'Dynamics of transference interpretations' (1955/6)

This postscript was added to the French publication of Paula Heimann's paper on 'The dynamics of transference interpretations' (1956) in *Bulletin de l'Association Psychanalytique de France* 5 (1969). It contains several revisions of her views presented in 1956 and has been translated into English for this book.

Postscript

Nearly fifteen years have elapsed since I wrote this paper[1] and of course later experience, stemming from my own work and from the study of the work of other psychoanalysts, has led me to modify the conclusions I expressed there. Those changes consist, on the one hand, of additions, enlargements, slight shifts of emphasis, but also, on the other hand, of important alterations concerning basic aspects in pathological psychic functioning, the earliest stages of development, and also the nature and course of later psychic growth.

To begin with I shall briefly examine these last points, for they concern my basic orientation and therefore provide the centre from which my views on the dynamics of transference interpretations extend and in which they both converge and authenticate each other.

Since my student days, I have been an enthusiastic supporter of the Freudian theory of life and death instincts, considered as the ultimate source of all instinctual processes. I still think that with this theory Freud presented an awe-inspiring concept – and in what fine language! – that has given us a glimpse of the relations between the various elements that make up the universe and which reconciles the contrasts between its various phenomena: attraction and repulsion, the expansion and contraction of the universe, animate and inanimate matter. However, I gradually came to mistrust this very enthusiasm

252

and to realize (as I have said elsewhere [Heimann 1968]) that my attitude was 'oceanic' rather than scientific; I have come to distinguish between the clinically verifiable elements of Freud's theory and the cosmic speculation that it involves.

What we can observe in our work as psychoanalysts is that our patients want to live, and to live well, to obtain the satisfaction of their various needs and instinctual wishes, and that this strikes us as quite 'natural'. But, before deducing from this a life instinct that evolved at the same time as a death instinct, it is safer to assume that the person wishes to survive; the individual's instinct for survival may be verified by observation, and by his reactions when his survival or the values of his way of life are threatened. Observation may also verify an individual's parental instinct, and here the psychoanalyst is at one with the naturalist, who sees it as an expression of the species' tendency to survival (an old distinction made by Freud between the ego instincts and the sexual instincts, and later between self-preservation and procreation).

In other words, one sees that a living person (and living creatures in general) want to go on living.

What, then, is the death instinct? There are many situations in which our patients tell us and show us that they want to be dead. I believe that it is more correct to say that they want to be dead than to say that they want to die; indeed, analysis reveals that the wish in question concerns a state that is painless, while the fact of dying is usually strongly invested with phantasies of pain. Behind the wish to be dead what one really finds is the wish to be free of pain, whether physical, or psychical, such as shame, guilt, intolerable fears, anxiety, depression, confusion, despair, and so on, or we find phantasy wishes to be revenged upon or to kill an object with which the patient has unconsciously identified. A fairly typical revenge phantasy, which is often pre-conscious, consists of imagining one's parents in a state of terrible guilt, suffering from remorse, accusing each other over their child's grave: here an Oedipal wish is concealed behind the wish to be dead.

This is not the place to give a more complete list of the pre-conscious and unconscious phantasies that underpin the conscious and unconscious wish to be dead; my main argument is that more careful investigations reveal a psychical condition that does not involve the theory of a death instinct.

Now it will be noted that Freud himself usually speaks of death instincts in the plural, and this in itself might suggest that he must have challenged the validity of the notion. (After all, when he introduced the dualism of life instincts and death instincts as being the primary source of the innumerable observable tendencies, he declared that he had only a lukewarm attitude to this idea.) Moreover, he referred to the death instincts by another term: 'destructive instinct(s)'. With this last concept we are back once again on the solid terrain of observable facts: both inside and outside the analytic situation, we encounter a destructive drive that is directed against both objects and self (indeed the first is often a roundabout way of arriving at the second, a fact that makes the Freudian theory of the struggle waged by the death instinct against the life instinct and of its ultimate victory so tempting).

We long ago abandoned the idea that destructiveness appears only as a result of the frustration of libidinal impulses, independently of the question, which has remained without an answer, as to the source from which this reaction of frustration manifests destructiveness. However, is it really from the tendency to destruction that one can posit the existence of a death instinct? Even at the time of my enthusiasm for the theory of the death instinct, I found it difficult to attribute to a wish to return to the inanimate state – that is to say, to the death instinct – something as strongly energetic as the wish to attack or to destroy an object, and I thought the 'negativism, refusal to perceive and cathect the object, turning away from it, denial, are characteristic expressions of the death instinct' (Heimann 1955/56).

Today I would insist even more on the difficulties there are in imagining that the inanimate condition may involve an energy-charged psychical residue; if we had to search for its manifestations, we would have to examine such states as negativism, indifference, contempt for pain, lack of interest in oneself and in all kinds of objects – in other words, something that was related to the absence of life. Thus we shall meet needs (physical and psychical), pleasure and pain, apathy, lack of reaction to stimuli, psychotic states of melancholic depression or of depression in schizophrenic patients, problems of great complexity involving early childhood experiences and imposed identifications (intrusions on the part of bad parents in early infancy) or desired, but ill-judged identifications, cumulative trauma (Khan 1964), and so forth; and I would hesitate to establish a direct link from these clinical phenomena to the concept of a 'primary' source. Furthermore, such a 'primary' source of all the life phenomena – life as a detour away from death – diminishes the specific conflicts of the *condition humaine*, the results of the leap from animal to man along the evolutionary spiral that, in my view, Teilhard de Chardin (1959)[2] has presented so convincingly.

The great achievement of *Beyond the Pleasure Principle* (1920g) lies in the fact that Freud puts an end to the confusion of concepts that had been maintained until the publication of that work; he does this by separating cruelty from libido, by admitting two primary drives. His speculation that they appeared when 'the properties of life . . . were raised from inanimate matter' (1920g: 38) may be confirmed or denied in a convincing way by research outside the domain of the psychoanalysts. The psychoanalytic situation can do neither of these two things, and furthermore, psychoanalysts are not experts in palaeontology, ethology, and so on. Personally, what I no longer find convincing is the relation between the hypothetical death instinct and the primary destructive drive.

Another change bearing on fundamental problems concerns the earliest phases of life and, consequently, the role of introjection and projection that I attributed in this article to the developmental process. The way in which these mechanisms are described in the article reveals restrictions and omissions – though they do not emerge easily on reading. In the article I gave excessive importance to object relations as the factor that complements the growth of the ego and shapes it; on the other hand, the ego's innate capacities, which at first are only potentialities for growth, and which are the driving force for the individual's development, achievement and cognitive function, I left in the shade..

Today I would like to stress strongly the need to distinguish between the ego mechanisms relating to the psychical context in which they are used and which decides whether they will serve defensive functions or functions of experimenting in the service of knowledge, the successful carrying out of a task of some specific creative aim. Hendrick was the first to draw attention to the fact that the ego mechanisms are not only defensive, but also executive.

By stressing the psychic context in which an ego mechanism functions, I also wish to insist on the motivation that sets it in motion and that determines its result. The difference between the defensive use and the creative or cognitive use of an ego mechanism lies in the quality and degree of consciousness that accompanies its functioning. As a defence mechanism, introjection proceeds in an unconscious way – for example, to remove the pain caused by the loss of an object – but, as a method of enriching the ego, this same mechanism is used with a conscious intention that also involves choice, discrimination, and so forth. Similarly, projection, when used unconsciously as a defence against guilt, shame, and other painful feelings, leads to delusion; but when employed consciously, it serves knowledge and makes it possible to evaluate an internal process, such as ideas and images: scientific and artistic activities have recourse to external means of projection.

The fact that one constantly encounters in the psychoanalytic literature new defence mechanisms that are indeed often no more than new names for known mechanisms, or in which the new element is used with a particular nuance brought out by the author, suggests that probably all the ego mechanisms may serve defensive aims that, in other circumstances, express a conscious choice of action. (I have developed these ideas in my article, 'Notes on the anal stage' [1962b].)

So much for fundamental modifications to my points of view. These modifications contain mainly what I said at the beginning of my article, and, as I have said, I do not claim to have exhausted this subject. If I now consider the principal content of the article, my ideas on the dynamics of transference interpretations, I would wish to add rather than to modify.

Interpretation is the only important tool that is specific to psychoanalysis. But if one wishes to understand how it functions, one must take into account both its history and the context in which it is presented. Freud established the analytic situation when he abandoned hypnosis and at the same time substituted for the attention that the patient and the therapist had previously given to a particular symptom, free association on the part of the patient and free hovering attention on the part of the analyst. If we bear the historical context in mind, we are protected against the danger of misunderstanding the adjective 'free' in so far as it could seem to deny the psychic determination of free association. Freud stressed the dual character of the analytical process, which is both research and treatment. Since then the analytic situation has been described under its dual aspect of the therapeutic working alliance and the transference neurosis. For my part, the two terms of the dualism should be, rather, the 'psychoanalytic milieu' and the 'psychoanalytic working team'.

I refer to the psychoanalytic milieu because this French term suggests both an environment and a centre, and that is what the psychoanalytic situation offers the patient – that is to say, an environment that nourishes his needs, his problems, his processes, and his internal conflicts. This environment repeats, to some extent, the patient's original environment, namely, being in the midst of the family where his psychic (and physical) development took place. The family circle, relatively constant and stable, may be compared to this psychoanalytic milieu thanks to the agreement made at the beginning of the analysis. I am referring here to the place, time-table, frequency, duration of analyst sessions, to the fees that the patient must pay, and I am including other information, in particular the 'fundamental rule' and the respective positions of the patient and analyst in the consulting room. In the analytic milieu, I also include the uninterrupted presence of the analyst and his continuous attention. Now, these features, of which the patient is not usually consciously aware, confer on the analytic situation the quality of something that belongs to the patient without having to be questioned by him, something relatively free from stimuli.

What the stability of the analytic milieu means for a patient becomes clear through the violent reactions that he manifests when interruptions and changes take place. I am not referring to interruptions caused by weekends and holidays, but by such changes as a redecoration of the consulting room (or a change of address on the part of the analyst). One day, when my room had been repainted and the furniture arranged differently, one of my patients said to me: 'I admit that it is more comfortable like this, but you know how much I hate any change.' He could have been the spokesman for all the patients except one, whose fundamental problems gravitated constantly around the search for something different or something new. This particular patient was immediately enthusiastic, on a conscious level for aesthetic reasons, on an unconscious level because my room ('I') had become something other and something new and, consequently, a good thing for the moment.

But, on the other hand, the psychoanalytic situation has an eminently variable, inconstant, dynamic character, rich in stimuli. This comes from the fundamental rule, from verbal exchange, associations–interpretations, and it is this that constitutes the psycho-analytic patient–analyst working team. The patient's silence, whether it is spontaneous or corresponds to the commentary or interpretation that the analyst is making, represents an action or an event that must be explored and ultimately transformed into an explicit verbal contact between them. Everything that the patient has said or not said has specific meanings depending on the circumstances. Of course, his thoughts do sometimes concern the milieu, but one hardly expects him to say something about this in each session; on the contrary, he will have a great deal to say on the process of psychic work deriving from the analytic situation, but also new things; he will have thoughts, feelings, phantasies, memories, desires, and fears to communicate.

The milieu reproduces, as I have said, the patient's original milieu. It is through the working team, through interpretations and especially transference interpretations (which are the subject of the article), that 'repetition becomes modification' and the patient's psychic development progresses. The psychoanalytic milieu really

257

repeats the original undifferentiation between the infant and maternal care, the infant's calm entourage, with gentle stimuli in the appropriate dosage coming from understanding parents. This allows the patient to re-live narcissistic illusions consistent with identifying with his loving parents, thus re-living an indubitable basic trust (which different authors have described in different terms), on which depends a favourable development, which both the infant in his family and the patient in the transference need if they are to overcome the pain and anxiety involved in the processes of growth and differentiation.

These processes, in which the loss of naïve primitive narcissism and that of the exclusive possession of maternal care are lived out, are reproduced in the analytic working team and they are reduced to verbal communication between patient and analyst.

It is within the working team that the processes of individuation, differentiation, and independent functioning, as well as the discovery of the ego's specific capacities are to be found and that whatever went wrong at the beginning may be corrected.

With all patients, there are moments or phases when verbal communication as such means severe frustration, when they receive it as indicating separation, distance, and otherness, and not as communion, which would be understood without mediation; and they do not appreciate the benefit to be obtained by the acquisition of language as a new means of making richer contact on an intrapsychic as well as on a inter-personal level. As we know, changes in the patient's psychic condition depend on the fact that he experiences a highly emotive understanding, a new awareness of himself, and this comes to him from the analyst's interpretations. However, evaluating the importance of an interpretation, we cannot allow ourselves to ignore the effects of the psychoanalytic milieu. This, given its constancy, represents a source of positive transference of another order than the violent, poignant, sudden, and temporary libidinal reactions produced by specific interpretations. The milieu and verbal contact are complementary factors. Since the analyst is alerted to the nature of the analytic situation, both of them, he and his patient, will be protected against a dogmatic or magical idealization on the part of either if taken separately.

What the analyst offers his patient in an interpretation (and sometimes in a mere exclamation or question in the form of 'Hm?' or 'Hm!', or again by picking up on a turn of phrase used by the patient, but which the analyst repeats with a different intonation), is the starting point of an exploration, a voyage of discovery and, since the exploration and the discovery begin with perception, it is the perception of the here and now processes which moves the patient on and provides the raw material of an interpretation. It is not up to the analyst to offer his patient a solution to his problems. But the interpretation must add something to what the patient already knew of himself. In other words, an interpretation (or a commentary belonging to the vast hierarchy of verbal communications that the analyst may make) links the verbalization of a particular, present problem with some illumination, which must nevertheless contain a questioning, an urging on, a request addressed to the patient's ego so that he may continue on his way, go on searching and advance; but, thanks to the illuminating element contained in the analyst's remarks, this movement will stem from a point that is already more advanced in relation to the patient's previous position. Without such an element of illumination, the patient would be doomed to going round and round in a circle – the vicious circle, the impasse with which he is all too familiar – and he would feel rejected and tormented. On the other hand, too many 'explanations' would shut the door to the patient's creative activity without benefiting him. Indeed, if the analyst's contributions to the working team excluded or ignored the patient's collaboration, this would mean for the patient that he was once again subjected to an authority that knew better than he in all matters; that would be to change his original dependence on his parents into a humble submission to his analyst. In fact, the patient's problems would not be resolved; it is only through a process of work carried out by oneself, though within one's relationship with the analyst, that one can arrive at a solution that will open up the path to other problems.

To work with the transference does not mean that the analyst refers to himself whenever he communicates something to his patient. Although he must be constantly alert to grasp the meaning of the transference (wish, drive, fear, and so on), he must also be attentive to the importance of events outside the psychoanalytic situation; for example, to emerging memories after a dream, and also to the need to do just what he pleases which is sometimes inherent in the patient's behaviour. Similarly, when the patient is engaged in a process of creative work, or in the work of mourning, the task of the analyst is that of a person who is simply there and remains vigilant. This is a part of his role as partner in the work.

It may be useful to stress that the term 'transference' is often used incorrectly (as psychoanalysts, we are sometimes so used to free association that we tend to express ourselves rather loosely) when we mean by the term the patient's feelings for the analyst. But the analyst is only one of the two interested parties in the transference, the other being represented by the patient's feelings for his original (past and present) object. That is why the task of the working team cannot but lead to memories real or imaginary, or to reconstructions of the past. And there is also a need for detour and preparation before the new representation of a past experience may be identified in its dynamic, meaningful development as it concerns the analyst.

What the patient plays out in the analytic situation may be a single, distinct experience or an entire phase of his life. I remember a phase that lasted for several weeks, during which a patient showed tenaciously that she knew more than I did, was more capable than I was, and surpassed me in every respect. After a while, and with the help of certain memories, we understood that she had been re-playing a phase in her life, before she had been allowed to go to school, when her brothers and sisters, all older than she, were those superior beings, admired and envied, who, day after day, acquired extraordinary knowledge.

An important problem concerning the contribution of the analyst to the work of the team has to take into account the extent of the patient's attention. It may be put on the same plane as the question of the optimal distance between the analyst's and patient's understanding. Clearly, the analyst usually possesses superior knowledge, but if he expatiates too long on a specific issue there is a danger that he will communicate more than the patient can usefully assimilate, either because his attention span is limited or because his capacity to assimilate new ideas is inadequate. (The word 'capacity' is used here in both its senses, referring to aptitude and volume.) When the analyst is 'too clever', he fails as a member of the team. Another important failure is due to bad timing: an interpretation given too early or too late will fail in its aim and increase the patient's resistances. In that case the analyst must examine his emotional disturbances, due to the transference or counter-transference.

To end, I would like to make a few brief observations about a problem that, to my knowledge, has not been properly discussed. I am thinking of the formulation of the interpretation – coming at the moment when the analyst believes that he knows what the interpretation ought to contain. If the function of the interpretation is, as I believe, to stimulate the patient's ego mechanisms, I maintain that the interpretation ought to be vivid, warm, personal, and not gloomy, didactic, schematic, since the latter are neither stimulating nor suggestive. But, as often happens, we are faced with a dilemma here: the vivid, non-schematic formulation may be felt as sadistic teasing or as a libidinal seduction, whereas the other formulation runs the risk of being felt as the expression of a coldness and

260

dogmatism that imposes silence. We must be aware, not only because of the content of the interpretation, but also because of its form, that what we intend to communicate to our patient may not be at all what he hears.

In short, I believe that we cannot claim to give an analytic recipe, but that we ought to speak in a way that is natural to us; this does not mean, however, that we cannot adapt to our patient's specific idiosyncrasies and needs in relation to the form as well as to the degree of his receptiveness, his capacity, and his present availability.

Translated by Alan Sheridan, London

Notes

1 [The following footnote was added to the French publication of the 'Postscript': 'Dr Paula Heimann was keen to write this postscript (the term, here, as we shall see, is used in its widest sense) on the occasion of the publication of her 1956 article in the *Bulletin*. We would like to thank her most warmly for it.']

2 In his introduction to the English edition (1959) of Teilhard de Chardin *The Phenomenon of Man*, London: Collins (1955), Julian Huxley emphasized his agreement with Teilhard de Chardin.

Opening and closing remarks of the Moderator to 'Discussion of "The non-transference relationship in the psychoanalytic situation"' (1969/70a)

The 'Opening and closing remarks' were Paula Heimann's contribution as moderator to the plenary session of the 26th International Psycho-Analytical Congress, Rome, 1969, that discussed the pre-published paper by Ralph R. Greenson and Milton Wexler, 'The non-transference relationship in the psychoanalytic situation', *International Journal of Psycho-Analysis* 50 (1) (1969). The contributions to the discussion were published in the *International Journal of Psycho-Analysis* 51 (2) (1970).

The authors' new contribution to psychoanalysis is stated boldly as a paradox: in order to facilitate the development, blossoming, and resolution of the transference neurosis, the analyst must facilitate the development of a relationship which is 'real' and not based on transference.

The analytic situation has two parts: the patient's 'transference neurosis' and the 'working alliance'. When the latter is in progress, the patient is not neurotic, fully related to contemporary matters, and works with his analyst on his problems constructively and unimpeded by his neurosis. The two components can alternate within one and the same session (as illustrated), but during the period of the 'working alliance' patient and analyst have a 'real' relationship with one another.

Mind you, the 'real' of the 'real' non-transference relationship is framed by inverted commas.

In contrast to the transference neurosis, the 'real' non-transference relationship is not to be subjected to analysis. To put it bluntly, it is not to be interpreted away. It is to be encouraged and maintained. Taken literally, analysis then depends on and presupposes *not* analysing certain sectors of the patient–analyst relationship. However, this first stark statement is followed by careful considerations which provide ample scope for debate, shared reconsideration and, possibly, revision of the original presentation. In my further remarks I shall refer to the authors' views (of which you have been reminded just now) very briefly as *theses* and oppose them – if I can – by *antitheses*, hoping that by acting as the Devil's advocate I shall highlight the controversial points.

Thesis 1. The analytic relationship is a relationship between two human beings who need to 'fit' with each other. The analyst's personality affects the analytic process, beneficially or harmfully.

No antithesis. This is Freud's teaching, amply confirmed.

Thesis 2. No patient, neurotic or psychotic, is regressed to the degree of being oblivious all the time to all of his analyst's personal traits. Total anonymity is neither possible nor desirable.

No antithesis. But a qualification, to be considered later, concerns the use which the analyst makes of these facts.

Thesis 3. Keeping to safeguards in order to avoid stifling an ongoing process of intellectual cognition or imagination in the patient, the analyst must acknowledge his errors of procedure or personality shortcomings which his patient has spotted.

No antithesis. Incidentally, why does it not occur to us to agree with a patient's praise?

Thesis 4. I quote: 'The two outstanding characteristics of transference phenomena are (1) it is an indiscriminate, non-selective repetition of the past, and (2) it ignores or distorts reality. It is inappropriate (Greenson 1967)'.

Antithesis. This definition is far too narrow. It acknowledges only Freud's first encounter with transference phenomena, when the unhypnotized patient 'confused' the therapist with his original objects. But in his later expositions Freud made important additions.

1 He separated from the erotic transference the mild positive transference which is closely related to confidence, trust, and sympathy, that is, to the basic ingredients of the *condition humaine*. Without 'basic trust' the infant would not survive; without 'basic transference' the patient would not accept his doctor's advice, the analytic patient not remain in analysis; but, of course, the maternal figure, the medical person, and the analyst must confirm and respond to this basic human factor.

2 Freud's second extension of the concept of the transference must be taken together with the fundamental rule, and concerns the effect on development.

With the establishment of the fundamental rule the patient's total personality, illness, and healthy mental functioning, waking life and dreams entered into the relationship with his analyst.

The therapeutic situation *changed from a symptom cure to a process of psychic growth*. Hence symptoms are outgrown rather than abreacted.

As a transference figure the analyst enables his patient to repeat his development. This repetition, however, results in change, in the liberation of growth potential, formerly stifled, because it takes place within the compass of the fundamental rule which demands from the patient – and grants him – spontaneity, while prescribing *responsiveness* to the analyst. The authors' clinical examples clearly illustrate this fact.

All development proceeds by spurts of advance alternating with regression, which may be pathological or 'normal' (Anna Freud) and 'in the service of the ego' (Kris).

In the analytic situation this may appear as emotional ambivalence coupled with oscillations between insight and flight from insight. It can occur within a single session (Michael) or over periods (Helen, Douglas).

Thesis 5. All object relations consist of different blendings of transference and non-transference components.

Antithesis. It is only the analytic relationship which is governed by the unique phenomenon of the fundamental rule.

Thesis 6. The authors object to the technique of 'only analysing' or 'only interpreting' transference phenomena.

No antithesis. But an amplification: from what I have heard or read of this procedure, it consists of an *automatic* translation of any and every experience with which the patient is concerned into his relation with his analyst – often in abstruse language.

This procedure raises the question whether it is psychoanalytic and whether it does deal with the patient's transference. Moreover, any 'interpreting only' *one* aspect of the patient's processes would not be an application of psychoanalytic metapsychology, nor does analysing the transference mean that the analyst refers to himself in every comment. Such a procedure repeats that of a possessive parent. The true and timely transference interpretation, however, has the outstanding advantage over other interpretative comments that it bridges the actual ego with its lost past within an intensely cathected, intensely lived object relationship. The object of this relationship *is a transference figure*, and this means that he is a person with an *inner stance* that keeps him persistently aware of being his patient's analyst (Fliess's 'work ego', Greenson's 'model of the patient').

I shall end with some questions.

Did Greenson introduce a far-reaching change in the concept of the psychoanalytic situation when he replaced the 'therapeutic alliance' with the 'working alliance'?

Did Wexler's work with psychotic patients underscore and extend this new orientation?

Does the new perspective not merely *attribute* to the patient in his relation to his analyst considerably more realism and rationality than has come my way, but in fact *achieve* this realism? Or have my limitations of grasp and synthesis led me to confuse problems of semantics or of shift of accent with problems of substance?

I look forward to learning from the discussants and the authors' reply.

Closing remarks of the Moderator (Paula Heimann)

I shall be very brief and list only summarily the main points of divergence that have been put forward in the discussion. These concern the problem of reality in the psychoanalytic situation and the closely related problem of the analyst's humanity as distinct from, and outside, the transference relationship between the patient and his analyst.

It appeared that greater clarity is needed to arrive at an understanding of the way in which 'reality' and 'humanness' (as posited in the paper) affect the way in which the analyst as a worker in the analytic situation listens to his patient, perceives what happens in him, and, as Freud put it, bends his own unconscious to that of his patient so as to gauge correctly the lines to be taken in the journey from the patient's conscious thoughts and feelings to his unconscious processes.

At times I felt that the comments raised revealed that the authors had been misunderstood – as indeed they had feared.

However, misunderstandings as well as concerns for the deeper exploration of issues which pertain to the concept of the psychoanalytic situation – all indicate that we have been considerably stirred by the paper, and this is, I think, what the authors wanted. We, in turn, may demand of them to keep our questions in mind as they continue their researches and provide us with more material to reconsider and test their ideas.

By way of a postscript I wish to register my impression that both the authors' presentations and the contributions by the discussants have suffered from the unspoken lack of agreement on the definition of what constitutes an interpretation. What turns the analyst's comment to his patient into the specific phenomenon, the dynamic tool, unique for psychoanalysis, to which we give the status of an interpretation and distinguish by this name? A number of conditional requirements seem to be used privately and hover around in the dim light of communications of a pre-conscious order. To mention a few which I believe to discern in what has been expressed today: the language in which the analyst's comment has to be couched; the contents which it has to verbalize; the level of the patient's psychic functioning which it should reach; the patient's affective state which it should pinpoint; and the amount of clarification which it should present at the given moment. It would have been of great help in our discussion of fundamental psychoanalytic issues – for example, the differences between a psychoanalytic and a physicianly procedure – if we had stated clearly how we define the concept of interpretation.

20

The nature and function of interpretation (1970b)

This paper is an edited version of a paper in thesis form which Paula Heimann gave in April 1970 in Latin America. We have edited the manuscript, which had many abbreviations and additions at the margins, for publication in this book. We found in Paula Heimann's literary estate several papers with extensive case material, marked 'Confidential', which seemed to have been prepared for seminars in Germany, and this paper brings together various aspects which were discussed in greater detail there.

What I shall say today will hardly be new. It is my aim to present ideas, whether they are new or old, in the form of simple statements in order to start a discussion on this important topic that demands a great deal from us every day.

I
Some aspects of the nature of interpretation

1 The nature of interpretation has to do with 'meaning' – compare Freud (1900) *The Interpretation of Dreams.*
2 It is a comment by the analyst to his patient.
3 This comment is the analyst's response to something from his patient, e.g., to:
   (a) a report on his experience(s) in the present or in the recent past;
   (b) recollection(s) from the earlier past;
   (c) an expression of feelings, wishes, fears, etc.;
   (d) a thought process in which the patient tries to solve certain problems;
   (e) material dealing with feelings and thoughts about the analyst;

(f) events, problems, wishes, or suggestions related to the 'psychoanalytic working team' or the 'psychoanalytic milieu';

(g) practical matters like a request for a change of time or fees, etc.;

(h) the patient's questions or other seemingly direct requests.

4 This element of response shows the analyst's endeavour to listen with participation – 'First position of the analyst's cognitive process' (Heimann 1978) – to follow and to understand his patient.

5 Following, understanding, and recognizing meaning is based on the analyst's listening in a specific manner, with psychoanalytic 'freely mobile' attention. Reik (1948) speaks of *Listening with the Third Ear* – I often feel with many more than three ears!

6 This specific listening differs from ordinary social listening: it corresponds with and responds to the patient's talking with 'free associations' – Freud's (1912e) analogy with a mirror.

(a) The analyst's attention is mobile so as to perceive the various modes of communication, the different levels of experience, the processes in the different psychic structures, and the relationship and interactions, be they co-operative or antagonistic, resulting from inter-systemic and intra-systemic conflicts.

(b) The analyst's attention does not pursue any line selectively from subjective motives or interests and is not determined by id impulses or superego demands. These are to a high degree eliminated, but I do not wish to say they are totally eliminated.

(c) In so far as the analyst's ego functions alone are determining his attention, his ego acts as the patient's 'auxiliary' or 'supplementary' ego.

(d) In so far as id and superego elements operate, they (should!) serve as additional organs for perceiving the patient's processes. It assists in understanding the patient's internal as well as external object relations.

(e) The analyst's attention thus interacts with his imagining and making images of how the patient treats his objects. This includes how the patient provokes them to specific ways of treating him/her.

(f) The psychoanalytic attention results from the analyst's training analysis and his theoretical training. These are continued as self-analysis, further learning from his own experience, from discussions with colleagues and also from reading the literature ('the mirror' must be kept clear!). Also, as Dr Perestrello[1] has pointed out, from his psychic structure and ego capacities, including intellectual grasp.

(g) The mirror analogy, however, holds only to a limited extent.

The analyst has feelings, but uses them for his work (his imagination and his counter-transference).

(h) Psychoanalytic attention thus focuses also on the analyst's own processes: his introspection helps to scrutinize and decode the patient's expressions, verbal or non-verbal, to prepare his rendering into language the impressions he has received and perceived from the patient.

II
The function of interpretation

Much about the functions of interpretation can be derived from its qualities, which I tried to describe in the preceding section. I shall now list some of its functions:

1 To make the patient aware of the meaning of his words, or his behaviour:
   (a) The deeper meaning of a patient's communication which may in itself be coherent and logical and yet may screen matters of a very different kind. It may refer to a chaotic state of irrational wishes, thoughts, feelings, fears, magical expectations, etc. ('Flight into reality and sanity' belongs here).
   (b) This apparently logical statement may serve
       (i) as a defence against the patient experiencing a deeper chaotic state that he feels would represent an immanent and actual danger;
       (ii) as a defence against confessing to the analyst the extent of his infantile modes of thinking and feeling; and
       (iii) as a defence against the extent of his dependence on the analyst.
   (c) I wish here to stress my view that the patient uses a hierarchy of means of expressing himself and of attempting to make contact with his analyst. He may intend to tell his analyst something, and he may be able to succeed by being clear, direct, and in full possession of his ego functions which constitute secondary process thinking or 'regression in the service of the ego' (Kris 1952). On the other hand, he may be too anxious, aggressive, teasing, or testing and therefore may use oblique expressions and allusions. He may even be in such a state of distress that he can only give a signal of his need.
2 An important function of the interpretation, then, is to make the patient aware of these different modes of relating to his analyst and the different kinds of expression used.

3 In connection with the interpretation being a comment by the analyst to his patient, its function is to establish contact with the patient;

    (a) to confirm the patient's capacity for making contact and acknowledge the wish for it;

    (b) to show the patient by the analyst's response that he has understood him;

    (c) to convey to the patient that his remarks (associations) and the analyst's remarks (interpretations) are an interacting and interdependent process (verbal interchange can serve as a model for all kinds of symbolic intercourse, including sexual intercourse).

4 In verbalizing the different kinds of communication the interpretation establishes links between the patient's different experiences. It thus fulfils an integrating function, and in the same process achieves both a widening of the ego's perceptive function and a strengthening of the ego.

5 This function helps to make the patient independent of the analyst and also of people in general.

6 So far I have listed the functions of interpretation which concern the patient's understanding (his cognitive processes and insight with affective cathexis). However, there is also a similar effect on the analyst's cognitive processes. I want to remind you here of Dr Perestrello's observation[2] that in the wake of interpreting, he becomes aware of ideas he had not thought about when he started. As I said at the time, this phenomenon is familiar to me. Taking this into consideration, we have to say that the function of an interpretation is to effect not only connections between the analyst and the patient, and within the patient's mind, but also that it effects and facilitates thought processes in the analyst. Thus interpretation is a means to facilitate thinking. (Perhaps this should have been put in the first section of these notes.) The 'word' is not only a designation of something that is there, it also creates new mental entities ('In the beginning was the Word', John 1:1). A fuller investigation would lead to the dynamics of language, with which I am not attempting to deal here. I may, however, briefly refer to my comments on speaking. In so far as it transforms inner images and thoughts into something that is communicated, I regard this as a creative act. Thus interpretation functions not merely as a presentation of the hidden, unconscious, or repressed meaning of the patient's communications and expressions (which may be signals, signs, fragments, or complete sentences, consciously or unconsciously intended to reach the analyst). Interpretation also

functions as an instrument of thinking: interpretation produces new thoughts.

7 In my view, the analyst's capacity to think and to think more freely than the patient, at least within the analytic situation (Fliess [1942] states that during the limited period of his work with his patient the analyst becomes an exceptional person), leads to his creatively transforming into a communication a process in the patient that was not a communication by its nature, not even unconsciously. The analyst does this by means of his interpretation, by revealing his creative understanding of his patient's needs. In doing this he carries out a maternal function. It is like the mother who recognizes her infant's need from his discharge motor activities at the earliest phase (I refer to my example of a ten-day-old baby in my comments [Heimann 1966] to Dr Kernberg's paper) before the infant has advanced to the stage of recognizing his mother as an object. By her ministrations the mother teaches her infant the meaning of his former primitive discharge and thus leads him to form the concept of communication. In the same way the analyst by his interpretation facilitates a process of psychic growth in his patient. Innate ego capacities are furthered by the mother, if she is, in Winnicott's terms, 'a good enough mother'. If she is not good enough, if she lacks in love and respect for her infant, if she narcissistically treats him as her possession or a source for her gratification, then instead of promoting his germinal ego capacities, she will stifle them and impose a 'false-ego' development. In analogy, if the analyst's interpretations are not in accord with his patient, he will not perform a creative act that liberates ego growth in his patient, but he will damage him. Owing to the strength of the transference, this damage may not be recognized by the patient, or at least not for a long time. Sometimes a narcissistic attitude ('object-disregarding narcissism') in the analyst may be suspected in so-called 'interminable analyses'.

8 Finally, the function of interpretation is dialectic: it strengthens the patient's transference and it reduces it. *En route*, it enables the patient to achieve ego identity with the capacity to appreciate and enjoy other people's ego identities, and thus maturity and mutuality in object relationships. This development includes a high degree of self-reliance and independence. As regards the attitude to psychoanalysis, this means the patient gains the ability for self-analysis: he then identifies with and assimilates the psychoanalytic method independent of his tie to his analyst.

III
The language of an interpretation

1 The analyst takes care to phrase his interpretation in a way that will be most meaningful to the patient.

2 Technical terms therefore are, as a rule, inappropriate, while ordinary language, the language in which the patient is used to think and which comes naturally to him, is meaningful to him.

> At an early phase in his analysis I said to a patient: 'You are not in contact with your depth.' The patient responded to this simple phrase very strongly: he repeated the phrase very thoughtfully, and throughout the analysis he returned to it. He said that it had impressed him very much and that it opened new vistas to him. He questioned himself in his relation to his perceptions and their evaluations, whether they concerned himself or other people, and particularly his work as a writer.

3 For an interpretation to fulfil its function it has to avoid encouraging, stimulating, and facilitating the patient's ego-syntonic defences; be these by intellectualization which pretends to be insight, or by 'pseudo-debility', the pretence that he cannot understand.

> A highly intelligent patient, a university graduate with a Ph.D., who had come to analysis because the girl with whom he was impotent had recommended it, often complained that she used to ask him whether he understood the transference. In his analysis transference phenomena were frequently interpreted, and he understood quite well that he treated me with the same feelings which he had for his father (predominantly from the beginning I represented his intelligent father and not his stupid mother) as well as for other figures of his past. However, he seemed unable to refer the thinking operation from his own experiences in the analysis to the term used by his girlfriend. On the surface this example illustrates emotionally conditioned inhibition of thinking, occurring outside the analysis. However, in view of the transference from this woman to myself (she had sent him to analysis), it also was an example, and was interpreted as such, of his demonstrating to me that he could not understand my interpretations.

4 In the course of an analysis certain key interpretations become a kind of special and private language between the patient and the

272

analyst, a shorthand writing, so to say, between them. When either of them says the specific phase, he/she brings into the actual work on a problem a complex and rich set of meaningful ideas which are strongly cathected.

5 This is one reason why interpretation is regarded as the most important single tool of psychoanalysis, but if we keep in mind that in the working-through process, in which former interpretations are associated and expanded by means of the actual new connections (see section II.4 above), factors belonging to the 'psychoanalytic milieu' naturally interact with the learning process stimulated and facilitated by the analyst's interpretation. A particular phrase which is a combination of familiar words (the everyday language in which the interpretation is formulated) widens the patient's cognitive process in a similar way to that in which originally his mother's and father's talking to him, to each other, or even 'thinking aloud' in his presence, did this in his original environment. Such widening – originally and hence in the transference repetition – may be experienced with positive or with negative feelings, contributing thus to the establishment of a pattern of learning. Here is an example of ambivalent learning:

> A very intelligent patient won a scholarship to a public school when he was eleven years old. In his first term there, he was so homesick that his father fetched him home from this boarding school, and sent him instead to a day school. He went there every morning returning home in the afternoon, as he had done before boarding. In his seventeenth year and later, when he took his Advanced Level examinations, he failed so that he could not go to university. When he reported this in his analysis, I suspected that he had failed on account of his unconscious determination not to follow in his father's footsteps and not to go to Oxford, as his father had done. In the course of his analysis this suspicion was amply confirmed, and his 'learning' difficulties also affected his attitude to the analysis. Once he told me how he learned the word 'typical'. He was long past infantile lack of sphincter control, when he one day let a piece of faeces drop on the floor. His mother picked it up, and his father, looking on, said: 'typical'. The child responded with a mixture of painful feelings like guilt, shame, anger with himself and with both his parents, and anxiety, etc. It was in this situation that he learned the word 'typical'. Indeed, he said, with much bitterness: 'This is how I learned what the word "typical" means.'

IV
The span of interpretation

1 It is one of the most difficult tasks of the analyst to gauge correctly his patient's capacity to maintain attention.

2 A great many factors determine how long the patient can listen to his analyst and take in with benefit what he/she says.

3 The same applies to the patient's capacity to encompass the range of his analyst's ideas: that is, his offer to establish contact both between the patient and himself, and also intrapsychic contact between the different levels of the patient's experience.

4 As I have already mentioned elsewhere (Heimann 1978), it needs a conscious self-training for the analyst to spot the moment at which the span and range of his patient's attention are about to end or have just ended.

5 Most patients tend to dissimulate their failure to follow and understand an interpretation at some time during their analysis, probably more often in the beginning. (I am here not concerned with hostile responses to interpretation.)

A patient who started his analysis in an abject state of anxiety which was triggered off by his girlfriend leaving him gave many indications of fear of separation related to the approaching holidays. I very carefully took these for interpretation and, in fact, he tolerated the holiday without disturbing anxieties. It seemed to me that he co-operated quite well. Only after the holidays and without an obvious thematic connection with the holidays did he tell me that he had been surprised about my interpreting his separation anxiety. As the analysis went on and he became secure and therefore more honest, he expressed protest when he felt that I exaggerated his feelings; for example, he protested when I said that he was terrified. He would only acknowledge a much milder degree of anxiety. However, one day he told me that he had been smoking hashish and that he had responded with a most intense state of terror. In this state he remembered many incidents of the analysis, both in content and in affect, and he told me that he then realized that my phrasing the interpretations in such strong terms had been fully justified. In his state of terror he wanted to phone and ask me to come to him, but he resisted this impulse with the thought that it was inappropriate. My impression was that he was able to feel a realistic consideration: 'I could not expect you to rush to me at two o'clock at night, and I thought you would quite rightly tell me to get a doctor!' In my opinion this was possible because the analysis had freed a sufficient amount of insight which enabled him to remember the many analytic incidents. One could say he maintained the therapeutic split between the observing and the experiencing ego.

6 I put the problem of gauging the span and range of a patient's attention first because in my experience it is less widely discussed than that of gauging the time for an interpretation. Although it is implicitly and widely acknowledged that interpretations should be short, I think it is useful to take the fact of the span and range of attention explicitly as the *decisive point of reference*.

7 To be understood may be regarded as the human being's overriding need and desire. To convey such understanding depends on the phase-adequate modes – this also holds true for the analyst–patient relationship.

I have by no means exhausted the topic of our discussion. This would not be possible for me to do in such a limited time. My aim was therefore to put forward a number of those points which may easily lead us further afield.

Notes

1 Dr Perestrello is a training analyst of the Brazilian Psycho-Analytic Society of Rio De Janeiro and was obviously present when Paula Heimann read her paper.

2 This again refers to Dr Perestrello's presence.

Sacrificial parapraxis – failure or achievement? (1975a)

This paper was written in honour of Richard Sterba on the occasion of his seventy-fifth birthday and published in the *Annual of Psychoanalysis*, vol. III, New York: International Universities Press, 1975.

In his paper 'The Multiple Determinants of a Minor Accident', Richard Sterba (1972) presents an intriguing inquiry into a parapraxis which he concludes by pointing to a gap in our theoretical understanding. As he will remember, I was so fascinated by his paper that I wrote to him about it, yet I did not know then what it really was that held me so much in its grip. When invited to contribute to this Festschrift, I knew without a moment's hesitation that I had to return to this paper, to take up the challenge of the questioning note on which it ends, and to find out what it was that so exercised my mind about it. I am thus doubly grateful for the invitation.

I

Parapraxes

Like so many psychological facts, parapraxes were generally neglected until Freud turned the torch of his scientific exploration on this phenomenon and brought to light its hidden meaningfulness and psychic function. The first generation of psychoanalysts was obviously fired by *The Psychopathology of Everyday Life*, followed Freud's example by analysing slips and bungled actions that came their way, and sent him instances to swell his collection. Later generations of analysts, however, have neglected the problem parapraxes pose. We seem content to look for the hidden meaning, as Freud has shown, but so far as I know, there has been no attempt at correlating parapraxes to specific aspects of psychoanalytic theory. All the more welcome is Sterba's paper, that points to this gap, explores the part which the ego and regression play in parapraxes, and offers an answer, albeit tentatively.

The publication of *The Psychopathology of Everyday Life* followed that of *The Interpretation of Dreams* by one year, but as Strachey[1] pointed out, Freud had already mentioned the solution of a parapraxis in 1898 in a letter to Fliess. He was thus preoccupied with this psychic phenomenon at the same time as he was struggling with the problem of dreams and of neurotic illness, and when discussing parapraxes, he showed their similarities with both the dream and neurotic symptoms.

Yet Freud made only a very modest claim concerning the scientific stature of *The Psychopathology of Everyday Life*. He said in a footnote: "This book is of an entirely popular character: it merely aims, by an accumulation of examples, at paving the way for the necessary assumption of *unconscious yet operative* mental processes, and it avoids all theoretical considerations on the nature of this unconscious" (p. 272).

The book was written before most of his major psychoanalytical and cultural works, but Freud was obviously content to have it reissued without link to his new discoveries, and with additions only of new examples, so that essentially the book remained as it was originally. In a sense this highlights its importance.

In my view, *The Psychopathology of Everyday Life* is twin to *The Interpretation of Dreams* – true, lighter in weight, but twin none the less. In his interpretation of parapraxes Freud shows that they serve the same function for psychic economy in the wakeful state that dreams serve in the condition of sleep. Impulses which we suppress and repress or have never allowed to reach consciousness can be lived out with impunity in the parapraxis, because the slip has been only transient and thus can be made good instantly, and in the dream where, so to speak, higher charges are at stake, because it occurs during sleep, whilst the motor apparatus necessary for action in the outer world is switched off. Thus we are all psychotic in our dreams, albeit not necessarily to the same degree in every dream, and we have a transient neurosis in our parapraxes. Here, too, not to the same degree in every one, and some slips, like losing or mislaying things which we need; or forgetting names, dates, and intentions; or certain bungled actions which damage other people as well as ourselves, we cannot afford with impunity. Both the dream can fail and the parapraxis can fail. The hallucinatory experience of a dream may continue into the wakeful state of a psychotic condition, and too many, too frequent, or enduring parapraxes lead over into an open neurotic condition. Symptomatic acts can transcend into neurotic symptoms.

By and large, however, it might be said that those people remain healthy who can restrict their most primitive impulses and primary-process thinking to the hallucinatory dream psychosis and their ambivalence conflicts to mild and transient parapraxes. I think we rightly worry about patients who never report dreams, never talk about their somatic processes, or never express hostile aggression or ruthless love demands. They are a caricature of normality.

Another exceedingly important trait that *The Psychopathology of Everyday Life* has in common with *The Interpretation of Dreams* is the demonstration that, contrary to the opinion current at the time, the frontiers between mental health and mental illness are not hard and fast. By diminishing the sharp divisions between mental health, neurosis, and psychosis, both works open new dimensions to the understanding of psychic life.

Freud named and grouped together the various parapraxes according to the specific function that was at fault. A look at his chapter headings shows this clearly. He inquired into the individual motivations that determined the occurrence of each slip. In his chapter on bungled actions, however, Freud gave a few examples which he named in accordance with the motive that prompted them. He called them "sacrificial acts". Here is the example that Sterba quotes as similar to his own slip action. Freud flung a slipper at a beautiful little marble statue of Venus and broke it into many pieces. Surprisingly for a collector, he remained utterly indifferent to the loss he had inflicted on himself. But we soon understand this as we read his analysis of the event. Preceding his bungled action he had received the news that the illness of one of his daughters was improving and not fatal, as he had dreaded. In smashing his little Venus statue, he had made a sacrifice as a thank offering. The determining motive for another sacrificial act was to avert worse disaster. Instead of breaking a friendship, he broke his latest acquisition, an Egyptian figure. He added that both could be mended!

When commenting on his smashing of the little Venus, Freud stated that it still was a mystery to him, even at the time of writing about it, how he decided on a sacrificial act so quickly, chose his target so appropriately, and aimed so accurately, feeling sure that had he set out with the conscious intention to hit only the little statue and none of the articles nearby, he would have failed.

Another type of sacrificial parapraxis mentioned by Freud relates to an old custom: on certain festive occasions some articles were broken deliberately, whilst a phrase was spoken to invoke good luck. This link with tradition is particularly pertinent to my ideas, and I shall return to it later. But I may here point to the need to distinguish between a fault in our mental functioning and an act of preserving a tradition that originates in a significant cultural event in the remote past. We need to reconsider our notion of regression.

These sacrificial parapraxes are clearly of a very different order from those slips that give transient relief in conflictual object relations, as in the example of the assistant asking his colleagues to "belch" instead of "clink their glasses" in honour of their revered chief.[2]

Dr Sterba's accident

Dr Sterba dropped the rear door of a Volkswagen station wagon on his forehead. The impact gashed the skin and cut a chunk out of it. The bone was not touched. He reacted with equanimity to the accident and was at first unwilling to recognize it as a parapraxis. Later, however, the true analyst's urge to analyse his actions asserted itself, and he found his mind particularly lucid whilst flooded by memories and thoughts.

I shall briefly summarize his findings.

Freud's discovery of the similarity between parapraxis and a dream is beautifully borne out by Sterba's interpretive procedure, when he first mentioned the event of the day preceding the day of the parapraxis.

This event was his daughter's marriage. He was delighted with her choice of a husband; he greatly liked his son-in-law and the new family. What crowned his happiness was the fact that his son-in-law was Jewish. It was one of the happiest days of his life.

Thus his first interpretation of his slip action was that it was a sacrificial act, a thank-offering, which he compared with Freud's smashing of the little Venus. However, he was unwilling to attribute very great significance to this meaning, and looked for other and more infantile unconscious determinants (again, similar to the way we regard a dream) and recognized the self-injury as an equivalent of circumcision, indicating impulses of rivalry with his daughter's husband. When telling a friend about the accident, he made a slip of the tongue, saying that a piece of his foreskin – skin of his forehead – was taken out. The whole and rich history of his relationship with Jewish people came into his mind, interwoven with his relationship to his family.

279

He grew up in a family who shared the general Austrian hostility against Jews which, after Hitler's advent, increased to violent hatred, particularly on the part of his older brother. In his schooldays he had no contact with his two or three Jewish classmates, who were mediocre and dull. Yet he greatly appreciated the attitude of the priest who taught religion, who included the Jewish boys in all his extra-curricular activities, who never used the word "Jew", already then a word of scorn, but instead spoke of "*de gente electa.*" (We may recognize here a forerunner of the guiding figures whom Sterba later collected in contrast to those who by kinship or convention were his mentors.)

Memories moved to young manhood, when for the first time he met Jewish young men whose intelligence and culture attracted him, and whom he found superior to his gentile colleagues. This was during his military service, in the officers' school. The Jewish companions were older and had more experience of life. From them he heard for the first time of Freud and his work. By contrast, the gentile Prussian major disgusted him with his cruel vulgarity. Sterba claims that it was largely due to a Jewish friend that he came out alive from the holocaust of the First World War.

On returning to civilian life and his medical studies, he decided to train in psychoanalysis, a decision that made his gentile colleagues recoil in horror.

The incident of his membership paper was remembered and led to the interpretation of initiation rites and castration fear. Further determinants belonging to the Oedipal constellation and sibling hostility came up, as he went on remembering how he increasingly associated himself with Jewish people and increasingly alienated himself from his family and their values – i.e. their growing enthusiasm for Hitler and Hitler's Germany. In view of these factors the instrument of the injury was meaningful: a German car became the punishing agency.

There are two outstanding events that proved his sense of belonging with his Jewish friends. One was his rejection of the invitation to read a paper to the Berlin Psycho-Analytical Society, which by then had been swallowed up by the German Psychotherapeutic Society after all Jewish psychoanalysts had been outlawed. Sterba accepted on the condition that he read a paper after a Jewish Viennese colleague. This, of course, put an end to the invitation. The other and most poignant event was the last time he saw Freud. A day after Hitler's army invaded Austria, the Board of the Vienna Psycho-Analytical Society met at Freud's house and every member was asked about his plans. Sterba, like all Jewish analysts, declared that he would emigrate – the supreme test of his electing to belong with the Jews. This memory continues to the – amazing – fact that the President of the International refused to help him since, as a gentile, he could have remained in Vienna. Without help, a refugee in Switzerland (notorious for her hostile attitude to refugees), exposed to persecution, and a repetition of this later in the United States – these experiences gave to the self-inflicted "circumcision" an added meaning of defiance and self-assertion against injustice and persecution. The Sterbas learnt in their own personal lives what generations of their elected people had suffered.

Having explored the determinants of his slip action, Sterba turned his attention to the role his ego played in it. And here he encountered the same problem which Freud had called a mystery. To achieve only a fleshwound, a "circumcision", and to leave the bone unharmed, this bungled action must have been controlled by superb ego functioning, an incredibly sharp gauging of the distance of head from door, and of the impact of that door on the head. Such precision without repeated careful practice does not occur under normal circumstances.

To account for the phenomenon Sterba looked for regression to an infantile capacity that might have been lost in the process of growing up. It is known that a child may have greater intellectual sharpness, greater sensitivity and creative imagination than later as an adult, but this is not the case with sensory-motor skills. They are not the prerogative of childhood; they have to be acquired. Ontogenesis thus did not seem to provide the answer.

Sterba then thought of one other situation in which such unusual excellence of ego functioning occurs. Quoting Pfister, he refers to mountaineers who, threatened by falling to their apparently unavoidable deaths, were able to save their lives by acting with incredible speed and skill to stop the fall. They report that they felt no fear and could marshall all their capacities for the task of survival.

Sterba himself reports a similar observation concerning a workman who was standing on a platform fixed by ropes to the roof. Suddenly one rope broke, and the platform swung into the vertical position. The man would have fallen to his death had he not in a split second dropped his tools, grabbed the bannister, and held on to it so that Dr. Sterba and his patient could pull him inside the consulting room.

Since, however, in the incident with the car door, Sterba was not in mortal danger, nor was Freud in the slip action with the little Venus statue, the explanation that maximal ego efficiency is available when survival is at stake did not apply.

Mild pressure by id and superego extracting a mild sacrifice, loss of an *objet d'art* in Freud's case and a harmless injury in Sterba's own, does not constitute a situation of emergency, releasing superperformance on the part of the ego. A "purely speculative hypothesis" makes Sterba return to the notion of regression – this time, however, not to a stage in ontogenetic development, but to the phylogenetic past. There are observations concerning primitives whose natural motor-sensory dexterity with their primitive tools far exceeds what civilized man can achieve, even with effort and practice.

I should like to quote Sterba's last paragraph in full. "Culturalization seems to make these faculties recede. May we assume that under the special circumstances mentioned above, the Ego has the possibility to reach into the phylogenetic past and be enabled in this way to acquire for a moment what seems to be superhuman motor and sensory faculties?" Let us note that he ends with a question.

It is the paradox that Sterba's consideration throws into relief so clearly. A parapraxis, a faulty action, is by definition due to a failure on the part of the ego. Yet at the same time, it reveals an unusual excellence of ego functioning. We know that psychoanalysis is full of paradoxes – "*Ça n'empêche pas d'exister.*" Nevertheless they present an irresistible challenge.

To start with, I feel reluctant to give up the connection with mortal danger. True, as Sterba states, neither he nor Freud were actually in any danger when they made the bungled actions described. However, we cannot dismiss the role of death in their thoughts. I have little doubt that the news of the improvement in his daughter's condition was very fresh in Freud's mind and that he still felt the dread of her impending death.

As regards Sterba, his powerful memories of his relations with Jewish people – the mortal danger threatening Freud and the other Jewish analysts and friends, when Hitler came into power, the many murders committed by Hitler, the war, and his own near death, the hardship the Sterbas suffered in Switzerland, and later the full persecution by people swearing to annihilate the Sterbas – death looms very large in the history of his rejoicing in his daughter's marrying a Jew, the day residue of his parapraxis.[3]

Next, the phylogenetic regression tentatively considered by Sterba is not pathological; it is exceedingly healthy. We remember here Kris's concept of regression in the service of the ego, which is helpful for certain ego interests. A broader concept of normal regression has been presented by Anna Freud (1966), who allocates to regression a regular function in development, alternating with obvious spurts of progression. Particularly germane to my ideas is her example of the sixth-form girls who were serious students in the early lessons but, when overburdened by a crowded timetable, "regressed" into silly giggles. The male teachers who took the lessons when they were overtired called them "a flock of silly geese." In fact they were not. Their "regression" was a healthy self-assertion against unreasonable demands which turned a learning situation into intellectual paralysis.

I conclude my present brief excusion into regression by underlining the normal forms of regression and their protective and productive functions. We might distinguish between regressing to an earlier mode of thinking and acting which would be pathological, and reactivating and reliving an earlier experience that contributes to maximal benefit to oneself.

Now a few comments on the incident with the workman. It made me think of many dreams encountered in analysis. If a patient had told me that he dreamt he fell from heaven, was in extreme danger of dying, could just hold on to an insecure support, and was finally saved by being pulled to safety through an opening, I would think that he had presented a birth fantasy, and images of very early life would float into my mind. Although this was not a dream, but a real event, I found myself thinking of early life, and this leads me to my section on narcissism.

II

Narcissism

The supreme feat of survival in mortal danger presupposes that mind and body, all mental and bodily systems, work in unison. When this is the case, the theory of the three structures, different in their functions with complex dynamics revolving upon conflict, seems not the best framework for the observation under discussion, since intrapsychic conflict would detract from the individual's marshalling all his capacities to achieve survival. In other words, I want to consider a regression to the state of undifferentiation, the very early infantile state. Absence of fear, as reported by mountaineers who saved themselves from almost certain death, points to the revival of certain elements of narcissism.

To return to the question of the theoretical framework, I would like to refer to Kohut (1971), who prefaces his erudite book with a comment on theory formation and distinguishes between experience-near and experience-distant abstractions. The theory of the systems id, ego, superego is less experience-near and denotes a higher level of theory-formation than the abstraction "Self".

Whereas many analysts consider the concept "Self" as not

sufficiently scientific, I find it most useful because it is closer to immediate experience and more comprehensive than the terms "Subject" or "Ego". The former is contingent on the reciprocal concept "Object", the latter on the connections with Id and Superego. Winnicott (1971) liked to work with the Subject-Object antithesis and combination and coined the term "Subjective Object". In my view this does not hold for the most primitive stage. The occasions which demand the application of the three structures with their inter- and-intrastructural conflicts are the analyst's daily bread, so to speak, when working with the transference problems of neurotic adult patients. Erikson's concept of "Ego-Identity" (1950) is highly meaningful, but again bound to a higher phase of development, one in which recognition of other identities has long been achieved and recurs with renewed intensity.

Thus to my way of thinking, the term "Self" is more fitting for earliest stages of development. It seems to me best in accord with Freud's description of primary narcissism (1911b, 1914c, 1925h).

Mahler (1969), drawing on extensive researches concerning psychotic children and normal development, adheres to Freud's view of early narcissism. She describes an early "normal autism", preceding the infant's symbiotic relationship with his mother, which gradually gives way to the separation-individuation process.

Early infantile thinking is dominated by the pleasure principle. Pleasure is good, and good is Me. Pain is bad, and bad is Not-Me. We may extend this to: "Me – mine – good (pleasurable) – allowed to exist – Yes," and "Bad (painful) – Not-Me – not mine – existence refused – No." It is an error, which I too made years ago, to think that Not-Me equates with the recognition of another person, a Not-Self. What it denotes is merely the omnipotent negation of pain, employing the mechanism of negative hallucination. This is possible thanks to the reality of the maternal figure (Freud 1911b: 219–20). However short-lived this omnipotence may be, its existence leaves traces which later experiences may revive.

In objective reality the infant survives the caesura of birth and long stretches of babyhood and childhood by virtue of other persons' love, sensitivity, and responsiveness to his needs, coupled with realistic judgements. In the infant's reality helplessness and dependence have no place; he lives in a global philosophy of an all-good world that is of his doing and belongs to him.

Favourable physiological and psychological endowment will intensify this philosophy; unfavourable endowment, early physical illnesses, or environmental distresses detract from it and give more weight to its interruptions by pain, hunger, tensions of any kind.

Such favourable endowment includes what Greenacre (1957, 1958) describes as the capacity for forming "collective alternates", a basic characteristic of the artist.

I have elsewhere (1962b) suggested that narcissism should not be regarded exclusively as an early position of the libido, but should be appreciated in the wider context of an experiential orientation with which the young infant meets all incoming stimuli. Like all psychic formations, narcissism is subject to the processes of maturation and development.

At least three types of narcissism can be distinguished: primary, naïve narcissism, the prerogative of the dawn of thought before the existence of Others than Self is appreciated; secondary, object-hostile narcissism, based on real or imagined wrongs perpetrated against the Self;[4] and creative narcissism, which, in addition to forms of narcissism specific to the creative person and the creative process (which I do not attempt to explore here), includes both the naïve, omnipotent narcissism and the object-hostile narcissism, the latter, particularly pronounced if there are objects who oppose the creative act.

All the forms of narcissism persist throughout life. Naïve narcissism is often met in highly sophisticated persons. Its hallmark is the surprise with which they react, when they meet with a view different from their own. The ease and interest, however, with which they can consider the new, divergent opinion, are free from object hostility. Equally, secondary narcissism with the propensity for feeling wronged is compatible with advanced thinking and mental health. It is hardly necessary to state that the extreme forms of narcissism like hypochondriasis and paranoia belong to the realm of pathology. This fact, however, does not contradict the view that narcissism is subject to development and compatible with health. A final, mature form does not interfere with mature object relations; on the contrary, a certain amount of mature narcissism encourages object relations and makes for positive enjoyment in encountering another Self with different qualities, felt as enriching, complementary, and congenial to one's own Self.

III

Collective alternates

Greenacre (1957) lists several basic characteristics for the artist, covering with this term all creative persons who are capable of expressing their creativity in real activities in any field of human endeavour.

These characteristics are a greater-than-usual sensitivity and responsiveness to sensory stimulation, unusual awareness of relations between various stimuli, which includes an unusually quick grasp of gestalts, unusual width and depth of empathy, and unusual intactness of the sensory-motor systems necessary for the actual performance of the creative act. Thanks to these capacities the artist forms collective alternates, finding or creating them from contemporary life, or history, or imagination.

In a net that spans eight centuries Greenacre comes up with several poets, a saint, and an explorer who, thanks to this gift for finding and creating collective alternates and identifying with them, were supreme achievers.

We might regard the mountaineers and the workman mentioned earlier as belonging to the category of "artist" as defined above. Their "superhuman" faculties that saved their lives include some of the characteristics attributed by Greenacre to the creative person, such as the unusual sensory response, the rapid perception of gestalt, the intactness of the sensory-motor apparatus: the branch on the route of the fall, or the bannister of the swinging platform to hold on to, the bit of glacier into which to thrust the pickaxe, are perceived and used in split seconds. Connoisseurs of sport will be able to point to artists in the area of physical prowess, not only in unusual situations of extreme danger.

What, however, do we know about the more than averagely gifted person from our work as analysts? In my experience it is less the achiever than the persons who, despite being highly gifted have failed to achieve, who turn to analysis for liberation of their talents. This request as motive for seeking analysis turns up surprisingly frequently in assessment interviews of patients applying for treatment at the London Clinic of Psycho-Analysis. It may be that the old fear that analysis would destroy talent has been overcome, but there may also be other motives, like shame about putting suffering from symptoms first and the expectation of having a better chance, when laying stress on cultural problems.

Amongst the factors that limit the potential artist from becoming an achiever, the obverse of their specially intense sensitivity and responsiveness to stimuli appears as paramount. This is their unusually intense and easily stirred narcissistic vulnerability. I should like to illustrate this with an example.

This was a woman, very gifted in her profession and in several forms of art. It appeared in her analysis that wherever she had worked, she had been immediately acknowledged as above average and had received offers of quick promotion. She either had not taken these up, realizing that they were not what she really wanted, or she had suffered, equally quickly, severe narcissistic hurts, and the flames of success rapidly turned into ashes.

Her childhood history was full of violence and tragedy, of physical and mental neglect and rejection. She had the capacity for forming collective alternates. In fact, her self-image revolved upon her having had a little basket into which she collected all the good things that her primary object(s) did not give her, but which she did obtain from other people – the maids in the house, visitors, people in the neighborhood, including the strange men who were called farm hands – from beautiful sights in a landscape, and later from art in its multiple forms.

But she also had an over average narcissistic vulnerability which so far had prevented her from having the success in her career to which she was entitled by virtue of her talents.

Her analysis with me started in a favorable way, although she might easily have construed an early rejection. That she did not do this, and that we were able to establish a solid working alliance that survived many a storm was essentially due to two factors: one in the preliminary interview she was enchanted by a vase with a little red rose on a table in my consulting room (as indeed I was too), and these little red roses and I, associated with them, were added to her collective alternates, her collection of good things; second, at an early stage in the analysis I presented the hypothesis that her distress at being put into the "last room" and left alone and helpless in her cot was mitigated by having within her field of vision a tree with its branches and leaves and seeing these in movement against a sky with changing colors. This reconstruction was in part based on her actual experience in the analysis: she could see from the couch a bit of sky and branches of a tree, which acted as a comfort for her disappointment that I did not live in a beautiful house, and that opposite my flat there was another nondescript block of flats. The equation between my consulting room and her nursery was clearly expressed when she suggested one day that I should paint my bookshelves and furniture white, and imagined with delight how good they would then look.

In a complex interaction of inner changes and external gratifications she became increasingly productive in her work. In her personal relations she discovered the pleasure from feeling kindness and fondness for and from other people, and the tendency to react with narcissistic hurt diminished. Further, she developed a sense of self, of justified self-assertion and claims, and could plan a future that would offer her scope for her talents, work satisfaction, and social and material rewards. I felt it as very significant that she now had developed a healthy narcissism and therefore could envisage making appropriate demands for respect and external acknowledgement as well as being ready to give on her part.

Earlier she had rushed into love affairs which could not give her the needed assurance of her value as a woman and a person, since she had never allowed herself the time necessary for an appraisal of the real person and of her motives for instant gratification.

These attempts at healing narcissistic wounds, therefore, had resulted in short-lived relationships, which she broke as easily as started, to discover later in the analysis how very little of herself had been engaged.

Now she was ready to allow time for the natural growth of a potential love relationship, but she was not willing to give up vital interests for the man's sake, as there were serious doubts about his ability to become a real partner in love.

Greenacre points out that the gifted infant will enrich the relationship with the primary object with the experiences from the wider fields of his sensitive responses. But the capacity for collective alternates has also the opposite effect; of achieving a greater than usual independence of the original objects and finding others outside the original milieu that correspond better and are more congenial to the gifted person.

This presupposes the capacity for undisturbed self-assertion.

IV

Self-assertion

With the recognition of the importance of a healthy and creative narcissism is correlated the notion of self-assertion.[5] Inability to develop the sense for self-assertion plays a crucial part in psychic illness. These patients either use what might be called corrupt or perverse forms of self-assertion, promiscuous relationships without affection, uncalled-for derogatory criticisms of other people, including those for whom they care and on whose good will they depend, or they confuse self-assertion with hostile aggression and impose inhibition on themselves which they attribute to their parents, indulging in a permanent sulk.

These patients, though, maintain areas of solid ego functioning, of satisfactory object relationships, and of sexual potency, although interspersed with actual perverse sexual activities or compulsive perverse fantasies. They feel, and certainly in analysis convey, personality restrictions and weaknesses or gaps in rapport.

It is obvious that the artist in Greenacre's sense must be capable of asserting himself and his talents despite the obstacles that might oppose him. The gifted person does overcome these obstacles and moves from his original milieu, if this is not congenial to himself, into another milieu of his choice.

We often see how our patients, incapable of healthy narcissism and healthy self-assertion, use phoney devices which of course do not succeed and may lead to a form of "false self". Originally Winnicott (1971) designated with this name persons who could show achievements, but only at the price of inner estrangement from their real selves. I have found false selves in patients who were unable to express their feelings of love or of admiration or their striving for warmth and color in their lives and relationships. In a defensive way they espied whatever possible weakness another person might have and, playing on these weaknesses in subtle ways, attacked these people and deprived themselves of the chance of a gratifying relationship, or they clung to a list of wrongs that their parents and later parental figures like former analysts had done them.

Here is one of many examples. Mr. E.'s analysis could roughly be divided into four phases. The first comprised the preliminary interview and the first two analytic sessions. In this first phase the basic elements of the analytic relationship were laid down, and I shall summarize them briefly. I made it clear to the patient that I was not willing to let him have another interminable and fruitless analysis, and that I expected him to take his share of responsibility for the analysis. I ended the preliminary interview by saying to him: "You have now seen me and we have discussed times and fees. It is now up to you to decide whether you want to have analysis with me." The patient was very surprised. He had obviously expected that I would make the decision without his sharing in it.

In the firstly analytic session we had a repetition of his uncommunicative talk of the preliminary interview. After listening in a baffled way, I realized that the patient was not addressing himself to me at all, but that he was performing a ritualistic incantation of which I was not meant to be a participant. And this is what I told him. In the next session without such an incantatory preamble, he told me that he felt in a dilemma. This amounted to something like this: if he talked about his external life, he did not give analysis its due, but if he talked about matters appropriate to analysis, he neglected his real problems. (What he said was in fact far more

289

confused than I have been able to reproduce it here. To me it was a phoney dilemma.) I said something like his denying that he was one and the same person in different aspects of his life.

In the following session the next phase of the analysis started; that is to say, he talked with involvement about his very serious problems. Ritualistic incantations did, of course, occur repeatedly, but he was himself now alerted to this form of escape and defense. The analysis proceeded in the usual way until a cataclysmic event occurred that threatened his business, his good name, and his livelihood. It was possible to make him realize that homicidal and suicidal wishes were no means of solving the problem. He realized also that he could not just throw his worries into my lap and expect magic solutions from me. He began to work very hard and continuously, and he was rewarded by saving his good name. Materially he incurred severe losses. The next phase of the analysis was characterized by his talking in great detail about his attempts to find new work and to acquire the necessary knowledge for the new undertaking.

Practically from the beginning there ran through the fabric of his analysis like a red thread the problem of self-assertion. The patient showed that neither had he ever been able to form the notion of self-assertion spontaneously nor could he grasp it responsively. Instead, he could only think in terms of violent actions. He complained to me that he never had been able to express aggression. This was an ever-recurring item in his ever-recurring complaints about his parents. Since practically in the same breath in which he depicted himself as incapable of expressing aggression (attributed to his traumatic upbringing by his parents), he expressed wildly sadistic fantasies occurring at the slightest provocation, and even without any discernible provocation, I tried to clarify what he meant by "expressing aggression", and suggested that he protested against the injunction not to act on his aggressive impulses which he obeyed for fear of retaliation. I also, when it seemed appropriate, spoke of his distress about his inability to assert himself in constructive ways. My patient remained tone deaf to these interpretations, despite his well-developed intellectual capacities and artistic leanings. He often explicitly appreciated my comments and interpretations; he liked the sessions and positively erupted with delight: "But you listen to me; you let me talk!" Nevertheless, he regarded me as nice old thing who, in contrast to his first analyst, did not persecute him, but he did not attribute any professional or intellectual acumen to me. I never gave him such erudite interpretations as his first analyst (a man) had done, and although they had done him no good, I came off badly in comparison. (That I did interpret his homosexual impulses and contempt for the penisless woman may be accepted without my producing the credentials.)

The third phase of this analysis was determined by his hard work to regain a viable position. Whilst in the preceding phase the sessions were filled by his anxiety-ridden descriptions of the oncoming disaster (always interspersed with infantile material of having been wronged), in this phase he spent most of the time telling me in detail about his new business undertakings which met with success.

Only in the following phase did the analysis reach greater depth. He now began to report dreams, often very bizarre, and frightening, with open homosexual and heterosexual incestuous contents which disturbed him deeply. He no longer liked coming to his sessions, nor did I continue to be the nice old thing. But he became very punctual and did everything possible not to miss any session.

It was in this last phase that he began to understand the notion of self-assertion and to distinguish it from that of destructive actions against other people.

The point I am trying to make is that, in this case, actions based on self-assertion, following very serious threats to his existence, preceded his conscious appreciation of this psychic process. Correlated with this insight, significant changes in his outer conduct of life occurred that took into account his wish to give expression to his cultural interests.

V

Sacrifice

Looking for a phylogenetic prototype of a sacrificial act valid for our Western culture, I turned to Genesis and the story of Abraham being "tempted" by God to sacrifice Isaac, his only son left to him.

I make no claim to base my ideas on Bible research, but allow myself to approach the story as a psychoanalyst. (What remnants of unremembered reading may be at work, I do not know.)

It may well be that several highly important steps in development took place in a relatively short period or are presented in a condensed way in symbolic and poetic language. Amongst these are the termination of slavery and the lesson that a servant has the same standing with God as his master. This is expresssed, we may surmise, in the covenant which God made with Abraham, when he

291

asked him to carry out the circumcision on himself, on all of the men in his employ, and on the "men bought" as well.

Still more momentous is the step to abolish the sacrifice of human life. There is an impressive build-up to depict the horror of human sacrifice. Abraham is shown as a good person as he pleads with God to save Sodom from destruction, if there are some righteous living that town. He engages in a veritable bargaining with God, starting with 50 innocent persons and coming down to 10 as the condition on which God agrees to spare the wicked town.

There is the moving narrative of the aging couple, Abraham and Sarah, being childless, and how Sarah, giving up all hope of having a child, suggests to Abraham to make her handmaiden pregnant so that his seed should bear fruit; how later, envy and jealousy between the women and the triumph which the master's mistress feels over her mistress cloud the former domestic happiness.

We are told of the wondrous promise of God's messengers, which God himself repeats, that Sarah will bear Abraham a son; how neither of them can believe it since she has ceased to menstruate. There is now some tension between God and Abraham, with Abraham quickly repenting. The miracle comes to pass, and Isaac is born.

The narrative gains in drama. Abraham arranges a feast for Isaac's weaning. This provokes the stepbrother's mockery. Sarah, now having a son of her own who healthily overcame the dangers of earliest infancy and proved her value as a mother, feels safe enough to give vent to her long-standing wrath about Hagar's arrogance. She demands that the maid and the maid's son be expelled. Abraham, albeit with grief in his heart, complies, begging God to take care of Ismael and receiving God's promise that He will do so.

The scene now seems set for the old parents to end their lives calmly, assured that their son will take over when the father retires. But as this event approaches with Isaac having outgrown his childhood and ready for his task, Abraham again hears God's voice, and this voice orders him to sacrifice his son.

The Biblical narrator succeeds in making us imagine vividly the horror and sadness in the old man's heart, his guilt towards his trusting son, his dread of telling his wife when the dreadful deed is done, the despairing outlook of an empty future. The drama ends as, at the last moment, God forbids Abraham to slay his son. Abraham puts a ram in his place.

I have ventured to depict the phylogenetic development of the concept of God and to show that this process started with a deity that found pleasure in blood sacrifices and thus justified the cruel strivings of the primitive mind. To use a term of an Oxford physicist friend of mine, "God-mindedness" is the prerogative of the human being. It undergoes vicissitudes and produces concepts in accordance with cultural progress. How difficult it was to give up the lust of killing is well described by the author of Genesis when he tells that Abraham killed a ram to please God.

From Abraham's time it took centuries until "God-mindedness" designed a God whose injunctions were of an ethical nature and demanded love and justice as guiding principles.

How tenuous this advance in "God-mindedness" is, how easily it can be reversed to the worship of barbarism in our "enlightened" times needs no documentation.

If I am right to regard the relinquishing of human sacrifice as the phylogenetic prototype of the sacrificial parapraxis, this would explain that this parapraxis is in a class by itself: it occurs only on unusual, profoundly moving occasions; it harms no other person than the individual himself who commits the bungled action; and this damage is slight. As a commemoration of a momentous step in cultural development, it bears witness to achievement rather than failure – as the analysis of its determinants shows: the life of a daughter being saved; a friendship being mended; a daughter moving into a new phase of life with all prospects of happiness.

The history of the last instance given in detail demonstrates the rejection of injustice and cruelty and the election of ethical values which includes our profession itself.

Notes

1 Editor's Introduction, p. xii, in SE 6.
2 Strachey's translation of Freud's works is inspired and inspiring. In this instance, however, I feel that his word "hiccough" is milder than the German word "*aufstossen*", whereas "belch" conveys the coarseness better, and that "drink" is not close enough to "*anstossen*" (Freud 1901: 54) in SE 6.
3 I hope Dr Sterba will not compare me with the German Professor of Literature who annotated Goethe's autobiography, and corrected Goethe's statement that his greatest love had been Lily, with the remark (in excruciating language): "Here Goethe is in error. This was the case for him with Frederika." In the train of ideas which Sterba's paper has set going in me, I must give a significant place to the theme of death. I hope to justify this idea.
4 Some authors define secondary narcissism with regard to the source of narcissistic feelings, i.e., narcissistic supplies offered to the infant by the

parental objects. I am here, however, concerned with the quality of the narcissistic condition, not with its sources.

5 I am aware that by stressing the importance of self-assertion I am not talking about an entirely new concept. The notion of healthy aggression has been indigenous in psychoanalysis from its very beginning. Yet with the associative links to our widened understanding of narcissism, my use of "self-assertion" is wider, although overlapping with the old concept of healthy aggression.

22

Further observations on the analyst's cognitive process (1975/7)

This paper is a slightly modified version of a paper which Paula Heimann read to the Canadian Psycho-Analytic Society in December 1975 in Montreal. It was published in the *Journal of the American Psychoanalytic Association* 25(2) (1977).

In recent times interest in the clinical situation has increasingly focused on the analyst, on what goes on in him and how he proceeds. Discussions of this kind have hitherto been largely confined to private study groups, seminars, and, of course, to supervision of students and young analysts.

Most of us learn probably more, and certainly more vividly, from exploring psychoanalytic technique than from erudite metapsychological expositions. Of course, both methods of guiding and checking our work are complementary to one another.

By establishing clarity about our own cognitive process we improve, above all, our own work. It is, in fact, part of our self-analysis. We also promote understanding between colleagues and also with workers in allied fields and with the interested public. In this way, I feel, we shall dispel misconceptions, illusions, and mysticism (the invidious return of religion) with regard to what we claim to be a scientific undertaking. That psychoanalysis is not only a science but also an art does not contradict the need for rigorous disciplined thinking. To move the "self-presentation" of the analyst at work from private to public exposition and debate means to show the strength and viability of psychoanalysis.

Some operational concepts

I wish to mention briefly the operational concepts presented by Fliess

(1942) and Greenson (1960) in their detailed investigation of the analyst's actual work with his patients.

Fliess offers the notion that the analyst develops a "work ego", thanks to which he becomes "a very exceptional person during his work with the patient", capable of enduring the manifold severe demands and deprivations which his function as analyst entails. For my purpose two facts are particularly relevant, as will become clear later: the role Fliess attributes to empathy; and the special relationship between the superego and the ego of the analyst during his work. This is characterized by the superego's limiting its critical functions and lending its specific powers to the ego.

Greenson's operational concept is "the working model of the patient" which the analyst builds up from the patient's communications and his own observations, impressions, etc., and against which he checks his actual conclusions. It is interesting that these two authors focus on different aspects of the psychoanalytic situation and in this way complement each other's findings. Greenson, like Fliess, proceeds from the concept of empathy, but he defines it differently from the way Fliess does. His illustration of the "working model of the patient" is taken from an instance in which his empathy had failed. By comparing his view of the patient in a given situation with the "working model" he had formed in the course of the preceding analysis, he came to realize his mistake and to correct it.

Many analysts attribute extremely high significance to empathy. In my view this concept is in danger of being overworked and overloaded. Fliess concludes that, although empathy is so often described as "putting oneself into another person's shoes" or "under his skin", etc., this does not in fact refer to a process of projection, but to the opposite: the analyst introjects his patient and identifies with him as a result of introjection. Such identification, however, must be only transitory. Fliess nevertheless sees it as the condition on which the analyst's understanding of his patient is based.

I do not agree with this view. The idea that we can only understand our patients by identifying with them does not take into account the danger of a *folie à deux* between patient and analyst. Fliess is obviously aware of such a possibility and therefore stresses the need to limit it. Moreover, to reduce identification to introjection means underrating the power of our imaginative capacities. I shall later come back to this problem.

It is interesting that Fliess in 1942 came to anticipate and reject the concept of "projective identification" which is now so much in vogue – to my regret, since I consider this notion a misnomer for a variety of psychic operations and, hence, erroneous and misleading.

Both concepts, the "work ego of the analyst" and the "working model of the patient", are significant and enriching contributions to the problem of the cognitive process in the analyst.

Ego configurations in the analyst's cognitive process

Holt's review, "The emergence of cognitive psychology" (1964), proved very stimulating and clarifying to my own thinking. It was not without surprise that I found psychology providing a definition of cognition so useful and, with certain additions, so applicable to the investigation of the analyst's cognitive process.

I quote the following passage from Holt's article:

> The scope of the term [i.e., cognition] is, to be sure, a good deal broader than thought processes: it comprises perceiving, judging, forming concepts, learning (especially that of a meaningful, verbal kind), imagining, fantasying, imaging, creating, and solving problems. One might try to summarize all this by saying that cognition deals with all aspects of symbolic behavior, in the broad sense, if it were not for the fact that the study of language is traditionally separated off into linguistics. (p. 650)

Clearly, we have here a list of ego functions. The fact that not only intellectual activity, but also "imagining, fantasying, and imaging" are given civic rights in the cognitive process is one reason why I saw the possibility of using this psychological definition as a scaffolding for a description and elaboration of what goes on in the analyst at work. I also wish to stress the usefulness, for my purpose, of separating off the function of speaking, as will soon become obvious.

First, a few additions to Holt's list. Even with these, the repertoire of ego functions operative in the analyst's cognitive work is not complete. To begin with, we need Freud's exposition of the secondary process related to perception (1911b). The ego functions that Freud, as I may remind you, connects with perceiving are: attention that actively seeks the outer world for its data and that leads to familiarity with them; further, those mental operations which constitute the system of storing perceptions: notation and memory. Freud then lists judgment (and here we make contact again with Holt's list). In the line Freud was pursuing in that paper, judgment essentially amounts to evaluating the external condition in respect of an internal impulse. This assessment will lead to action, if such action is appropriate, or to the delay of action, if the external condition is

297

judged to make satisfaction of the wish impossible and, instead, likely to produce painful, dangerous, frightening results.

The sequence of ego functions Freud describes is not restricted to problems set by the stirring of a drive. In other words, the wish in question may not be of an instinctual order, and the external condition may be the mental/emotional state of another person.

A further amplification of Holt's list of ego functions follows from Beres' work. I am referring to his article of 1960, from which I quote a passage on imagination. "I would define imagination as the capacity to form a *mental representation* of an *absent* object, an affect, a body function, or an instinctual drive. I am here defining a *process* whose *products* are images, symbols, fantasies, dreams, ideas, thoughts, and concepts. It is essential to distinguish the process from the products" (p. 327).

I have earlier expressed my misgivings about the view that neglecting the power of imagination makes understanding another person contingent upon introjection and identification. Beres' definition of imagination allocates to this ego function a most significant part in the process of cognition. We understand another person by forming a mental image of him, by grasping with our imaginative perception his problems, conflicts, wishes, anxieties, defenses, moods, etc. When we identify ourselves with the other person, we experience a change of our ego that may not at all further our awareness of him. In the psychoanalytic situation, instead of patient and analyst, there are two patients, as Gitelson (1952) pointed out with a humorous reference to his own student days.

Beres states that his definition differs from the usage of ordinary language, "which makes imagination a phenomenon associated with creativity and unreality, beyond the realm of ordinary thought processes". Instead, he sees "imagination as a ubiquitous component of human psychic activity unique to man" (p. 327). In my view, however, acknowledging that imagination is "a ubiquitous component of human psychic activity unique to man" does not contradict the general connection with creativity. It is true, though, that the term creativity is often, albeit tacitly, reserved for capacities that lead to mental achievements of a special kind and high order.

According to Beres, imagination may occur within primary-process activity or secondary-process activity. It is not opposed to reality; in fact, one of its most important applications is precisely adaptation to reality. In this connection a remark by Chagall (in McMullen 1968) may be quoted. He said: "Our whole inner world is reality, perhaps even more real than the apparent world. To call everything that seems to be illogical a fantasy or a fairy tale is to admit that one does not understand nature" (p. 198).

I will now add another ego function to Holt's list, one which indeed only the practicing psychoanalyst knows from direct experience, or perhaps it would be more correct to speak of a whole dimension of cognition. I am referring to the countertransference.

As you know, this is a controversial concept, since many analysts simply equate countertransference with transference. In my view, as I have stated elsewhere, Freud, master of words as he was, would have said "transference" if he had meant it. The prefix "counter" characterizes the phenomenon as a *specific response* to the patient. However, leaving linguistics aside, Freud's remarks (1910d, 1915a) clearly describe an analyst's unconscious reaction to his patient, not a preformed attitude applied to him. Unfortunately, Freud never defined his concept more fully, and it is possible to read different meanings in his words. He was concerned only with a disturbance in the analyst's condition.

I have suggested that the countertransference represents a highly significant tool for the analyst's work. For longish stretches in his interaction with his patient, the analyst uses this cognitive instrument with ease, in an autonomous manner, one might say, and his countertransference therefore does not impinge painfully on his consciousness. Two comparisons come to mind. Once the child has mastered his tools for locomotion, he need not give special attention to the action of moving about and instead directs his conscious interest to the data in the environment in which he moves. Another comparison is with the patient in what Freud (1914g: 151) called the mild positive transference, which enables him to cooperate with the analyst without resistance.

In general we know that our organs and functioning demand our attention only when something has gone wrong with them. Thus, when our countertransference transmits to us that it has failed, that we do not understand our patient, that we encounter emotions of undue strength, positive or negative, undue gratification or elation, on the one hand, or undue distress, anxiety, fear, anger, etc., on the other, then we are forced to turn our attention to it, to explore it, trace the origin of the disturbance. I would say the hallmark of the disturbed countertransference is the sense of something alien to his ego that the analyst experiences. Essentially, what has happened is that he failed to perceive consciously some important process in his patient when it was actually happening. This missed perception, which the analyst recovers by analysing his disturbed counter-transference, this time lag between conscious and unconscious perception, amounts to an *unconscious* introjection of his patient, and an *unconscious identification* with him. Once the analyst has recognized this, the sense of disturbance disappears, he has repaired his working tool, reestablished his "work-ego", rediscovered his "working model" of his patient. Thanks to this piece of self-analysis on the spot, inside the psychoanalytic situation, he has done what Freud demanded: he has recognized and mastered his (disturbed) countertransference.

The process in his patient that the analyst has failed to notice in good time is very often the impulse to intrude, invade, occupy the analyst (mind and body) – a phenomenon well-known in the history of wars between nations. Some analysts adduce the notion of the "mechanism of projective identification" to explain this situation. Intrusion, however, is not an ego mechanism, but an interpersonal *action*. Further, the motives behind such action are by no means always hostile as in the political analogy. They are complex and manifold and often include the "return to the womb" phantasy. The patient's motives will get the better of the analyst if the analyst unconsciously yields, colludes, allows himself to be overwhelmed, fails to use perception as a barrier against adverse stimuli. In the last analysis, such incidents can be traced to the original infant–mother fusion. For this reason, too, it happens particularly with very helpless, very regressed patients. They do exert a particular appeal, and to use Wangh's formulation (1962), they have the capacity to evoke a proxy. They also have the capacity of "driving another person crazy", as Searles pointed out (1959). A "crazy", confused, helpless analyst does not function well.

In his work with his patient – that is, within the psychoanalytic situation – the analyst alternates between listening and talking. I suggest that in each of these positions he uses specific *ego configurations*. With this term I wish to designate a constellation of ego operations in which a special set of closely linked ego functions has primacy over the others. This ego-function(s) primacy I see as analogous to the drive primacy at specific developmental stages.

Before turning to the analyst as he listens or talks, I wish to add some ego functions, so far not mentioned, that are of great importance for the analyst at work. I list them in loose order.

Nunberg's "synthetic function" (1930), the organizing operation that combines a quantity of diverse data into an entity, which can be integrated by the ego, enriching and protecting it from being disrupted by a mass of unmanageable stimuli. It can be seen as the mature counterpart to the barrier against stimuli.

The function of "containing", a notion that has gained much

300

popularity in recent years and should therefore be treated with caution! If it is at all different from Freud's concept of "storing", it is because it suggests greater immediate availability of the stored perceptions. At least I use it here in this sense. By containing his impressions of his patient's initial communications, verbally or gesturally or behaviorally, in a particular session, the analyst is able to gain the perspective of his trend of progression, his actual "developmental line", to borrow Anna Freud's (1965) concept from child analysis, and see whether this line is consecutive, coherent, or changes course, and also whether such change is constructive or evasive and defensive. Moreover, as the analyst follows his patient's movements, he learns something about the rhythm and tempo of his patient's psychic processes. Sometimes the events in a single session demonstrate on a small scale the prognosis of the whole analysis.

Recognition that very often a patient's first comments represent the chapter heading for the whole hour.

Spotting the innuendos and allusions in the patient's remarks. Discerning the re-enactment of parts of a dream.

Detecting primary-process elements, even though they are beautifully covered by a completely realistic and rational statement.

Finally, I would mention listening simultaneously on several levels. Reik spoke of the "analyst's third ear" (1948). I think he needs more than three.

The analyst as participant observer, listening

When listening, the analyst's ego configuration is determined by the priority of his mobile *attention* and its attending functions, described earlier when I referred to Freud's paper of 1911. Such attention hovers freely around the patient, perceiving the hierarchy of clue or sign, signal, direct or allusive verbal communication, gestures, and behavior, starting from the first moment of their meeting. Mobility and seeking further refer to data of earlier sessions, in particular the most recent one. He takes notice, stores, contains, and remembers. He moves from the patient's "psychic surface" to his depth. This corresponds to Greenson's "model of the patient". While listening to his patient, the analyst follows him with a kind of silent "running commentary". (Some years ago in a discussion with Pearl King, I discovered that she, too, used this designation.) Such "running commentary", in my experience, is by no means fully verbalized, or in completed sentences. To quote Greenson (1970): describing his route towards an interpretation this astute and empathic clinician

301

said, "All this flashed through my mind quickly and was not as carefully thought out as it sounds here" (p. 543). The analyst's inner comments contain superficial pre-conscious – that is, dim – elements, sharp flashes, that may disappear as suddenly as they came, from unconscious or deep pre-conscious levels, "regressions in the service of the ego", here in relation to an object, the patient. They lead to "trial interpretations" which, however, may never reach expression to the patient, because in further listening they are relinquished and superseded by others. They have to be forgotten. Forgetting, too, is an important ego function which plays its part in concentrating on a problem and pursuing it creatively. The analyst's attention must remain mobile, must not get stuck.

In addition to this "running commentary", I often find that a remark of my patient's sets off an image of three concentric bands similar to the circles produced by a stone's being thrown into water. The first of these bands centering on my patient's associations presents what my patient consciously thinks, feels, imagines, fears, etc., and consciously wants me to know; the second and third deal with unconscious experiences related to his original object(s) and to the analyst in the transference from them and from his own early self.

This is one example of the role imaging assumes in the analyst's cognition, and helps to build up "a working model of the patient". I would like to mention a special instance of imaging, albeit of a different kind, that is more easily reported. One day, listening to a patient talk about present-day events and relationships apparently of no great import, I suddenly envisaged her as a little girl, near her mother, unconsciously aware of her mother's pathology, consciously puzzled, but trying to pretend with her mother that nothing of significance was in progress. When using this image, I suggested that she had noticed her mother's odd attitude and had been bewildered, she immediately confirmed by bringing highly relevant memories which she had not mentioned earlier. There is, of course, the danger that a patient, particularly one who appreciates fantasies, may accept the analyst's fantasy reconstruction only by virtue of his suggestibility. In this case, I watched carefully, but did not find evidence for any such suspicion, or for the possibility that this matter had come up in her earlier analysis.

As participant observer, listening, the analyst functions also as his patient's biographer, of his original and his analytical past, but since this biographer deals with a living and developing person, he is also imaging and imagining his patient's future. Indeed, in the analytical situation, present, past, and future meet.

Further, there is the more immediate future of the patient and of the analyst–patient relationship, with which the analyst has to be concerned, namely, his decision to change over to becoming the active partner of a dialogue, talking. In connection with the primacy of attention, judgment for action comes into play, and this action is the analyst's interpretation, or to put it more generally, his verbal comment to his patient.

Mobile attention and its related or constituent functions have primacy during the listening and determine the occurrence of the "running commentary", the "trial interpretation," and the images I have mentioned. These in turn contribute significantly to the cognitive process, since they involve the elements of "forming concepts, learning, creating, and solving problems" of Holt's list, as well as the specific psychoanalytic functions I have added earlier. All these processes are instrumental for arriving at the judgment for the correct time, content, and form for the analyst's verbal action. This leads me to consider the second position of the analyst.

Before doing so, however, I feel the need to avoid misunderstanding about my use of the term "positions" of the analyst. I hope I have not given the impression that I see the analyst heaving himself heavily and pompously from one "position" to the other or occupying either for a set time. It is true, though, as many analysts have said, that the transition from receptive listening to actively coming to the fore with valid comments can quite often be felt as a very difficult task. The patient expects something from his analyst. It is by no means always easy to fulfil this expectation, to say the right thing.

The analyst as partner of a special dialogue

It may well be said that the way in which an analyst listens to his patient is also of a special kind, yet I would maintain that the analyst's remarks to his patient highlight the difference between the psychoanalytic and an ordinary social dialogue.

Whilst the patient's verbal communications are spontaneous, left to his own choice even within the accepted understanding that he is expected to express his thoughts as they occur as "free associations", it is equally understood that he will very often not do so, not be capable or willing to do so. Further, what he talks about are what concerns *him*: his feelings, worries, problems, fears, wishes. His conscious interest at times is the analyst's person and life outside the analysis, and he does feel frustrated, angry, hurt, and the like, if his curiosity is not satisfied. Such incidents do not detract from the fact that the patient is the *central* figure in the dialogue – in the psychoanalytic situation – that the analysis revolves around him.

The analyst, on the other hand, does not start a theme spontaneously, but follows his patient. He does not communicate his worries or ask for help. There is no need to elaborate this point any further. It can be stated briefly that the analyst's verbal comments amount to *therapeutic* interventions, and are thus charged with special responsibility. His task as partner in this dialogue can be divided schematically in two parts, which, though, interact and influence one another. The first relates to an inner process, to himself, so to say, the other to his patient. Before he can attempt verbal rapport with his patient, he has to give the thoughts in his mind an outer existence, if you want, transform an inner speech into an address to his patient. The silent running commentary must be turned into spoken comments, the mute trial interpretations into audible propositions.

The primacy of ego functions in these activities lies with those that are involved in organizing a mass of impressions and thoughts, with sifting and discerning the hierarchy of significance and temporal order, with imparting clarity and appropriate form, etc. All these functions converge toward a definitive (for the time being) formulation that can be expressed to the patient. As mentioned earlier, many of the ideas engendered by listening are incomplete, dim, and hazy. It does appear that private inner speech and spoken language are different – for many of us painfully so, for especially linguistically gifted individuals less so. But it is probably more correct to stress in the first place the talent for conceptual clarity and creativeness and give linguistic skill a place of second order. The gift of the gab, in fact, can be quite dangerous!

To these inner, self-related operations we add explicitly those that focus on the patient, such as assessing whether he is ready to be receptive, whether he is in a co-operative or defensive-resistant mood, and, further, the kind and degree of his regression, etc., so as to anticipate his reactions in terms of fear, rage, or relief.

Now, however, after describing the analyst's inner work to arrive at a sound verbal communication, I want to remind you that we do by no means speak to our patients exclusively in discursive language.

We use, in fact, a range of utterances, meaningful monosyllabic sounds like "Eh?" "Ah!" "Hm," etc., on the one hand, and correctly formed complete sentences on the other. In between, there is the single word chosen by the analyst, or one that the patient had used and which the analyst repeats, with, however, a different inflection, which suggests a new meaning and arrests the patient's attention.

In one case the course of the analysis changed dramatically when, out of my patient's long soliloquizing lecture, I picked up his word "bedeviled" in a questioning tone. This patient was a Roman Catholic, and in his own view a devout believer. I felt certain that he had severe religious scruples about seeking analysis and, moreover, from a Jewish analyst instead of turning to a priest, but I had found it impossible to open up this area. It was in the twentieth session that the opportunity offered itself. He started the hour by referring with apppreciation to "our session yesterday" – it was the first time he made such a personal remark, explicitly bringing us together. In passing, he made a comment on the light in my room, but he then moved away, leaving me miles behind. My repeating his word "bedeviled" led to the emergence of a system of fantasies that centered around the devil as the most important and superior of all the beings created by God and nearest to the creator himself. My patient was identified with him. On this level, thus, there was no conflict about rejecting a priest. In addition, he raised me to the stature of devil too. His remark about the light in my room could now be recognized as characterizing me as Lucifer, another manifestation of the devil. No wonder he had included me in his own experience! I shall not withhold from you the fact that my patient was the first born, and that he unconsciously projected his family situation into the religious sphere. His scruples came to the fore only in the further analysis.

Indeed, a question may serve as a more dynamic intervention than a careful explanation. Here is an example taken from another analysis. I ended a session in which my patient's tendency to procrastinate had again been central without yielding to insight, by saying: "The question is, what do you expect to happen between today and tomorrow?" This comment affected him much more and had a more liberating effect than many of my earlier interpretations.

The greater my analytical experience, the less do I like explanations. Certainly, they are at times necessary – I prefer to think of clarifications and elucidations rather than explanations – but there is a great danger that they turn into pedantic, dull, and dulling statements instead of offering a challenge to the patient's own creative functioning. I positively dislike "because" interpretations and aim at finding formulations of a more vivid character, or I just play back to my patient what he has said in words or gestures so as to induce a "new look" in him. A very artistic patient – perhaps pandering to my preferences – once supplied me with the concept of "village explainer" (a quotation from Gertrude Stein), and indeed I do not want to be one. Maybe I simply cannot do it well.

The problem of what constitutes a "good" interpretation is too wide to be explored here fully, or even adequately, but I shall put forward a few ideas. We often hear praise of the short interpretation and condemnation of the long one. In my view, the value of an interpretation cannot be measured with an inch tape. We are so much exposed to the injunction to talk only sparingly to our patients that even an analyst as original and controversial as Masud Khan expressed surprise when he found that his patients could follow with benefit a lengthy reconstructive interpretation (1974). A short interpretation that just hits the bull's eye is certainly very impressive, but it may fail by not substantiating the reasons for the analyst's statement. In such a case the patient's infantile wishes for an omniscient parental authority may be endorsed and gratified, but he will not be liberated from his past and helped towards independent critical judgment. With artistic patients, interpretations usually can be quite brief, even only start, when they will take over and move forward to another point of interest or problem on their own. If, however, the alternative lies between the analyst's appearing to his patients as a human being, a bit pedantic because, like other mortals, he is subject to the ordinary laws of thinking, or as a divine authority, I would prefer the first. My hope, though, is that my comments and interpretations will enable my patient to experience the psychoanalytic process as illuminating and inspiring and that his own creative activities will be facilitated.

Turning again to the ego configuration in the analyst when he is engaged in preparing his comment to his patient, I believe that quite naturally there is some loss of his mobile attention, which he used so much and easily in his role as participant listener. To some degree his attention is now focused on his formulations and does not hover around his patient. Transforming inner images into words is a creative act, which by necessity brings some narcissistic elements into operation. The analyst therefore needs to train himself specially and consciously to keep his eye on his patient and to notice his reaction *during* his interpretation and not only afterward.

I have made it a rule to tell my patients, when the occasion arises, that I expect them to interrupt me and not to go on being quiet, when their interest is taken up by some process in their mind. This is perhaps another fundamental rule that well deserves general discussion. It is particularly necessary in the analysis of withdrawn patients, as was brought home to me with great strength when I analyzed a severely schizoid adolescent with suicidal impulses and an appalling sense of loneliness. I was naturally, from the very beginning, aware of the danger of his actually withdrawing from contact with me, and I never relaxed watching him when I was talking. Often, I stopped to point out that he seemed to have wandered away, and this enabled him to come back, even if only to confirm my observation – but without his knowing where he had been. Sometimes such re-establishment of rapport made him actively wish to hear the missed communication. But it was less any specific idea that mattered than his experience that lost contact could be recovered.

Later in the analysis, the transference meaning of some of these incidents could be discovered. His father was in the habit of giving the boy long lectures about matters that did not interest him. Unfortunately, these included psychoanalysis. (Of course, the father was not an analyst.) Whenever my patient felt that my remarks were, as he later told me, "psychoanalytic", I became his father, and he used the defenses that he had developed against his father's intrusions. Once this genetic factor had emerged, the patient's tendency to withdraw diminished. It goes without saying that more and more of his highly complex and conflictual relation with his father was subjected to analysis and worked through.

When the therapeutic alliance between patient and analyst has a positive character, the small narcissistic element on the part of the analyst, which I mentioned earlier, does not disturb the analytic dialogue or the patient's trust in his analyst.

This leads me to another consideration. I said that I do not regard pedantic interpretations as good enough to set a spark to the patient's own ego functions. I want to add now that I am also against an analyst taking too much trouble and being too anxious to find just the right phrase for this patient. Young analysts are often too self-critical about what they say to their patients and, at the same time, overlook the power of the negative transference or of infantile defiance or paranoid episodes in a nonpsychotic patient. It is not only lack of love on the part of the speaker that turns his words into "sounding brass or a tinkling cymbal", as St Paul said; the hearer's hatred brings about the same effect.

Highly critical situations arise, when suddenly and unexpectedly a patient re-enacts in the transference an intensely hostile and negative experience with his original object. Obviously, it is this regressive process that has to be tackled as such, and the actual stimuli for the arousal of paranoid reactions have to be discovered. Without this work, even if the analyst talked with the tongue of angels, he could not expect to effect a change in his patient.

The analyst as his own supervisor

No analyst worth his salt fails to scrutinize his work. He acts as his own supervisor. He has to provide himself with an account of a session or a series of sessions, and this means that he has to recall and record what happened in them. Obviously, then, memory has the primacy in his ego configuration. As we go on, though, we shall see that the ego's reality testing versus superego assessment is a high runner-up in the hierarchy of ego functions.

Human memory is not an automatic device that recalls everything. It is selective, as was also the analyst's perception of the events in the session. No analyst will claim that nothing escapes his attention, however mobile he endeavors to keep it. Moreover, his capacity to remember is strongly influenced by emotional motivation clashing with cognitive interests.

In many ways the analyst's position when recalling and recording[1] his work is similar to the one in which he is concerned with subjecting the data of his perception to spoken formulations. Again he shifts from considering what *he* saw, felt, thought, and said to what *his patient* expressed and needed, and, further, what he can learn about both himself and his patient for his future work.

To list some of his cognitive concerns: he wants to pursue more fully certain themes that the patient mentioned, but that remained tangential in the course of the session; to define the difference between his therapeutic function in a particular session and the specter of conflicts that were lit up sporadically; the glimpses which he gained of childhood experiences down to earliest somatopsychic events that, as such, are beyond recall, but need to be reconstructed and articulated as a significant source of rapport between patient and analyst and understanding for the patient's development. There are, further, the analyst's interests in the practice and theory of psychoanalytic technique and in metapsychology; ambition in these fields; stimuli received from colleagues and the literature; flashes that he experienced on various occasions and that the material of recent sessions may substantiate; his wish and need to investigate more fully countertransference disturbances which occurred during a session, and thus to carry his self-analysis to deeper levels. Many more considerations could be listed. But I think I have said enough to make it clear that the analyst, when recalling a session, does more than only record, only remember data. He reconstructs, re-creates, does research, trains himself. He also prepares scientific communications of his observations and experiences and speculations.

Memory is unreliable and given to falsifications under the pressure of fears and wishes. The recording analyst, as I said, acts as his own supervisor, and we are all familiar with the fact that we come up against feeling puzzled, angry, guilty when "supervising" our attitude and procedure in a session. "Why did I interpret this and not that? How could I have overlooked something so important – so profound – so *obvious!*"

In passing, I would like to say that it is precisely the obvious that we tend to overlook. What is extraordinary and striking impinges forcibly on us.

At this point it will help us to return to Fliess's concept of the analyst's work ego. It is formed and maintained by the superego's refraining from criticizing and inhibiting it. By putting its judicious powers at the ego's disposal, it increases the range of the ego's cognitive functions and facilitates their activities. This is the main reason why, during his actual contact with his patient, the analyst becomes a very special person.

Once this contact is ended, however, and the analyst is in the third position of recalling and recording sessions with his patient, it appears that the superego returns, with a vengeance, so to say, severely castigating the analyst's work, falsifying his memories and his actual cognitive evaluations. It behaves like a superstrict parent who is afraid that, in considering special circumstances, he has allowed his child too much freedom. It is here that the analyst's reality sense has to assert itself by fostering his awareness of the difference in his position now, when outside his contact with his patient (recalling and recording the events of a session), and when actually with his patient, acting and reacting to him under the powerful influence of his patient's transference, regressive processes, and the manifold variations of the psychoanalytic scene caused by his patient's free or defensive associative movements.

When acting as his own supervisor, the analyst's reality testing is of decisive importance in order to distinguish genuine errors he made from the deceptive wisdom of hindsight, emanating from the superego. Otherwise, instead of benefiting from his exploration, he will merely suffer unproductive and false feelings of guilt.

Scrutinizing his psychoanalytic data in close proximity to actual psychoanalytic sessions, not under superego pressure or from the distant height of theory; comparing recent with past events are part of the analyst's cognitive process, fruitful research that will widen his understanding and skill. As a by-product, his self-supervision will teach him how to supervise others, particularly beginners who treat their supervisor as their superego. Once again we have here evidence for Freud's wisdom when he demanded the analysis of the analyst; we achieve effective insight only from what we experience ourselves.

The analyst's cognitive process is not confined to the three positions I have outlined. However, it would burst the frame of this paper if I went on to examine his ego configurations, when he acts as teacher, reader, author, or discussant in scientific meetings or study groups with his colleagues. Beyond this, because his work concerns human beings, his arena of cognition and learning is that of all forms of human expression and achievement, unlimited as is civilization itself.

Notes

1 In accordance with British tradition, I am speaking of analysts who do not take notes during the session.

23

On the necessity for the analyst to be natural with his patient (1978)

This paper was written in German in honour of Alexander Mitscherlich on the occasion of his seventieth birthday. It was published in *Provokation und Toleranz. Alexander Mitscherlich zu ehren*, Frankfurt am Main: Suhrkamp, 1978, and has been translated into English for this book.

Introduction[1]

The observations that I am going to report are in accord with Alexander Mitscherlich's untiring efforts, struggles, and disappointments, as is shown by the list of his publications. The spectrum ranges from 'Medicine without humanity' (*Medizin ohne Menschlichkeit*) to 'The desolation of our cities' (*Die Unwirtlichkeit unserer Städte*). They could be collected under the title 'Naturalness, Honesty, and Creative Effort: The Foundations of Humanity and of Psycho-Analysis'. We can furthermore learn from him that courage is a prerequisite for a naturally humane way of acting.

My contribution should be considered a kind of picture book. The pictures are taken from my clinical work with patients and students. I hope they will stimulate the onlookers and remind them of their own experiences. Yet, since pictures are ambiguous, I will also give my own commentaries. Many readers may well have a different opinion. Because of the personalities of those involved, every analysis is unique.

Driven by his suffering, the patient turns to the analyst in the hope of finding help. The analyst can provide help if he himself originally came to analysis as someone who was ill – and in some regards still is ill – but had the courage to do without falsehood and tricks, in this way making something creative out of his illness.

311

I recall Heine's irreverent verse:

> Krankheit war wohl der letzte Grund
> Des ganzen Schoepferdrangs gewesen.
> Erschaffend wurde ich gesund
> Erschaffend konnte ich genesen.

(Heinrich Heine, *Neue Gedichte*, 'Schoepfungslieder VII')

> Illness was ultimately the reason
> for my entire creative fervour.
> Labouring I became well,
> Labouring I was able to recover.
>
> (Translated by Michael Wilson)

We analysts go through this process time and again.

I am completely aware that my demand that the analyst be natural contains many traps and dangers. But it is simply a fact that our profession is by nature confronted by difficulties and suffering. Whoever wants an easy job, working from 9 a.m. to 5 p.m., should not become an analyst, and whoever has mistakenly entered the profession should get out again as quickly as possible, in his own interest and in that of his patients.

I also realize that my examples may lead to misunderstandings, such as that I am opening the gates for wild analysis. But this danger is also a part of our profession. The deeper we go into the history of psychoanalysis and the psychoanalytic movement, the more we become aware that identity crises have been linked with the development of analysis from the beginning, even though the term 'identity crisis' itself was not coined until much later. Is it possible that the practitioners of this new, unsettling, and often attacked mode of thinking, somewhere between science and art, provoked such crises over and over again by attempting to cover up – out of their own anxieties – their natural humanity?

Freud's case histories read like novels, about which he was almost apologetic, but he did not change them or himself because he himself acted in a natural way. He suffered with his patients. I can think of his description of Fräulein Elisabeth von R.'s condition as she recalled in analysis that at her sister's deathbed the thought had come to her that her brother-in-law was now free and she could marry him (Freud 1895d: 157). Another case history (Katharina) shows that Freud surrendered his desire for scientific satisfaction when he saw that his patient did not want to examine a specific symptom after she had gained relief. He noted how her facial expression had changed for the better and that she had understood his question but was not inclined to give a direct answer. He respected the limits that Katharina set (Freud 1895d: 132). I refer, further, to an entry he made after one session with the Rat Man, 'He was hungry and was fed' (Freud 1909d: 303).

Freud never attempted to be a 'superman' above everything human. Again and again he recognized and admitted his mistakes. We have long been freed of the naïve view that analysis is concerned with curing symptoms. Freud's failure as a hypnotist during his work with Breuer (who was so good at it), his discovery of transference, his self-analysis, his case histories, and many of his theoretical formulations show that he viewed the analytic experience as a liberation to naturalness and honesty. His shortest and most intense formulation of the goal of analysis is the re-creation of the capacity for pleasure and work. Yet this goal cannot be achieved if we analysts are unnatural, suppress our own feelings (for example, our counter-transference), or pretend that we are 'neutral'. In my opinion, there is only a short distance from the neutral analyst to the neuter.

From a supervision

Dr G. was an experienced psychiatrist, a gifted candidate in psychoanalytic training, intelligent, and warm-hearted. He reported how his patient had arrived for analysis: punctual but wet all over and blue from the cold. It was an evening when an especially icy rain beat down on the streets. The patient mentioned in passing that he had arrived at the analyst's house a quarter of an hour early (as he often did) but that he preferred to walk around outside than to come too early. Then he went on to other problems.

Dr G. described the course of one session, and I listened. His interpretations were, so to speak, entirely correct and also contained a reference to the patient's anxiety and inhibition. But Dr G. did not feel comfortable with his actions and suspected that I disagreed with him. So I asked him what he felt when he saw the patient completely wet and blue in the lips. Didn't he think of offering the patient something hot to drink? The student immediately confirmed that this had in fact been his first impulse. And he would have done so with a patient in his psychiatric practice, but while in psychoanalytic training he thought he was only permitted to give the patient interpretations.

It is true that many analysts do in fact insist that an analyst can only offer interpretations. This is one of the taboos I referred to earlier. Once I even heard a highly educated analyst recommend that we avoid asking direct questions and instead always make some kind of interpretation in the hope that the necessary information would be given. I believe that this kind of manipulation is based on a serious misunderstanding. It overlooks the strength of the unconscious, the dynamic of the contact between analyst and patient, and the hidden processes that are an integral part of analysis and give it vitality.

Why can't I simply and honestly ask my patient for the information I need to understand his associations if he can easily provide it? Of course we all have our own peculiarities, but dogmas are at a different order of magnitude. I am often a failure at disregarding ideas if I suspect, although I am uncertain, that they are important. In such situations it has often happened to me that somatic language has thwarted my intentions (or made the decision for me!). My stomach growled suddenly and audibly. If the patient made a reference to it, it was usually easy to mention the suppressed comments and to examine them with the patient.

In this connection I would like to refer to another bit of nonsense. This is the equation that five hours a week equal analysis and that fewer than five are sins. In this regard, I recall Willi Hoffer,[2] who was by no means a wild or heretical analyst. He told a committee discussing the criteria for the admission of regular members that he knows analysts who achieve more with a single hour per week than many others do with five a week. This was, of course, not meant to encourage analysts arbitrarily to reduce the amount of time provided to patients, especially if there were no corresponding reduction in fee (see Greenson 1974). It is noteworthy that Freud, who was accustomed to working six hours a week with his patients, expressly said that some patients require no more than three hours.

I certainly do not underestimate the importance for the analytic process of how the patient experiences interpretations, and I will have more to say about this later. Here I would like to state that – in contrast to Balint[3] and Winnicott,[4] who correctly emphasized the human element in the contact between analyst and patient and did not adhere to dogmas – I have never found it necessary to show patients my understanding of their anxieties by means of physical contact, such as holding their hand or head. Colleagues who follow Balint and Winnicott in this regard believe that I have never had patients in severe regression or never permitted patients to experience a deep but therapeutically necessary regression in which only physical contact is meaningful.

However, to return to the student I supervised, the interpretations

314

that he substituted for his first and natural feeling that the patient needed a hot drink more than anything else were really 'substitutes'. The interpretations were lame; they lacked vitality. And the student knew it. To prevent any misunderstanding, I am not claiming that the analyst's mistake caused any lasting harm or that the patient was driven into a case of influenza. He was a young man who had spent his early childhood in the country, where he must have been exposed to wind and weather. The important point is the violation of the natural way of acting; that is, the violation of the fundamental principle and goal of analysis. Each participant in the analytic process seeks and struggles for both, internal and external truth. The acknowledgement of reality, to which all psychic progress and opportunities for happiness are tied, requires that each exhibit a natural honesty.

From the analysis of an elderly patient

Some years before the beginning of the analysis from which I will describe several episodes, Mrs N. called me and requested an appointment because of her depression. In the interview I found that the patient had been depressed for many years. Furthermore, her marriage had been very unhappy, and she was waiting for her divorce settlement. She said that at present she was completely penniless. The referring doctor had apparently assumed that the patient was familiar with the costs of a private analysis, and therefore had not discussed this aspect with her. The subject of recommending analysis without discussing with the patient the cost in terms of time and money should be paid more attention than is possible in this paper. In my opinion it is dishonourable to send a patient unprepared to an analyst; it is also destructive to both patient and analyst.

I considered whether I should name a *pro forma* fee for the consultation or none at all, and decided for the latter. An unrealistically small sum would have promoted her dishonesty. If she were really as poor as she claimed, she could have sought therapy within the framework of the National Health Service instead of turning to an analyst in private practice.

One aspect of Freud's genial understanding of the patient–analyst relationship was that he insisted on the analyst making it clear to the patient from the very beginning that the patient also has to accept responsibility for the analysis and make commitments; that is, that it is not a matter of one person giving and another taking. Proceeding in this way does not eliminate a patient's phantasies, which in the last

315

resort arise from the area of transference, but at least the analyst then does not provide any false encouragement; the analyst is not 'seduced'; that is, he does not play along.

Years later Mrs N. came again, this time not as a beggar but able to pay a suitable fee. The patient's appearance was impressive, and she definitely had presence and qualities which had made her very useful to her former husband and she herself had greatly enjoyed all the honours that accompanied his position.

Several weeks into her analysis, although her comments provided little information, I noticed the swelling of her abdomen. I do not know if she had willingly or consciously chosen a position on the couch that made an overpowering visual impression. But that was my impression. I remembered that she had complained not long before that it was impossible for her to slim, which certainly seemed necessary. So I said: 'Naturally you can't keep to your diet, you're in your fifth month.' The patient started, in authentic indignation, 'But Doctor!' It was clear that she wanted to finish the sentence with, 'You're crazy,' but she did not get that far. She fell silent because she suddenly recalled something that she had repressed for a long time. The experience had happened nearly forty years before. She had had a relationship with a man she implicitly described as a completely unreliable character. She had had an abortion because her lover said it was not right to have children during the war. 'Let's wait until the war is over, and then we can plan to have children and offer them a good life.' She had gone along with him. But not much later she discovered that she was pregnant again, or rather that she had missed her period and was afraid that she was pregnant. A month later she had her period and calmed down. When she missed her period once more a month later, she comforted herself with the thought that missing a period once did not mean that she had conceived. It was impossible for her to maintain this belief, however, when she missed her next period as well. She consulted a doctor, who informed her that she was in her fifth month of pregnancy, which ended in a frightful operation.

Mrs N. came from a Roman Catholic family. Every year since that abortion she entered a state of catastrophic depression and despair on this date; in other words, she followed the Roman Catholic ritual of remembering a beloved deceased person. She commemorated this day and knew, but on the other hand did not know, why she was suddenly overcome by such despair.

She had not mentioned this abortion when on an earlier occasion she had spoken about the four abortions which she had to terminate pregnancies from this man. After hesitating for a long time she had finally married him, against her mother's advice, but divorced him after the war when he said that it was a crime to have children after Hiroshima.

In making my interpretation I violated the rules and followed my feelings by neglecting the patient's verbal communication and treating my view of her abdomen as something more important. Naturally I cannot prove it, but I am convinced that the patient would not have spontaneously mentioned this very important abortion and that this would have slowed the progress of the analysis. I am also convinced that the climate of the analytic situation would have been greatly burdened if I had felt it forbidden to follow my natural observation and had to force myself into the Procrustean bed of analytic rules.

Another important point was our ages. The patient was sixty-nine and a half years old, and I even older. Neither of us could afford the luxury of wasting time. In her transference phantasies the patient viewed me, as she spontaneously remarked, as her sister Lena, whom the mother had entrusted with the task of raising the patient since she was very small. But this did not make us any younger. We cannot arbitrarily force the pace of analysis, as we in fact cannot force anything, but we also do not have the right to slow it down either. A quick, intuitive interpretation that hits the mark is very impressive but has to be judged with caution. The dangers associated with it are larger than with an interpretation that is slowly worked out and carefully follows the patient's associations. The patient's reaction is, of course, the test of each interpretation. A patient's reactive associations sometimes seem even more important to me than freely made ones. In any case, critical self-observation, continued self-analysis, and self-supervision are essential. As so often, both in analysis and in the human condition, there is a paradox: only tamed naturalness is creative. With growing experience we acquire the criteria for distinguishing both a patient's authentic understanding and our correct intuitive interpretations from impulsiveness, naïve or wild. Finally, in my opinion intuitive interpretations and, similarly, spontaneous behaviour (such as the offer of a hot drink mentioned previously) acquire a function with a secondary autonomy.

A second such episode occurred a few weeks later. The patient reported how she had much earlier had a new idea about educational problems faced by gifted children. One day a friend told the patient about her very gifted daughter. The patient described the achievements of this adolescent in bright colours. She had passed all the admission examinations for university with excellence, and was admitted to one of our most famous universities. While listening to the list of

317

achievements that the patient enthusiastically recited, I became more and more concerned. As she crowned her picture of this outstandingly gifted child with the comment, 'And you could talk with her like with a seventy-year-old,' I made the interpretation that she had been talking about herself, adding that her enthusiasm simply made me shiver.

My patient again reacted with indignation. Again she started to protest with the phrase 'But Doctor . . .', and again she suddenly went quiet because a long-repressed memory surfaced. I shall follow her description. She had always been an outstanding student, but when she was sixteen years old her teacher asked her mother to come to school and informed her to her surprise and horror that her daughter's achievements had fallen drastically for some time. Her failure was a reaction to a catastrophe in the family. Her brother, Fred, had lost the family's money by gambling and speculating only a few years after the death of their father. At that time the patient had renounced her creativity, just as she later repeatedly sacrificed opportunities to have children and also her intellectual productivity. (During her marriage she had forgone her own professional development in favour of being in the role of her husband's wife.) The patient did not make any comments about her mother not noticing that she was depressed.

She then told me the details of Fred's story. Shortly before his birth her mother had had a miscarriage and was too exhausted to nurse him. A wet nurse was hired, a Protestant red-head. Thus Fred had a red-haired, Protestant nurse. The patient did not know what had happened to the nurse's own child, but she did know that the nurse usurped the mother's place and took the baby. One day when the baby was eleven months old, the mother wanted to hold the baby but the nurse refused to give him to her and threatened her with a poker. The nurse was fired, and the baby thus simultaneously lost both the breast that fed him and the mother image closest to him.

Fred's development was a disappointment to his parents. He refused to go on to higher education and was satisfied to open a shop. Furthermore, to his parents' great horror he married a red-haired woman who was not Roman Catholic and who already had a small boy, probably illegitimate. The marriage did not last long, and then Fred began his career as a gambler and speculator. Although he had always been good and generous towards his younger brothers, he failed when he should have supported his widowed mother. He even robbed her.

Fred's story is like a Greek drama. The red-haired nurse determined his fate. He looked for and found her, complete with a little boy, sided with her in opposition to his parents, and left her just as she had left him after a period of love and generosity. He identified with her low cultural level, defying his parents in this regard as well. Like her, he was generous towards young boys, his younger brothers. He revenged his nurse and himself on his mother by usurping her money and leaving her without support.

It is conspicuous that the patient never mentioned her father while she was unfolding the drama of the red-haired nurse. He was no longer alive at the time her teacher informed her mother about her failing achievement. He died when she was eleven years old. She probably experienced a depression then too (unnoticed by her mother?), although she did not say anything about it.

Without a doubt everyone who views this unusually rich picture will draw his own conclusions. The important item for me at the time was her renouncement of achievements that gave her satisfaction and recognition. Concerning her father, I soon had the impression that, in contrast to many signs and observations, she retained an excessively ideal image of her father, just as she later did of her husbands in both of her marriages.

I shall now return to my interpretation. The communication of my feelings in violation of the rules appeared to me as something natural. I was somewhat surprised myself, and thought more about it later. The description of one's self in another person is a well-known strategy of our patients, a compromise between the desire for frankness and resistance to it, and it is usual to tell this to our patients. I could have done this without mentioning my feelings. Thus I later tried to find formulations omitting my feelings, but I did not like any of the interpretations; they all seemed a little cramped. My self-supervision did not produce anything better. As detailed elsewhere (Heimann 1964), I am against an analyst communicating his feelings to his patient and giving him an insight into the analyst's private life, because this burdens the patient and distracts him from his own problems.

While I did not find a better interpretation than that I had given my patient, I recognized that the statement that I shudder at a fifteen-year-old having the mental calibre of a seventy-year-old in reality does not disclose anything about my private life, just as little as my statement that the patient was identified with the girl.

I now come to the question of why the patient was able to overcome her repression. To find the answer I must briefly describe what I knew about her story at the time. In making an interpretation we analysts always make use of more material than is provided at any one time. The patient introduced her family with the key word 'remarkable'. Her father had been a very successful businessman until the political circumstances forced him to emigrate from their native country. In his first marriage he had six children, all of whom were finally united with the family. After the death of his first wife he married a much younger woman. This second wife was also pregnant six times, against her wishes. As already mentioned, Fred was born after a miscarriage. The mother did not want any more children after she had already had four. The patient remembered arguments in which her mother attacked her father for being sexually inconsiderate. It must be remembered that coitus interruptus was the only means of contraception at that time. The family thus also consisted of numerous children from her father's first marriage, their husbands and wives and numerous children (from several marriages), and my patient's mother had to take care of them in various ways. The patient was the unwanted youngest child, and her mother left it to Lena to care for her. Several of the patient's siblings and half-siblings were actually exceptionally talented, but not Fred. He was especially significant to her because they shared – even if for different reasons – the lack of early maternal care and attention. Fred was not an unwanted child, but the mother could not nurse him because she was physically too exhausted, and she could not take care of him much because the wet nurse kept him from her. My patient, in contrast, was the result of a later and very much unwanted pregnancy.

The patient had hardly mentioned Fred in her associations about her family. Everything she told me following my interpretation was completely new to me. Knowing his story it can be assumed that he was too much an object of conflicts, in part a less talented *alter ego*, but also envied because their mother loved him and wanted him. This repressed experience was also marked by insufficient maternal love. The mother had not noticed her daughter's depression; it was a stranger, the teacher, who made her aware of her daughter's condition.

When I now attempt to answer the question why my interpretation led the patient to free herself of the repression that had lasted so long, I come to precisely the affective element – that is, how feelings are offered. At the beginning of the analysis my patient spontaneously said that I was exactly like her sister Lena. In the situation in which I expressed my concern about her – the so exceptionally talented girl – I repeated her experience with the teacher. I believe that the patient unconsciously identified me with the teacher, and that she therefore had the courage to recognize the repressed element and share it with me. It is not necessary here to go into the over-determination expressed in the Fred saga. I shall limit my comments to my role as the concerned teacher, because it corresponded to the character of my unusually talented patient who required analysis to free her unused talents and who had the courage to start analysis and to learn something new at the age of sixty-nine.

It is fitting to identify an analyst with a teacher who has the qualities of careful observation and empathy. Even Freud himself occasionally referred to analysis as a late re-education, which unfortunately was misunderstood in the sense of a one-sided and instructional education.

We offer our patients the chance to alter their past and their present personality by acting as their supplementary ego (Heimann 1956). In the process we utilize the various and multifaceted signals provided by our patients. Our theoretical knowledge helps us to decide which signal is the most important at the moment. Yet this knowledge is inseparable from our emotional perception, which we communicate to our patients when we make interpretations. Words deserve our attention: we choose from the patient's communication what feels authentic and share it through our interpretations.

We also perceive, however, what the patient does *not* say, signal, or imply, or did not experience in an adequate way. In both situations – when we respond either to something the patient signalled or to something he did not signal – we follow less the example set by the parents (that is, in earliest childhood the mother figure), than the *principle* embodied by the maternal function, which originally was performed in a manner that may have been for the better or for the worse. This function means, among other things, that the mother, as supplementary ego, offers the child concepts that it does not have itself. The mother teaches the child new concepts of thinking and thus sets it on the path of progress. To prevent a false development it is decisively important for the new concepts to be appropriate to the child's ego, personality, and disposition, and for them not to have the quality of an attack or of something alien that would distort the natural course of the child's development.

Even before the child understands words, it feels what its mother's expressions, tone of voice, and gestures communicate. Later it associates words to its pre-verbal impressions.

Natural empathy and intuition – thanks to which we are able to perceive what our patients did not say, what is wrong, or what they were deprived of – are rooted in our own personal experience of early privations and subsequent illnesses.

The shock-like rejection with which my patient initially reacted to my interpretations indicates that she had experienced too little of the educational function of loving maternal care, too little natural stimulation and confirmation of her unused talent. This is the ultimate reason for the ease with which she sacrificed her original and productive achievements.

When a patient responds to an interpretation with the feeling, 'I've known this all the time', he is not only referring to the overcoming of his repression(s). He is also referring (without knowing it) to the fact that he experienced something totally new, in so far as a previously suppressed element of his natural character has now become reality. Because it corresponds to his natural disposition, he believes that he has always been in possession of it, so that he has 'known it all the time'.

The necessity for the analyst to be natural with patients is genetically founded. Since the experiencing of psychoanalysis represents a developmental process, it links the natural element with the creative and lends analysis its artistic, creative character. Both patient and analyst experience growth. The interdependence – that is, the mutual influence which patient and analyst have on each other in the psychoanalytic process – deserves to be studied in detail, but this does not belong within the framework of this paper. The precondition for this interdependence is that we do not tend to attribute a predominance to either the instincts or the intellect. The same applies to both the microcosm of the psychoanalytic situation and the macrocosm of the real world: the capacity to harness both tendencies is the only means to put them in the service of natural humanity.

Translated by Michael Wilson, Ph.D., Heidelberg, West Germany

Notes

1 Through an unfortunate combination of circumstances I did not become aware of the deadline for my contribution until it was actually already too late. Thus the scientific secondary process, which enables us to put our original and personal thoughts into a form that can be printed, has not had sufficient influence on how I have formulated my remarks.

The thoughts that I am now putting to paper are not temporary in nature, however. They refer to the clinical situation, which is the origin and touchstone of psychoanalysis; they are, furthermore, the consequence of a suggestion that Alexander Mitscherlich made to me two years ago. At that time I showed him a paper I had given in a foreign country. Although he agreed with its contents, he was critical that the title did not fit the text and suggested that the title express my demand that the analyst should act in a more natural manner. I had in fact discussed the taboos and holy cows that ruin our procedure, and condemned every form of behaviour in an artificial manner towards patients. He gladly agreed to accept the article for *Psyche* if I made the minor revisions that would be made necessary by the change in title. For a moment I thought I would make these revisions, but then I changed my mind. I do not want to put a warmed-up dish on his table full of birthday presents. Thus what I am going to report in this paper are fresh observations.

2–4 Michael Balint, Willi Hoffer, and Donald Winnicott were senior training analysts of the British Psycho-Analytical Society.

24

About children and children-no-longer (1979/80)

This paper was written in response to an invitation by J-B. Pontalis to contribute to a volume of the *Nouvelle Revue de Psychanalyse* devoted to 'The Child'. The contributors were asked to talk about their responses when being with a child. The paper was published in *Nouvelle Revue de Psychanalyse* 19 (1979). An altered English version of this paper was published in a book in honour of P. J. van der Leeuw's seventieth birthday: *Psychoanalytici aan het woord*, Deventer: Van Loghum Slaterus BV, 1980. It is this English text that is published here.

I shall start with the first ideas that came into my mind immediately after reading J-B. Pontalis's[1] invitation to take part in a project that I warmly welcome. The word 'ideas' is not quite correct. What occurred to me were pictures, scenes, memories of contact with children outside my professional activities.

A young mother visited us with her four-months-old baby daughter. After welcoming her and her baby, we, the hosts, were the recipients of her attention. Not having seen us for some time, she had many things to tell us. I noticed that the baby in her arms felt excluded and tried repeatedly to make her mother turn to herself. She was positively wooing her mother, and persevered, for what seemed to me a very long time, without crying or expressing disappointment or anger in other ways. And thus her mother did not notice her. But, after a while, I could not bear it any longer, I did not wish the child to reach the limit of her tolerance. Knowing that my young friend would not take my intervention amiss, I did intervene, and the baby became joyful, when her mother turned to her lovingly. This mother would qualify for Winnicott's designation of 'ordinary devoted mother', or rather more than that. The interchange between her and her little daughter appeared to be of great happiness, and as such an experience very familiar to both of them.

Another scene revisited. I was looking after a boy aged eighteen and a half months, while his mother was in the maternity home giving birth to her second son. Her pregnancy, the birth of his brother, the place where this took place, had been told him in various ways, and also that Mummy would soon come home with his baby brother. The child had shown longing for her and distress only on the first morning without her. It was spring in name, but not in fact. Thinking that children need fresh air, I took him out in his perambulator, which was of the advanced kind so that he could sit and look around freely, while yet wrapped up warmly. After doing some shopping I decided that we had enough of fresh air, and I said, more to myself than to my ward, that it was now time to go home. The child looked at me, pronated his left wrist and looked down at it, then up to me and said with a smile: 'Two'. I did not know how far he could count, but between us, 'two' was his highest number. It related to my dressing him, when 'two' meant: second foot into sock, second leg into trousers, second arm into sleeve. I was surprised about his reaction to what I had regarded merely as my thinking aloud. Later, back home, I happened to look at my watch, and the meaning of the child's gesture earlier in the street then occurred to me. I tested it by asking him much later in an entirely different context for the time. He repeated action, word, and smile. I am not sure whether the child was really so very bright or whether I, child-no-longer, was rather dim.

I now come to an experience with another advanced toddler. As a welcome visitor to the family I spent a night in their house. I was awakened suddenly by the little boy getting into my bed. I assumed that he had woken up from an anxiety dream, and I was pleased and touched by his taking it for granted that I should welcome him even in the middle of my sleep. I caressed him, said something comforting and put my arm around him, as he nestled against my body, practically into it. He fell asleep immediately, and I heard him breathe quietly and rhythmically. What I noticed next was a pleasurable increase of warmth over much of my body, and this warmth came from my bedfellow, my self-invited guest. Why did he wet? His anxiety was over. Of course, I do not know what he was dreaming, but I do not believe that, had he dreamt of a fire needing extinction, he would have slept so peacefully. I regarded his wetting as an erotic gesture after relief from anxiety and as a response to my loving welcome. He continued to sleep and lay quite still. I, however, awake with many thoughts about the child, did not lie still, and as I moved, and air wafted into the wet bed-clothes, I felt a most disagreeable cold and clammy dampness that drove me out of the bed.

I had often wondered why children appear not to be disturbed, when they wet their bed or napkins. In the present instance I could argue that by being in deep sleep, and staying motionless, the child remained in the pleasantly warm medium. However, this is not a sufficient explanation. The capacity for locomotion, crawling, and sometimes even walking, is well established before bladder control. Children still with napkins around them, when moving about, so that the initial warmth is lost by the access of air, do not show displeasure.

I now mention an experience with a child, in which I was not actively involved. Three children whose ages ranged from about seven to one-and-a-half years were engaged in some game, when the youngest left the group and went to his mother. A wordless dialogue took place. Both went out of the room and returned with a chamber pot, which the mother put down somewhat remote from the other children, who took little notice. Obviously the little boy had informed his mother – again without words, which I should have heard in view of the short distance between the room and the bathroom – that he wanted to see what happened when he defecated. He positioned himself over the pot, straddling it, and bent forward to see clearly. His facial expression revealed intense interest. What did he see? First of all, the lower part of his body and his penis, certainly a familiar and pleasurable sight. He waited with fascination for the moment in which he actually passed his stool. But what happened then did not please him at all. As his stool fell down, his face changed to grave disappointment and disdain. He immediately rejected the pot with his stool and turned away with disgust. What I witnessed was a young researcher's project ending with mortification.

My last offering deals with two brothers, O. and Y. The time is Christmas, and I spend the holidays with the children's family. In an English home the major presents are put around the Christmas tree to be opened on Christmas day after breakfast. Minor presents are packed in the Christmas stocking, which is suspended from the children's beds, when they are asleep, to be found when they wake up. (I suspect that this arrangement is meant to secure some rest for the hard-pressed parents.) I am woken up in the night by some noises from the dining room downstairs. Entering the room I see O. and Y. in their pyjamas and without slippers. The room is icy. The coal fire has expired. I get busy, fetching an electric fire, warming some milk (a great mistake, since these children never drank warm milk), and try to persuade them to go back to bed. O., aged four years and two-and-a-half months, says reassuringly that it is quite all right, Mummy has given permission. Y., aged two years and nine months, just says one word: 'Bicky', which his brother translates for me as 'biscuit'. O. with clear open eyes, looking straight at me, had said a lie, I learned later. Y., slow in using words, had lived for a very long time with the two words: 'No', and 'More', and the occasional combination 'No more'. Since I found that this vocabulary in fact covered all contingencies, I used to wonder whether and why he would ever use other words. There was never any doubt about his high intelligence. However, once, when the family visited me for lunch, he surprised us by saying a whole sentence. This was: 'I want Daddy to sit next to me.' The way he pronounced this correctly constructed sentence made it sound as if it were one word. He shot it out with great speed, leaving no intervals between the words. Maybe, he wanted to outwit big brother by announcing his claim at the earliest moment and in the quickest way. In the incident at Christmas he again uttered only one word: 'Bicky'. But there were more factors to be considered. He had a bad cough and thus was physically not at his best. Moreover, he was bored. He was left far behind his big brother's absorption with the toys and, I think, he was relieved when his father appeared and made the boys return to bed.

Some professional thoughts

I shall now try to assess my spontaneous private experiences with children from a psychoanalytical point of view.

The four-months-old baby girl showed a high degree of tolerance to her mother's neglect. Altogether, as I mentioned elsewhere, I have found that children have far more patience with their parents' failings than is generally acknowledged. Such forbearance is by no means always beneficial to the child. It is, of course, overdetermined. The child's sense of need and helplessness makes him deny his perception of his parents' faults or illness. As he cannot afford to admit that the powerful and all-knowing parent, as he needs his parent(s) to be, makes in fact gross mistakes, he prefers to attribute to himself the cause and guilt for privations. In these cases idealization serves as a defence against fears of annihilation and despair, states that fleetingly occur even in the life of children in a loving home. But idealization is also part of being acutely in love (Verliebt-sein), as Freud has shown, and these states too are not rare in childhood, when a joyful experience, say, with his mother, makes the child feel an acute intensification of love together with gratitude. (We may think of the kinship between gratitude and gratification.) Such joyful elation is the child's natural prerogative. Melanie Klein's theory of the 'manic defence' against feelings of guilt ultimately due to pre-natal, inborn envy, one of the seven deadly sins, fails to appreciate primary *joie de vivre* (1957). It has moreover a distinctly religious quality, but religion should be kept outside psychoanalysis.

In the eighteen-and-a-half-months-old boy, who told me the time, I see cognitive functions in an autonomous learning process. The elements, which Freud (1911b) lists as constituting realistic secondary process thinking, are at work here, such as active attention, perception, storing of observations in the memory system, and ready recall. In addition, he correctly interpreted my wish for the comfort of the home, which my remark and, I assume, my facial expression too revealed. Something was added to his cognitive achievement when he offered it as a gift, and the whole event was pleasurable, as shown in his smile. Without my understanding it at the time, he not only proved himself an apt partner in a discourse on time; by using the highest number belonging to our relationship, he moreover expressed sympathy with me and my wish to be home. The experience of 'the other', a person different from himself – in contrast to me he did not feel cold – here meant an enrichment of thinking, learning, and applying knowledge.

The Latin saying that we learn for life, not for school, bypasses psychological truth. Children do learn for and with the teacher, whom they like. With an uncaring and uncared-for teacher the child is stupid, becomes stupid, chooses to appear as stupid. Or he may secretly learn from motives of defiance. But knowledge gained in this way and produced with hostile triumph is so much charged with conflict and hurt that it gives little benefit to either child or child-no-longer.

To return to my companion: the word 'two' itself was associated with pleasant memories of motor activities and bodily skill, which are themselves highly prized by children. In certain situations adults too indulge in such pleasures, as is shown by the widespread enthusiasm for sport and ever-new forms of sport, of challenge to bodily prowess, mastery over danger.

Actual pleasure in locomotor freedom and control may recall former helplessness in the many situations of waiting passively and in infinite boredom to be picked up and taken to places to see new and interesting things. Moreover, as Freud pointed out, movement serves as a cognitive tool in discerning whether a perception belongs to the outside or to the self. I believe that it is not sufficiently appreciated how much boredom is suffered by children from early infancy onwards. It is only partly acknowledged in the concept of 'stimulus hunger', which, however, omits the child's wishes to seek and find stimuli actively on his own. To admit the importance of such deprivations helps us to understand the toddler's pleasure in teasing the adult. As mentioned elsewhere (1962b), all the toddlers whom I have known, chose to go where, they knew, the adult would not like it, such as opening the gates of other people's gardens and strolling about and picking flowers there, walking in the opposite direction, trying to cross the road, and so on. Such teasing is done in good humour, and will deteriorate into hostile defiance only if the adult is lacking in understanding and does not in turn show a sense of humour.

The new achievement of locomotor capacities links the movement of the whole body with that of the stool within the body, as is well expressed by the English word 'motion'. It might be better to speak of an anal–motor and anal–aggressive phase rather than globally call the phase anal–sadistic, and so leave room for exploring the conditions which change aggression to sadism, such as undue restrictions and deprivations of various kinds which the child has suffered. Early locomotor sadism may well later lead to suicidal daring in the pursuit of sport. As regards my visitor at night I now emphasize his realism, his good sense, when he chose to disturb me rather than his parents or any other member of the household.

The incident with the two brothers invites many thoughts. I called O.'s assertion that his mother had given him permission to play with his toys, a lie. I think this is a typical example of an adult's failure to tune in with a child's interpretation of a situation. Toys in the Christmas stocking are meant to be played with, when waking up. This is what he was doing. That he invoked his mother and not his father reveals a preference too obvious to need an explanation, but it may also have more and other reasons. From the child's point of view I was lying when I expressed an opposition to his playing. This leads me to add some points to the theme of the child's tolerance *vis-à-vis* his parents. I refer to their only too frequent inconsistencies. In connection with toys there is indeed a good deal of pretence on the part of the parents. One familiar example, very amusing to the observer, but exasperating to the child, is the good father who gives his son a kite and goes with him to the park. Who then plays with the kite? It is the father, not the son. The latter may do some minor chores to help Daddy fly the kite. Another pet toy that a father buys for himself, when ostensibly giving it as a present to his son, is the electric train. It is again the father who assumes the dominant role in running it. Altogether, I have often wondered whether toys are wanted by children or by children-no-longer, quite apart from the manufacturers. Toys often serve as a placebo, because mother or father have no time or inclination to be with their children and engage in common activities with them. Often a child prefers to be busy with a parent and do something practical that is needed and important for the household and assures him of respect for his abilities. But this has to be in accordance with his choice. I do not mean that children like to be told to do errands when they would rather play. I do not deny the value of toys that challenge a child's wits, nor the need for remedial toys.

The sibling complex

From my encounter with the two brothers I select the problem of the younger child, who follows his older sibling's example. The older boy was fascinated by his toys, the younger one was clearly bored. In this incident he made no attempt to imitate his brother. He did so on other occasions, even when he was obviously not sharing his brother's fun, being by age and interest not on the same level.

The danger that the younger child might be driven into a precocious false self struck me very much, when I supervised the analysis of a three-year-old boy, whose presenting symptoms were inability to hear, talk, or understand. His sister, seventeen months younger, was his superior in every respect and, by general consent in the family, used to annex his possessions. She also tried to usurp his analysis by entering the analytic room and claiming attention. The analyst was capable of coping with both children and yet analysing her patient. When the latter had improved and could hear, talk, and carry out activities adequate to his age, we became worried about the formerly so bright little girl, who was now left behind and out of her depth. It became clear that the analyst was faced with a family problem, each member in turn becoming the 'mute, sad-eyed child', for whom she very skilfully arranged appropriate and successful therapies (Elles 1962).

I use the term 'sibling complex' in analogy with the Oedipus complex. Incidentally, I regret that 'complex' is no longer fashionable. The relationship between siblings, a child's chronological position amongst his siblings, reactions to parental preferences or neglect, comparisons, spontaneous or induced, of looks, talents, achievements, health, and so forth – all this is of very high significance, and not only because the sibling represents a parent.

Modern youth has invented the 'generation gap'. I used to be amused. Do they believe that there was no gap between their parents and grandparents? Were parents and children of the same age in the bad old times? But I have come to think that they are justified, when they claim more attention to their peer group as such, to their achievements, problems, conflicts. What is at stake is not only the adolescent's Oedipal rebellion.

It is noteworthy that Freud chose *King Oedipus*, the tragedy between the generations, to illustrate our fundamental and ubiquitous human predicament, but omitted *Oedipus at Kolonos* and *Antigone* (Politzer 1972). The last play of Sophocles' trilogy portrays with great clarity the drama within the same generation. We are used to think of Antigone as the selfless daughter, whose only aim in life is loving care for her unhappy father. It is with some surprise that we learn in the last of the Theban plays that she none the less has a sexual life: she is betrothed to Haemon, Creon's son. But when her father has reached his predestined end, gently and with the grace that is due to his majesty, when she is free to return to Thebes and marry, she sacrifices everything, her love for Haemon and her life, to her brother Polynices, who killed and was killed by the other brother, Eteocles. Defying Creon's order, she buries Polynices with the sacred rites to save him from humiliation and divine wrath.[2]

If it was the author's intention to depict the unmitigated and unmitigatable, the unredeemed and unredeemable horror of incest between son and mother, then he must show that this union is an outrage against nature and cannot produce life, a new generation. This generation must die, sweeping more deaths with them. Ironically, nature, blessing the incestuous couple with four healthy children, proved herself far less pernickety than her human interpreters. Biology and psychology are often not in agreement.

The differences in the characters of these four siblings are impressive, with Antigone as the richest, profoundest, and most fascinating personality (does the author's Oedipus complex shine through?), the brothers as personifications of hateful ambition and rivalry, rather than persons, illustrating the Oedipus and the sibling complexes, and Ismene as somewhat insipid, obedient, 'reality-adapted' – a bit of the dull, goody-goody child, whom we find in many nurseries. Acknowledging the importance of the sibling complex does not mean neglecting the Oedipus complex. They interact and intertwine throughout, in life no less than in Sophocles' trilogy.

Children's distress

Reflecting on the children whom I have described, I realize that all of them experienced some distress, frustration, privation. With one exception, to which I shall turn later, there was not a massive, dramatic trauma. The events that occurred were, so to say, of the stuff of which ordinary life is made.

I repeat briefly. A four-months-old baby has to share her mother's attention with other persons. This will have happened before I saw it, and it will happen again. A first-born is separated from his mother, who has another baby. Children have occasional nightmares. Parents expect some discipline and do not allow their children to play in the middle of the night. Freud showed to an unwilling public that it is an illusion to believe that children live in paradise. But frustration was followed by gratification. The baby girl regained her mother's love focusing on her. Although without his mother, the young sage, who knew the time, had a good deal of fun and interest from the substitute mother. Loneliness and fears in the night gave way to security and erotic pleasure with the chosen companion. The toys from the Christmas stocking had been sampled with joy. It is possible to think that, when deprivation is followed soon by happiness, a pattern may be laid down of 'bad things go and good things come'. We may regard this as the psychological equivalent to physiological immunity. Although it is impossible to measure another person's pain, on the basis of psychoanalytical findings, I believe that these disappointments were not severe enough to form the 'cumulative trauma' (Khan 1963). Indeed, the cases described by Khan suffered deprivations of a different order.

As a severe trauma, the exception, I regard the blow to the young researcher's creative scientific spirit. He experienced a humiliation, not through somebody else's doing, whom he might have blamed, attacked, or disobeyed; his frustration originated within himself. And he knew it. In the same incident he had a most satisfactory experience with his mother, who understood him so well in their wordless dialogue. I do not think that this gratification could compensate for the failure of his project. The former continued or repeated early infantile modes of living, the latter was an attempt to reach forward, and its failure may well have left behind a nagging doubt about his intellectual capacities.

332

Learning about chidren

What did I learn from my relationship with children? I attempt a brief summary. Children acquire a good deal of patience and tolerance towards their parents and other adults. They persist in the pursuit of an aim. Such perseverance should not be confused with the neurotic compulsion to repeat. Even if it were neurotic, you have not got to rush your child at once to a psychoanalyst. The apparent severity of a symptom can be deceptive and not call for professional help (A. Freud 1968). The child invests repetition itself with pleasure. By contrast, the no-longer-child gets bored with repetition, needs new things, becomes addicted to changes, be these in clothes, furniture, sport, words. Watch women shopping for clothes or at the hairdresser or in the beauty salons, and men at the corresponding places! I suggest that they are possessed by the illusion that their whole life will be changed for the better – that they themselves will become new – young, beautiful, potent, and so forth. A whole industry is built on this illusion.

The child is faithful. A story read or told must keep its original text, and alterations are rejected. The child asks, wants to know the answers, persists here too, unless intimidated by the adult. He is inventive, which often gives to his questions a twist which the grown-up did not expect and which makes him all the more unwilling to be bothered by this inconvenient, inquisitive child. This is beautifully portrayed by John Habberton (1876). A great range of emotional and intellectual cognitive processes occur in the child, which are unrecognized at the time. ('Oh, he is only a child!') The child puts up with the adult's unrelatedness to his cognitive faculties, with their inconsistencies, mood changes, lack of attention, and so on, frequent even in a 'good enough' milieu. In fact, what makes the milieu 'good enough' is largely the child's tolerance, persistence in learning, resourcefulness, and autonomous thinking. I omit the abuse of physical power by parents because the children whom I mentioned and others, from whom I learned, were not exposed to physical brutality.

All these qualities of the child can be summed up in the concept 'openness to life'. That is what makes children so attractive. I have often wondered, why are babies and young children so adorable, whereas adults very rarely are? My answer is that the adult has so often given up, is 'resigned', suppresses his curiosity, accepts what is there, but with resentment and in apathy. He offers little to life – seizes little from it. No wonder this adult is dull. It might prove useful to give the vicissitudes of infantile curiosity a prominent place in the investigation of the discomforts of civilization. I think that visually the young child's openness to life shows in the round lines of a baby's and young child's face, which artists have not failed to exploit fully. I think of the curves of forehead, cheek, nose, chin, these half-circles that remain open – like question marks. Of course, it should be put the other way round: the child-no-longer learned the question mark from the younger children. For good measure I add the enchanting, humid, glistening pink of the new-born's nails. I cannot attribute to this feature the quality of a question – or can I? I can claim that to ask, put a question, means also to make a demand, and I applaud nature for her wisdom, that made her endow her most helpless human creation with maximal appeal, the demand for love and care.

I am aware that the examples which I have given do not substantiate all of my conclusions. I have drawn on a wider field of relationships with children. I am also aware of not having described unpleasant children.

Editorial demands and strictures

So far, I realize, I have reacted only to J-B. Pontalis's personal letter, and that was easy, child's play, so to say. Indeed, without being aware of it at the time, I behaved like a child, and by playing showed what I do, in fact, consider characteristic for children: they respond immediately and easily to a benevolent invitation to express their thoughts, to be active and creative. Beyond this, I hold that we cannot make a valid contribution to a discourse unless we allow ourselves to identify with its subject-matter. Perhaps this is only my own idiosyncratic reaction. I talk of problems concerning human beings. Such identification, however, will be constructive only if checked by disciplined self-awareness, by having trained oneself to search for clarity and to be sensitive to unclear thinking – considerations that bring to mind the theme of the counter-transference. However, I am here not concerned with the psychoanalyst at work. In passing, though, the threads that link a therapist's counter-transference with an adult's capacity to identify in a controlled manner with a child deserve to be explored.

As I now study the demands and strictures issued by J-B. Pontalis, the editor, things at once become different. I encounter difficulties with which I am only too familiar. An empty page stares at me, and my mind goes blank. The Project wants to collect the ideas which psychoanalysts have about children, not about patients who happen to be of child age. I now register annoyance at the thought that it is necessary to urge analysts to be clear about their notions of the infant, infancy, and the infantile – or rather more than that: to urge analysts to have such notions. It is indeed necessary. How often, when supervising a child analysis, did I see that the analyst met a child for the first time in the role of patient! I now see that the page is no longer blank, nor could my mind have been, since after all I did write down some ideas. Is it significant that they are hostile? I answer in the affirmative. Perhaps, I have again identified with a child, this time, when confronted with a stranger, not knowing how to start a dialogue, or with parents who for reasons of their own were unable to initiate contact or respond gladly to the child's attempts at reaching them.

Agreements and objections

As I vent criticisms, I would comment on the widespread error which treats the condition of the regressed adult as identical with his original childhood. Something extremely important is here overlooked. The regressed person, adult or child, suffers from a breakdown of advanced functions, suffers from destructive processes affecting developmental achievements. This implies narcissistic hurts, wounds to self-esteem, shame, a sense of being let down by oneself, failure in many respects. The new helplessness reactivates old demands on others, and awareness of the loss of independence creates a vicious circle.

Another error which I regret is related to the mother–infant observation that forms part of the English psychoanalytic training. The student regularly visits a mother to observe her, as she deals with her baby. He is instructed to refrain from making comments, to comport himself as if he were not there or just part of the furniture. Since I disapprove of the 'uninvolved and neutral' analyst, I also am against the uninvolved mother–infant observer. It is worth mentioning here the reaction of two analysands of mine to this item of their training. Both were devoted and interested young fathers. Dr A. said that, if he saw the mother do something harmful to her baby, he would 'interfere' and explain to her why she must not do such a thing to her child. Dr B. reported that the baby was always asleep at the appointed time, but that the mother was very glad to see him. In other words, he had plenty of occasion to observe her flirting with him. I myself thought that this was not a bad thing, and that she would probably be a better mother if she was less bored with her life and looked forward every week to some entertainment – which, after all, was due to her baby. However, I am far from objecting to students learning something about the mother–infant couple. On the contrary, as I said earlier, it is very necessary. What I am opposed to is the condition that the student should be 'uninvolved and neutral'. It should be left to the mother and her visitor to decide how he should participate. I wonder, though, whether this method of observing the mother–infant couple is really good. I fully sympathized with a young mother who flatly refused to allow what she regarded as an interference with a most intimate and delicate relationship.

Scientific criteria

I have long been puzzled about the origin of the ideal of the 'neutral' analyst. If you read Freud's case histories (and reports by former analysands of his, Blanton 1971, H.D. (Hilda Doolittle) 1956), it is obvious that Freud felt with and for his patients. At the same time it is very clear that Freud maintained his distance (with one baffling exception, Holland 1969), thus protecting himself and his patients from uncontrolled counter-transference reactions. To his patients such distancing meant a disappointment. Freud here anticipated the findings of later child analysts, for example, Winnicott (1971) who defines the mother's task as distancing herself from her child and disillusioning him, when the earliest period of total adaptation to her child needs to be ended.

The notion of the uninvolved analyst may stem from Freud's description of the eighteen-months-old boy, who invented the game of 'fort' and 'da' (1920g). Freud there set the custom, which generally has been followed, of not revealing what his personal relation with the little boy was, and how he came to live under the same roof with him. He analysed the multiple functions and motives of this game to lead to his new idea that there are psychic processes beyond the pleasure principle. I used to regret this reticence, suspecting that we analysts, children-no-longer, are afraid of owning up to having feelings, afraid lest the sages would pounce on us and denounce our lack of 'scientific' spirit that they make incumbent upon emotional detachment. However, I came to realize that such silence was determined by a different and highly important consideration: discretion must be maintained in the interest of the children and families concerned. Indeed, who would want to find himself made known to the public, a vast and uninvited audience?

I turn now to a pet objection of mine. I refuse to acknowledge the validity for psychoanalysis of current scientific criteria, since their root lies in a mode of thinking that antedates Freud's discoveries of the Ucs and its influence on all spheres of mental functioning. In contrast to myself, Daniel Lagache, whose untimely death has deprived psychoanalysis of a brilliant worker, took the trouble of investigating the reason why the scientific status of psychoanalysis is not recognized (English translation 1966). He found that it is the quantity of material with which psychoanalysts deal that misleads the judgement of the scientists, who themselves have not to work through such a multitude of data in their researches. I am still inclined to criticize these scientists. They fail to acknowledge the need to cope with both, the chaff and the wheat, in order to extract the latter from the former.

What I respect is the judgement of mathematics, because this science has influenced the thinking of mankind from time immemorial, and mathematical concepts, I believe, are unlimitedly wide and inclusive and yet of exact specificity. To my delight my friend Professor Matte-Blanco offered me a mathematical confirmation for my assertion in a recent paper (1977), that a 'neutral', unfeeling analyst is not far from being a 'neuter' and cannot affect the psychoanalytic process. When I mentioned this idea, including a disrespectful smile to him, he wrote down for me a number of mathematical formulae. I select the proposition that deals with addition, since this applies most easily to the relation of patient and analyst. It runs as follows:

> Any number, if added to another number, gives a third number as a result, for example: $1 + 1 = 2$. There is, however, one and only one exception: 0. Zero added to any number leaves the number unchanged, for example: $1 + 0 = 1$. In mathematics it is said that 0 is the (unique) neutral element in the operation of addition.

This is exactly what I maintain: 1 is the patient, and 0 is the 'neutral' analyst, who will not bring about something new. His patient will remain unchanged, without benefit from the analysis, and possibly in a worse condition.

I am probably again behaving like a child when I persevere with my emphasis on feelings as a cognitive and practical tool. The verb 'affect' in the phrase 'affect the psychoanalytic process' denotes something sober like expediency. It is identical with the noun that means feeling, emotion, and is very close to 'affection', love, but also not far from 'affectation', which signifies pretence and falsehood. Playing with words starts in childhood but maintains its charm for children-no-longer.

Put in another way: playing is learning, and learning can be joyful. I also hold that a valid lecture need not be pompous and heavy.

Exact interpretations

Pontalis castigates as 'a genetic illusion' the assertion that it is possible to catch the constituents of the Ucs *in statu nascendi*. I have not met this in the psychoanalytic literature, or I have forgotten it. I myself once recommended that the analyst should verbalize a process in the patient as it is just taking place. I do not think that Pontalis refers to this, although I am now stung into wondering whether my observation implies such a genetic illusion in view of my conviction that the patient relives his past in the psychoanalytic space and time. What I had in mind was the element of immediacy, and genetic considerations were outside my frame of ideas. But with some sophistry and well-oiled rhetoric it could be proved that, if I believe that the patient relives his past in the present, and if I believe that interpretations can move pre-conscious into conscious thinking, then it follows that I believe it is possible to catch 'the constituents of the Ucs'. Nevertheless, I continue with the matter with which I am concerned now: the patient's need to feel that his analyst tunes in with him. We are familiar with the patient who responds to his analyst's comment with the remark: 'It is funny that you should be saying this. I was just thinking (exactly what the analyst said).' With the word 'funny' he does not consciously mean a thing of fun, something gay, merry, and so on. Other patients call such an experience 'strange'. I feel that these patients tell us about their childhood and indict their parents of lack of understanding. Thus they became used to not being understood, and when now the analyst behaves in a different way, it is odd and strange. Strange refers also to the child's experience that the familiar figure, mother or father, when failing to understand him, turned into a stranger, and in turn treated the child as if he had been an unknown stranger. In keeping with such disappointments in childhood is the defensive trick of some patients to tell their analyst something important only when it is no longer hot, so that the analyst cannot touch him, cannot hurt him.

This leds to the question of what it is that makes an interpretation valuable, makes it click, a living experience. It is not, I suggest, verbal exactness. Freud clearly opposed the idea of accurately reporting the events of an analytic session (1912e). Not only is it in fact impossible, since too many things happen. It is not even desirable, it would be deadly pedantic. I know a psychotherapist who decided against training as a psychoanalyst, and used his personal analysis in a rather original form of psychotherapy. He was utterly flexible. His patients were free to lie on the couch, or sit or move about. They also could bring friends or relatives to their sessions. With their agreement he used a tape recorder. If there was some uncertainty about what had been said or by whom, he, again with his patient's agreement, played back the doubtful passage. I do not think that listening again to their voices and phrases was likely to deprive that session of vitality. In fact, I appreciate his work. I myself, though, could not do it. Maybe, I prefer a bit of a muddle to the use of a gadget. I must contradict my last sentence. I do not like muddled thinking at all, although I am guilty of it only too often as just now. I meant to express my strong dislike against introducing any gadget into the psychoanalytic relationship. I probably should not be able to handle it correctly.

Freud also negated the idea that it is ever possible to analyse a dream completely – a view shared by Blum and Khan (1976), two analysts whose analytic thinking differs widely from one another. I understand Freud to believe that we anyhow catch unconscious processes only approximately, but for achieving dynamic rapport between patient and analyst such approximation is sufficient, it is 'good enough'. It enables the patient to gain insight, inner sight – that is, intrapsychic contact, rapport with himself within his relation with his analyst. This new experience of inner and outer rapport also throws light on the pleasure element in the word 'funny' ('It is funny your saying this'). Psychic enrichment gives pleasure, sometimes even if the content of what we learn about ourselves may be first of all of a painful nature.

To acknowledge the limited, approximative nature of our discoveries and interpretations does not contradict the high subjective and objective value of the emergence of a memory, in particular one related to early infantile life. We seem to price our early and earliest selves very highly. The return of a hitherto forgotten memory, be this an event or an idea or an emotion, or the occurrence of a link between so far unconnected psychic items is rightly appreciated as a 'touchstone' for the value of the psychoanalytic experience, for both patient and analyst. It is an encouragement, it gives hope and trust, does effect a change in the patient. It is an experience that confirms, more than that, it affirms the reality of the psychoanalytic process. It is also a reward for the work done, the pains suffered, by both.

The crucially important experience, which I just mentioned, happens often as a direct response to a specific verbal interpretation.

339

Yet, in contrast to some authors who extol the unsurpassed importance of the word – for example, Maud Mannoni (1967), following Lacan – I want to warn against singling out the word as the exclusive vehicle of communication and meaning and neglecting other phenomena that occur at the same time. Listening as well as vocalizing goes together with muscular and sensory modalities and actuates memories of similar experiences down to those of oneness with mother, when the infant did not differentiate her from himself. I do not mean that those earliest memories are recalled as such. The analyst's words evoke feelings and a re-enactment of the infant's early learning by identifying with his mother. Considering earliest undifferentiation, it would be more correct to speak of his identifying her with himself.

I remember a patient who, after a successful interpretation, of which I was quite proud, applauded herself, her unconscious, not me, not my perceptiveness, my giving name and shape to something that, until she heard my comments, had been inchoate in herself, and thus not within her conscious grasp, not leading to creative insight. I shall not analyse here her contemporary wish to reduce me or my reaction to it.

Thinking about words makes me pick up Pontalis's remark about the pejorative use of 'infantile'. The Anglo-Saxon languages offer an easy distinction between the factual and the hostile reference to the child. The first is 'childlike' ('kindlich'), the second 'childish' ('kindisch'). I may say to a child, when irritated, 'Don't be childish!', and meaning, 'Do not pretend that you are stupid, just because you are a child'. I should not say, 'Don't be childlike'. The pejorative use of the word 'infantile' betrays the ambivalence to children of those who are no longer children. They either denigrate childhood or sentimentally idealize it by attributing creativity exclusively to the child. One is as incorrect as the other. Faulty thoughts lead to ugly language. When I hear interpretations like 'the child part' of the patient, I wince. Why do we not speak of infantile impulses, wishes, fears, modes of thinking, and so on?

There is another reason for my reacting strongly against the expression 'child part'. This relates to the word 'part'. Although I have spent more time of my life in England than in Germany, I still notice peculiarities of the English language which do not strike those who are born and bred in it. I once had a collection of oddities which greatly surprised my English friends. The word 'part' in 'child part' stirs in me associations to the coy, circumlocutory expression 'private parts' for genitals. Why are they more private than other parts of our body? I may show myself as indecent and moreover obstinate, but I am absolutely sure that the genitals are not meant for 'private' use. Nature designed them for use with another, and society deprecates masturbation. In more respectable and dull language: biological and social considerations lead to the conclusion that masturbation cannot be regarded as the most appropriate sexual activity.

I do not like the phrase 'the child in you, him, her, them, us', unless there is a special dialectic need. It is correct only in statements about a pregnant woman. Next, I object to the 'part object' as a description of the child's relationship. Again the idea is wrong, and hence the language. Who is ever related to the whole person! (I dislike also 'object' for person, except when we are concerned with the subject/object antithesis.) When I have a discussion, I focus on my partner's ideas. I may know a great deal about him, his job, his hobbies, his quirks, and so on, but at this point in time they do not interest me, and, if all these data, which I know, were actively operating in my mind, if thus I were related to the 'whole' person, I should go crazy, and there would be no discussion.

Being still bothered by the concept of a 'genetic illusion', I wonder whether I have accepted it, when stating that I have the same type of 'object relationship' that the child has. No, I must negate this. I have denied that the child has a 'part object relationship'.

Psychoanalytic literature offers a phrase like 'To begin with the child relates to his mother as a need satisfying object'. I prefer this formulation, provided that the need for intellectual stimulation and responses from a very early age onwards is included. When did the eighteen-and-a-half-months-old start to integrate the variety of observations into a concept of time? What I saw was the end result; its beginnings were hidden.

My last paragraphs make it obvious how much words matter to me. Indeed, I shall be the last person to doubt the strength and might, the charm and magic of words. But precisely for these qualities words are dangerous. Their power can easily be misused. An analyst's words can carry suggestive influences, intoxication, indoctrination, and some analysands lose conceptual thinking as they acquire a vocabulary. The psychoanalytic process is not kept moving only by words. An analyst's silent participation is at times crucial, and words are impossible. In some situations my silence was far more telling than any word could have been. In fact, I had no words, and I should have been ashamed had I spoken. The patient himself may be so immersed in his grief or horror that he does not consciously notice his analyst or his analyst's silence. Later he will need words, often also then remember and appreciate his analyst's wordless gift of sympathy and empathy. I believe that I merely re-phrase what Freud called psychoanalytic tact.

Psychoanalysis aims at enabling patients to achieve lucid intellectual sharpness as well as rich, free feelings and imagination. By liberating the patients from the ravages of their past experiences, from their fears, guilt, and inhibitions, it assumes the quality of a learning process and facilitates the unfolding of their creative potential. Psychoanalysis is a reciprocal process. Analysts learn from their patients, as children-no-longer learn from children. In both situations there are dangers. I deprecate the systematic explorations undertaken by a child's parent, of which there are published records. If a child is taken to an analyst, whatever explanation his parents give him, the child knows *ab initio* that the stranger will do things for a purpose; he recognizes the professional nature of the analyst and of his meeting with him. He may come to like his analyst and to appreciate what happens in his session. This indeed is usually the case with a 'good-enough' child analyst, and the child develops an inkling of psychoanalysis. If, however, his parent assumes a professional attitude, watches his child systematically, functions as a scientist, I consider that this parent abuses his child's trust and treats him as a guinea-pig. I further want to ban all those films about deprived children which inflict deprivations in the very act of filming. Psychoanalysts in the name of science have inflicted cruelty – true to the tradition of spreading the word of the loving God by persecution.

On the part of the child analyst we not infrequently find a possessive attitude to the child patient. His parents are treated as a nuisance or worse. They are intimidated against wanting to know whether their child makes progress. However, fanaticism and incompetence are not restricted to child analysts; this truism is yet worth mentioning. Not only the power of language is dangerous; so is that of the transference. Psychoanalysts can never overestimate the power of the transference.

Equally damaging to the child are the jealous parents who interfere with his therapy by subjecting him to questions about himself and the therapist. This is another of the frequent examples where the child-no-longer fails to respect the child.

What are the appropriate sources for furthering our understanding of children? Of course, we come to the artists and poets who, as Freud acknowledged, are the precursors of psychoanalysis. Although they alone did not achieve enough, we are helped by turning to them. I earlier mentioned one particularly enchanting tale of children and adults, but there are many other authors who portray children's life with respect and understanding. As regards the psychology of children-no-longer I refer to Jane Austen, who died about four decades before Freud's birth. She used the word 'unconscious' in a strictly psychoanalytic sense. I single her out of the unlimited range of literature, because she depicts no grand dramatic events, but rather the miniatures of everyday domestic life.

To end, I mention one vitally important function which an adult has, when being with a child, and he needs no professional training for it, merely ordinary experience of life and good sense. He has to protect the child from harming himself. If the child-no-longer is in good contact with his own childhood, he will be able to prevent the child from damaging himself without humiliating him or discouraging his imagination and inventiveness.[3]

Notes

1 This article has a history. Its original version appeared in the *Nouvelle Revue de Psychanalyse* 19 (1979), entitled 'L'Enfant'. It was a direct and very personal reply to J-B. Pontalis, editor of the *NRP*, who asked for a contribution from me with so much warmth and friendship, so much encouragement and advance appreciation that I identified with the subject-matter, and felt I was treated as a child. Part of the writing then proved very easy.

However, he also attached an 'Avant Projet' to his invitation with guidelines and views which I regard as representative for our colleagues of the Association Psychanalytique de France, which are worthwhile discussing.

In the present essay I have omitted sections that were specifically addressed to Pontalis, but I have referred to the 'Avant Projet', when intrinsically relevant. Other modifications are the natural result of my looking critically at something I had written some time earlier after an interval had passed. Precisely because of its origin I regard my article as fitting to be offered for the Festschrift of a colleague and friend.

2 I follow the translation of E. F. Watling, *Sophocles, the Theban Plays*, Penguin Classics.

3 [Paula Heimann was asked by J-B. Pontalis, the editor of the *Nouvelle Revue de Psychanalyse*, to write about her feeling-responses when she was with children. In his introduction to the issue entitled 'L'Enfant', he singled her out as the contributor who had retained over her long experiences with children a natural way of being attuned to them. In his view, if analysts and also others do not maintain an ability to meet children with an open, questioning mind, then all communications with them are bound to become closed.]

Complete bibliography of Paula Heimann's publications

English language publications

Heimann, P. (1942) 'A contribution to the problem of sublimation and its relation to processes of internalization', *International Journal of Psycho-Analysis* 23: 8–17.

—— (1949) 'Some notes on the psycho-analytic concept of introjected objects', *British Journal of Medical Psychology* 22: 8–15.

—— (1950) 'On counter-transference', *International Journal of Psycho-Analysis* 31: 81–4.

—— (1952a) 'A contribution to the re-evaluation of the Oedipus complex – the early stages', *International Journal of Psycho-Analysis* 33: 84–92.

—— (1952b) 'Preliminary notes on some defence mechanisms in paranoid states', *International Journal of Psycho-Analysis* 33: 208–13.

—— (1952c) 'Notes on the theory of the life and death instincts', in M. Klein, P. Heimann, S. Isaacs, and J. Riviere *Developments in Psycho-Analysis*, London: Hogarth Press and the Institute of Psycho-Analysis (1952: 321–37).

—— (1952d) 'Certain functions of introjection and projection in early infancy', in M. Klein, P. Heimann, S. Isaacs, and J. Riviere *Developments in Psycho-Analysis*, London: Hogarth Press and the Institute of Psycho-Analysis (1952: 122–68).

Heimann, P. and Isaacs, S. (1952e) 'Regression', in M. Klein, P. Heimann, S. Isaacs, and J. Riviere *Developments in Psycho-Analysis*, London: Hogarth Press and the Institute of Psycho-Analysis (1952: 169–97).

Heimann, P. (1954) 'Problems of the training analysis', *International Journal of Psycho-Analysis* 35: 163–8.

—— (1955a) 'A contribution to the re-evaluation of the Oedipus complex –

344

the early stages' (revised version of 1952a op. cit.) in M. Klein, P. Heimann, and R. E. Money-Kyrle (eds) *New Directions in Psycho-Analysis*, London: Tavistock Publications (1955: 23–38).

—— (1955b) 'A combination of defence mechanisms in paranoid states', (revised version of 1952b, op. cit.) in M. Klein, P. Heimann, and R. E. Money-Kyrle (eds) *New Directions in Psycho-Analysis*, London: Tavistock Publications (1955: 240–65).

—— (1956) 'Dynamics of transference interpretations', *International Journal of Psycho-Analysis* 37: 303–10.

—— (1960) 'Counter-transference', *British Journal of Medical Psychology* 33: 9–15.

—— (1962a) 'Contribution to discussion of "The curative factors in psycho-analysis"', *International Journal of Psycho-Analysis* 43: 228–31.

—— (1962b) 'Notes on the anal stage', *International Journal of Psycho-Analysis* 43: 406–14.

—— (1964) 'Comment on Dr Katan's and Dr Meltzer's papers on "Fetishism – somatic delusions – hypochondria"', *International Journal of Psycho-Analysis* 45: 251–3.

—— (1966b) 'Comment on Dr Kernberg's paper on "Structural derivatives of object relationships"', *International Journal of Psycho-Analysis* 47: 254–60.

—— (1968) 'The evaluation of applicants for psycho-analytic training', *International Journal of Psycho-Analysis* 49: 527–39.

—— (1970a) 'Opening and closing remarks of the Moderator to "Discussion of 'The non-transference relationship in the psychoanalytic situation'"', *International Journal of Psycho-Analysis* 51: 145–7.

Heimann, P. and Valenstein, A. F. (1972) 'The psychoanalytical concept of aggression: an integrated summary', *International Journal of Psycho-Analysis* 53: 31–5.

Heimann, P. (1974a) 'A discussion of the paper by Charles Brenner on "Depression, anxiety and affect theory"', *International Journal of Psycho-Analysis* 55: 33–6.

—— (1974b) 'Discussion of "The effects of the psycho-analyst's personality on psycho-analytic treatment" by E. A. Ticho', *The Psycho-Analytic Forum* 4: 152–7.

—— (1974c) 'Discussion of "Psycho-analysis of the rich, the famous and the influential" by C. W. Wahl', *The Psycho-Analytic Forum* 5: 109–18.

—— (1975a) 'Sacrificial parapraxis – failure or achievement?' *Annual of Psychoanalysis*, New York: International Universities Press, 3: 145–63.

—— (1975b) 'From "cumulative trauma" to the privacy of the self', *International Journal of Psycho-Analysis* 56: 465–76.

—— (1975c) 'Obituary: Lois Munro 1907–1973', *International Journal of Psycho-Analysis* 56: 99–100.

—— (1977) 'Further observations on the analyst's cognitive process', *Journal of the American Psychoanalytic Association* 25: 313–33.

—— (1980) 'About children and children-no-longer', in *Psychoanalytici aan het woord*, Deventer: Van Loghum Slaterus BV, pp. 289–307.

French language publications

Heimann, P. (1969b) 'Dynamique des interprétations de transfert' (avec un postscriptum), *Bulletin de l'Association Psychanalytique de France* 5: 171–8.

—— (1975d) 'Daniel Lagache – temoignage personnel deuil et souvenir', in 'Documents et debats – homage à Daniel Lagache', *Bulletin Intérieur de l'Association Psychanalytique de France* 11: 27–45.

—— (1979) 'Libres propos sur les enfants et ceux qui n'en sont plus', in 'L'Enfant', *Nouvelle Revue de Psychanalyse* 19: 77–97.

German language publications

Heimann, P. (1959) 'Bemerkungen zur Sublimierung', *Psyche* 13: 397–414; also in *Psychologie des Ich*, Darmstadt: Wissenschaftliche Buchgesellschaft (1974: 239–61).

—— (1966a) 'Bemerkungen zum Arbeitsbegriff in der Psychoanalyse', *Psyche* 20: 321–61.

—— (1969a) 'Entwicklungssprünge und das Auftreten der Grausamkeit', in A. Mitscherlich (ed.) *Bis hierher und nicht weiter. Ist die menschliche Aggression unbefriedbar?*, Munich: R. Piper & Co. Verlag (1969: 104–18).

—— (1969c) 'Gedanken zum Erkenntnisprozess des Psychoanalytikers', *Psyche* 23: 2–24.

—— (1978) 'Über die Notwendigkeit für den Analytiker mit seinen Patienten natürlich zu sein', in *Provokation und Toleranz. Alexander Mitscherlich zu ehren*, Frankfurt am Main: Suhrkamp (1978: 215–29).

Italian language publications

Heimann, P. (1981a) 'L'importanza del transfert e controtransfert nel rapporto medico–paziente', *Neuropsichiatria Infantile* 235–6: 117–28.

—— (1981b) 'La sfida di Freud al coraggio e alla creativita dell' individuo *Neuropsichiatria Infantile* 242: 707–20.

Bibliography

References in [ ] refer to Introductory memoirs and Editor's introduction only.

Abraham, K. (1916) 'The first pregenital stage of the libido', in *Selected Papers on Psycho-Analysis*, London: Hogarth Press and the Institute of Psycho-Analysis, 9th edn (1965: 248–79).

—— (1920) 'The narcissistic evaluation of excretory processes in dreams and neurosis', in *Selected Papers on Psycho-Analysis*, London: Hogarth Press and the Institute of Psycho-Analysis, 9th edn (1965: 318–22).

—— (1921) 'Contributions to the theory of the anal character', in *Selected Papers on Psycho-Analysis*, London: Hogarth Press and the Institute of Psycho-Analysis, 9th edn (1965: 370–92).

—— (1924a) 'The influence of oral erotism on character formation', in *Selected Papers on Psycho-Analysis*, London: Hogarth Press and the Institute of Psycho-Analysis, 9th edn (1965: 393–417).

—— (1924b) 'A short study of the development of the libido, viewed in the light of mental disorders', in *Selected Papers on Psycho-Analysis*, London: Hogarth Press and the Institute of Psycho-Analysis, 9th edn (1965: 418–501).

Arlow, J. A. (1949) 'Anal sensations and feelings of persecution', *Psychoanalytic Quarterly* 18: 79–84.

Balint, A. (1936) 'Handhabung der Übertragung auf Grund der Ferenczischen Versuche', *Internationale Zeitschrift für Psycho-Analyse* 22: 47–58.

Balint, M. (1954) 'Analytic training and training analysis', *International Journal of Psycho-Analysis* 35: 157–62.

—— (1958) 'The three areas of the mind', *International Journal of Psycho-Analysis* 39: 328–40.

—— (1968) *The Basic Fault*, London: Tavistock Publications.

Beres, D. (1960) 'Perception, imagination, and reality', *International Journal of Psycho-Analysis* 41: 327–34.

Berman, L. (1949) 'Countertransferences and attitudes of the analyst in the therapeutic process', *Psychiatry* 12: 159–66.

Bibring, G. (1954) 'Training analysis and psycho-analytic training', *International Journal of Psycho-Analysis* 35: 169–73.

Bird, B. (1962) 'On the selection of psycho-analytic candidates', *Report to the American Psycho-Analytic Association* (mimeographed).

Blanton, S. (1971) *Diary of my Analysis with Sigmund Freud*, New York: Hawthorn Books.

Blum, H. P. (1976) 'The changing use of dreams in psycho-analytic practice: dreams and free association', *International Journal of Psycho-Analysis* 57: 315–24.

Bonnard, A. (1958) 'Pre-body ego types of mental functioning', *Journal of the American Psychoanalytic Association* 6: 581–611.

[Bott Spillius, E. (ed.) (1988) 'Introduction to part two: projective identification', in *Melanie Klein Today*, London: Routledge (1988: 81–6).]

Bowlby, J. (1960) 'Grief and mourning in infancy and early childhood', *The Psychoanalytic Study of the Child* 15: 9–52.

Brierley, M. (1951) *Trends in Psycho-Analysis*, London: Hogarth Press and the Institute of Psycho-Analysis.

[Coltart, N. (1986) ' "Slouching towards Bethlehem" . . . or thinking the unthinkable in psychoanalysis', in G. Kohon (ed.) *The British School of Psychoanalysis*, London: Free Association Books.]

Console, W. (1963) 'A study of one hundred consecutive applications', *Report to the American Psychoanalytic Association* (mimeographed).

Doolittle, H. (1956) *Tribute to Freud*, Oxford: Carcanet Press (1971).

Eissler, K. (1953) 'The effect of the structure of the ego on psychoanalytic technique', *Journal of the American Psychoanalytic Association* 1: 104–43.

—— (1965) *Medical Orthodoxy and the Future of Psychoanalysis*, New York: International Universities Press.

Elles, G. (1962) 'The mute sad-eyed child: collateral analysis in a disturbed family', *International Journal of Psycho-Analysis* 43: 40–9.

Erikson, E. H. (1950) *Childhood and Society*, New York: Norton.

Fairbairn, W. R. D. (1941) 'A revised psychopathology of the psychoses and psychoneuroses', *International Journal of Psycho-Analysis* 22: 250–79.

—— (1943) 'The repression and the return of bad objects', *The British Journal of Medical Psychology* 19: 327–41.

—— (1944) 'Endopsychic structure considered in terms of object-relationships', *International Journal of Psycho-Analysis* 25: 70–93.

—— (1946) 'Object-relationships and dynamic structure', *International Journal of Psycho-Analysis* 27: 30–7.

Fenichel, O. (1945) *The Psychoanalytic Theory of Neurosis*, New York: Norton.

Ferenczi, S. (1909) 'Introjection and transference', in *First Contributions to Psycho-Analysis*, London: Hogarth Press and the Institute of Psycho-Analysis (1952: 35–95).

—— (1914) 'The ontogenesis of the interest in money', in *First Contributions to Psycho-Analysis*, London: Hogarth Press and the Institute of Psycho-Analysis (1952: 319–31).

—— (1925) 'Psychoanalysis of sexual habits', in *Further Contributions to the Theory and Technique of Psycho-Analysis*, London: Hogarth Press and the Institute of Psycho-Analysis (1950: 259–97).

Fisher, C. (1965) 'Psychoanalytic implications of recent research on sleep and dreaming', *Journal of the American Psychoanalytic Association* 13: 197–270.

Fleming, J. (1961) 'What analytic work requires of an analyst: a job analysis', *Journal of the American Psychoanalytic Association* 9: 719–29.

Fliess, R. (1942) 'The metapsychology of the analyst', *Psychoanalytic Quarterly* 11: 211–27.

Fox, H., Daniels, E., and Wermer, H. (1964) 'Applicants rejected for psychoanalytic training', *Journal of the American Psychoanalytic Association* 12: 692–716.

Freud, A. (1936) *The Ego and the Mechanisms of Defence*, London: Hogarth Press and the Institute of Psycho-Analysis (1937).

—— (1965) *Normality and Pathology in Childhood*, New York: International Universities Press.

—— (1966) 'Some thoughts about the place of psychoanalytic theory in the training of psychiatrists', *Bulletin Menninger Clinic* 30: 225–34.

—— (1968) 'Indications and contraindications for child analysis', *The Psycho-Analytic Study of the Child* 23: 37–46.

Freud, S. (1893–95) *Studies on Hysteria, Standard Edition of the Complete Psychological Works of Sigmund Freud* (SE), London: Hogarth Press (1950–74)

—— (1893a) *Studies on Hysteria*, I 'On the psychical mechanism of hysterical phenomena: preliminary communication' (1893) Breuer and Freud SE 2: 3–17.

—— (1895d) *Studies on Hysteria*, II 'Case histories', SE 2: 19–181.

—— (1900a) *The Interpretation of Dreams*, SE 4/5.

—— (1901b) *The Psychopathology of Everyday Life*, SE 6.

—— (1905c) *Jokes and their Relation to the Unconscious*, SE 8.

—— (1905d) *Three Essays on the Theory of Sexuality*, SE 7: 135–243.

—— (1908b) 'Character and anal erotism', SE 9: 169–75.

—— (1908c) 'On the sexual theories of children', SE 9: 209–26.

—— (1908e) 'Creative writers and day-dreaming', SE 9: 143–53.

—— (1909d) 'Notes upon a case of obsessional neurosis', SE 10: 155–318.

—— (1910–19) *Papers on Technique*, in *Collected Papers II*, London: Hogarth Press and the Institute of Psycho-Analysis (1924: 285–402).

—— (1910a) 'Five lectures on psychoanalysis', SE 11: 9–55.

—— (1910d) 'The future prospects of psycho-analytic therapy', SE 11: 141–51.

—— (1910h) 'A special type of choice of object made by men', SE 11: 165–75.

—— (1911b) 'Formulations on the two principles of mental functioning', SE 12: 218–38.

—— (1912e) 'Recommendations to physicians practising psycho-analysis', SE 12: 111–20.

—— (1913c) 'On beginning of treatment' (further recommendations on the technique of psycho-analysis I), SE 12: 123–41.

—— (1914g) 'Remembering, repeating and working-through' (further recommendations on the technique of psycho-analysis II) SE 12: 147–56.

—— (1914c) 'On narcissism: an introduction', SE 14: 73–102.

—— (1915a) 'Observations on transference love' (further recommendations on the technique of psycho-analysis III), SE 12: 159–71.

—— (1915c) 'Instincts and their vicissitudes', SE 14: 117–40.

—— (1915d) 'Repression', SE 14: 146–58.

—— (1915e) 'The unconscious', SE 14: 166–215.

—— (1917a) 'A difficulty in the path of psycho-analysis', SE 17: 137–44.

—— (1917c) 'On transformations of instinct as exemplified in anal erotism', SE 17: 127–33.

—— (1917e) 'Mourning and melancholia', SE 14: 243–58.

—— (1919a) 'Lines of advance in psycho-analytic therapy', SE 17: 159–68.

—— (1920g) *Beyond the Pleasure Principle*, SE 18: 7–64.

—— (1921c) *Group Psychology and the Analysis of the Ego*, SE 18: 69–143.

—— (1922b) 'Some neurotic mechanisms in jealousy, paranoia and homosexuality', SE 18: 223–32.

—— (1923b) *The Ego and the Id*, SE 19: 12–66.

—— (1925h) 'Negation', SE 19: 235–9.

—— (1926d) *Inhibitions, Symptoms and Anxiety*, SE 20: 87–174.

—— (1927c) *The Future of an Illusion*, SE 21: 5–56.

—— (1930a) *Civilization and its Discontents*, SE 21: 64–145.

—— (1931a) 'Libidinal types', SE 21: 217–20.

—— (1933a[32]) *New Introductory Lectures on Psycho-Analysis*, Lecture XXXII, 'Anxiety and instinctual life', SE 22: 81–111.

—— (1937c) 'Analysis terminable and interminable', SE 23: 216–53.

—— (1937d) 'Constructions in psycho-analysis', SE 23: 257–69.

—— (1940a[38]) *An Outline of Psycho-Analysis*, SE 23: 144–207.

—— 1940e[38]) 'Splitting of the ego in the process of defence', SE 23: 275–8.

Gitelson, M. (1948) 'Problems of psychoanalytic training', *Psychoanalytic Quarterly* 17: 198–212.

—— (1952) 'The emotional position of the analyst in the psychoanalytic situation', *International Journal of Psycho-Analysis*, 33: 1–10.

—— (1954) 'Therapeutic problems in the analysis of the "normal" candidate', *International Journal of Psycho-Analysis* 35: 174–83.

—— (1964) 'On the identity crisis in American psychoanalysis', *Journal of the American Psychoanalytic Association* 12: 451–76.

—— (1963) 'On the present scientific and social position of psychoanalysis', *International Journal of Psycho-Analysis* 44: 521–7.

Greenacre, P. (1956) 'Re-evaluation of the process of working through', *International Journal of Psycho-Analysis* 37: 439–44.

—— (1957) 'The childhood of the artist: libidinal phase development and giftedness', in *Emotional Growth*, vol. II, New York: International Universities Press (1971: 479–504).

—— (1958) 'The family romance of the artist', in *Emotional Growth*, vol. II, New York: International Universities Press (1971: 505–32).

—— (1961) 'A critical digest of the literature on the selection of candidates for psychoanalytic training', *Psychoanalytic Quarterly* 30: 28–55.

—— (1966) 'Problems of training analysis', *Psychoanalytic Quarterly* 35: 540–67.

Greenson, R. (1960) 'Empathy and its vicissitudes', *International Journal of Psycho-Analysis* 41: 418–24.

—— (1965) 'The working alliance and the transference neurosis', *Psychoanalytic Quarterly* 34: 155–81.

—— (1966) 'That "impossible" profession', *Journal of the American Psychoanalytic Association* 14: 9–27.

—— (1967) *The Technique and Practice of Psychoanalysis*, London: Hogarth Press and the Institute of Psycho-Analysis, pp. 151–5.

—— (1970) 'The exceptional position of the dream in psychoanalytic practice', *Psychoanalytic Quarterly* 39: 519–49.

—— (1974) 'The decline and fall of the fifty-minute hour', *Journal of the American Psychoanalytic Association* 22: 785–91.

Grunberger, B. (1959) 'Étude sur la relation objectale anale', *Revue Française de Psychanalyse* 23: 177–204.

Habberton, J. (1876) *Helen's Babies* (full reference unobtainable).

Hartmann, H. (1939) *Ego Psychology and the Problem of Adaptation*, New York: International Universities Press (1958).

—— (1950) 'Comments on the psychoanalytic theory of the ego', *The Psychoanalytic Study of the Child* 5: 74–96.

—— (1955) 'Notes on the theory of sublimation', *The Psychoanalytic Study of the Child* 10: 9–29.

——(1956) 'The development of the ego concept in Freud's work', *International Journal of Psycho-Analysis* 37: 425–38.

Heimann, P. (1942) 'A contribution to the problem of sublimation and its relation to processes of internalization', *International Journal of Psycho-Analysis* 23: 8–17.

[——(1949) 'Some notes on the psycho-analytic concept of introjected objects', *British Journal of Medical Psychology* 22: 8–15.]

——(1950) 'On counter-transference', *International Journal of Psycho-Analysis* 31: 81–4.

[——(1952a) 'A contribution to the re-evaluation of the Oedipus complex', *International Journal of Psycho-Analysis* 33: 84–92.]

[——(1952b) 'Preliminary notes on some defence mechanisms in paranoid states', *International Journal of Psycho-Analysis* 33: 208–13.]

——(1952c) 'Notes on the theory of the life and death instincts', in M. Klein, P. Heimann, S. Isaacs, and J. Riviere *Developments in Psycho-Analysis*, London: Hogarth Press and the Institute of Psycho-Analysis (1952: 321–37).

——(1952d) 'Certain functions of introjection and projection in early infancy', in M. Klein, P. Heimann, S. Isaacs, and J. Riviere *Developments in Psycho-Analysis* (1952: 122–68).

——(1954) 'Problems of the training analysis', *International Journal of Psycho-Analysis* 35: 163–8.

——(1956) 'Dynamics of transference interpretations', *International Journal of Psycho-Analysis* 37: 303–10.

——(1959) 'Bemerkungen zur Sublimierung', *Psyche* 13: 397–414.

——(1960) 'Counter-transference', *British Journal of Medical Psychology* 33: 9–15.

——(1962a) 'Contribution to discussion of the "curative factors in psycho-analysis"', *International Journal of Psycho-Analysis* 43: 228–31.

——(1962b) 'Notes on the anal stage', *International Journal of Psycho-Analysis* 43: 406–14.

——(1964) 'Comment on Dr Katan's and Dr Meltzer's papers on "Fetishism – somatic delusions – hypochondria"', *International Journal of Psycho-Analysis* 45: 251–3.

——(1966b) 'Comment on Dr Kernberg's paper on "Structural derivatives of object relationships"', *International Journal of Psycho-Analysis* 47: 254–60.

——(1966) 'Problems of therapeutic interventions', Presidential address, Medical Section, British Psychological Society, unpublished.

——(1968) 'The evaluation of applicants for psychoanalytic training', *International Journal of Psycho-Analysis* 49: 527–39.

——(1969c) 'Gedanken zum Erkenntnisprozess des Psychoanalytikers', *Psyche* 23: 2–24.

——(1970a) 'Opening and closing remarks of the Moderator to "Discussion of the 'non-transference relationship in the psychoanalytic situation' " ' ', *International Journal of Psycho-Analysis* 51: 145–7.

[——(1975a) 'Sacrificial parapraxis – failure or achievement?', *The Annual of Psychoanalysis* 3: 143–63.]

[——(1977) 'Further observations on the analyst's cognitive process', *Journal of the American Psychoanalytic Association* 25: 313–33.]

——(1978) 'Über die Notwendigkeit für den Analytiker mit seinen Patienten natürlich zu sein', in *Provokation und Toleranz, Alexander Mitscherlich zu ehren*, Frankfurt am Main: Suhrkamp (1978: 215–29).

[——(1979) 'Libres propos sur les enfants et ceux qui n'en sont plus', in 'L'Enfant', *Nouvelle Revue de Psychanalyse* 19: 77–98.]

Heimann, P. and Isaacs, S. (1952e) 'Regression', in M. Klein, P. Heimann, S. Isaacs, and J. Riviere *Developments in Psycho-Analysis*, London: Hogarth Press and the Institute of Psycho-Analysis (1952: 169–97).

Hendrick, I. (1943) 'Work and the pleasure principle', *Psychoanalytic Quarterly* 12: 311–29.

Hoffer, W. (1959) 'A reconsideration of Freud's "primary narcissism" ', (unpublished).

Holland, N. H. (1969) 'Freud and H.D.', *International Journal of Psycho-Analysis* 50: 309–15.

Holt, R. (1964) 'The emergence of cognitive psychology', *Journal of the American Psychoanalytic Association* 12: 650–5.

Holt, R. and Luborsky, L. (1955) 'The selection of candidates for psychoanalytic training', *Journal of the American Psychoanalytic Association* 3: 666–81.

——(1958) 'Applications to the selection of candidates for psychoanalytic training', in *Personality Patterns of Psychiatrists*, New York: Basic Books.

Isaacs, S. (1948) 'The nature and function of phantasy', *International Journal of Psycho-Analysis* 29: 73–97.

James, M. (1960) 'Premature ego development: some observations upon disturbances in the first three years of life', *International Journal of Psycho-Analysis* 41: 288–94.

Jones, E. (1911) 'The pathology of morbid anxiety', in *Papers on Psycho-Analysis*, 4th edn, London: Bailliere, Tindall & Cox (1938: 407–32).

——(1918) 'Anal-erotic character traits', in *Papers on Psycho-Analysis*, 5th edn, London: Bailliere, Tindall & Cox (1948: 413–37).

——(1927) 'The early development of female sexuality', in *Papers on Psycho-Analysis*, 5th edn, London: Bailliere, Tindall & Cox (1948): 438–51.

——(1937) 'Love and morality', *International Journal of Psycho-Analysis* 18: 1–5.

Katan, M. (1964) 'Fetishism, splitting of the ego, and denial', *International Journal of Psycho-Analysis* 45: 237–45.

Khan, M. M. R. (1963) 'The concept of cumulative trauma', *The Psychoanalytic Study of the Child* 18: 286–306.

—— (1964) 'Ego-distortion, cumulative trauma and the role of reconstruction in the analytic situation', *International Journal of Psycho-Analysis* 45: 272–8.

—— (1974) *The Privacy of the Self*, London: Hogarth Press and the Institute of Psycho-Analysis.

—— (1976) 'The changing use of dreams in psycho-analytic practice: in search of the dreaming experience', *International Journal of Psycho-Analysis* 57: 325–30.

[King, P. H. M. and Steiner, R. (forthcoming) *Freud–Klein Controversies – 1941 to 1946*, London: Routledge.]

Klein, H. (1965) *Psychoanalysts in Training: Selection and Evaluation*, New York: Columbia University Press.

Klein, M. (1932) *The Psycho-Analysis of Children*, London: Hogarth Press and the Institute of Psycho-Analysis.

—— (1935) 'A contribution to the psychogenesis of manic-depressive states', *International Journal of Psycho-Analysis* 16: 145–74.

—— (1940) 'Mourning and its relation to manic-depressive states', *International Journal of Psycho-Analysis* 21: 125–53.

—— (1945) 'The Oedipus complex in the light of early anxieties', *International Journal of Psycho-Analysis* 26: 11–33.

—— (1946) 'Notes on some schizoid mechanisms', *International Journal of Psycho-Analysis* 27: 99–110.

—— (1948) 'A contribution to the theory of anxiety and guilt', *International Journal of Psycho-Analysis* 29: 114–23.

[—— (1956) 'A study of envy and gratitude', in J. Mitchell (ed.) *The Selected Melanie Klein*, Harmondsworth: Penguin (1986: 211–29).]

[—— (1957) *Envy and Gratitude*, London: Tavistock Publications.]

Kohut, H. (1964) 'Values and objectives', *Journal of the American Psychoanalytic Association* 12: 842–5.

—— (1966) 'Forms and transformations of narcissism', *Journal of the American Psychoanalytic Association* 14: 243–72.

—— (1971) *The Analysis of the Self*, New York: International Universities Press.

Kramer, M. K. (1959) 'On the continuation of the analytic process after psychoanalysis', *International Journal of Psycho-Analysis* 40: 17–25.

Kris, E. (1952) 'The image of the artist', in *Psychoanalytic Explorations in Art*, New York: International Universities Press, pp. 64–84.

—— (1962) 'Decline and recovery in the life of a three-year-old; or: data in psychoanalytic perspective on the mother–child relationship', *The Psycho-Analytic Study of the Child* 17: 175–215.

Kubie, L. (1937) 'The fantasy of dirt', *Psychoanalytic Quarterly* 6: 388–425.

Lagache, D. (1966) 'Psychoanalysis as an exact science' in R. M. Loewenstein *et al.* (eds) *Psychoanalysis: a General Psychology*, New York: International Universities Press 1966: 400–34.

Lampl-De Groot, J. (1954) 'Problems of training analysis', *International Journal of Psycho-Analysis* 35: 184–7.

Langer, M. (1962) 'Selection criteria for the training of psychoanalytic students', *International Journal of Psycho-Analysis* 43: 272–6.

Langer, M., Puget, J., and Teper, E. (1964) 'A methodological approach to the teaching of psychoanalysis', *International Journal of Psycho-Analysis* 45: 567–74.

Lantos, B. (1955) 'On the motivation of human relationships', *International Journal of Psycho-Analysis* 36: 267–88.

Leeuw, P. J. van der (1962) 'Selection criteria for the training of psychoanalytic students', *International Journal of Psycho-Analysis* 43: 277–82.

Lewin, B. and Ross, H. (1960) *Psychoanalytic Education in the United States*, New York: Norton.

Little, M. (1951) 'Counter-transference and the patient's response to it', *International Journal of Psycho-Analysis* 32: 32–40.

Lorenz, K. (1963) *On Aggression*, London: Methuen (1966).

McMullen, R. (1968) *The World of Marc Chagall*, London: Aldus Books.

Mahler, M. S. (1969) *On Human Symbiosis and the Vicissitudes of Individuation*, New York: International Universities Press.

Mannoni, M. (1967) *L'Enfant, sa 'maladie' et les autres*, Paris: Editions du Seuil; English translation, *The Child, his Illness, and the Others*, London: Tavistock Publications (1970).

Matte-Blanco, I. (1941) 'On introjection and the processes of psychotic metabolism', *International Journal of Psycho-Analysis* 22: 17–36.

——(1975) *The Unconscious as Infinite Sets*, London: Duckworth & Co.

Menninger, W. C. (1943) 'Characterologic and symptomatic expressions related to the anal phase of psycho-sexual development', *Psychoanalytic Quarterly* 12: 161–93.

Milner, M. (1950) *On Not Being Able to Paint*, London: Heinemann (1957).

Nunberg, H. (1930) *Principles of Psychoanalysis*, New York: International Universities Press (1955).

——(1931) 'The synthetic function of the ego', *International Journal of Psycho-Analysis* 12: 123–40.

Ophuijsen, J. H. van (1920) 'On the origin of the feeling of persecution', *International Journal of Psycho-Analysis* 1: 235–9.

Politzer, H. (1972) 'Oedipus in Kolonos', *Psyche* 26: 489–519.

Reik, T. (1948) *Listening with the Third Ear*, New York: Farrar & Straus.

Riviere, J. (1936) 'On the genesis of psychical conflict in earliest infancy', *International Journal of Psycho-Analysis* 17: 395–422.

——(1952) 'The unconscious phantasy of an inner world reflected in examples from literature', *International Journal of Psycho-Analysis* 33: 160–72.

[Rosenfeld, H. (1987) 'Afterthought: changing theories and changing techniques in psychoanalysis', in *Impasse and Interpretation*, London: Tavistock Publications, pp. 265–79.]

Rycroft, C. (1956) 'The nature and function of the analyst's communication to the patient', *International Journal of Psycho-Analysis* 37: 469–72.

Sachs, H. (1947) 'Observations of a training analyst', *Psychoanalytic Quarterly* 16: 157–68.

Sandler, J. and Rosenblatt, B. (1962) 'The concept of the representational world', *The Psycho-Analytic Study of the Child* 17: 128–45.

Schlesinger, H. J. (1965) 'Contribution to Panel Meeting on "memory and repression"', reported in: *Journal of the American Psychoanalytic Association* 13: 622–4.

Schmidl, F. (1955) 'The problem of scientific validation in psycho-analytical interpretation', *International Journal of Psycho-Analysis* 36: 105–13.

Searles, H. F. (1959) 'The effort to drive the other person crazy – an element in the aetiology and psychotherapy of schizophrenia', in *Collected Papers on Schizophrenia*, New York: International Universities Press (1965: 254–83).

Segal, H. (1955) 'A psycho-analytical approach to aesthetics', in *New Directions in Psycho-Analysis*, London: Tavistock Publications (1955: 384–405).

Sharpe, E. F. (1930) 'Certain aspects of sublimation and delusion', in *Collected Papers on Psycho-Analysis*, London: Hogarth Press and the Institute of Psycho-Analysis (1950: 125–36).

—— (1935) 'Similar and divergent unconscious determinants underlying the sublimation of pure art and pure science', London: Hogarth Press and the Institute of Psycho-Analysis (1950: 137–54).

—— (1940) 'Psycho-physical problems revealed in language: an examination of metaphor', London: Hogarth Press and the Institute of Psycho-Analysis (1950: 155–69).

Spitz, R. A. (1958) 'On the genesis of superego components', *The Psycho-Analytic Study of the Child* 13: 375–404.

Spitz, R. A. and Wolf, K. M. (1949) 'Autoerotism: some empirical findings and hypotheses on three of its manifestations in the first year of life', *The Psycho-Analytic Study of the Child* 3/4: 85–119.

Stärcke, A. (1920) 'The reversal of the libido-sign in delusions of persecution', *International Journal of Psycho-Analysis* 1: 231–4.

Sterba, R. F. (1972) 'The multiple determinants of a minor accident', *Israel Annals of Psychiatry and Related Disciplines* 8: 111–22.

Stout, G. F. (1920) *The Groundwork of Psychology*, London: Kegan Paul.

Strachey, J. (1934) 'The nature of the therapeutic action of psychoanalysis', *International Journal of Psycho-Analysis* 15: 127–59.

—— (1937) 'Symposium on the theory of the therapeutic results of psychoanalysis', *International Journal of Psycho-Analysis* 18: 139–45.

[Symington, N. (1983) 'The analyst's act of freedom as agent of therapeutic change', *International Review of Psycho-Analysis* 10: 283–91.]

Teilhard de Chardin, P. (1955) *The Phenomenon of Man*, London: Collins (1959).

Waelder, R. (1962) 'Selection criteria for the training of psychoanalytic students', *International Journal of Psycho-Analysis* 43: 283–6.

Wangh, M. (1962) 'The evocation of a "proxy"', *The Psycho-Analytic Study of the Child* 17: 451–69.

Watling, E. F. (trs.) (1969) *Sophocles, the Theban Plays*, Harmondsworth: Penguin.

Weiss, E. (1935) 'Todestrieb und Masochismus', *Imago* 21: 393–411.

Winnicott, D. W. (1945) 'Primitive emotional development', *International Journal of Psycho-Analysis* 26: 137–43.

—— (1958) 'The capacity to be alone', in *The Maturational Processes and the Facilitating Environment*, London: Hogarth Press and the Institute of Psycho-Analysis (1965: 29–36).

—— (1960a) 'The theory of the parent–infant relationship', in *The Maturational Processes and the Facilitating Environment*, London: Hogarth Press and the Institute of Psycho-Analysis (1965: 37–55).

—— (1960b) 'Ego distortion in terms of true and false self', in *The Maturational Processes and the Facilitating Environment*, London: Hogarth Press and the Institute of Psycho-Analysis (1965: 140–52).

—— (1971) *Playing and Reality*, London: Tavistock Publications.

Name index

Abraham 291–3
Abraham, K. 12, 61–2, 70, 105, 132; and anality 169, 172; and infantile sexuality 91, 92, 93, 171–2
Alexander, F. 2
Arlow, J. 173
Austen, J. 343

Balint, A. 73
Balint, M. 22, 24, 136 n. 1, 232, 243, 246, 314, 323 n. 2
Beres, D. 298
Berlin Psycho-Analytical Society 2, 3, 280
Berman, L. 79 n. 1
Bibring, G. 232, 241
Bion, W. R. 20, 234
Bird, B. 232, 249
Blanton, S. 336
Blum, H. P. 339
Bonnard, A. 135
Bowlby, J. 248
Breuer, J. 46, 313
Brierley, M. 147
British Psycho-Analytical Society 1–3, 5–6, 240, 323; Controversial Discussions of 5, 10–11, 18, 25 n. 2; Independent Group of 8, 13, 23, 25

Chagall, M. 298
Coltart, N. 23

Console, W. 232
Copernicus, N. 47

Darwin, C. 47
Doolittle, H. 336

Eissler, K. 201, 233, 243, 247, 248
Eitingon, M. 2
Elles, G. 330
Erikson, E. H. 213, 284

Fairbairn, W. R. D. 65, 223
Fenichel, O. 2
Ferenczi, S. 24, 61, 70, 73, 169, 171, 172
Fisher, C. 194
Fleming, J. 232, 234, 239, 250
Fliess, R. 232, 234, 240, 251 n. 2, 271; and trial identification 235, 237, 296; and work ego 236, 239, 264, 295–6, 309
Fliess, W. 277
Fordham, M. 151, 153, 154, 157, 159
Fox, H. 232
Freud, A. 7, 149, 170, 226, 233; and child analysis 301, 333; and regression 264, 282
Freud, S. 67, 102, 105, 121 n. 4, 165, 201, 226–8; and anality 169, 171, 174; on analyst's role 5, 11, 73, 114, 151, 265, 268, 336; and analytic process 104, 108, 110, 192–3, 256, 338;

Subject index